PUBLIC IN PUBLIC HISTORY

Public in Public History presents international research on the role of the public in public history: the ways people perceive, respond to and influence history-related institutions, events, services and products that deal with the past.

The book addresses theoretical reflections on the public, or multiple publics, and their role in public history, and empirical analyses of the publics' active responses to and impact on existing forms of public history. Special attention is also paid to digital public history, which facilitates the double role of the public—as both recipient and creator of public history. With a multinational author team, the book is based on various national, but also international, experiences and academic traditions; each chapter goes beyond national cases to look transnationally. The narratives built around their cases deal with issues such as arranging a museum exhibition, managing a history-related website, analyzing readers' comments or involving non-professional public as oral history researchers.

With sections focusing on research, commemorations, museums and the digital world, this is the perfect collection for anyone interested in what the public means in public history.

Joanna Wojdon is an associate professor at the Institute of History, University of Wrocław, Poland.

Dorota Wiśniewska is a research assistant at the University of Wrocław, Poland, and initiator of the International Public History Summer School in Wrocław.

Global Perspectives on Public History
Edited by Dr. Kristin O'Brassill-Kulfan, Rutgers University

This series explores the work of public historians and the contested histories they engage with around the world. Authored by both scholars and practitioners, volumes focus on cases where complex histories and diverse audiences meet and examine public representations of history. The series aims to link professional discussions of different historical methodologies with broader dialogues around commemoration, preservation, heritage and interpretation in diverse geographical, cultural, social and economic contexts. The coexistence of both global and regionally specific volumes in the series highlights the wide range of innovative new projects and approaches on offer. These books will provide students, researchers and practitioners with new case studies and helpful analytical tools to confront the (mis) representations of history they encounter in their work and as members of twenty-first-century communities.

Contested Commemoration in U.S. History
Diverging Public Interpretations
Edited by Melissa M. Bender and Klara Stephanie Szlezák

Public in Public History
Edited by Joanna Wojdon and Dorota Wiśniewska

PUBLIC IN PUBLIC HISTORY

Edited by
Joanna Wojdon and
Dorota Wiśniewska

 Routledge
Taylor & Francis Group

NEW YORK AND LONDON

First published 2022
by Routledge
605 Third Avenue, New York, NY 10158

and by Routledge
2 Park Square, Milton Park, Abingdon, Oxon, OX14 4RN

Routledge is an imprint of the Taylor & Francis Group, an informa business

Library of Congress Cataloging-in-Publication Data
Names: Wojdon, Joanna, 1973- editor. | Wiśniewska, Dorota, 1991–editor.
Title: Public in public history / edited by Joanna Wojdon and Dorota Wiśniewska.
Description: New York, NY: Routledge, 2021. | Series: Global perspectives on public history
Identifiers: LCCN 2021003867 (print) | LCCN 2021003868 (e-book) | ISBN 9780367641030 (paperback) | ISBN 9780367641047 (hardback) | ISBN 9781003122166 (e-book)
Subjects: LCSH: Public history.
Classification: LCC D16.163.P87 2021 (print) | LCC D16.163 (e-book) | DDC 900—dc23
LC record available at https://lccn.loc.gov/2021003867
LC e-book record available at https://lccn.loc.gov/2021003868

ISBN: 978-0-367-64104-7 (hbk)
ISBN: 978-0-367-64103-0 (pbk)
ISBN: 978-1-003-12216-6 (ebk)

Typeset in Times New Roman
by codeMantra

CONTENTS

CONTRIBUTORS

Sugandha Agarwal is a recent graduate in Communication from Simon Fraser University, Canada. Her research interests include forced migration, refugees and mobility. Previously, she worked as a research assistant on a forthcoming volume on Canadian media and migration. She is currently a Sahapedia-UNESCO research fellow in New Delhi, India.

Dorota Choińska holds an MA in Public History from the University of Wrocław, Poland. She is currently enrolled in a double doctoral program at the Open University of Catalonia and the University of Wrocław. She conducts a research on Polish refugees in Spain during the Second World War.

David Dean is Professor of History and co-director of the Centre for Public History at Carleton University, Canada. His recent publications include *Migration and Stereotypes in Performance and Culture* (2020) and *The Companion to Public History* (2018). He co-edits *International Public History* and is currently writing *Performing Public History* for Routledge.

Alexander Khodnev is a professor and chair of the World History Department, Yaroslavl State Pedagogical University, Russia. His research interests include history of international organizations and public, popular and applied history. His recent journal articles include "Cultural Transfer of the Age of Enlightenment (textbook on universal history by A. L. Schlozer)" (2020) and "Social-Cultural Practices of Public History in the USA" (2019).

Olga Konkka is a teaching assistant at Bordeaux Montaigne University, France; associate researcher at the Center for Modern and Contemporary Worlds Studies; and a postdoctoral fellow of the French Holocaust Memory

Foundation. Her main research interest is teaching of the twentieth-century history in Russian schools.

Marta Kopiniak is a PhD student at the University of Wrocław, Poland, and guide at the Depot History Center. She is currently working on her thesis focusing on the history of public participation in museums.

Tihana Kušter is a PhD candidate of the Premodern History at the University of Zagreb, Croatia, and the founder/editor of the public history website www.povcast.hr. Her current interests are digital history, data modeling and historical network analysis. She holds an MA in History and Art History.

Agata Moskwa graduated from the University of Wrocław, Poland (BA degree: Indology; MA degree: Public History). Her research interests include the issues of remembrance and politics of memory in Asia, particularly in Japan and South Korea.

Ricardo Santhiago is an assistant professor at the Federal University of São Paulo, Brazil (Unifesp). His work has appeared in various academic journals and includes a dozen of authored and edited books. He is a founding member of the Brazilian Public History Network.

Jakub Šindelář is a Modern History PhD student at Charles University in Prague, Czechia. His dissertation explores the reception analysis of historical narratives and representation of WWI through video games and Let's Play videos. His research and teaching concern the representations of modern European history in audiovisual media.

Linda S. Thomas received her ALM in Religion in May 2021 from the Harvard University Extension School, Cambridge, MA, USA. She holds an MA in History from Villanova University and a MA in Applied Linguistics from UMass Boston. She works full-time as an Academic Coordinator at Harvard University in Cambridge, MA.

Paweł Ukielski is an assistant professor at the Institute of Political Studies, Polish Academy of Sciences, Warsaw. He is the Deputy Director of the Warsaw Rising Museum (2004–2014 and since 2016). His publications include *Aksamitny rozwód. Rola elit politycznych w procesie podziału Czechosłowacji* [*The velvet divorce. The role of political elites in the division of Czechoslovakia process*] and *Pamięć Polski, pamięć sąsiadów. Pamięć Europy* [*Memory of Poland, memory of neighbours. Memory of Europe*].

Caitlin White is a PhD candidate in Public History at Trinity College, Dublin, Ireland, researching expressions of Irish identity after partition with Dr. Anne Dolan. Hailing from Nenagh, Co. Tipperary, her research interests include commemoration, memory, democratizing access to knowledge and promoting historical engagement.

Dorota Wiśniewska is a research assistant at the University of Wrocław, Poland, and initiator of International Public History Summer School in Wrocław. Her research interests focus primarily on women's history. She recently published an article in *Gender & History* on Polish Women's Political Attitudes during the Great Sejm (1788–1792).

Joanna Wojdon is an associate professor at the Institute of History, University of Wrocław, Poland, where she is also a Chair of the Department of Methodology of Teaching History and Civic Education, and a coordinator of MA program in Public History. She has authored an award-winning *White and Red Umbrella: Polish American Congress in the Cold War Era (1944–1988)* (Helena History Press, 2015). Her recent publications include *Textbooks as Propaganda. Poland under Communist Rule. 1944–1989* (Routledge, 2018) and *Communist Propaganda at School. Reading Primers of the Soviet Bloc. 1949–1989* (Routledge, 2021).

Ewa Woźniak-Wawrzyniak has graduated from the MA program in Public History at the University of Wrocław, Poland, and currently is a PhD candidate in history, researching the image of Poland after the collapse of the communist regime presented in contemporary Polish school textbooks. She works as a guide in the Depot History Centre in Wrocław.

Alexandra Zaremba is PhD candidate at American University, Washington, DC, USA, working on national identity construction, museums and memory in Yugoslavia. She holds an MA in Public History from Duquesne University and recently published a chapter on the politics of memory in Jasenovac Memorial Museum (Palgrave Macmillan, 2020).

1

PUBLICS, PUBLIC HISTORIANS AND PARTICIPATORY PUBLIC HISTORY

David Dean

Public history, as the call for papers for the 2019 conference on *The Public in Public and Applied History* which inspired this collection of essays conveniently set out, is about history in the public realm. It is, to quote the organizers, "history *for* the public, *by* the public, *with* the public, *about* the public or *in* the public sphere."[1] But who is or who are "the public"? In this chapter, I will consider what public historians have in mind when they speak about

FIGURE 1.1   Canadian History Hall © archer10 (Dennis), public domain.

"the public" and briefly discuss debates surrounding the notion of publics and the public sphere. A case study will be offered demonstrating how a major public history institution in Canada, the Canadian Museum of History, sought to operationalize publics during a vital moment of transition (Figure 1.1). My discussion will draw on the work of scholars working in the fields of public pedagogy and participatory performance which may prove instructive for public historians, and concludes with the proposition that thinking about "publics" rather than a single, unitary public is a useful step forward in our understanding of what we mean by putting the word "public" in front of "history."

The Public in Public History

What do we have in mind when we speak of history *for, by, with* or *about* the public? The various prepositions employed signal both the range of approaches adopted by public historians in their analyses and creations of representations of the past and raise a number of theoretical and methodological issues. Is the public (or are publics) passive consumers of the historical representations created by public historians? This is what history *for* the public implies. The public receives history curated in whatever form (books, exhibits, films, podcasts, walking-tours, etc.) by recognized (and certainly self-identified) authorities or experts who have been professionally trained as historians or in an allied field and are usually working in institutions (government departments, museums, universities, etc.). This is history in the public realm functioning as discipline and knowledge, where historical productions are generated for the public and which sees the public as needing information and instruction. This can take the form of official state narratives or, conversely, counter-narratives: both see publics as passive consumers of the historical representations that are produced. Unpacking history *for* the public in this way resonates with the first of Gert Biesta's threefold typology of public pedagogy: "pedagogy *for* the public that is *aimed* at the public."[2]

To be sure, and particularly in the past few decades, such "top-down" public histories have involved varying degrees of public consultation. This can take place prior to the final production—often, to be rather cynical about it, designed to anticipate problems that might render the professional institution vulnerable to criticism—or afterward by way of evaluation and feedback to assist in shaping the next production. Representations—particularly those in museums and galleries, living history performances and reenactments—might even involve degrees of audience participation and interaction, but here too the public act as participants in representations firmly controlled and established by the professionals. The public may in such instances be active rather than passive consumers, but they are consumers, nonetheless.

Such a position is also implied in talking of history *about* the public. Here, the public serves as both the subject and object of the historical production in question. As in history *for* the public, the expert historian or specialist in an allied discipline or professional field is seen, by themselves and by others, as existing outside the public they are addressing. Indeed, these specialists claim that their training and experiences enable them to distance themselves from both the past they seek to represent "objectively" and the public for whom their representations of the past are intended.

History *with* the public on the other hand recognizes that the public has a role to play in producing representations of the past. The preposition "with" suggests a moving away from the public playing the role of a consumer who might (if they are fortunate) be consulted or invited to participate, to one where they play a significant role in shaping historical representation. History *with* the public means that the public helps to shape the subject and nature of the production and to set the research agenda and is involved in the development and enactment process. The public works toward determining the storylines and narratives and is involved in strategies and technologies of representation and reception. Public histories in these instances are truly collaborative exercises, where the professional is just one contributor to the historical production and may not even play the most significant role in determining outcomes. Public historians in histories *with* the public often find themselves playing the role of facilitator and cheerleader, and this involves often complex processes of sharing and shared authority.

History *by* the public, which to a degree mirrors Biesta's second type of public pedagogy ("pedagogy *of* the public that is done by the public itself"),[3] suggests histories that are created without the involvement of such professionals altogether—particularly professionally trained historians—or at the very least that they play a very supplementary role as sources (perhaps even as consultants) for historical representations initiated by others. This reverses the role of the public in histories *for* and *about* the public and firmly places experts as a constituent part of the public. To put it another way, this is "bottom-up" history, often generated outside official institutional structures, and they might be supportive of, or in harmony with, "top-down" histories or antagonistic and resistant to them.

Whether history is produced *for*, *about*, *with* or *by* the public, public historians tend to conceptualize the audiences of historical representations as a single, unitary public. This is captured in the phrase "the public," sometimes qualified as "the general public," or even the elitist phrase "the ordinary public," which explicitly marks the public historian, and perhaps others—such as curators, filmmakers, and actors participating in the process of historical creation—as existing outside the public she or he has in mind. This is another frequent sense of the word: public history practitioners talk about needing to find "an audience" as if there is a public "out there" that somehow needs to be accessed.

Publics, Counter-Publics and the Public Sphere

Where is this public to be found? Although the call for papers evoked Jürgen Habermas's concept of the public sphere, it is surprising how absent his work has been from discussions by public historians seeking to offer a definition of public history. Habermas saw the public sphere as "a realm of our social life in which something approaching public opinion can be formed [...] Citizens behave as a public body when they confer in an unrestricted fashion [...] about matters of general interest."[4] Habermas located the emergence of the public sphere in conversations taking place in clubs, societies, newspapers and periodicals of the eighteenth century. The concept of the public sphere generated much debate over issues such as to what degree elements of the public sphere could be detected earlier than the eighteenth century, how inclusive the liberal public sphere really was, how there were alternative means of civic engagement and how well it served as a mode of analysis for non-European cultures.

One of the most frequently cited critiques was that offered by Nancy Fraser who supported the position that it was more useful to think about "a multiplicity of publics" rather than "a single public sphere."[5] Habermas's unitary comprehensive public sphere may have been dominated by the bourgeois, male, educated and well-off elite, but they were not wholly constitutive of it. Subordinate groups formed alternative publics which Fraser called *"subaltern counterpublics"* (italics in original), parallel "discursive arenas where members of subordinate social groups invent and circulate counter discourses to formulate oppositional interpretations of their identities, interests, and needs."[6] These counter-publics might function "as bases and training grounds for agitational activities directed towards wider publics."[7] Whatever form their activities took, alternative publics expanded the public sphere.[8]

Who were these alternative publics and counter-publics? Most were associated with subaltern groups and can be characterized as social movements such as those working for workers' rights, women's rights, civil rights and so on. Such "emergent publics," as Ian Angus helpfully calls them, sometimes succeed in challenging dominant publics, achieving an expansion of the public sphere.[9] As Fraser pointed out, subaltern, counter or alternative publics were not necessarily socially progressive; as Michael Warner has recently observed, contemporary alt-right activists are also "publics in waiting."[10]

Warner's work on counter-publics takes as a given that publics are constructed through discourse. He notes several "senses" of the (English) noun "public" that are often "intermixed." There is the sense of *the* public as "a kind of social totality," of "people in general."[11] Whether framed as the nation, a city, a community or a group, the assumption is that it includes everyone within its compass and there is no real alternative English word for this sense of public: "crowd" or "audience," for example, do not capture the same degree of social totality. On the other hand, when we think of "concrete" publics, these words do work as substitutes because a public in this sense is brought together to experience itself in a specific place, bounded by space, place, and event, "assembled in common visibility and common action."[12] A third sense of public is the one "that comes into being only in relation to texts and their circulation," and this is Warner's primary concern as he proceeds to explore print cultures and "broadcast publications" from the eighteenth century onward.[13]

Warner illuminates our understanding by identifying seven aspects to our understanding of *a* public. First, he argues that a "public is self-organized." It is "a space of discourse organized by nothing other than discourse itself," existing only for the purpose for which it is organized. "It exists *by virtue of being addressed*."[14] To paraphrase Warner's argument, a self-organized public exists by being addressed through text, visual, audio or digital means; it is imagined but always open-ended since its composition is never completely known.

It follows then that, second, a public is necessarily "a relation among strangers." Strangers in the context of a public are not alien but belong to a shared social imaginary: they "are on a path to commonality." The peculiarity that public discourse necessarily requires stranger relationality is explained by a third feature, namely that public speech "is both personal and impersonal."[15] In being addressed as a public, we experience it both personally—as it is addressed to us in particular—and impersonally—as we are addressed as strangers. Fourth, a public, because it exists through being addressed, requires "active uptake."[16] In other words, to exist, a public requires addressees to be attentive and active—even passively or accidentally.

The fifth and sixth characteristics of a public are that anything that addresses publics must circulate and that publics "act historically according to the temporality of their circulation."[17] These observations should remind us of Habermas. "Writing to a public," Warner argues, "helps to make a world insofar as the object of address is brought into being partly by postulating and characterizing it" and it follows that a public "can only act in the temporality of the circulation that gives it existence."[18] Warner's final suggestion is that a public "is poetic world making":

> There is no speech or performance addressed to a public that does not try to specify in advance, in countless highly condensed ways, the lifeworld of its circulation: not just through its discursive claims—of the kind that can be said to be oriented to understanding—but through the pragmatics of its speech genres, idioms, stylistic markers, address, temporality, mis-en-scène, citational field, interlocutory protocols, lexicon, and so on. Its circulatory fate is the realization of that world. Public discourse says not only "Let a public exist" but "Let it have this character, speak this way, see the world in this way." It then goes in search of confirmation that such a public exists, with greater or lesser success—success being further attempts to cite, circulate, and realize the world understanding it articulates. Run it up the flagpole and see who salutes. Put on a show and see who shows up.[19]

The successful creation of a public depends then on the identification of stranger participants and consequent circulation that binds them together. These many publics are thought to constitute *the* public, but the apparent unity of *the* public is an illusion because some publics are more able than others to frame themselves as the normative, dominant, universal public. Sub-publics, counter-publics, and alternative publics function nevertheless in the same way as dominant publics. Warner describes the dynamic between publics and counter-publics as an "oscillation," as counter-publics try to be the dominant public or withdraw in order to embrace difference that allows for experimentation. The public sphere is in effect an assemblage of multiple publics.[20]

The ability of counter-publics to experiment and innovate resonates with Biesta's third form of public pedagogy, the enactment of *becoming* public. This is activist, experimental and demonstrative: "activist in that it aims to create real alternatives of being and doing, experimental because it is about inventing new ways of being and doing, and demonstrative because it shows that it is possible to do things differently."[21] Indeed, Glenn Savage, another scholar of public pedagogy, drawing on Warner, has identified three categories of publics: political publics, popular publics and concrete publics. Political publics for Savage are those that identify with a particular nation-state, their sense of belonging (whether real or imagined) tied to a defined national community. Popular publics are everyday cultural lives that are less spatially referenced than political publics and where history is engaged with in sites and forms quite different from the official ones. Indeed, popular publics are often formed as counterpoints to political publics. Concrete publics are, as with Warner, those contained by an event or experience in a shared space such as museums, or cinemas, or theaters where publics are self-selected "addressees who have chosen to be addressed."[22]

Public Historians, Publics and Popular History

After acknowledging the complexity of the term public, Ludmilla Jordanova suggests that "Among other things, public history is *popular* history—it is seen or read by large numbers of people and has mostly been designed for a mass audience."[23] As Faye Sayer puts it, when public historians think about the public they have in mind the "population and community as a whole."[24] Sayer and Thomas Cauvin in their single-authored (English language) introductions to the field, like Cherstin Lyon, Elizabeth Nix and Rebecca Shrum in their jointly written introductory text (also in English), all point out that when the field formally emerged in the 1970s, particularly in the United States, it was seen as non-academic history.[25] Whatever the origins of particular historical representations—official, state or institution-based ("top-down") or grassroots ("bottom-up"), professional or amateur, national or local, community or family-based—the distinguishing feature was that the public was the target audience and they engaged with historical representations as consumers, as Jerome de Groot put it in the title of his important account of history, heritage and historians in contemporary popular culture.[26]

De Groot's deep analysis of the almost inexhaustible variety of ways in which the public consumes history and heritage reminds one of the earlier works of Raphael Samuel who explored the ways in which the past plays a vibrant and positive role in contemporary English life.[27] Both, of course, acknowledge that different people participated and consumed the past differently. In the United States, between 1989 and 1998, Roy Rosenzweig and David Thelen differentiated the public systematically in their exploration of the "popular uses of history in American life" (the subtitle of their book, *The Presence of the Past*).[28] Their survey revealed that Americans engaged with the past in a variety of ways: visiting museums and historic sites, watching history on television and film, reading history books and talking about the past with family and friends. Asking respondents about these forms of engagement, Rosenzweig and Thelen were also interested to find out which ones their interviewees thought to be the most "trustworthy" as well as which ones made them feel most connected to the past. The American survey inspired one in Australia carried out between 1999 and 2003 by Paul Ashton and Paula Hamilton, and most recently one in Canada led by seven historians who formed "the pasts collective" whose results were published in 2013.

In order to succeed, each of these surveys had to identify respondents, and they did so by differentiating the public in a number of ways. Rosenzweig and Thelen unpacked the public by ethnicity and race: White Americans, African Americans, Mexican Americans and Native Americans. They also analyzed their results through the lenses of age, education, gender and income. The Australian survey followed suit, though with a more generalized process to uncover the experiences of the continent's indigenous peoples (Aborigines and Torres Strait Islanders), and distinguished groups within the largely white, settler community.[29] Similarly, the Canadian survey assessed results by age, education, gender and income, but added parenthood and religion as categories of analysis.[30] Furthermore, the Canadian survey carried out three additional surveys focusing on Saskatchewan aboriginals (First Nations, Metis, Inuit), New Brunswick Acadians (French-speaking peoples many of whom were deported by the British in the eighteenth century) and Francophone Quebecois.

Public historians then, seeking to understand how the public engages with history, why they do so, which forms and venues of historical representation they trust and which make them feel most connected to the past, have found it necessary to identify specific publics in order to meet the objectives of their surveys. Whatever the omissions and absences (sexuality, ability, generations, etc.), by recognizing the inadequacies of generalizing about the public the surveys have contributed to the project of recognizing the plurality of publics in the public realm and differentiating publics in public history. They also found it useful to operationalize their interviewees depending on the ways in which they engaged with the past and the sites where these activities and experiences took place. For example, those watching historical films were "audiences"; those listening to teachers and professors, "students"; those researching family or community histories, "amateur historians"; and those frequenting museums, "visitors." This is not just a matter of introducing some linguistic variation to make their books more readable, but each of these terms shares something and means something different. Each, especially the first and last (audiences, visitors), has long been delineated by public history practitioners working in institutions outside the academy.

Operationalizing Publics

Academic historians of course care about the audiences of their work. They want to be read and seen. They hope their lectures and conference presentations might have a reach beyond the classroom or conference panel. They tweet the appearance of a new article or book in the hope of generating broader interest and dream of their monograph being adapted for stage or screen. If not fame and fortune, they certainly hope their work will generate enough public indicators to assist in securing funding for their next project or promotion within their institution. When all is said and done, though, the audiences of their work are consumers rather than producers; success is not determined primarily by popularity but by peer assessment. Indeed, poor reviews have little consequence beyond creating embarrassment and generating indignation—the academic historian simply turns to the next project.

Public historians working outside academia can, by contrast, have their work shaped and even determined by publics. Museum directors and curators can be forced from their positions by adverse public reaction, especially when supported by, or even fueled by, the media or politicians. In Canada, this happened in the case of the Royal Ontario Museum's *Out of Africa* exhibit and the Canadian War Museum's gallery display on the Allied bombing campaign during the Second World War.[31] Such controversies undoubtedly have influenced curatorial work and management oversight subsequently.

It has, of course, always been good curatorial practice to think through the potential audiences of exhibits. Curators of what was then the Canadian Museum of Civilization (now the Canadian Museum of History) when proposing new exhibitions to management for approval, funding and resources had to distinguish stakeholders, communities, target audiences and general visitors when offering a "market" analysis:

3.1. A description of stakeholders in the exhibition with special emphasis on the groups that have a special interest in the exhibition.
3.2. A description of the stakeholders who will be consulted during the development of the exhibition (e.g., cultural community).

3.3. A description of the specific target audiences (general public not accepted).

3.4. A discussion of the elements of the exhibitions that will appeal to the museum's general visiting public (i.e., those not necessarily initially interested in the subject or theme).[32]

This process for exhibit approval reveals that the museum distinguished between the "general visiting public" and visitors who had a particular interest in the exhibited content. It also identified various types of "stakeholders": groups who had a particular interest in the subject of the exhibit and those groups that needed to be consulted. Third, it reveals an acknowledgment that curators needed to identify "specific target audiences."

This operationalization of publics took on even greater importance when the Canadian Museum of Civilization became the Canadian Museum of History, a transition that took place between 2012 and 2017. The most significant change was that the Civilization Museum's Canada Hall was to be replaced by a "proper" History Hall which would, as the official announcement put it, celebrate "national achievements and accomplishments." Along with a stronger political focus and a clearer chronological framework, the Civilization Museum's mandate to promote "critical understanding" was replaced with an obligation to encourage "appreciation and respect."[33] The museum engaged in an extensive range of consultations before and during the makeover. These included charettes (collaborative meetings of historians, curators, designers and the museum's architect, Douglas Cardinal), public events, focus groups and expert panels.

What these processes revealed was a need to develop a sophisticated understanding of "the public" who would be visiting the museum. To quote from the final Exhibition Concept document that appeared just over three years before the museum opened its doors, "identifying audience needs" would "help shape the extensive research into a visitor experience."[34] Deep research into the potential audiences of the museum leads to a few key conclusions as to what visitors want from a museum that will be no surprise to anyone familiar with the several national surveys discussed earlier. Visitors want to learn and discover something new, they want "authentic, object-based experiences," and they tend to visit museums in groups (couples, families, tourists, school groups), which requires the museum to be a place that encourages and facilitates social interaction. Setting aside those visiting as part of a formally organized tour group and those visiting as part of an educational group visit (either during the school year as part of their formal curriculum or toward the end of the year when the visit was meant to be a fun day out on a school trip), the museum broke down "the public" into four key visitor types.

The first were "Sightseers." They often visited as family members and were driven to the museum to discover something new about Canadian history. They wanted to learn, but also to have fun, and to do so together (parents, children, etc.). The museum had to offer an experience that was varied, that would satisfy all members of the group and that would "allow for the creation of shared memories." The second group was "Families." Always visiting as a family, their motivation differed from Sightseers in that they really were looking for a fun day out. Knowledge-seeking was a very low priority; more important was an enjoyable "socially mediated learning experience" that gave them the opportunity "to connect as a family." The third group was "Museum Enthusiasts." These visitors usually came with other adults and tended to be frequent museum goers. They were using their leisure time as an opportunity to learn more, discover new things and deepen their personal interest in history. Finally, there were the "History Seekers." They were committed to learning more about Canadian history, because they were either professionals or amateur history buffs. They came "looking to satisfy their own quest for knowledge." Unlike the first two groups, and much more so than the third, they were seeking "content-rich, object-based experiences."[35]

The museum thus determined that particular audiences needed specific things and the challenge was to appeal to everyone. The new History Hall is much more fluid, dynamic and colorful, full of bright spaces, dotted with interactives and exhibits featuring innovative digital work. It features thousands of original, authentic objects displayed in a rich environment that at times is text light. The Hall is divided into three chronologically arranged galleries (pre-contact to 1763, 1763 to 1914, and 1914 to the present) contained within architect Douglas Cardinal's flowing spaces resonating with his design for the museum's exterior. "History" now begins with indigenous peoples, and troubling stories are addressed more openly, particularly those of the twentieth and twenty-first centuries. Even so, as John Walsh has observed, "the Canadian History Hall largely follows a chronology of linear historical time marked by the grand events that dominate settler histories of the nation state."[36]

Despite the care taken to deconstruct "the public" into a variety of "publics," the museum resorted to seeing those same publics as essentially passive consumers of the historical representations the museum had to offer. Very occasionally, interspersed among the static displays, there is a carefully orchestrated activity, but interactives are few and far between in this museum and largely directed to children. In other words, the museum ended up with a traditional understanding of public participation. It was public history *for* the public, *about* the public and aimed *at* the public.

In her influential book, *The Participatory Museum*, Nina Simon argues that museums can function as dynamic spaces.[37] As Susan Bennett and Catherine Hughes have shown, animating exhibits through performance is one way of doing this and it is revealing that not long before the announcement was made about the transition of the Canadian Museum of Civilization to the Canadian Museum of History, the former's in-house theater company, *Dramamuse*, was disbanded.[38] This company researched, scripted and performed original works that spoke directly to the spaces in the Canada Hall. Interacting with the reconstructed spaces around them, the stories were often edgy and challenged visitors to think through about past lives lived, contested spaces and controversial histories. These included stories about female servants in early modern Quebec (performed in the seventeenth century town square) and the trauma of the residential school system (told in the reconstructed Wildcat Café in Yellowknife, Northwest Territories). Eliminating such site-specific, contested histories from the gallery's floors anticipated the later shift in the museum's mandate from "critical understanding" to "appreciation."[39]

Theater and performance artists, practitioners and scholars have been at the forefront in thinking through scenarios of public participation because of the dynamic, interdependent and often intimate relationship between performers and audiences. As Thomas Ostermeier, artistic director of Berlin's Schaubühne theater put it, reflecting on the effects of COVID-19 global pandemic in closing the theaters, "as long as there is no interaction between stage and audience there is no theatre."[40] Richard Schechner, who founded New York-based *The Performance Group* in 1967, staged performances involving audience participation in what has been described as "environmental theatre." In his foundational text, *Performance Theory*, Schechner argues that audiences are active participants from the moment they approach the theater to the time they leave.[41]

Since these beginnings, it might be said that engaging audiences actively during the performance has become a frequently-resorted-to strategy in the theater playbook. Take, for example, Ostermeier's 2012 production of Henrik Ibsen's *An Enemy of the People* written in 1882. Ibsen's play focuses on the fate of what today we would call a whistle-blower. Dr. Thomas Stockmann, medical officer of a small-town spa, discovers that the waters are contaminated and his campaign to reveal the truth leads to family disintegration (his brother is the mayor) and personal suffering. Ostermeier's production made explicit the topicality of the play when Stockmann's public lecture on the subject offers the view that the real culprit is not the excesses of capitalism but the complacency of liberal thinking in contemporary German democracy. His opinions are put to the audience for a vote and they overwhelmingly support him. This provokes a lively audience/stage discussion, facilitated by the actor playing the editor of the newspaper who had decided not to publish Stockmann's damning report, before seamlessly returning to Ibsen's plot.[42] Such collaborative moments, where audiences actively participate and interact with what is happening on stage, resonate with many forms of public history practice.

Pablo Helguera, in his discussion of socially engaged art, distinguishes nominal, directed, creative and collaborative forms of participation.[43] Nominal participation is when publics are passive consumers of the historical product. There may be moments of directed participation, where publics follow instructions to complete tasks that have been carefully constructed and designed by the experts responsible for content delivery that contribute to the shaping of the work. Creative participation is where participants are provided with the necessary tools, such as content, to shape the historical representation, and are free to do with it what they wish within the structures established by the expert curator or artist. Lastly, Helguera posits "collaborative participation" where everyone shares responsibility for developing the product. With these last two forms of participation, we have public history *with* the public and *by* the public. Distinguishing types of participation returns us also to the value of speaking about publics in the plural rather than the ("general," "ordinary," "broad") singular, unitary public.

Conclusion: Doing Public History

Reading the introductory essay to a collection of essays on public pedagogy, recently I came across a paragraph which captured very nicely some of the dilemmas we face in defining and making sense of what we mean by public history. Substituting "history" for "pedagogy," among a few other word changes and additions (indicated in bold), it would go something like this:

> Public **history** has been largely constructed as a concept focusing on various forms, processes and sites of **historical representation** occurring beyond or outside of formal **history.** It involves learning **about the past** in institutions such as museums, zoos and libraries; in informal **historical** sites such as popular culture, media, commercial spaces and the internet; and through figures and sites of activism, including public intellectuals and grassroots social movements.[44]

This altered paragraph stands very well against definitions of public history offered on the website of the National Council on Public History and by the many authors of textbooks and handbooks on the field.[45]

Public history *has* been largely defined by its forms and sites, and if one peruses the pages of the long-established journal, *The Public Historian*, over the past three and a half decades, article after article focuses on representations of the past: how they are made, who is making them, and why, and how the public is variously engaged. Public history also *has* often been described as applied history, history practiced by historians (professionally trained or not) working outside the academy, often regarded by those employed by universities as unfortunate second cousins. Public history, in other words, was something to be engaged with outside the practice of history proper ("formal history"). Public historians, when asked what they do, often turn very quickly to talk about the sites of their work rather than speak of theories, methodologies or approaches.

Yet it is precisely those historical theories, methodologies and approaches that signify that public history is a field of historical enquiry. In my department, all students in our undergraduate and graduate public history programs take the same historical theory and methodology courses as their colleagues specializing in other fields and concentrations. We proceed from an assumption that all historians need to be familiar with, for example, how to use archival sources, but they all also need to think through what constitutes an archive. Public and non-public historians alike need to know how to interpret photographs, paintings and film or how to read landscapes, explore material culture and engage with intangible heritage. They all need to become familiar with approaches that challenge established historical conventions or have challenged them in the past. While it is likely that students in public history will choose to write the past in film, in podcasts, in fiction, in graphic novels, in video games, etc., rather than the more traditional essay or thesis, such a decision is by no means exclusive to them. Thus, although this chapter has focused on the "public" in public history, it is also important to acknowledge that we public historians are part of a larger discipline with a long and varied genealogy. Thinking through what we mean when we call what we do public *history* as opposed to, say, public *memory* or public *pedagogy* will allow us to understand our field more clearly. It will help us to recognize the nature of its contribution to the discipline and help us identify what it shares with other fields of history, and what not.

What does seem clear is that public historians especially acknowledge, encourage and value the participatory role of publics in history-making. Furthermore, they are more likely to work collaboratively with publics and this forces them to confront their own subjectivities, to challenge their assumptions about expertise and authority and to think deeply about accountability more than other historians. These issues come sharply into focus when public historians encounter the many representations of the past that populate the public sphere which have been initiated and created without the involvement of trained historians. Some are relatively harmless even though they may be superficial or uncritical, miss complexity or prioritize entertainment value over historical veracity. Others are deeply troubling because they commemorate or celebrate dark histories or deliberately misuse the past to support agendas in the present. Historians can choose to ignore, ridicule and dismiss such representations or to critically engage with them, producing alternative, better histories. Whatever action they take, historical representations produced by non-historians invite questions central to the field. What makes a historian a public historian? Is it their training as historians or that they do history in the public sphere, or both? Do the histories produced by non-historians count as public history? Do those who make them become public historians as a consequence of their history work even though they have no training in the discipline?

It might be said that all history is public history in that it addresses publics. It might also be said that historians have always practiced history publicly. They have done so in varying ways and forms at all times and in all cultures. Yet, if all history might be said to be public history, it does not necessarily follow that all history is practiced publicly in the same way and to the same extent. *Going Public: The Changing Face of New Zealand History* was an important collection of essays that appeared just as the twenty-first century began. The editors, Bronwyn Dalley and Jock Phillips, assembled a group of historians each of whom in different ways and for various reasons had ended up "going public" in their history work, reshaping it to address larger concerns and broader audiences, in particular the increasing numbers of university-educated people at a time of "growing cultural nationalism" in Aotearoa/New Zealand.[46] A decade and a half later, another important essay collection appeared with the same main title: *Going Public: The Art of Participatory Practice*. Edited by Elizabeth Miller, Edward Little and Steven High, respectively professors of Communications, Theatre and History, this book brought "socially engaged practitioners in theatre, documentary media, the visual or multimedia arts, and oral history into conversation to explore how and with whom we collaborate, and why."[47] These complementary yet significantly different approaches to the historian's craft under the same title signal a shift from public history as history *for* and *about* publics to public history as history made *by* and *with* publics. It marks a move from a practice where historians speak *to* wider audiences to one where they work *with* them as collaborators and partners and in doing so embrace interdisciplinarity. One of the most important contributions of public historians to the broader discipline has been to trouble what we mean by doing history in the public sphere and by insisting on the value of history-making that is both participatory and more inclusive.

Notes

1 https://www.academia.edu/36603067/Call_for_Papers_The_PUBLIC_in_Public_and_Applied_History. This chapter began its life as one of three keynote presentations at the conference, and the others were by Cord Arendes who considered why public historians had written so little about the "public" and Jerome de Groot who explored what constituted "history" in public history practice. See also Cord Arendes, "What Do We Mean by 'Public'?", *Public History Weekly* 7, no. 27 (2019), https://dx.doi.org/10.1515/phw-2019-14181. I owe much to the presentations and conversations at the conference.

2 Gert Biesta, "Making Pedagogy Public: For the Public, of the Public, or in the Interest of Publicness?", in *Problematizing Public Pedagogy*, ed. Jake Burdick, Jennifer A. Sandlin, and Michael P. O'Malley (New York, London: Routledge, 2014), 21–23.

3 Ibid., 21–23.

4 Jürgen Habermas, "The Public Sphere: An Encyclopedia Article (1974)," *New German Critique* 3 (Autumn 1974): 49. Originally published in German in 1964. The major work is of course *The Structural Transformation of the Public Sphere: An Inquiry into a Category of Bourgeois Society* (Cambridge: Polity Press, 1989). Originally published in German in 1962.

5 Nancy Fraser, "Rethinking the Public Sphere: A Contribution to the Critique of Actually Existing Democracy," in *Habermas and the Public Sphere*, ed. Craig Calhoun (Cambridge, MA, London: MIT Press, 1992), 136–137.

6 Ibid., 123.
7 Ibid., 123–124.
8 Revisiting this early work many years later in a lucid discussion about transnational, diasporic and global public spheres, Fraser summarized the many and varied criticisms of *The Structural Transformation* and pointed out that its essential Westphalian framework (investing the state with absolute sovereignty over a nation) had rarely been questioned. See Fraser, *Scales of Justice: Reimagining Political Space in a Globalizing World* (Cambridge: Polity Press, 2008), 76–99.
9 Ian Angus, *Emergent Publics: An Essay on Social Movements and Democracy* (Winnipeg: Arbeiter Ring Publishing, 2010).
10 Fraser, "Rethinking," 124; "Publics and Counterpublics with Michael Warner – Conversations with History," University of California Television (UCTV), YouTube, April 18, 2018, https://www.youtube.com/watch?v=5PCTL1qidtg.
11 Michael Warner, *Publics and Counterpublics* (New York: Zone Books, 2002), 65.
12 Ibid., 66.
13 Ibid., 65–66.
14 Ibid., 67.
15 Ibid., 74–76.
16 Ibid., 87.
17 Ibid., 96.
18 Ibid., 91, 96.
19 Ibid., 114.
20 Warner, *Conversations*.
21 Biesta, "Making Pedagogy," 23.
22 Glenn C. Savage, "Chasing the Phantoms of Public Pedagogy. Political, Popular and Concrete Publics," in *Problematizing Public Pedagogy*, 80–90.
23 Ludmilla Jordanova, *History in Practice* (London: Hodder, 2000), 140.
24 Faye Sayer, *Public History: A Practical Guide* (London: Bloomsbury, 2015), 7.
25 Sayer, *Public History*, 7–13; Thomas Cauvin, *Public History: A Textbook of Practice* (New York, London: Routledge, 2016), 10–12; Cherstin Lyon, Samantha Nix and Rebecca Shrum, *Introduction to Public History: Interpreting the Past, Engaging Audiences* (Lanham: Rowman & Littlefield, 2017), 1–3.
26 Jerome De Groot, *Consuming History: Historians and Heritage in Contemporary Popular Culture* (New York, London: Routledge, 2008).
27 Raphael Samuel, *Theatres of Memory: Past and Present in Contemporary Culture* (London, New York: Verso, 1996).
28 Roy Rosenzweig and David Thelen, *The Presence of the Past: Popular Uses of History in American Life* (New York: Columbia University Press, 1998).
29 Paula Hamilton and Paul Ashton, *Australians and the Past* (Perth, Western Australia: University of Queensland Press, 2003).
30 The Pasts Collective, *Canadians and Their Pasts* (Toronto: University of Toronto Press, 2013).
31 David Dean, "Museums as Conflict Zones: The Canadian War Museum and Bomber Command," *Museum & Society* 7, no. 1 (2015): 1–15; Shelley Butler, *Contested Representations: Revisiting into the Heart of Africa* (Toronto: University of Toronto Press, 2007).
32 Canadian Museum of Civilization, *Exhibitions and Programmes, Exhibitions Management and Development Process* (Hull, Quebec: Canadian Museum of Civilization, 2001), Appendix 1 – Approach Paper.
33 Dean, "Politics and Memory in Canada's New History Museum," *Memoria e Ricerca, Rivista di storia contemporanea* 25, no. 1 (2017): 117–134.
34 Canadian Museum of History, *Exhibition Concept* (Gatineau, Quebec: Canadian Museum of History, 2016).
35 Ibid.
36 John Walsh, "Canadian History Hall: A Review," *The Canadian Historical Review* 100, no. 2 (June 2019): 280–285.

37 Nina Simon, *The Participatory Museum* (Santa Cruz: Web 2.0, 2010).
38 Susan Bennett, *Theatre & Museums* (Houndmills, Basingstoke: Palgrave Macmillan, 2013); Catherine Hughes, *Museum Theatre: Communicating with Visitors through Drama* (Portsmouth, New Hampshire: Heinemann, 1998).
39 "Museum of Civilization closes curtain on actor troupe," CBC [Canadian Broadcasting Corporation], August 16, 2011, https://www.cbc.ca/news/canada/ottawa/museum-of-civilization-closes-curtain-on-actor-troupe-1.1035433; "Civilization museum's $25M rebranding to focus on history," CBC, October 16, 2012, https://www.cbc.ca/news/canada/ottawa/civilization-museum-s-25m-rebranding-to-focus-on-history-1.1225802.
40 "Thomas Ostermeier and Mark Ravenhill in discussion with Peter Boenisch," YouTube, April 27, 2020, https://www.youtube.com/watch?time_continue=2&v=nrETP86byvs&feature=emb_logo.
41 Richard Schechner, *Performance Theory* (New York, London: Routledge, 1988), 72.
42 *"Ein Volksfeind* (An Enemy of the People)," *The Theatre Times*, accessed September 22, 2020, https://thetheatretimes.com/ein-volksfeind-an-enemy-of-the-people.
43 Pablo Helguera, *Education for Socially Engaged Art: A Materials and Techniques Handbook* (New York: Jorge Pinto Books, 2011), 14–15.
44 Jake Burdock, Jennifer A. Sandlin, and Michael P. O'Malley, "Breaking without Fixing: Inhabiting Aporia," in *Problematizing Public Pedagogy*, 2. The original reads: "Public pedagogy has been largely constructed as a concept focusing on various forms, processes, and sites of education and learning occurring beyond or outside of formal schooling. It involves learning in institutions such as museums, zoos, and libraries; in informal educational sites such as popular culture, media, commercial spaces, and the Internet [sic]; and through figures and sites of activism, including public intellectuals and grassroots social movements."
45 "About the field," National Council on Public History, accessed September 22, 2020, https://ncph.org/what-is-public-history/about-the-field.
46 Bronwyn Dalley and Jock Phillips, introduction to *Going Public: The Changing Face of New Zealand History* (Auckland: Auckland University Press, 2001), 10–11.
47 Elizabeth Miller, Edward Little, and Steven High, introduction to *Going Public: The Art of Participatory Practice* (Vancouver, Toronto: University of British Columbia Press, 2017), 3.

Bibliography

"About the field." National Council on Public History. Accessed September 22, 2020. https://ncph.org/what-is-public-history/about-the-field.
Angus, Ian. *Emergent Publics: An Essay on Social Movements and Democracy.* Winnipeg: Arbeiter Ring Publishing, 2010.
Arendes, Cord. "What Do We Mean by 'Public'?" *Public History Weekly* 7, no. 27 (2019). https://dx.doi.org/10.1515/phw-2019-14181.
Bennett, Susan. *Theatre & Museums.* Houndmills, Basingstoke: Palgrave Macmillan, 2013.
Burdick, Jake, Jennifer A. Sandlin, and Michael P. O'Malley, eds. *Problematizing Public Pedagogy.* New York, London: Routledge, 2014.
Butler, Shelley. *Contested Representations: Revisiting into the Heart of Africa.* Toronto: University of Toronto Press, 2007.
Canadian Museum of Civilization. *Exhibitions and Programmes, Exhibitions Management and Development Process.* Hull, Quebec: Canadian Museum of Civilization, 2001.

Canadian Museum of History. *Exhibition Concept.* Gatineau, Quebec: Canadian Museum of History, 2016.

Cauvin, Thomas. *Public History: A Textbook of Practice.* New York, London: Routledge, 2016.

"Civilization museum's $25M rebranding to focus on history." *CBC,* October 16, 2012. https://www.cbc.ca/news/canada/ottawa/civilization-museum-s-25m-rebranding-to-focus-on-history-1.1225802.

Dalley, Bronwyn, and Jock Phillips, eds. *Going Public: The Changing Face of New Zealand History.* Auckland: Auckland University Press, 2001.

Dean, David. "Museums as Conflict Zones: The Canadian War Museum and Bomber Command." *Museum & Society* 7, no. 1 (2015): 1–15.

Dean, David. "Politics and Memory in Canada's New History Museum." *Memoria e Ricerca, Rivista di storia contemporanea* 25, no. 1 (2017): 117–134.

De Groot, Jerome. *Consuming History: Historians and Heritage in Contemporary Popular Culture.* New York, London: Routledge, 2008.

"*Ein Volksfeind* (An Enemy of the People)." *The Theatre Times.* Accessed September 22, 2020. https://thetheatretimes.com/ein-volksfeind-an-enemy-of-the-people.

Fraser, Nancy. "Rethinking the Public Sphere: A Contribution to the Critique of Actually Existing Democracy." In *Habermas and the Public Sphere,* edited by Craig Calhoun, 109–142. Cambridge, MA, London: MIT Press, 1992.

Fraser, Nancy. *Scales of Justice: Reimagining Political Space in a Globalizing World.* Cambridge: Polity Press, 2008.

Habermas, Jürgen. "The Public Sphere: An Encyclopedia Article (1974)." *New German Critique* 3 (Autumn, 1974): 49−55.

Habermas, Jürgen. *The Structural Transformation of the Public Sphere: An Inquiry into a Category of Bourgeois Society.* Cambridge: Polity Press, 1989.

Hamilton, Paula, and Paul Ashton. *Australians and the Past.* Perth, Western Australia: University of Queensland Press, 2003.

Helguera, Pablo. *Education for Socially Engaged Art: A Materials and Techniques Handbook.* New York: Jorge Pinto Books, 2011.

Hughes, Catherine. *Museum Theatre: Communicating with Visitors through Drama.* Portsmouth, New Hampshire: Heinemann, 1998.

Jordanova, Ludmilla. *History in Practice.* London: Hodder, 2000.

Lyon, Cherstin, Samantha Nix, and Rebecca Shrum. *Introduction to Public History: Interpreting the Past, Engaging Audiences.* Lanham: Rowman & Littlefield, 2017.

Miller, Elizabeth, Edward Little, and Steven High. *Going Public: The Art of Participatory Practice.* Vancouver, Toronto: University of British Columbia Press, 2017.

"Museum of Civilization Closes Curtain on Actor Troupe." CBC, August 16, 2011. https://www.cbc.ca/news/canada/ottawa/museum-of-civilization-closes-curtain-on-actor-troupe-1.1035433.

Rosenzweig, Roy, and David Thelen. *The Presence of the Past: Popular Uses of History in American Life.* New York: Columbia University Press, 1998.

Samuel, Raphael. *Theatres of Memory: Past and Present in Contemporary Culture.* London, New York: Verso, 1996.

Sayer, Faye. *Public History: A Practical Guide.* London: Bloomsbury, 2015.

Schechner, Richard. *Performance Theory.* New York, London: Routledge, 1988.

Simon, Nina. *The Participatory Museum.* Santa Cruz: Web 2.0, 2010.

The Pasts Collective. *Canadians and Their Pasts.* Toronto: University of Toronto Press, 2013.

"Thomas Ostermeier and Mark Ravenhill in Discussion with Peter Boenisch." YouTube, April 27, 2020. https://www.youtube.com/watch?time_continue=2&v=nrETP86byvs&feature=emb_logo.

University of California Television (UCTV). "Publics and Counterpublics with Michael Warner – Conversations with History." YouTube, April 18, 2018. https://www.youtube.com/watch?v=5PCTL1qidtg.

Walsh, John. "Canadian History Hall: A Review." *The Canadian Historical Review* 100, no. 2 (June 2019): 280–285.

Warner, Michael. *Publics and Counterpublics.* New York: Zone Books, 2002.

PART I
Museums and Their Publics

2

WARSAW RISING MUSEUM—ON, WITH AND FOR A PARTICIPATORY PUBLIC

Paweł Ukielski

On July 31, 2004, thousands of people came to a former tramway power plant located in the Wola district in Warsaw for the solemn opening of the Warsaw Rising Museum—the institution that was created in an extremely short period of time, but nonetheless had already managed to build its "trade mark" and to foster a broad desire within the public to confront imagination with reality. It was a milestone in Polish museology as it is the first

FIGURE 2.1 Interactive part of the exhibition in the Warsaw Rising Museum, © Warsaw Rising Museum.

historical museum in Poland to open after 15 years of independence follow-ing the fall of Communism. It is also a modern, narrative and interactive museum which has created a new approach both to the idea of historical exhibition and to the activity of institutions as such. It has proposed a revo-lutionary change in comparison to earlier, much more conservative methods of presentation, focused on objects rather than the education and populari-zation of history within the broader public. The shift from a visitor-observer to a visitor-participant approach has irreversibly changed the concept of the museum in Poland and public expectations toward it.

This "revolution" has brought significant change of attitude toward mu-seums, especially the historical ones. Since then, many new institutions have been established (just to mention only a few of them: the POLIN Museum of the History of Polish Jews in Warsaw, the European Solidarity Center and Museum of the Second World War in Gdańsk, the Depot History Center in Wrocław, the Emigration Museum in Gdynia, the Silesian Museum in Katowice and the Dialogue Center Upheavals in Szczecin) and the annual number of visitors to Polish museums has more than doubled.[1] The Warsaw Rising Museum itself, during 15 years of functioning, has had either stable or growing annual numbers of visitors, exceeding half a million (visitors to the main exhibition only) or 700,000 (including accompanying events) and never recording a visible decrease.

In this chapter the role of the public in the functioning of the Warsaw Rising Museum will be analyzed. The analysis will be conducted based on documents, and secondary sources centered mostly on statements and remarks by the muse-um's management and staff. Another source of information will be the author's memory, as he himself had participated in the whole process of the museum's creation and was its deputy director in the years 2004–2014 and since 2016.

With the Public(s): The Public(s) in the Creation Process

Guidelines for the creation of the museum had already been written in June 2003 by the initiation team. In the document, the authors stressed various goals of the institution: educational, social, museological and popularizing. Six target groups of the museum were defined, which were:

- Children;
- Students of primary, middle and high schools as well as university students;
- Insurgent environments, veterans and their families;
- Tourists, both from within Poland and abroad, and in particular Poles from abroad;
- Students, researchers and ordinary people whose focus of interest is modern Polish history;
- Soldiers on active service.[2]

As was stated in the document, "from an exhibition point of view, those are groups with disjunctive features, and therefore the project has been prepared in such a manner that each of them would find an adequate message or set of information."[3] Paweł Kowal summarized it aptly: "We decided on the concept of the museum for 'grandparents and grandchildren.'"[4]

The "grandparents" were the most important target group in the process of creation. It would be impossible to create a popular museum referring to the history of the Warsaw Rising without the veterans, as it is their story. Therefore, on the one hand, one of the core foundations of the museum was to pay homage to the insurgents.[5] On the other hand, however, it was also important to refer to the most modern museums in the world, avoid "museological boredom" and use a broad variety of means of communication.[6] Those factors appeared difficult to combine. At that time, not only were the veterans elderly people, but they were also those who had been waiting for the museum for decades, enduring falsifications of history during the Communist period and unfulfilled promises during the 14 previous years of an independent Poland. They had been meeting each other for many years, debating about the most important event in their lives (the Warsaw Rising of 1944) and their individual visions of the desired exhibition had been founded. Naturally, each of the visions was different.

The first reaction of the insurgents was quite reserved, as they had no reason to believe that, after many years of no progress in building a museum, it would actually happen this time. As Jan Ołdakowski recalled of his first meeting with veterans in July 2003:

> I talked enthusiastically about my new mission, they listened—cold and ruthless. And then a regular fire began. All questions started with the phrase "and why not?" Why is Mr. X or Mrs. Y not involved in this project? Why is the museum not dedicated to "Zośka" and "Parasol" battalions? Why… And so on for the following two hours.[7]

However, when the veterans realized that works were proceeding quite quickly and the opening of the museum was becoming a reality, their attitude changed. They turned out to be more flexible than expected, as they accepted the modern vision of the exhibition. Some of them said: "We know this history, do it in the way that would attract those who do not know it," while others told us: "We do not fully understand what you mean, but if youngsters would come, do it your way."[8]

The role of veterans from the very beginning was significantly greater than just a mere "target group." They were treated as co-hosts of the museum, people who would build the specific atmosphere of the place, those participants of history (both of the "great" one and the personal ones), whom visitors could meet in the museum. In the Guidelines, it was defined as follows: "The museum should be a place of communication not only between today's veterans and visitors, but between youngsters of those days with the contemporary youth."[9] They also had "consultative power"—not only through discussions on the shape of the exhibition, but also to determine what ideas were acceptable to them and what might offend or distress them. Thanks to such consultations, they could explain that the use of the symbol for the Polish Underground State ("Fighting Poland"—a letter "P" with an anchor) for promotional purposes is acceptable, whereas armbands are reserved for insurgents only and should not be used in any kind of cultural, social or anniversary event.[10]

After the opening of the museum, the veterans became frequent visitors to the institution. They participated in anniversaries, numerous events, meetings with youth, but they also visited the exhibition—however, their manner of exploring it differed from that of other visitors'. As Jan Ołdakowski has described it:

> How can one recognize an Insurgent in the Warsaw Rising Museum? He is turned with his back to the exhibition and faces the visitors. Because he had known and seen everything that is in display cases, it is the children's reactions that really "turn him on."[11]

One of the biggest concerns during works on the museum was communication with the public. Creators of the project decided to work in full transparency and to inform the public about every step in the process. As described in the Guidelines:

> We propose the implementation of the concept of a "museum growing in front of the inhabitants of Warsaw," a "museum visible on all streets of Warsaw, on the subway and in the trams," as an element of communication with the inhabitants of Warsaw and involving them in the discussion about the Rising, contemporary patriotism and finally the museum project itself.[12]

Close co-operation with the media, especially local ones, was therefore of crucial importance. The team led an open and broad policy of information, resulting in a great number of press, radio and TV items about the emerging museum, and, after some time, it led to a self-identification of numerous journalists with the project.[13]

Simultaneously, several public actions aiming at the activation of the society were held. In the public collection of memorabilia held on November 9–11, 2003, several hundred people (insurgents and their families) came to donate about two thousand items. The aim of this policy was to create an awareness of the emerging institution and a sense of its importance among the broad public (with special stress placed on Varsovians). The collection of memorabilia became a success not only because of the number of exhibits acquired, but also as a turning point in the veterans' attitude toward the project and the scale and tone of media reports.[14] The first visible fruits came within a few months—according to a poll conducted in December 2003 more than 12 percent of Poles regarded Warsaw Rising Museum as number one on their list of "must see" places to visit, even though it was a museum that had not yet come into being.[15] All those activities combined: the work with veterans, the collection of memorabilia and the broad actions of information aimed at building "circles of loyalty." The first circle was constituted of insurgents, as they were "waiting for the museum and were emotionally involved." To cite Jan Ołdakowski again: "Historical narrative museums are museums of witnesses—as it is they and their families who are waiting for the commemoration of the event in which they took part."[16] The second circle is described as: "All those who believe that events presented in the museum are significant for the history of Poland or important to understand some aspects of it or to comprehend local history."[17] Paweł Kowal labels the second circle as "Varsovians" who were waiting for "the most Varsovian museum."[18]

The decision-making process has been described by Paweł Kowal:

> We had two strategies to choose from for informing people about the museum: a big surprise opening upon completion, or remaining in regular contact with the journalists and thus Varsovians. Large museum projects around the world frequently make use of the big surprise opening. Their authors kept silent about their work until the opening day. This is somewhat reminiscent of work on a new product aimed at surprising the market, or a new periodical in which all information is protected until the printing of the first issue. Who doesn't know the joy of an artist from the surprised faces during a vernissage? It is worth applying this method, particularly when we are certain of its success, as the museum subject is appealing to society and there are no financing problems. So, it seems that from a time perspective, we should have chosen just such a path. Ultimately, we decided to build the museum in the open. We assumed that we don't have any secrets to hide from the public. As Varsovians have waited years for this museum, we decided to build it together with them. In this way, we sensed the opportunity for the smooth functioning of the museum in the future.[19]

It should be added that the biggest concern was neither money nor public support for the project, but time. Due to the extremely short time for the creation of the institution, its exhibition curators were aware that only the providing of extensive information about every step would absolve them if something failed.

For the Public(s): Exhibition as a Means of Communication

For a museum, an exhibition is its calling card or trademark. Paweł Kowal, who took part in several foreign study visits at the beginning of the project recalls: "We were told that if we want youth to visit a museum, it would have to be like a computer program or a modern television."[20] Therefore, from the very beginning, a great variety of tools for communication were planned: "As forms of expression the scenographic visual means, photography, computer animations, film materials, music, and internet should be broadly used."[21] Everything was subordinated to the aim to "avoid 'museological boredom.'"[22]

In a competition for a concept of the exhibition, the winning project was created by a team of three designers, each with different skills and experience: interior designer Mirosław Nizio, computer graphic designer Jarosław Kłaput and theatrical scenographer Dariusz Kunowski. Their diversity became a strength of the project, as they combined a variety of skills and artistic sensitivity as well as solutions from different art fields.

The main idea of the exhibition was to create an atmosphere, to make visitors feel that after entering the museum and closing the door they are leaving the contemporary world behind and entering history. As the designers have stressed in their concept: "We want the visitors to cross the barrier of passive observation, of standing aside, so that they feel drawn into the whirlwind of events for a moment, feel similar [to Insurgents'] emotions."[23] Therefore, for example, visitors do not walk on a plain floor typical of museums but on a cobbled street instead, and a symbolic monument placed in the center, emitting heartbeat audible from every part of the exhibition. Designers have described it as follows: "We designed the exhibition as if it had human features—it has a voice, an image, it moves, trembles, emits heat..."[24]

All those means of communication used in the exhibition aim at the creation of an interactive museum. This notion needs some explanation as it is often identified with the term "multimedia," which is a considerable oversimplification. The idea of an interactive museum, as one of the basic assumptions of the Warsaw Rising Museum creators, has meant a museum that is establishing interaction between a visitor and history. Multimedia constitutes only one feature among many different approaches to visitors and should not be treated as an end in itself. Therefore, to keep the display attractive, a proper balance between different means of presentation is crucial. Multimedia cannot overwhelm it because firstly, today people have a lot of multimedia equipment at home and it will not attract them to museums—they still prefer the older-style exhibits that build deeper connection with the past; and secondly, multimedia constitutes the part of exhibition that is aging most quickly.

It might be considered to be a paradox in a narrative museum, but in the Warsaw Rising Museum there is no strictly indicated tour route. Each visitor is able to find his or her own unique way of going through the exhibition, and decides upon the order of visiting numerous thematic parts of it. The visitors are encouraged to arrange their own path through the past events.[25] However, they are not left completely alone—calendar pages (one for each day of the Warsaw Rising with a short description of what happened on that particular day) constitute a kind of signposting throughout the whole exhibition. Small sheets of paper, stylized as old-school calendars, play two roles. First, they help in understanding the time lapse and the moment of history visitors "are in." Second, they are leaflets to be collected—an attentive visitor is able to gather 71 sheets with all the most important events from the Warsaw Rising and take the collection home.[26] Calendar sheets became very popular among the public, and are one of the most interactive parts of the exhibition—every week several visitors write letters or e-mails asking the museum to send them sheets they missed during the visit. They are a kind of trademark of the museum, as people leaving the exhibition can be recognized because they are carrying a collection of them.

One of the biggest challenges that the exhibition's curators had faced was the question of the text information in the museum. On the one hand, it was obvious that written information is one of basic elements of each exhibition—it delivers certain knowledge to visitors, explains objects and describes the broader context. On the other hand, as stated above, to attract youngsters, it was necessary to "combine modern TV with a computer program," which meant less text. It seemed clear that in the modern era, people do not like reading long dissertations, and thus texts should be more like headlines and less like academic treatises. Therefore, a decision was made to have text information structured into four categories (apart from the calendar pages), each with its own non-extendible number of characters. The structure was as follows:

- Basic information (900 characters, with extension to circa 3,000 characters for a leaflet);
- Detailed information (600 characters);
- Photo/exhibit description (250 characters);
- Biography (1,000 characters; this category of texts is presented in special drawers all over the exhibition, which is another interactive solution applied in the museum).

To give visitors an even stronger impression of dynamics and to break down the barrier between them and history, it was decided to write all the texts in the present tense. Great attention was also paid to using texts that are easy for any visitor to comprehend.

Foreign visitors were one of the target groups, and thus the exhibition is bilingual (Polish and English), which is a quite obvious and common practice in modern museology, and so is the accessibility of guided tours in several languages. For this latter purpose, the museum initiated cooperation with embassies, proposing to translate and record the text of museum's audio guides. As a result, in a relatively short time, the museum had them available in more than 20 languages.[27]

The Warsaw Rising Museum's exhibition was created in two phases. Its first part, covering the narrative story from the beginning of the Second World War through the occupation of Poland and the Warsaw Rising with its multiple aspects, to the ending with the demolition of Warsaw, the POW camps where Insurgents were sent after the Rising and communist rule after the war, was opened in 2004. The second part, with the full-scale replica of a Liberator B-17 bomber, a sewer replica, the theme of "Germans in Warsaw" and the 3D cinema hall has been open to the public since 2006 (although not all elements were ready then). The second phase was in progress while the museum was already hosting visitors, who were encouraged to share their opinions. Therefore, the second part is more "participatory." The idea of building a replica of the plane came from numerous discussions with veterans, who wanted to pay tribute to airmen who flew to Warsaw to deliver airdrops. The sewer and "Germans in Warsaw" sections, on the other hand, were the results of surveys among visitors, who suggested that those elements should be presented in a more detailed way.

The second part of the exhibition has another feature distinguishing it from the first, narrative part—it is much less "dense." The narrative line which opened in 2004 contains a great deal of information and incentives attracting visitors' attention on various levels and with different senses, especially at the beginning of the route. The basic aim of such a construction of the exhibition was to overwhelm the audience from the very beginning, to strengthen their feeling of immersion in history. Another goal was to induce people to return to the museum, as they leave the exhibition with a feeling that once was not enough and they have missed some interesting parts of the story. This intention proved to be successful—according to a survey conducted in 2015, almost 40 percent of the museum's visitors were not on their first visit to the exhibition.[28]

The "Liberator Hall" constitutes a different zone—it is much less intensive, with a lot of space. This part is, as designers described it in their project, "a place of quiet reverie and reflection."[29] It is the last part of the museum, and therefore the exhibition is constructed following the rule "from more to less intensive." The different nature of this space also gives an opportunity to organize cultural events of different kinds for hundreds of people. The same possibility is also given by the Freedom Park—the outdoor space with grass and trees beside the museum. It is an integral part of the exhibition, where the Remembrance Wall and memorial monuments are located. It provides even more possibilities for taking a deep breath during a visit to the museum, but also for organizing events for several thousand people. This is where the annual meeting of the President of Poland with veterans takes place.

By the Public: Participatory Practices

Discovering New Information in Collaboration with the Public

The Warsaw Rising is one of the most important events in Polish history of the twentieth century, and thus it is not surprising that there is an enormous literature about it. Nevertheless, we still lack a lot of detailed information— even the precise number of victims (both soldiers and civilians) is unknown. The Warsaw Rising Museum from the very beginning has been working to gather as much information as possible in cooperation with the public.

The beginning of the process started before the opening of the museum— with the abovementioned public collection of memorabilia, which has been conducted as an ongoing and permanent practice since, and with consultations with veterans. In the spring of 2004, before the museum's opening, the Veteran's Room was opened. Insurgents could meet there, along with the volunteers, to give their memoirs and deliver information about their own and their friends' and colleagues' fate.[30] Moreover, soon after the museum's opening, the Oral History Archive was established.

All those actions were broadly communicated through the media to encourage people to share their memories, documents, memorabilia and information. All the information is used in commemorative projects, including a flagship project—the Remembrance Wall located in the Freedom Park beside the museum. Its idea was to commemorate all fallen insurgents with their names carved in stone. Together with the inflow of information, which is verified by historians, the list is extended every year. In 2020, it has reached 11,511 names.[31]

To extend the action of gathering information, the museum developed another project enabling a broad audience to share their knowledge— "Insurgent Biographies." It is an online dictionary of insurgents founded on an open collaboration basis (the method popularized by Wikipedia). The project not only gives possibilities of adding an insurgent or amending information about one of them, but also to attach documents or photographs. All the information is verified by historians and the museum's database is expanding—in August 2020, it contained 56,097 records.[32] A similar method and pattern of gathering information was applied to civilian victims of the Warsaw Rising. After years of research and completing data from people, the database contains 53,488 names, which is far less than half of the expected number.[33] The project is accompanied by cyclical exhibition "Let's keep their memory alive" held every year since 2015.[34]

The action "Recognize" was of a similar character. It accompanied the creation of the film "Warsaw Uprising" —the first non-fiction war drama.[35] Using documentary material had a significant shortcoming—numerous people who appeared in the newsreels were unknown. Therefore, the audience was asked to support the museum by recognizing people that appeared in the film. As Jan Ołdakowski described it: "It was creating the cast for the movie *à rebours* [...] The cast was completed 70 years ago. The only task for the Warsaw Rising Museum was to identify the characters."[36] A gallery with unidentified people was published both on the official museum website and as a Facebook profile. As a result, altogether about 130 persons out of about 400 were identified.[37]

The Museum as an Inclusive Cultural Center

In the establishing document written in June 2003, creators of the museum wrote that it "should also play the role of a 'center,' where youngsters, students, tourists and veterans will spend their time, where different activities are proposed to them."[38] This implies that from the very beginning, the Warsaw Rising Museum was perceived in the modern way—not as a mere permanent exhibition with temporary exhibitions from time to time, but as a cultural center with numerous events of different kinds that would attract various target groups. Jan Ołdakowski defined it as an idea of a "polyphonic museum."[39]

The idea was strengthened with the decision of the Mayor of Warsaw, Lech Kaczyński, that the same team that had been building the museum should organize the 60th anniversary of the Warsaw Rising celebrations.[40] These celebrations were supposed to be "different from all the previous ones."[41] The idea was to prepare a much more "inclusive" set of commemorative events, to gather as broad an audience as possible, and to offer different people with different sensitivities a chance to find their own modes of expression. The primary concept was to create a custom of celebrating together as a community.[42]

The subsequent years confirmed the position of the Warsaw Rising celebrations as a leading anniversary on the map of important events in Warsaw. They are organized to last several days and cover a great variety of events. Most of those organized by the museum already have the status of annual events, but at the same time each anniversary is marked by spectacular exclusive events: a concert connected with a record release, a theater play premiere at midnight on August 1, a bicycle parade or a location-based photo game "Your Film from the Rising."[43] The participation of veterans, who are honorary guests of the celebrations, is fundamental as, apart from being honored, they also create an opportunity for the youngsters to meet the insurgents in person. The culmination of the events is the meeting of the insurgents with the President of Poland and the Mayor of Warsaw in the Freedom Park beside the museum.[44]

Two anniversary events are of a particularly participatory nature. The social action "Freedom Binds" takes place annually exactly on August 1 at 5 p.m.—the precise anniversary of the break-up of the Rising. Scouts and the museum volunteers hand out pins with the symbol of Fighting Poland to passers-by in hundreds of remembrance places in Warsaw. The action involves hundreds of the museum's collaborators and thousands of Varsovians and tourists.[45]

Another event which has become very popular and attracts many thousands of people every year is the collective singing of Insurgent songs with an orchestra and choir.[46] The action named "Varsovians sing (un-)prohibited songs" quickly became one of the "trademarks" of the anniversary celebrations and the museum itself, and is broadcast by the main program of public television, with an audience of between two and three million viewers.[47]

The museum did not limit its cultural activities to anniversary celebrations or even the Warsaw Rising topic only. Shortly after opening it established its branch, the Stefan Starzyński Institute, named after the legendary Mayor of Warsaw who was killed by the Germans during World War II. The idea of the Institute, however, is not to focus on the history of the war, but on contemporary Warsaw—its identity, dynamic development, architecture, urban planning, culture and diversity.[48] It is based on the conviction that the importance of the Warsaw Rising for the city, its inhabitants and identity is significant enough to legitimize the existence of a cultural branch of that kind within the framework of the museum.

The flagship of the Institute is its "Innocent Sorcerers" Warsaw Festival which has taken place every year in November since 2006. Each year, the Festival have been dedicated to a different decade of the twentieth century or to a special topic, and all events have been subordinated to the main thematic line. Subsequent years have also had different artists and their work as the leitmotiv of the Festival program. A diverse set of events has been proposed each year—dancing, silent discos, theatre plays, workshops, debates, concerts, city-games and performances.[49] In 2010, the Festival was granted the prestigious cultural award WDECHA in the category of "Event of the Year."[50]

The Institute organizes numerous other events—series of lectures, workshops or walk-throughs of different kind, competitions and podium discussions. Similar activities are also organized by other departments of the museum (educational, historical and promotional, as well as other branches of the museum), the Warsaw Fotoplastikon (stereoscopic theatre) and the Cells of the Secret Service (an exhibition devoted to communist persecutions against the Home Army soldiers). All those activities, both larger- and smaller-scale, deliver a broad variety of possibilities for any interested visitor.

Social Media—New Possibilities of Participation

The second decade of the twenty-first century has been marked by the rapid development of social media and a significant increase in its influence on shaping people's activities. The museum has been developing together with them and from the very beginning has used them broadly and explored emerging possibilities. In 2020, social media was one of the basic means of the museum's interaction with the public. Over 420,000 followers in all social media channels (Facebook: 336,000[51]; Instagram: 48,000[52]; Twitter: 25,000[53]; YouTube: 15,000[54], as of August 21, 2020) are an excellent base for active communication with the public and building public engagement. Creating such a large group of followers was a result of several years of interactive work—dedicated projects and campaigns in individual channels of communication.

The developed social media communication has proved to be extremely useful during the COVID-19 pandemic and subsequent lockdown. From the first day of the closing of schools and cultural institutions (March 16, 2020), the museum decided to use the live streaming option, thanks to which direct contact with recipients was established. Despite the closure of the exhibition for visitors, they have been provided with contact with the institution, which (especially at the beginning of the lockdown) enjoyed great interest. The subject matter of the broadcasts was varied and adapted to various groups of the public: from history lessons where the core curriculum was implemented, through lectures on the architecture of Warsaw, to a virtual tour of the Warsaw Rising Museum. From March to June 2020, 185 live broadcasts were organized with a total of 3,090,326 views.[55] Interaction was a crucial element of all the broadcasts: viewers could ask questions to the hosts, producers reacted to viewers' suggestions and topics for subsequent meetings were selected together with the public.

The three months of live broadcasting culminated in the Great Streamers Quiz, which the museum conducted on June 10, 2020 on Twitch, the video game streaming platform. Popular gamers prepared mini history lessons for their viewers. While playing their favorite games, they shared the knowledge prepared in cooperation with the museum, and then provided the viewers with a special quiz to check how much information they remembered. The reach of the campaign in social media was 42,750 users, 75,200 of streams displayed and 555,600 minutes of streaming watch time. Altogether, 300 people took part in the quiz, and the best of them received prizes (gaming equipment: chairs, mice, and mouse pads).[56]

Social media, a tool that was already a relevant means of communication and interaction in previous years, proved its usefulness during lockdown even more. Some activities initiated due to the pandemic will probably become a part of the "everyday life" of the museum, as live streaming combined with interaction is planned to be continued in the future.

Modern Volunteering as the Highest Level of Participation

One of the closest "circles of loyalty" in the museum has been volunteering. Established at the very beginning of the process of creation of the new institution, it was a novelty in Poland, as volunteers were introduced to a modern system—with an agreement, rights and duties and responsible tasks to complete. In the beginning, it was a group of a dozen or so people who were assisting in the process of the creation of the museum. Later, after the opening, the number increased significantly. The organizational scheme of their work was based on the pattern of American museums, which at the time had not yet become popular in Poland.[57]

From the very beginning, two iron principles had been established in the museum. First, volunteering is not a path to getting a job. Those two worlds do not mix—either a person is a volunteer or an employee. The rule is strictly respected to avoid any unclear situations and to keep real enthusiasm among the volunteers. Second, volunteers do not get "stupid work," such as fetching things, making copies or making coffee. They get genuine, important and responsible tasks that can satisfy their need for action and a sense of mission.[58]

In 2019, about 200 volunteers collaborated with the museum on a regular basis; in July and at the beginning of August, including the preparations and anniversary celebrations, this number temporarily tripled. They are mostly young (almost two thirds are under 26), but elderly people are also volunteers (almost 10 percent are over 65), which makes it an inter-generational group, where they can profit from each other's experience. Over 60 percent of the volunteers work for more than a year, which means they prefer a long-term relationship with the institution. The vast majority of them (71 percent) are female. Between January and November 2019, volunteers participated in 1,007 events and worked for circa 32,500 hours.[59]

Volunteers collaborate with almost all departments of the museum. They have trainings and workshops, after which they can become, for example, guides in the permanent exhibition, educators in the Little Insurgent Room or interviewers in the Oral History Archive.[60] It is worth underlining that almost all interviews in the Archive that had been gathered so far were conducted by volunteers. Until mid-2020, the Archive had about 4,000 interviews with insurgents and civilians who were in Warsaw during the Rising.[61]

Reasons for volunteers to start collaboration with the museum are various. Youngsters often want to get experience and work on interesting projects where some responsibility is entrusted in them. Usually, they are either connected to the Warsaw Rising and insurgents by family ties (in the first few years of the museum's existence, some insurgents were volunteers as well) or simply interested in history. They are commonly devoted to the values that stood behind the Rising—patriotism, respect for independence, democracy and freedom. Older volunteers are often already retired and want to feel needed, have responsible duties and share life experience with younger people.[62] Some of them say that throughout the years, they have created a powerful, intergenerational group of friends rather than just co-workers.

The trans-generational ties emerge not only between younger and older volunteers but also between volunteers and veterans. The action "Call the

Grandparents" can serve as an example. It was organized by the museum immediately after the COVID-19 lockdown was announced in Poland in March 2020. The Warsaw Rising Museum established a system of scheduled phone calls to all living veterans—employees and volunteers were calling them to explain the situation, ask about their needs and in some cases to organize help. The director of the museum, Jan Ołdakowski, publicly called on others to do the same for elderly people.[63] As a result, the museum has a large group of devoted people who are not only ready to work for it, but has also created a special, close "circle of loyalty" strongly bound to the institution with a special atmosphere of co-creating it and participating in its development.

Conclusion

The Warsaw Rising Museum was the first Polish modern, narrative and interactive historical museum created after 1989. Since the very first document, its aims and methods of communication were defined to be as inclusive and participatory as possible. The idea was brought to life from the very initial stage of the creation process, as the public was involved through consultations and numerous open actions (such as the collection of memorabilia) and broadly informed by the media about the emerging institution. As a result, the interactive exhibition was opened as a culmination of the 60th anniversary of the Warsaw Rising celebrations.

The museum has developed a great variety of activities to attract people. It has become a broad cultural center, an institution that gathers a great number of documents and data to discover new facts about history, and a popular center for volunteering. Social media has been an important means of communication for many years and became even more important during the COVID-19 pandemic. All those activities were developed to attract the public and to encourage them to participate, either by visiting the exhibition or by participation in the events organized by the museum. It might be considered as a "revolution" in Polish museology, where for decades the focus had been on the objects rather than on the public.

After the opening, the museum soon became a "must see" in Warsaw, exceeding the expectations of its creators. What is even more important, it has become a trendsetter among Polish museums—it has been a reference point not only for newly created institutions, but also for many existing ones that have decided to transform their programs of events and exhibitions toward greater openness to the public.

Modern museology all over the world has already followed this direction of development for several decades. The paradigm of a participatory public is one of the fundamental ideas of museums, and—in a broader view—cultural institutions.

Notes

1 According to data published by the Main Statistical Office in Poland, in 2018 the number of visitors to Polish museums exceeded 38 million, while in 2004 it was about 17.5 million. See *Kultura w 2018 r.* (Warsaw, Cracow: Główny Urząd Statystyczny, 2019), 74, https://stat.gov.pl/obszary-tematyczne/kultura-turystyka-sport/kultura/kultura-w-2018-roku,2,16.html; *Kultura w 2004 r.* (Warsaw, Cracow: Główny Urząd Statystyczny, 2005), 129, https://stat.gov.pl/obszary-tematyczne/kultura-turystyka-sport/kultura/kultura-w-2004-r-,2,2.html?pdf=1.

2 Jan Ołdakowski, Paweł Kowal, in cooperation with Joanna Bojarska and Lena Dąbkowska-Cichocka, *Podstawowe założenia programowe i organizacyjne Muzeum Powstania Warszawskiego w Warszawie ul. Przyokopowa 28* (Warsaw, 2003), 9, document in author's collection.

3 Ibid.

4 Paweł Kowal, "How We Built the Museum," in *Guidebook to the Warsaw Rising Museum*, ed. Lena Dąbkowska-Cichocka et al. (Warsaw: Warsaw Rising Museum, 2007), 7.

5 Ołdakowski et al., *Podstawowe założenia programowe*, 5.

6 Ibid., 4.

7 Piotr Legutko, *Jedyne takie Muzeum. Odzyskana Pamięć o Powstaniu Warszawskim* (Cracow: Znak, 2014), 116.

8 Ibid., 118.

9 Ołdakowski et al., *Podstawowe założenia programowe*, 5–6.

10 Legutko, *Jedyne takie Muzeum*, 118–119.

11 Ibid., 121.

12 Ołdakowski et al., *Podstawowe założenia programowe*, 7.

13 See for instance Kamil Zubelewicz, ed., *Księga prasowa Muzeum Powstania Warszawskiego*, vol. 1 (Warsaw: Muzeum Powstania Warszawskiego, 2004).

14 Legutko, *Jedyne takie Muzeum*, 93; Agnieszka Sopińska-Jaremczak, *Operacja Muzeum* (Warsaw: Fronda, 2014), 43–46.

15 Agnieszka Panecka, ed., *Polityka historyczna. Historycy – politycy – prasa* (Warsaw: Muzeum Powstania Warszawskiego, 2005), 272.

16 Ołdakowski, "Dlaczego powstają muzea historyczne narracyjne," in *Muzeum i zmiana. Losy muzeów narracyjnych*, ed. Paweł Kowal and Karolina Wolska-Pabian (Warsaw: Muzeum Powstania Warszawskiego; Cracow: Towarzystwo Autorów i Wydawców Prac Naukowych "Universitas," 2019), 76.

17 Ibid.

18 Legutko, *Jedyne takie Muzeum*, 121.

19 Kowal, "How We Built," 8–9.

20 Ibid., 8.

21 Ołdakowski et al., *Podstawowe założenia programowe*, 4.

22 Ibid.

23 Jarosław Kłaput, Dariusz Kunowski, and Mirosław Nizio, *Muzeum Powstania Warszawskiego ul. Przyokopowa 28 w Warszawie. Prezentacja koncepcji na ekspozycję Muzeum Powstania Warszawskiego*, 3, document in the author's collection.

24 Ibid.

25 Sometimes, the way of presentation of the narrative line in such a manner is criticised and not all visitors accept it. See some critical opinions on Tripadvisor, accessed August, 27, 2020, https://pl.tripadvisor.com/Attraction_Review-g274856-d1154437-Reviews-Muzeum_Powstania_Warszawskiego-Warsaw_Mazovia_Province_Central_Poland.html.

26 Sopińska-Jaremczak, *Operacja Muzeum*, 129–130.

27 In 2020 it was 26 foreign languages (plus Polish): Azeri, Bulgarian, Chinese, Chroatian, Czech, Danish, Dutch, English, Finnish, French, Georgian, German, Hebrew, Hungarian, Indonesian, Italian, Japanese, Macedonian, Polish, Portugese, Romanian, Russian, Slovak, Slovenian, Spanish, Swedish, Ukrainian; see "Visit us," Warsaw Rising Museum, accessed August 27, 2020, https://www.1944.pl/en/article/visit-us,4993.html.

28 *Cykliczne badanie opinii osób zwiedzających Muzeum Powstania Warszawskiego*, 6, document in author's collection.

29 Kłaput, Kunowski, Nizio, *Muzeum Powstania Warszawskiego*, 3.

30 Legutko, *Jedyne takie Muzeum*, 115.

31 "Wirtualny Mur Pamięci," Warsaw Rising Museum, accessed August 27, 2020, https://www.1944.pl/wirtualny-mur-pamieci.html.

32 "Powstańcze Biogramy," Warsaw Rising Museum, accessed August 27, 2020, https://www.1944.pl/powstancze-biogramy.html.

33 "Ofiary cywilne," Warsaw Rising Museum, accessed August 27, 2020, https://www.1944.pl/ofiary-cywilne.html.

34 "Marsz Pamięci i otwarcie wystawy *Zachowajmy ich w pamięci*," Warsaw Rising Museum, last modified August 4, 2005, accessed August 27, 2020, https://www.1944.pl/artykul/marsz-pamieci-i-otwarcie-wystawy-zachowajmy-ic,4331.html.

35 The movie was the first in the world to attempt to combine original historical footage with a scenario written recently. The footage taken during the Warsaw Rising was colorized and remastered and then used to illustrate a story. See Jan Komasa, dir., *Warsaw Upising. 87 minutes of truth* (Warsaw Rising Museum, Polski Instytut Sztuki Filmowej, 2014), http://warsawrising-thefilm.com.

36 Iza Michalewicz, Maciej Piwowarczuk, *Powstanie Warszawskie. Rozpoznani* (Warsaw: Muzeum Powstania Warszawskiego, Agora, 2014), 5.

37 Ibid. Interestingly, four persons recognized themselves. See Michał T. Wójciuk, "Muzeum Powstania Warszawskiego i kombatanci – integracja pokoleń a funkcje wychowawcze na przykładzie projektów oraz 'wydarzeń' zrealizowanych w latach 2004–2016," in *"Ojczyzna obrońcy swemu." Weterani i kombatanci jako problem polityczny i społeczny w Polsce XX wieku*, ed. Marek Kornat, Marcin Kruszyński, and Tomasz Osiński (Lublin, Warsaw: Instytut Pamięci Narodowej, 2017), 436.

38 Ołdakowski et al., *Podstawowe założenia programowe*, 4.

39 Ołdakowski, "Dlaczego powstają muzea," 74.

40 *Guidebook to the Warsaw Rising Museum*, 20.

41 Sopińska-Jaremczak, *Operacja Muzeum*, 115.

42 Ibid., 122.

43 The idea of the game is to follow the route and photograph historical scenes and places in the city. There are four categories of competition: detail, object in motion, portrait and reportage.

44 See for instance "Programme of the 75th Warsaw Rising Anniversary Ceremonies," Warsaw Rising Museum, https://f.1944.pl/UserFiles/4/d/7/4d7037b054f10a5a5179-6b6d607bb556.pdf.

45 "Akcja społeczna: Wolność łączy," Warsaw Rising Museum, last modified July 31, 2019, accessed August 27, 2020, https://www.1944.pl/artykul/akcja-spoleczna-wolnosc-laczy,4929.html.

46 "Warszawiacy śpiewają (nie)ZAKAZANE PIOSENKI," Warsaw Rising Museum, last modified July 29, 2020, accessed August 27, 2020, https://www.1944.pl/artykul/warszawiacy-spiewaja-nie-zakazane-piosenki,4928.html.

47 According to Polish public television.

48 "Oddziały Muzeum," Warsaw Rising Museum, last modified July 28, 2020, accessed August 27, 2020, https://www.1944.pl/artykul/oddzialy-muzeum,4515.html.

49 See for example the program of the 14th edition "XIV Festiwal Warszawski Niewinni Czarodzieje: Wiech, Bareja, Kondratiuk," Warsaw Rising Museum, last modified October 25, 2019, accessed August 27, 2020, https://www.1944.pl/artykul/xiv-festiwal-warszawski-niewinni-czarodzieje-wi,4953.html.

50 "Muzeum zdobyło kolejną WDECHĘ!" Warsaw Rising Museum, last modified February 2, 2011, accessed August 27, 2020, https://www.1944.pl/artykul/muzeum-zdobylo-kolejna-wdeche,3356.html.

51 Facebook profile of the Warsaw Rising Museum, accessed August 27, 2020, https://www.facebook.com/1944pl.

52 Instagram profile of the Warsaw Rising Museum, accessed August 27, 2020, https://www.instagram.com/1944pl.

53 Twitter profile of the Warsaw Rising Museum, accessed August 27, 2020, https://twitter.com/1944pl.

54 YouTube channel of the Warsaw Rising Museum, accessed August 27, 2020, https://www.youtube.com/1944pl.

55 Based on data from the Promotion Department of the Warsaw Rising Museum.

56 Ibid.

57 Wolska-Pabian, "Nowe zadania muzeów narracyjnych," in *Muzeum i zmiana*, 95.

58 Legutko, *Jedyne takie Muzeum*, 126.

59 Data after presentation prepared by the Volunteering Department of the Warsaw Rising Museum, document in author's collection.

60 "Wolontariat," Warsaw Rising Museum, accessed August 27, 2020, https://www.1944.pl/artykul/wolontariat,4526.html.

61 Information from the Oral History Department of the Warsaw Rising Museum.

62 Wolska-Pabian, "Nowe zadania," 95–96.

63 "Zadzwoń do dziadka," Warsaw Rising Museum, last modified March 13, 2020, accessed August 27, 2020, https://www.1944.pl/artykul/zadzwon-do-dziadka,5017.html.

Bibliography

Cykliczne badanie opinii osób zwiedzających Muzeum Powstania Warszawskiego. Document in author's collection.

Kłaput, Jarosław, Dariusz Kunowski, and Mirosław Nizio. *Muzeum Powstania Warszawskiego ul. Przyokopowa 28 w Warszawie. Prezentacja koncepcji na ekspozycję Muzeum Powstania Warszawskiego.* Document in author's collection.

Komasa, Jan, dir. *Warsaw Upising. 87 minutes of truth.* Warsaw Rising Museum, Polski Instytut Sztuki Filmowej, 2014. http://warsawrising-thefilm.com.

Kowal, Paweł. "How We Built the Museum." In *Guidebook to the Warsaw Rising Museum*, edited by Lena Dąbkowska-Cichocka et al., 7–11. Warsaw: Warsaw Rising Museum, 2007.

Kultura w 2004 r. Warsaw, Cracow: Główny Urząd Statystyczny, 2005. https://stat.gov.pl/obszary-tematyczne/kultura-turystyka-sport/kultura/kultura-w-2004-r-,2,2.html?pdf=1.

Kultura w 2018 r. Warsaw, Cracow: Główny Urząd Statystyczny 2019. https://stat.gov.pl/obszary-tematyczne/kultura-turystyka-sport/kultura/kultura-w-2018-roku,2,16.html.

Legutko, Piotr. *Jedyne takie Muzeum. Odzyskana Pamięć o Powstaniu Warszawskim.* Cracow: Znak, 2014.

Michalewicz, Iza, and Maciej Piwowarczuk. *Powstanie Warszawskie. Rozpoznani.* Warsaw: Muzeum Powstania Warszawskiego, Agora, 2014.

Ołdakowski, Jan. "Dlaczego powstają muzea historyczne narracyjne." In *Muzeum i zmiana. Losy muzeów narracyjnych*, edited by Paweł Kowal and Karolina Wolska-Pabian, 73–77. Warsaw: Muzeum Powstania Warszawskiego; Cracow: Towarzystwo Autorów i Wydawców Prac Naukowych "Universitas," 2019.

Ołdakowski, Jan, and Paweł Kowal, in cooperation with Joanna Bojarska and Lena Dąbkowska-Cichocka. *Podstawowe założenia programowe i organizacyjne Muzeum Powstania Warszawskiego w Warszawie ul. Przyokopowa 28*. Warsaw, 2003. Document in author's collection.

Panecka, Agnieszka, ed. *Polityka historyczna. Historycy – politycy – prasa*. Warsaw: Muzeum Powstania Warszawskiego, 2005.

Sopińska-Jaremczak, Agnieszka. *Operacja Muzeum*. Warsaw: Fronda, 2014.

Warsaw Rising Museum. "Akcja społeczna: Wolność łączy." Last modified July 31, 2019. Accessed August 27, 2020, https://www.1944.pl/artykul/akcja-spoleczna-wolnosc-laczy, 4929.html.

Warsaw Rising Museum. Facebook. Accessed August 27, 2020. https://www.facebook.com/1944pl.

Warsaw Rising Museum. Instagram. Accessed August 27, 2020. https://www.instagram.com/1944pl.

Warsaw Rising Museum. "Marsz Pamięci i otwarcie wystawy *Zachowajmy ich w pamięci*." Last modified August 4, 2005. Accessed August 27, 2020. https://www.1944.pl/artykul/marsz-pamieci-i-otwarcie-wystawy-zachowajmy-ic,4331.html.

Warsaw Rising Museum. "Muzeum zdobyło kolejną WDECHĘ!" Last modified February 2, 2011. Accessed August 27, 2020. https://www.1944.pl/artykul/muzeum-zdobylo-kolejna-wdeche, 3356.html.

Warsaw Rising Museum. "Oddziały Muzeum." Last modified July 28, 2020. Accessed August 27, 2020. https://www.1944.pl/artykul/oddzialy-muzeum,4515.html.

Warsaw Rising Museum. "Ofiary cywilne." Accessed August 27, 2020. https://www.1944.pl/ofiary-cywilne.html.

Warsaw Rising Museum. "Powstańcze Biogramy." Accessed August 27, 2020. https://www.1944.pl/powstancze-biogramy.html.

Warsaw Rising Museum. "Programme of the 75th Warsaw Rising Anniversary Ceremonies." https://f.1944.pl/UserFiles/4/d/7/4d7037b054f10a5a51796b6d607bb556.pdf.

Warsaw Rising Museum. Tripadvisor. Accessed August, 27, 2020. https://pl.tripadvisor.com/Attraction_Review-g274856-d1154437-Reviews-Muzeum_Powstania_Warszawskiego-Warsaw_Mazovia_Province_Central_Poland.html.

Warsaw Rising Museum. Twitter. Accessed August 27, 2020. https://twitter.com/1944pl.

Warsaw Rising Museum. "Visit us." Accessed August 27, 2020. https://www.1944.pl/en/article/visit-us, 4993.html.

Warsaw Rising Museum. "Warszawiacy śpiewają (nie)ZAKAZANE PIOSENKI." Last modified July 29, 2020. Accessed August 27, 2020. https://www.1944.pl/artykul/warszawiacy-spiewaja-nie-zakazane-piosenki, 4928.html.

Warsaw Rising Museum. "Wirtualny Mur Pamięci." Accessed August 27, 2020. https://www.1944.pl/wirtualny-mur-pamieci.html.

Warsaw Rising Museum. "Wolontariat." Accessed August 27, 2020, https://www.1944.pl/artykul/wolontariat, 4526.html.

Warsaw Rising Museum. "XIV Festiwal Warszawski Niewinni Czarodzieje: Wiech, Bareja, Kondratiuk." Last modified October 25, 2019. Accessed August 27, 2020. https://www.1944.pl/artykul/xiv-festiwal-warszawski-niewinni-czarodzieje-wi, 4953.html.

Warsaw Rising Museum. YouTube. Accessed August 27, 2020. https://www.youtube.com/1944pl.

Warsaw Rising Museum. "Zadzwoń do dziadka." Last modified March 13, 2020. Accessed August 27, 2020. https://www.1944.pl/artykul/zadzwon-do-dziadka, 5017.html.

Wójciuk, Michał T., "Muzeum Powstania Warszawskiego i kombatanci – integracja pokoleń a funkcje wychowawcze na przykładzie projektów oraz 'wydarzeń' zrealizowanych w latach 2004–2016." In *Ojczyzna obrońcy swemu." Weterani i kombatanci jako problem polityczny i społeczny w Polsce XX wieku*, edited by Marek Kornat, Marcin Kruszyński, and Tomasz Osiński, 419–448. Lublin, Warsaw: Instytut Pamięci Narodowej, 2017.

Zubelewicz, Kamil, ed. *Księga prasowa Muzeum Powstania Warszawskiego*. Vol. 1. Warsaw: Muzeum Powstania Warszawskiego, 2004.

3

FOR THE PUBLIC, BY THE PUBLIC, ON THE PUBLIC

The Triple Role of the Public in School Museums of History in Russia

Olga Konkka

One of the common elements of various definitions of public history suggested by scholars and institutions presents this field as being "outside of academia,"[1] which can be understood as "outside of universities and schools." However, in late Soviet and post-Soviet Russia, as well as in some other post-Soviet states, public history has found its way into schools, through a unique and unexplored phenomenon called "school museums." Indeed, many Russian secondary schools, as well as youth activity centers, have their own museums. If we use Pierre Nora's theoretical framework of *lieux de mémoire* ("sites" or "realms" of memory), we should consider these museums, along with textbooks or commemorations, as "symbolic elements of the memorial heritage of [a] community."[2]

In many countries around the world, educational institutions may host different kinds of "sites of memory" in the broad sense of the term.[3] For example, since the First World War, many French schools have monuments commemorating former students and teachers killed during the war.[4] All over the world, schools having experienced tragic events maintain commemorative plaques dedicated to the victims. We can also think of trophy cases in many American schools, which say something about their history as well.

The Russian educational system for almost two centuries has been fostering the creation of museums hosting multiple and rich exhibitions. As well, they may cover history that goes far beyond the past of a particular school, or even a village, town or region. Although these museums are located within the school buildings and are used as curricula support, they fulfill larger functions and involve different publics.

What Is a "School Museum"?

It is difficult to give a simple explanation of why in Russia, unlike many other countries, schools are interested in having their own museums.

FIGURE 3.1   Museum of no. 65 Krasnaya Polyana school, Sochi, Krasnodar Krai, Russia, © Olga Konkka.

Indeed, many Russian schools have quite ill-equipped (if any) gymnasiums, computer laboratories or science laboratories. School library collections are also often quite poor, and many school buildings are desperately in need of renovation. And yet, about a quarter of Russian schools have museums. This fact may be partly explained by a long tradition, as school museums were quite common in the Russian Empire. Firstly, schools followed the example of the universities which had natural science and other collections.[5] Secondly, this educational system was largely inspired by the German one, and many German schools used to have museums,[6] which some wish to be reinstated.[7]

The very first Siberian museum was a school museum founded in Irkutsk in 1782.[8] By the end of the nineteenth century, there were more than 150 school museums in Russia. Teachers organized conferences where they exchanged their experience, and published tutorials explaining how to start a museum. At first, their collections, considered as pedagogical tools that allowed to teach "other than through books,"[9] were mostly focused on natural history. Later, when a new subject, regional studies (*kraevedenie*), was added to school curricula, ethnographical collections became popular as well.[10] In spite of all the changes that the Russian educational system has undergone since the 1917 Revolution, regional studies were still considered as an important part of young Soviet citizens' education. In the 1930s, Soviet educational authorities encouraged schools to create exhibitions presenting local productions and crafts.

However, after the Second World War, this trend changed, explaining the fact that the vast majority of current school museums are historical. Starting from the 1950s, many educational institutions wished to commemorate former students who gave their lives on the battlefields, and celebrate those who had been decorated. Teachers or Pioneer leaders together with pupils created "corners of military glory" displaying photographs and newspaper articles. Later, these collections were enriched with many other items, such as uniforms, helmets, weapons, ammunition, as well as letters and common articles presenting the everyday wartime life. These spaces grew and became museums. In the 1970s and 1980s, the "Great Patriotic War" victory began to be commemorated largely through ceremonies and new monuments. During the same period, hundreds of new school museums were created all over the USSR, bringing their number to about 4500,[11] while guidelines for a new "museum pedagogy" were discussed on a national level.[12] During the decade following the USSR's collapse, in spite of the state's withdrawal and lack of funding for secondary education, some schools still decided to start a museum,[13] and, as earlier, most of the exhibitions were focused on the history of the war. This trend persisted into the 2000s and 2010s, when patriotic education has become one of the priorities for the government, resulting in the opening of an even larger number of new school museums. In some regions, hosting a museum that "contributes to students' patriotic upbringing" can even help a school to improve its ranking.[14] The school museums licensing and registration procedure (*pasportizatsiya*) created in the 1970s allows them to obtain official status and increases their visibility.

Some open-access, yet very partial data analyzed for the current research are available for 5204 school museums located in 42 out of 85 federal subjects of the Russian Federation. The estimated total number of these museums can then be extrapolated to approximately 11,000, which is confirmed by certain other sources.[15] Knowing that there are around 41,300 schools in Russia,[16] this means that about 26.6 percent of them have museums. Of course, this rate is not constant: while some old museums disappear (sometimes together with schools, especially in rural areas), other new museums are created. The open-access database informs that 33 percent of the museums included there were established during the Soviet era, 21 percent were founded in the 1990s and 46 percent in the twenty-first century.

Russian school museums explore different fields and subjects. Some school museums are literature or art museums (including ethnic art). Some are natural science museums focused on archaeology, biology, geology, etc. Other museums aid in learning more about physics, chemistry or astronomy. Moreover, many school museums combine several fields (e.g., geology, archaeology and history).

However, as is demonstrated by the quantitative analysis of the above-mentioned database, as well as of some additional data[17] including a sample of more than one hundred school websites, a large majority of school museums are exclusively history museums, and this chapter is focused on this most common type. These museums may present national or local history, military and war history, ethnography, the biography of a famous person, history of a particular school or history of education in general. History museums aim to help teachers, providing additional visual support for some of their classes, and serving as an environment for extracurricular activities. Sometimes, but not always, they help to add a local dimension to national history curricula.

Bringing Together Different Stakeholders

Teachers are, without any doubt, key figures of Russian school museums: they create and run these places. Without teachers' enthusiasm and personal involvement, certainly none of the thousands of school museums would exist. History museums are usually run by history teachers, although there are some exceptions: those who teach literature, geography or civil defense may be found among educators in charge of school museums as well. While deciding to create a new museum, the teacher often chooses a subject or a historical period that he or she is keen on. While this does ensure that the teacher willingly devotes time to the initiative, if after the teacher's leaving or retirement, another member of the school staff does not share this interest, the museum risks being abandoned. However, this might also provide an opportunity for opening new exhibitions. After all, thousands of currently operating museums were established several decades ago and have known several generations of teachers. Moreover, teachers are not the only ones to create and run these places.

Students play an important role in the school museums' functioning. The fact that the exhibitions are created and visited by the same public makes them unique, and breaks the traditional "professionals-for-audience" paradigm that characterizes most museums. From the threshold of Russian school museums history, namely from the end of the nineteenth century, they have been perceived as places created by teachers and pupils together. At that time, museum collections often presented local skills, crafts and products, and students were the ones who created exhibits during special workshops.[18] After the 1917 Revolution, many museums were enriched and expanded, thanks to the "Students' Movement for Tourism and Regional Studies" that emerged in the 1930s. Some school museums are still supplied by regional studies clubs.[19] Another large youth movement that has contributed largely to current school museums' collections is known as "search brigades" (*poiskovye otryady*). They have partly inherited from the "Red Pathfinders" movement founded in the late 1950s and officially supported by the Komsomol since 1965.[20] Search brigades are often created and guided by teachers, with a mission to organize expeditions to the Second World War battlefields in order to dig up, identify and re-bury the soldiers' remains. They also search for objects such as weapons, ammunition, helmets and badges. Unlike "black diggers," who organize illegal excavations in order to sell these objects, search groups seek to restore them to the soldiers' descendants, or donate them to museums and to school museums in particular. Therefore, many search brigades have established partnerships with schools, even though their members are not necessarily in the secondary education system: among them, there are many university students and working adults. Since the early 1990s, these kinds of expeditions were often organized as part of the whole set of activities provided by "military and patriotic," "military and historical" or "military and sport" clubs that have emerged all over Russia.[21] Some of the search teams or patriotic clubs are registered at the educational institutions and operate as a part of their offers of extracurricular activities.

However, the pupils' role is not solely an issue of finding or creating exhibits. Indeed, specially trained students fulfill the role of guides in the majority of school museums. This work may be more or less formal. In some schools, the teacher in charge of the museum simply picks some students that he or she considers capable of the task, and instructs them in a quick tour what they have to reproduce in front of the visitors. In other schools, museology is an official extracurricular activity or an elective course, and students receive long high-quality training, participate in regional and national seminars and competitions, and sometimes even wear a special uniform. Educators consider this activity as an opportunity to introduce students into disciplines such as history, archaeology and museology, which may even have an impact on their future career choices. It is useful to learn more than what is suggested by curricula, develop public speaking skills and, for those rare schools that have a chance to welcome international visitors, to practice foreign languages.

Alongside teachers and students, Russian school museums may benefit from the support of external stakeholders. Many museums are officially governed by a Museum Council, composed of teachers, students and external members like the staff of a local state museum. In the 1970s and 1980s, when many educational institutions decided to start museums, they willingly contacted state museums to ask them to donate items from their reserve collections.[22] Since then, some school museums cultivate partnerships with state museums, who, among other kinds of support, provide training for teachers and students, offering them skills in management, storage and preservation of their collections.

Many war museums maintain strong ties with local veteran associations, who gladly donate wartime photographs and letters, as well as their decorations,[23] and sometimes explicitly ask schools to start a museum. As well, gifts may come from students' families and other locals who want their family relics to be exhibited in a school museum. If a school museum is fully or partially dedicated to a famous person, for example, a war hero or a writer, relationships with their family or descendants may be particularly close and long-lasting. For example, number 24 Krasnodar school museum[24] hosts a large exhibition on Timofey Khryukin and is named after him. This local-born colonel-general of the Soviet Air Force during the Second World War was twice decorated as a Hero of the Soviet Union. Khryukin's son who lives in Moscow was surprised to discover that a school museum has put his father's life story at the center of its collection. Since then, he has become one of the major benefactors of the museum, sharing items such as copies of documents from the family archive.[25] However, social media posts explaining how to retrieve a family relic from a school museum suggest that sometimes families prefer to have their ancestor's belongings returned to their home. School museums can also benefit from other types of donations than exhibits, such as money for renovation and furniture. The interviewed teachers[26] mentioned having received financial support from a local deputy or a wealthy alumnus.

Therefore, Russian school museums involve many different publics, who contribute to these places in different ways. Through this support, they acknowledge the importance of school museums as local "realms of memory" and the value of history that they convey. Those who donate items to school museums consider that they deserve to become part of heritage, and thus actively contribute to public history. Indeed, the school museums' mission goes far beyond the scope of curricula support.

Sharing History with Different Categories of Visitors

The majority of school museums' visitors are comprised of students of the school concerned. In general, students visit the museum of their own institution several times during their school years. Moreover, since the 2000s, these places host an increasing number of commemoration practices, such as "courage lessons"—patriotic activities usually involving war memory. A school museum can also attract groups of students from neighboring schools: if the latter have their own museums, partnerships and exchanges may be established. Many secondary school museums are visited by nursery school classes and host thematically connected activities adapted for a younger age.

Multiple school websites testify that a school museum is a privileged place for welcoming school guests, such as officials, writers and foreign delegations. The vast majority of war museums host meetings with war veterans, who "appreciate an opportunity to communicate with the children."[27] During the "open house day," schools are proud to show their museums to their prospective students' families and to local inhabitants. Moreover, some school museums choose to join the Night of Museums cultural event which is becoming increasingly popular in Russia.

If an average Russian school museum rarely has the chance to welcome visitors other than students and neighborhood residents, some museums present their collections to a much larger public. Opened in the 1960s, no. 65 Krasnaya Polyana school is the unique educational institution of the village area located in the Caucasus Mountains, about 40 km from Sochi. The school has always been proud of its regional history museum, known as one of the largest and richest school museums of the Krasnodar Krai. Started in a classroom, it grew and moved into a separate building of 277 m² in 2005. Among many other items, the museum exhibits archaeological findings from ancient Caucasus civilizations, such as a sword which dates from the first century, jewelry found in a burial place of the fifth or sixth century, and medieval sabers. However, the largest exhibition is dedicated to the Second World War, and namely to the Battle of the Caucasus. The museum owns a rich collection of weapons, personal belongings, as well as uniforms of Soviet and German soldiers and officers. Shortly after its relocation, a singular event gave a new boost to the museum, extending its public to visitors from all over Russia and abroad. In 2007, when Sochi was elected to host the 2014 Winter Olympic and Paralympic games, Krasnaya Polyana was chosen as a place for the alpine skiing events of the competition. During the preparation and delivery of the Olympics, no. 65 school museum welcomed hundreds of new visitors such as athletes, supporters and military units responsible for the security of the event. After the Olympics, given that the Krasnaya Polyana area was home to the major Russian mountain and ski resort, its school museum has been visited by even more numerous guests. Many tourists and groups attending different events organized in the huge hotel complex that was built for the Olympics used this opportunity to learn about the region and its history. In addition, the museum often opens its doors to groups from the educational center Sirius located near Sochi, which welcomes about 600 gifted teenagers from all over Russia monthly.[28] According to the school's official website, the museum has been visited by more than 900,000 people.[29]

Another example worth mentioning is the museum called "But the Muses were not silent" located in a separate three-floor building belonging to no. 235 Saint Petersburg school, specializing in arts and aesthetics. At the beginning of the 1960s, when the school was located in another building, it had a museum composed of simple makeshift exhibits telling stories of composers, artists, poets, writers and their creations. The school's relocation in 1967 coincided with the period when, 15 years after the "Leningrad case" fabricated by Stalin against local communist leaders, public discussion about the siege of Leningrad was made possible again. The first official place of commemoration of these tragic events, Memorial complex on Piskaryovskoye Cemetery, was inaugurated in 1960, followed by a special exhibition in the Leningrad History Museum which opened in 1964.[30] Educational institutions were also encouraged to start historical museums and "military glory halls" commemorating this period. Responding to this call, no. 235 school teachers and students decided to dedicate their new museum to literature, poetry, music, theatre and fine arts during the siege. They started an important research activity in order to find out as much as possible about the intelligentsia and cultural life in wartime Leningrad. Thanks to their great enthusiasm and personal involvement, and since they were the first ones to be interested in this aspect of the city's history, they managed to get hold of many rare and authentic documents and objects. Multiple testimonies of the survivors of the siege were also recorded by teachers and students. Paradoxical as it may seem, the key leader of the research effort and the first director of the museum was a sports teacher, Evgenii Lind. The new museum opened in 1968, but since then and until today, the research work has continued. In the mid-1970s, a new two-floor building specifically designated for the museum was constructed.[31] In 2005, after a difficult period when the school desperately needed renovation and its museum was almost abandoned, the institution moved again into its original building.[32] Today, the museum contains about 20,000 original documents and items. Among them, there are musical instruments and theater costumes, paintings and sketches, propaganda and satirical posters of "TASS Windows" and "Baltic Searchlight," editions of *Leningrad* and *Zvezda* magazines published during the war, concert programs, including handwritten ones, catalogs of exhibitions, theater and invitation tickets, leaflets and more than 2,000 books. The museum also holds some documents and original scores of famous composers, in particular Dmitry Shostakovich after whom the school was officially named in 1996. It exhibits original paintings and sculptures by famous artists, such as Mikhail Zvyagin whose works are exhibited in the State Russian Museum, in the Berlin Wall Museum and in Princeton University. It also contains manuscripts and personal items of writers, such as a table that belonged to Olga Berggolz and counterfoils of her bread ration cards from December 1941. Since none of the other Saint Petersburg museums offer so much information about cultural life in the besieged city, and no Russian museum is explicitly dedicated to art during the war, the no. 235 school museum is visited every year by hundreds of people from all over the world and welcomes university students for internship. The museum has its own website[33] providing detailed information on the museum's history, collections and latest news. Thanks to a partnership with the President's museum, the website offers a possibility of high-definition and close-to-reality virtual visits.

Of course, this example presents a particularly rich and outstanding museum, whereas the majority of Russian school museums hardly possess any rarities and do not attract any visitors other than locals. It is also important to mention that the above-described museums are located in separate buildings. This provides many more opportunities for welcoming the external public. Indeed, due to strong counter-terrorism and anti-crime measures, many city departments of education strictly prohibit access to schools for any unauthorized person. Therefore, school museums are confronted with a contradictory situation: they would like to open up their collections to a larger public, yet they are located in strictly secured buildings. Village schools are less concerned by the problem, and teachers in charge of museums are happy to show these local "realms of memory" to rare visitors. In her recently published travel report book *Zimnik*, Diane Slëzkine narrates her visit to some of these museums.[34] The major concept of the French author's trip consisted in following an itinerary that, according to one of the most challenging and unlikely transport projects, might become a part of a new Paris–New York rail link by 2030. The journey brings Slëzkine to Yakutia, from where the future train would take a tunnel under the Bering Strait to reach Alaska. She stops in Tomtor, a rural locality of Oymyakonsky District, better known as a part of historical region of Kolyma. In this settlement considered as one of the world's coldest inhabited places, she is invited to visit what she calls the "Gulag museum," located in the only school of the area. Even though the official website of the educational institution prefers to call it a "museum of literature and regional studies,"[35] the exhibition room created in 1992 is indeed focused on poets and writers who were prisoners of the former Soviet camps of the area. Among them is Varlam Shalamov, who spent the last two years of his Siberian exile in Tomtor, where he wrote one of his famous books of poems, *The Blue Notebook*. Since its foundation, the museum has been run by Maria Boyarova, an enthusiastic teacher who has also published a book on the men of letters who were forced to settle in Kolyma.[36] In Vitim, another locality of Yakutia situated on the Lena River, the author of *Zimnik* visits another school museum and meets the enthusiastic teacher in charge of it:

> The place looks very modern… but nothing is formal here: in fact, the museum is rather original. It is the inhabitants' museum, they come here to offer whatever might tell the history of the past, of their

family… Many objects were donated by students who discovered them while exploring abandoned villages.

This museum also provides a lot of information on those who were deported to this area for political reasons.[37]

In Tomtor and Vitim, as in many other remote Russian localities, a tourist willing to visit a museum should most likely look for a school. However, unlike the above-mentioned museums, the exhibitions don't necessarily cover local history, especially its most tragic pages.

Using History as an Instrument of Patriotic Upbringing

In her book entirely dedicated to Russian museum pedagogy, Marina Yuhnevich notes that in the 1980s, when school museums rapidly spread all over the USSR, they chose various fields and themes, but strangely enough,

> by no means could one say that the majority of school museums are dedicated to the place where they are situated, to the local people, or to the history of the school (which would be the most consistent with the interests and capabilities of their creators).[38]

Indeed, many history school museums fail to take advantage of their geographic location and explore the past of their neighborhood, town or village. More than 70 percent of Russian school museums are entirely or partially dedicated to the Great Patriotic War. Even though they are slightly more widespread in the Western regions of Russia, especially in the areas of famous battles, many are located in Siberia and in the Far East as well, far from the former frontline. Obviously, a war museum could also tell a wartime history of any Russian city or village, presenting local soldiers sent to the front, women and children suffering from hard work and malnutrition, factories and kolkhozes involved in the gigantic war effort, together with the nearby Gulag camps. Unfortunately, this kind of approach to war history is quite rare in school museums. Only some of them, located in the eastern part of European Russia or behind the Ural Mountains, cover this particular part of the school history if its building was temporarily converted into an evacuation hospital. However, the general problem of the vast majority of Russian school museums about the war is that they almost exclusively focus on its military aspects, such as battles, operations, commandment of the Army or war heroes. Therefore, many museums choose to speak about the war events that took place hundreds and thousands of kilometers from where the school is situated. They tend to ignore the fact that the history of everyday life during the war experienced by people of different statuses might be as interesting and worth mentioning as the heroism of frontline soldiers. This is one of the explanations for the school museums of Western Russia providing so little information about life under occupation that these regions would have experienced during the war. For instance, in spite of the fact that, according to the latest estimations, between 2,600,000 and 2,800,000 of about 6,000,000 European Jews were exterminated in the Soviet Union,[39] according to the official records no Russian school museum is entirely or even partially dedicated to the Holocaust.

This raises another problem, that of the events chosen to be covered by school museums, as well as their general approach to Russian history and official historical policies. While analyzing themes and exhibition titles of school museums situated in different parts of Russia, one can notice that most of them are comparatively silent when it comes to dealing with a tragic and conflictual past, especially with the events that have deeply affected local history. Of course, there are tragedies that cannot fail to be mentioned. For instance, the museum "Memory" of the unique school of Vidyayevo, a closed locality in Murmansk Oblast not far from the Barents Sea, contains an exhibition dedicated to the crew of the submarine Kursk which tragically sank in 2000.[40] Indeed, most of the families of the crew members were stationed in the village. Likewise, the museum of the new school of Beslan (which, symbolically, has no number) is today a major place of commemoration for the victims of the number 1 Beslan school hostage crisis which occurred in September 2004, causing the death of at least 333 people including 186 children. Portraits of all the victims are exhibited in a separate hall of the museum, which has since 2004 opened a few other sections.[41]

However, a large majority of Russian school museums fail to mention tragic events of the past that have impacted on local and regional history. Therefore, we can also speak of these "realms of memory" as "realms of oblivion." The first and the most obvious example of this amnesia is the memory of the Gulag and repressions of the Soviet period. Only 33 museums (0.6 percent) among those which are registered in the open databases contain exhibitions on the repressions, Great Terror, camps or deportations. If we consider ethnic-based deportations ordered by Stalin in the 1930s and 1940s, we manage to find information about only four museums that mention these deportations, even though they have deeply impacted some localities and ethnicities and created some several million victims. Russian school museums are also silent when it comes to the two severe famines of the twentieth century: the first happened shortly after the Civil War, while the second was caused by collectivization. The latter tends to be presented as a new and sometimes positive milestone in local history,[42] rather than a brutal reform that cost thousands of human lives. Finally, when it comes to dealing with the recent Chechen wars in Chechnya, we can speak of a real "oblivion policy." School museums, as well as other forms of public history of the republic, prefer to focus on the Great Patriotic War rather than on this recent and traumatic past.[43] Among nineteen Chechen museums included in the database, nine contain exhibitions on the Great Patriotic War while only two mention the recent local wars between Chechen separatists and the federal army.

In general, the narratives provided by Russian school museums (analyzable thanks to exhibition titles, textual components of the exhibitions' displays, information folders available on some school websites, etc.) tend to adopt the point of view that was official at the time when each of the presented events occurred. Thus, the presentation of the past is sometimes contradictory even within a single museum. For example, exhibitions highlighting local religious heritage (Orthodox, Muslim or Buddhist) can be found alongside the exhibitions that give a positive overview of the Soviet past, even though the Soviet State had sought to eradicate any form of religion. Likewise, in many former Cossack areas, school museums try to bring out both of the quite irreconcilable elements which are the legacy of communism and the Cossack heritage.

However, the narrative that dominates, whether or not the museums were created before the collapse of the USSR, is the one that perfectly reflects Soviet memory policies. For instance, in spite of multiple actions undertaken by the Russian government since 1991 to rehabilitate historic figures and other features of the former Russian Empire, school museums that deal with the Revolution and the Civil War take sides with the Bolsheviks. Likewise, even though according to the current legislation no ideology or political parties are admitted in public schools, 427 (8.2 percent) of the accounted museums pay tribute in some way to the communist youth movements (Oktyabryata, Pioneers and Komsomol). Communist organizations are part of almost any Russian school's history. However, titles of some exhibitions suggest a positive vision of these movements, as, for example, "The glorious Pioneers movement" (Museum located in Tatarstan, founded in 1979), "Beautiful Pioneer years, my Komsomol youth" (Museum located in Tatarstan, founded in 2002), "Being Pioneer means being the first" (Museum located in Krasnoyarsk region, founded in 2007, and museum located in Smolensk region, founded in 2005), "Pioneers, our past and our future" (Museum located in Tatarstan, founded in 2002). In some schools, the very idea to start a museum in the 1990s came from the unwillingness to abandon the attributes of the Pioneer movement (flags, Lenin's portraits, issues of the *Pioneer Pravda* newspaper, drums and horns) that almost every Soviet school used to have.[44] A new museum seemed to be a perfect place to store and cherish this heritage of the recent past.

The last example of this attachment to Soviet narratives is related to the war in Afghanistan (1979–1989). This war, the most unpopular in the national history, according to the public opinion polls,[45] is mentioned in many school museums. Teachers, students and families wanted to commemorate those who, soon after having graduated, were sent "across the river," as they used to say, and returned in zinc-lined coffins. However, it is quite surprising to observe that in five school museums, all of which were established after the end of the Soviet period, exhibition titles speak of those who "fulfilled their international duty." This formulation comes from the Soviet propaganda which presented every participation of the Soviet troops in an international conflict as a "proletarian duty." It was used in spite of the official (although increasingly controversial) vision of the Soviet operation in Afghanistan formulated in 1989 and condemning it "from a moral and political point of view."

Conclusion

About 11,000 currently existing school museums cover Russia, from Kaliningrad Oblast to Kamchatka and Sakhalin. The majority hold no rarities or valuable exhibits. The exhibitions' design often reveals the amateurism of their creators, while rooms and furniture look rather modest and need renovation. However, they are the only museums to tell the story of many little-known prominent people, such as war heroes, men of culture or outstanding teachers. They are the unique "realms of memory" of multiple neighborhoods, towns and villages. In some localities, they are the only museums within a radius of hundreds of kilometers.

Russian school museums are created and run by the public, not only teachers and pupils, but many other categories: higher education students and adults participating in expeditions and excavations, alumni, students' families and local people who donate whatever they consider as belonging to "history" and worth exhibiting, war veterans and cultural associations, state museums sharing their expertise and collections, and local authorities and businessmen offering administrative and financial support.

Russian school museums operate for different categories of publics. They share their piece of history with students of the school and of other educational institutions, with war veterans' associations, military units, school partners and guests, and sometimes tourists and visitors coming from far away. Even though school museums are created first and foremost for teaching and learning, different case studies show that their mission goes far beyond the framework of education.

But should we consider that school museums also narrate the history of various categories of publics? This is a more complex question. Indeed, some school museums include social history of different population groups. In several localities, they do not hesitate to dedicate exhibitions to those who were imprisoned, executed, deported, exiled, forced to do slave work or starved to death. Teachers in charge of these museums consider that each part of history deserves to be told. However, the majority of Russian school museums prefer to ignore these tragedies and to depict a glorious Soviet past of a neighborhood that suffered from repressions, of a village that was emptied of its population through deportations or of a town built by Gulag prisoners. However, we should also take into account the fact that Russian public opinion currently tends to justify state policies and wars of the past regardless of their human cost. In particular, the Soviet period is considered today as the best period of the national history by 75 percent of Russians,[46] while Stalin is becoming one of the favorite national historic figures. Persecutions against the Memorial Society struggling to preserve the memory of the repressions have been met by almost general indifference. From this point of view, school museums certainly tell the history that the majority of the Russian public wants to hear and to pass on to future generations.

Notes

1 Robert Kelley, "Public History: Its Origins, Nature, and Prospects," *The Public Historian* 1, no. 1 (1978): 16–28.
2 Pierre Nora, preface to *Realms of Memory: Rethinking the French Past*, trans. Lawrence D. Kritzman (New York: Columbia University Press, 1998), xvii.
3 According to Pim den Boer, Nora's *lieux de mémoire* are "mnemotechnical devices, but extremely ideological, full of nationalism, and far from being neutral or free of value judgments. Most *lieux de mémoire* were created, invented, or reworked to serve the nation-state." However, Astrid Erll suggests that this concept "lends itself particularly well to the study of a wide array of phenomena"; Astrid Erll, Ansgar Nünning, and Sara B. Young, eds., *Cultural Memory Studies: An International and Interdisciplinary Handbook* (Berlin, New York: Walter de Gruyter, 2008), 10, 21.
4 Hugues Marquis, "Un aspect de l'implication de l'École dans la Grande Guerre: l'hommage aux 'maîtres morts pour la France' dans l'académie de Poitiers (1914–1930)," *Annales de Bretagne et des Pays de l'Ouest. Anjou. Maine. Poitou-Charente. Touraine*, no. 122–2 (June 30, 2015): 119–137.
5 Olga Petrushkina, *Shkol'nye Muzei: Uchebnoe Posobie* (Samara: MGPU, 2016).
6 Branko Šuštar, "Shkol'nye Muzei Evropy: Mnogoobrazie Podhodov," *Voprosy Muzeologii* 6, no. 2 (2012): 80–96.
7 Peter Gautschi, "A Museum for Every School!" *Public History Weekly* 4, no. 8 (March 10, 2016), https://dx.doi.org/10.1515/phw-2016-5589.
8 Evgeniĭ Leonov, "Istoricheskiĭ Aspekt Poyavleniya i Razvitiya Shkol'nykh Muzeev v Rossii," *Vestnik Kemerovskogo Gosudarstvennogo Universiteta Kul'tury i Iskusstv*, no. 17–2 (2011), 39–49.
9 Marina Yuknevich, *Ya povedu tebya v muzeĭ* (Moscow: Rossiĭskiĭ institut kull' turologii, 2001), 13.
10 Petrushkina, *Shkol'nye Muzei*, 11.
11 Yuhnevich, *Ya povedu tebya v muzeĭ*, 103.
12 Ibid., 5.
13 Several sources report a closure of multiple school museums in the 1990s, but their number is unknown.
14 "O shkol'nyh muzeyah na vysokom urovne," MPGU, last modified December 18, 2017, accessed April 23, 2020, https://www.mgpu.ru/o-shkolnyh-muzeyah-na-vysokom-urovne.
15 Aleksandr Ozerov, "Shkol'nye Muzei v Sisteme Vospitaniya Uchashihsya," *Vestnik Detsko-Yunosheskogo Turizma* 4, no. 1–2 (2010), 16.
16 Natal'ya Bondarenko, Leonid Gohberg, and Natal'ya Kovaleva, *Obrazovanie v Cifrah* (Moscow: NIU VShE, 2019), 37.

17 For instance, the detailed catalog of school museums of Krasnodar, created by the city department of education, was analyzed.
18 Yuhnevich, *Ya povedu tebya v muzeĭ*, 99–100.
19 Ekaterina Sayaparova, "Shkol'nye Muzei Buryatii: Istoriya Formirovaniya, Tradicii i Innovacii," *Voprosy Muzeologii* 6, no. 2 (2012): 97–104.
20 Nina Tumarkin, *The Living & the Dead: The Rise and Fall of the Cult of World War II in Russia* (New York: BasicBooks, 1994), 14; Ekaterina Mel'nikova, "Rukami Naroda: Sledopytskoe Dvizhenie 1960–1980 gg. v SSSR," *Antropologicheskiĭ Forum*, no. 37 (2018): 20–53.
21 See Marlene Laruelle, "Patriotic Youth Clubs in Russia. Professional Niches, Cultural Capital and Narratives of Social Engagement," *Europe-Asia Studies* 67, no. 1 (January 2, 2015): 8–27.
22 Yuhnevich, *Ya povedu tebya v muzeĭ*, 102.
23 The Krasnodar city department of education prohibited conservation of war decorations in school museums, since their security cannot be guaranteed. Indeed, one of the interviewed teachers mentioned that her school museum had been robbed and decorations stolen, certainly to be resold on the black market.
24 A field research of the Second World War school museums in Krasnodar region was conducted thanks to a post-doctoral scholarship of the French Holocaust memory foundation (Fondation pour la Mémoire de la Shoah).
25 Interview with Elena Deshevyh, teacher in charge of no. 24 Krasnodar school museum, October 2019.
26 Three teachers in charge of school museums, two in Krasnodar and one in Sochi, have been interviewed in October 2019.
27 Interview with Anzhela Leshukova, teacher in charge of no. 30 Krasnodar school museum, October 2019.
28 Interview with Marina Bondarenko, teacher in charge of no. 65 Krasnaya Polyana school museum (Krasnodar Krai), October 2019.
29 "Shkol'nyĭ istoriko-kraevedcheskiĭ muzeĭ Krasnaya Polyana," accessed April 23, 2020, http://65.sochi-schools.ru/shkolnyj-istoriko-kraevedcheskij-muzej-krasnaya-polyana.
30 *Osnovnye Polozheniya Koncepcii Muzeĭno-Vystavochnogo Kompleksa "Oborona i Blokada Leningrada"* (Saint Petersburg Committee for Culture, n.d.).
31 "Svedeniya o Muzee," accessed April 22, 2020, http://spbmbmus.ru/Our.html#bottom.
32 Elena Shul'gina, "Blokadnyĭ Muzeĭ v Osade," *Novaya Gazeta*, July 4, 2002, http://novayagazeta.spb.ru/articles/315.
33 http://spbmbmus.ru/.
34 Diane Slëzkine, *Zimnik: du Baïkal au Béring* (Courtomer: Les Carnets de l'aléatoire, 2017), 56–58.
35 "Informaciya o Shkole," accessed April 23, 2020, https://tomshkola.ucoz.ru/index/o_110_letii_so_dnja_osnovanija_tomtorskoj_shkoly/0-2.
36 Maria Boyarova, *Moĭ Kraĭ, Vospetyĭ Muzoĭ Stradaniya i Lyubvi* (Yakutsk: Bichik, 2009).
37 Slëzkine, *Zimnik*, 144–145.
38 Yuhnevich, *Ya povedu tebya v muzeĭ*, 101.
39 Ilya Al'tman and Maria Gileva, "Istoriya Holokosta v Voprosah i Otvetah," *Prepodavanie Istorii v Shkole* 5 (2019): 10–17.
40 "Shkol'nyĭ Muzeĭ 'Pamyat,'" accessed April 23, 2020, http://xn---51-5cdlanizql9ai3kve.xn--p1ai/muzey-pamyat.
41 Evgeniya Priemskaya, "My vyhodili na rabotu s eshche ne snyatymi shvami," *Izvestiya*, last modified September 1, 2019, accessed April 23, 2020, https://iz.ru/915865/evgeniia-priemskaia/my-vykhodili-na-rabotu-s-eshche-ne-sniatymi-shvami.

42 See, for example, the website of the museum of Klochki village school (Altai Krai), which offers a perfectly communist pro-collectivization and anti-kulak discourse: "Shkol'nyĭ kraevedcheskiĭ muzeĭ istorii sela Klochki," accessed April 23, 2020, https://muzklochki.ucoz.ru/index/kollektivizacija/0-32.

43 Aude Merlin, "Remembering and Forgetting in Chechnya Today: Using the Great Patriotic War to Create a New Historical Narrative," in *Chechnya at War and Beyond*, ed. Anne Le Huérou, Aude Merlin, Amandine Regamey, and Elisabeth Sieca-Kozlowski (London, New York: Routledge, 2014), 37–57.

44 See, for example, Vladimir school no. 2 website: "Shkol'nyĭ muzeĭ 'Istoriya shkoly,'" accessed April 23, 2020, http://shkola2.ouvlad.ru/shkolnyj-muzej-istoriya-shkoly.

45 "Spravedlivye i Nespravedlivye Voĭny," *Levada Tsentr*, last modified March 19, 2014, accessed April 23, 2020, http://www.levada.ru/19-03-2014/spravedlivye-i-nespravedlivye-voiny.

46 Elena Muhametshina, "Tri chetverti rossiyan schitayut sovetskuyu ėpohu luchsheĭ v istorii strany," *Vedomosti*, March 23, 2020, https://www.vedomosti.ru/society/articles/2020/03/23/825985-tri-chetverti.

Bibliography

Al'tman, Ilya, and Maria Gileva. "Istoriya Holokosta v Voprosah i Otvetah." *Prepodavanenaksie Istorii v Shkole* 5 (2019): 10–17.

Bondarenko, Natal'ya, Leonid Gohberg, and Natal'ya Kovaleva. *Obrazovanie v Cifrakh*. Moscow: NIU VShE, 2019.

Boyarova, Maria. *Moĭ Kraĭ, Vospetyĭ Muzoĭ Stradaniya i Lyubvi*. Yakutsk: Bichik, 2009.

Erll, Astrid, Ansgar Nünning, and Sara B. Young, eds. *Cultural Memory Studies: An International and Interdisciplinary Handbook*. Berlin, New York: Walter de Gruyter, 2008.

Gautschi, Peter. "A Museum for Every School!" *Public History Weekly* 4, no. 8 (2016). https:// dx.doi.org/10.1515/phw-2016-5589.

"Informaciya o Shkole." Accessed April 23, 2020. https://tomshkola.ucoz.ru/index/o_110_letii_so_dnja_osnovanija_tomtorskoj_shkoly/0-2.

Kelley, Robert. "Public History: Its Origins, Nature, and Prospects." *The Public Historian* 1, no. 1 (1978): 16–28.

Laruelle, Marlene. "Patriotic Youth Clubs in Russia. Professional Niches, Cultural Capital and Narratives of Social Engagement." *Europe-Asia Studies* 67, no. 1 (January 2, 2015): 8–27.

Leonov, Evgeniĭ. "Istoricheskiĭ Aspekt Poyavleniya i Razvitiya Shkol'nyh Muzeev v Rossii." *Vestnik Kemerovskogo Gosudarstvennogo Universiteta Kul'tury i Iskusstv*, no. 17–2 (2011): 39–49.

Marquis, Hugues. "Un aspect de l'implication de l'École dans la Grande Guerre: l'hommage aux 'maîtres morts pour la France' dans l'académie de Poitiers (1914–1930)." *Annales de Bretagne et des Pays de l'Ouest. Anjou. Maine. Poitou-Charente. Touraine*, no. 122–2 (June 30, 2015): 119–137.

Mel'nikova, Ekaterina. "Rukami Naroda: Sledopytskoe Dvizhenie 1960–1980 Gg. v SSSR." *Antropologicheskiĭ Forum*, no. 37 (2018): 20–53.

Merlin, Aude. "Remembering and Forgetting in Chechnya Today: Using the Great Patriotic War to Create a New Historical Narrative." In *Chechnya at War and*

Beyond, edited by Anne Le Huérou, Aude Merlin, Amandine Regamey, and Elisabeth Sieca-Kozlowski, 37–57. London, New York: Routledge, 2014.

MPGU. "O shkol'nyh muzeyah na vysokom urovne." Last modified December 18, 2017. Accessed April 23, 2020. https://www.mgpu.ru/o-shkolnyh-muzeyah-na-vysokom-urovne.

Muhametshina, Elena. "Tri chetverti rossiyan schitayut sovetskuyu èpohu luchsheĭ v istorii strany." *Vedomosti*, March 23, 2020. https://www.vedomosti.ru/society/articles/2020/03/23/825985-tri-chetverti.

Nora, Pierre. *Realms of Memory: Rethinking the French Past*. Translated by Lawrence D. Kritzman. New York: Columbia University Press, 1998.

Osnovnye Polozheniya Koncepcii Muzeĭno-Vystavochnogo Kompleksa "Oborona i Blokada Leningrada" (Saint Petersburg Committee for Culture, n.d.).

Ozerov, Aleksandr. "Shkol'nye Muzei v Sisteme Vospitaniya Uchashchihsya." *Vestnik Detsko-Yunosheskogo Turizma* 4, no. 1–2 (2010): 16.

Petrushkina, Olga. *Shkol'nye Muzei: Uchebnoe Posobie*. Samara: MGPU, 2016.

Priemskaya, Evgeniya. "My vyhodili na rabotu s eshche ne snyatymi shvami." *Izvestiya*. Last modified September 1, 2019. Accessed April 23, 2020, https://iz.ru/915865/evgeniia-priemskaia/my-vykhodili-na-rabotu-s-eshche-ne-sniatymi-shvami.

Sayaparova, Ekaterina. "Shkol'nye Muzei Buryatii: Istoriya Formirovaniya, Tradicii i Innovacii." *Voprosy Muzeologii* 6, no. 2 (2012): 97–104.

"Shkol'nyĭ istoriko-kraevedcheskiĭ muzeĭ Krasnaya Polyana." Accessed April 23, 2020. http://65.sochi-schools.ru/shkolnyj-istoriko-kraevedcheskij-muzej-krasnaya-polyana.

"Shkol'nyĭ kraevedcheskiĭ muzeĭ istorii sela Klochki." Accessed April 23, 2020. https://muzklochki.ucoz.ru/index/kollektivizacija/0-32.

"Shkol'nyĭ muzei 'Istoriya shkoly.'" Accessed April 23, 2020. http://shkola2.ouvlad.ru/shkolnyj-muzej-istoriya-shkoly.

"Shkol'nyĭ Muzeĭ 'Pamyat.'" Accessed April 23, 2020. http://xn---5l-5cdlanizql9ai3kve.xn--p1ai/muzey-pamyat.

Shul'gina, Elena. "Blokadnyĭ Muzeĭ v Osade." *Novaya Gazeta*, July 4, 2002. http://novayagazeta.spb.ru/articles/315.

Šuštar, Branko. "Shkol'nye Muzei Evropy: Mnogoobrazie Podhodov." *Voprosy Muzeologii* 6, no. 2 (2012): 80–96.

Slëzkine, Diane. *Zimnik: du Baïkal au Béring*. Courtomer: Les Carnets de l'aléatoire, 2017.

"Spravedlivye i Nespravedlivye Voĭny." *Levada Tsentr*. Last modified March 19, 2014. Accessed April 23, 2020. http://www.levada.ru/19-03-2014/spravedlivye-i-nespravedlivye-voiny.

"Svedeniya o Muzee." Accessed April 22, 2020. http://spbmbmus.ru/Our.html#bottom.

Tumarkin, Nina. *The Living & the Dead: The Rise and Fall of the Cult of World War II in Russia*. New York: BasicBooks, 1994.

Yuhnevich, Marina. *Ya povedu tebya v muzeĭ*. Moscow: Rossiĭskiĭ institut kull'turologii, 2001.

4

STUDENTS AS THE MUSEUMS' PUBLIC

Marta Kopiniak

Museums and Their Publics

The museum we know today has come a long way from the *museion* of antiquity and the modernistic, universal museum of the nineteenth century. In 2019, the International Council of Museums (ICOM) proposed the following definition of a museum:

FIGURE 4.1   Exhibition "Wroclaw 1945–2016" in the Depot History Center in Wrocław during Independence Day Celebrations in 2019, © M. Biodrowski, Depot History Center.

> [...] democratising, inclusive and polyphonic spaces for critical dia-
> logue about the pasts and the futures. Acknowledging and address-
> ing the conflicts and challenges of the present, they hold artefacts and
> specimens in trust for society, safeguard diverse memories for future
> generations and guarantee equal rights and equal access to heritage
> for all people. Museums are not for profit. They are participatory and
> transparent, and work in active partnership with and for diverse com-
> munities to collect, preserve, research, interpret, exhibit, and enhance
> understandings of the world, aiming to contribute to human dignity
> and social justice, global equality and planetary wellbeing.

The above definition was not, in the end, officially approved, but it is a sign
of the direction in which the understanding of museums is heading.[1] This
change has been precipitated by the radical shift in the museum world which
began with Peter Vergo's *The New Museology*, published in 1989, where he
postulated making these institutions more active and dynamic, to concentrate on the relationship with visitors, rather than with the collection.[2]

In the following years, the digitalization age had an impact on both museums and the public's approach toward museums. Digital tools have become
the basic form of providing information to visitors while also allowing even
the smallest and most remote museums to communicate with a worldwide
audience, consisting of countless publics.[3] In turn, different publics can engage with museums from all over the world, take part in world-spanning
discussions on matters important to them and influence the narrative of
institutions that without the internet would not be accessible to them.

The most recent breakthrough in implementing digital tools in museums
is the deployment of Web 2.0 tools that have helped to create and define
a new type of relationship between museums and the public. As Web 2.0
is defined by its focus on user-generated content, this relationship is based
on online sharing with extensive use of social networking, podcasts, wikis
and blogs. This allows the public to take an active part in creating museum
content, which ultimately transforms *visitors* into *contributors*.[4] Those tools
have contested and redefined the roles that museums assign to the public—
not a so long while ago visitors were considered potentially harmful to the
museum collections. Their place was in the middle of the museum exhibition, in pensive contemplation, consuming the knowledge carefully chosen by professionals.[5] Currently, they are seen not only as visitors who are
welcome and necessary for the very existence of the museums, but are encouraged to participate in various forms of transfer of authority from the
institution to members of the public.

Many institutions incorporate the public's contributions as an addition
to their regular activity, amplifying the voices of the publics for marketing
and identity purposes, and some give them an even more central role. For
example, the public's help is employed in selecting works to be exhibited,

or in "folksonomy" where social and community tagging is used for index-ing digital documents.[6] This "participatory revolution" is part of a larger change—the immersion of museums into the digital age with new gener-ations of visitors who are expecting an experience curated especially for them. This ties inseparably to university students, as they are a major part of this generational change—constituting a majority of Millennials in recent years and starting to amass the representation of Generation Z.[7]

It is the purpose of this analysis to describe students as the museums' public—the way in which students perceive museums and what they expect of them and the museums' approach to this specific public. For the purposes of this analysis, I have described a historical museum as any institution that meets the basic requirements for museums (collecting, conserving, exhibit-ing) and brings the history of its artifacts to the present while not focusing solely on their physical or artistic properties and values (so as to exclude art or science museums).

Students as the Museums' Public

The online questionnaire that was the basis of this analysis was designed in April 2018 and was open to the public during May and June of that same year. It was published in three Facebook groups created for students of Uni-versity of Wrocław, University of Gdańsk and University of Silesia in Kato-wice. Respondents were asked to provide responses based solely on their own experiences with history museums. Answers from the questionnaire were later addressed in June 2019 in interviews with six students who were the first to respond to a call for participants.

The questionnaire was divided into three parts, with the last includ-ing general, demographic questions. It consisted of questions about age, gender, years of study and place of residence. The two former parts were two different paths that were presented to respondents depending on their answer to the first question: "When did you last visit a museum?" Ques-tions included there varied in character: respondents were asked single and multiple-choice questions, scale questions and open-ended questions. Questions included in the questionnaire were created as part of a discus-sion among fellow students, partially for the purpose of proving or disprov-ing our own assumptions based on personal experiences with museums.

There were 266 answers to the questionnaire, filled out by respondents aged from 18 to 55 years old. Although the age range might seem wide, most answers (80 percent) came from students between the ages of 20 and 25 years old. 80.5 percent of the overall number of respondents were female, 19.2 per-cent were male and the rest did not identify with any gender. As the age of respondents suggests, most of them were bachelor and master's students—they constituted 54 and 34 percent of all respondents, respectively. A large number of respondents—over 60 percent—declared their place of residence was a city with over 100,000 inhabitants. 23.3 percent lived in cities with less than 100,000 inhabitants, while 15.8 percent declared as living in villages.

The first group emerging from the questionnaire, making up 22.6 percent of the overall number of respondents, is characterized by its negative view of museums as institutions alien to them and their interests. It is also a group, whose members do not find that exhibitions, events or even whole museums would interest them; therefore, they do not feel the need to visit those institutions. They had visited museums as children on school trips, with parents or other family members but mostly not by their own choice—that is the experience of 80 percent of non-visitors. If visiting a museum is not easy and pleasant, they simply opt not to visit. Barriers perceived by non-visitors, which seem to be subjective, include issues with transportation, ticket prices and lack of time. When asked what would encourage them to visit museums more often, respondents commonly mentioned "lower prices." However, there were no specific margins or insights as to what would be considered a sufficiently low price. This relates to another issue—since non-visitors would not consider money spent on a museum ticket worthwhile, they would also consider time spent in a museum as wasted. 45.2 percent of respondents living in villages had not visited a museum in the previous year. Compared to 16.7 percent of respondents living in cities above 100,000 inhabitants, it is clear that the availability of museums and mobility of individuals have a great impact on the frequency of museum visits. It looks as if non-visitors simply preferred other—more affordable, accessible or simply more entertaining—ways of spending free time and they would choose cinema, concerts or theatre over a museum. The questionnaire has confirmed what is known from previous scholarly research on the barriers and issues that contribute to perceiving museums as unapproachable.[8]

Accidental visitors are the next group that can be distinguished on the basis of the gathered data. They are the largest of the three, comprising 41.7 percent of the whole number of respondents. It is the most diverse group, including respondents that have visited one, two and three museums in the previous year, and one that constantly remains open to what museums have to offer. However, its members are not sure if museums are the answers to what they are looking for. They require emotional engagement from their recreational activities, and similarly to non-visitors, their first choices are concerts, theatre or cinema—events that are certain to provide this much needed emotional engagement. They, however, do not consider a museum to be a place where they would experience gripping emotions. What differentiates them from non-visitors is the openness to the museum experience during which they want to engage with history first-hand, lose themselves in the past—touch, smell and taste it. The accidental visitors want exhibitions and events where they can see and engage with a reconstruction (or even better, an original) of a garment, interior or an object. They are consumers of culture, so it is quite hard for them to pass up on an opportunity to use free tickets—22.5 percent of members of this group had visited museums with free tickets. Close proximity of museums is another aspect encouraging visits—accidental visitors have visited museums local to them such as the Museum of the Second World War in Gdańsk, the Silesian Museum in Katowice and Pan Tadeusz Museum in Wrocław. The preference for local museums is clear, as the respondents of the questionnaire were students of universities from those same three cities. They treat museum visits as any other social outing where they have an opportunity to socialize with friends and colleagues. It can be clearly seen in interviews conducted with students—company is essential to a museum visit.

Accidental visitors correspond with the visitors' profile identified by Prentice et al. who have found in their research that museums were not visited out of specific interest, but rather to gain general knowledge—more out of curiosity or as a part of a day out with a group than to see a specific artifact or learn a specific thing.[9]

This group is also similar in nature to the one described by Falk and Dierking as Facilitators: a group socially motivated and "focused on enabling the learning and experience of others in their accompanying social group."[10] The experience and emotional engagement that they seek are not included, however, in Falk and Dierking's typology, and therefore, this group cannot be fully identified with Facilitators.

The last group—enthusiasts, making up 35.7 percent of the total number of respondents—is characterized by its most intense attitude toward museums. Those are the individuals that guide their steps toward those institutions wherever they find themselves—they had visited four or more museums in the year previous to filling out the questionnaire. They visited several museums in a single day or several in a single week, sometimes several a month—always in the plural, regardless of the circumstances. Whether they are on vacation, on an exchange or they find some free time on a regular day—they will choose to visit a museum. 60 percent of respondents from this group visited a museum on holiday, while 86.2 percent did so in their general "free time." They make the most of the opportunities offered by the cities they live and study in, well aware that such occasions might not repeat themselves—63 percent of them visited museums in the cities they study in and 32.6 percent in the city they live in. They are also usually inhabitants of the largest cities—above 100,000 citizens. They approach museums enthusiastically, although not without critical thinking—they have seen so many of them, that they have opinions on many matters relating to museums and are able to comment on positive and negative aspects of any museum they visit. They do not see a museum visit as a social situation, but rather as an opportunity to learn and develop their interests while having a good time. This third group seems to match Falk's and Dierking's Explorers: "curiosity-driven visitors with generic interests in the content of the museum" who expect there to be something at the museum that "will grab their attention and fuel their curiosity for learning." Above the characteristics of Explorers, Enthusiasts are exceptional in their intense search for museums in every circumstance they find themselves in.

Marylin Hood offers a typology similar to the one that emerged from my analysis—she distinguishes frequent visitors and occasional visitors, with the former wanting to learn something, do something worthwhile and wanting the challenge of the new, while describing the latter as wanting social interaction, feeling the need to feel comfortable in their surroundings and wanting to participate actively.[11] It is clear to see that while the students' approach and attitude toward museums are based on those general profiles, this public's approach has some distinct elements to it, that separates them from the "general public." Those distinct elements are in part connected to a generational characteristic that in recent years has made quite a career—the famous Millennials are the people that still make up a large percentage of the public of students. For example, research indicates that Millennials look for and expect good value[12]—a concept clearly visible in the outcome of the above analysis. Another idea that is close to Millennials' hearts, especially visible with accidental visitors, is prioritizing interaction over things[13]—they want to feel, not accumulate objects. Millennials are also characterized by the desire for events to be flexible and social, strongly embedded in social media and the internet overall.[14]

Millennials are closely followed by Generation Z, entering the students' stage. The relation of Generation Z to cultural institutions like museums is yet to be thoroughly analyzed, and most characteristics are being created on the basis of anecdotal evidence. All of them have been born in a world where the internet exists, and many of them have made use of it from a very young age. This is one of the challenges museums face in creating experiences this generation would be interested in.

Museums and Their Approach to Students

We now know that students do visit museums, we know the patterns they follow and that they fit into the ongoing revolution of museums. Being aware of the students' attitude toward museums, let us now focus on the museums and their approach toward students. Four of Wrocław's museums that represent four different models of organization and a range of methods of functioning will be used in this analysis: the National Museum in Wrocław, Wrocław City Museum, the Depot History Center and "Pan Tadeusz" Museum of the Ossoliński National Institute.

All of these museums are among the most popular in Wrocław according to the Tripadvisor website.[15] Three of them, with the exception of the Depot History Center, are located in the city center. Otherwise, the chosen museums are mostly characterized for their differences toward each other: in the topics they unravel within their exhibitions, organizing bodies, the

ways in which they tell their stories and many others. This has enabled me
to examine if and how those fundamentally different museums cater to the
same public of students and deal with the challenge of it.

The National Museum in Wrocław is the institution with the longest
history—it was created as a state museum in 1947 and was transformed into
a National Museum in 1970.[16] Wrocław City Museum was created in the
year 2000, as a result of merging a couple of different institutions: the Archeological Museum, the Museum of Medalist Art and the Historical Museum with its branches—the Military Antiquities department and the Old
Jewish Cemetery.[17] The two remaining museums "Pan Tadeusz" Museum[18]
and the Depot History Center[19] were both opened in the same year of 2016.
The National Museum is a state-operated institution, Pan Tadeusz Museum
is led by the National Ossoliński Institute foundation,[20] while the City Museum is led fully by the city. The Depot History Center is operated by the
Remembrance and Future Center, which is partially funded by the state and
partially by the city of Wrocław.[21]

The museums also differ in the collections they possess and the contents
and forms of exhibiting those collections. The most traditional of them is
the National Museum, whose collection consists of over 200,000 objects that
represent all aspects of art, as well as many documents and books. They are
all presented in the museum's main building within the frame of six permanent exhibitions: "Silesian stone sculpture between the twelfth and sixteenth
centuries," "Silesian art between the fourteenth and sixteenth centuries,"
"Silesian art between the sixteenth and nineteenth centuries," "Polish art
between the seventeenth and nineteenth centuries," "European art between
the fifteenth and twentieth centuries," and "Miracle-Workers"—an exhibition devoted to crafts and decorative art, art of the Orient and contemporary
ceramics and glass.[22] All but the "Miracle Workers" exhibitions are quite
conservative—their main focus lies in the objects. The text within the exhibitions is confined only to captions beneath objects. This pattern has changed
in the "Miracle Workers" exhibition, as it is quite a new addition to the museum and has been designed with current museum trends in mind.

The Historical Museum section of the City Museum was created in 2008
and is located in a modernized and renovated Royal Palace. Its permanent
exhibition, "1000 years of Wrocław," presents objects that illustrate the history of the city from the early Middle Ages until the present day. At the
beginning of the exhibition, visitors are greeted by a short film outlining
the 1000-year history of Wrocław, which is then explored in depth within
the exhibition space using objects from the Museum's collection as well as
some interactive technological devices.

A vastly different idea of a museum exhibition is represented by the
Depot History Center. The exhibition there is divided into two sections: the
first talking about the overall post-Second World War history of Wrocław
and the second focusing on Wrocław's Solidarity movement. Neither section

focuses on objects or artifacts, but rather on the scenography that has been designed to elicit emotions in order for the visitors to feel the history, as opposed to just reading about it. It is important to note that most of the engaging elements of the exhibition are not digital—they are primarily objects that the visitors can touch, pick up or manipulate to receive a reaction (i.e., a radio that can be manipulated to play a certain broadcast). The Depot History Center does not rely heavily on screens and digital engagement media.

It is opposite to what "Pan Tadeusz" Museum has done with its exhibition. Within the exhibition "Manuscript of 'Pan Tadeusz'" (a poem universally considered to be a masterpiece of Polish literature and one of the most important elements of Polish culture, based on the story of the Lithuanian noblemen during the Napoleonic wars), the museum has exhibited the only existing manuscript of the poem and artifacts related to it, with the use of over 100 applications and multimedia presentations. The second section of the museum consists of the exhibition "Mission: Poland,"—the cabinets of witnesses to history of the Second World War and the Cold War: Władysław Bartoszewski[23] and Jan Nowak-Jeziorański[24] are filled with both memorabilia and artifacts as well as numerous digital tools. The connection between "Pan Tadeusz" and the heroes of the cabinets may be controversial; however, the quality of both exhibitions cannot be questioned.

Both the Depot History Center and "Pan Tadeusz" Museum easily fit into the definition of a history museum as an institution that brings the history of its artifacts to the present while not focusing solely on their physical or artistic properties and values. The situation is slightly different when it comes to the City Museum and the National Museum, as they have a more traditional approach to exhibiting their artifacts. However, I would argue that recent changes made to those museums' exhibitions and new parts of those exhibitions signify a more modern approach, thus placing those museums within the proposed definition.

The analysis of the museums' offerings started with the accessibility of their permanent exhibitions. Two of the basic elements that amount to accessibility are opening hours and ticket prices, with particular attention to student tickets.

The National Museum was open in 2019 from 10 a.m. until 6 p.m. seven days a week in the summer, and from 9 a.m. to 5 p.m. during the week and 10 a.m. to 6 p.m. on Fridays and weekends during the rest of the year. The Depot History Center was open from 9 a.m. to 5 p.m. Tuesday to Wednesday, from 10 a.m. to 5 p.m. on Thursdays and from 10 a.m. to 6 p.m. on weekends. "Pan Tadeusz" Museum and the City Museum were open from 9 a.m. to 5 p.m. on weekdays and from 10 a.m. to 6 p.m. on weekends.

The Depot History Center and "Pan Tadeusz" Museum both offer discounted student tickets (for students under the age of 26, due to national legislation). At the Depot History Center, it is 5 zł (around $1.25), half the price of a regular ticket, and at "Pan Tadeusz" Museum, it is 10 zł (about $2.50), also half the regular price. At the National Museum, students can visit the institution for just 1 zł upon presenting a valid student ID card, and the City Museum makes no charge at all for entry to its permanent exhibitions—this applies to everyone, not just students.

Both opening hours and ticket prices have been highlighted by students as factors with a strong influence on the frequency of their museum visits. Longer opening hours and lower ticket prices were mentioned as incentives for visiting among non-visitors. And although there is some variety that can be seen when it comes to ticket prices, all of the analyzed museums have very similar opening hours, varying only slightly.

The differences occur with respect to events organized by museums. Those analyzed below took place between June 1, 2018, and May 31, 2019, and, subject to the possibilities of the internet websites for the particular museums, information about them was gathered by browsing the museums' websites or their social media profiles with the assumption that museums take care to provide the most accurate information they can online.

The largest number of events—318—was organized by the National Museum, by far surpassing all the other analyzed museums. The next in line is "Pan Tadeusz" Museum with 150 events; the third, with 94, is the Depot History Center; and the last is the City Museum with 58. Apparently, all the analyzed institutions work diligently to provide additional opportunities to engage with the public. But how many of those events provide the public with real engagement? For the purpose of this paper, an engaging event is one that requires or offers a chance for the visitors to express themselves in some way: be it a discussion, a workshop or any other form of possible engagement.

As can be seen above, the largest number of events, both in general and as interactive ones, took place at the National Museum. However, at the same time, it has the lowest percentage of those that we can classify as engaging, only just under 30 percent of all events. Additionally, most of those engaging events (57 out of 95) were geared toward children under the age of twelve. Those include workshops organized as part of larger programs such as "Winter break at the museum" or in relation to permanent and temporary exhibitions. A large number of workshops were related to an exhibition exploring the art of the Viceroyalty of Peru—children were invited to create

	Depot History Center	Pan Tadeusz Museum	National Museum	City Museum
Engaging events/all events	52/94	62/150	95/318	33/58
(percentage of engaging events)	(55.3%)	(41.33%)	(29.87%)	(56.9%)

FIGURE 4.2 Data on events in analyzed museums.

their own pieces inspired by those shown in the exhibition or to create objects tied to the culture of Peru or the Inca civilization. A separate category were workshops for teenagers organized as part of a series devoted to different styles in art. Events organized with adults in mind constitute only 7.54 percent of the whole, including those without a link to the museum itself: European Night of Museums, celebrations of the centennial anniversary of Polish independence, the long May weekend[25] and Slow Art Day. The most numerous events for adults at the National Museum were guided tours with volunteers, exploring different parts of the main exhibition. Similarly, there were numerous occasions on which the National Museum worked in cooperation with other institutions, such as "Irish Day" (although described as a "family occasion") or a theatre performance. The actions taken by the National Museum were often repeated—they used the same ideas and frameworks many times.

Events organized by "Pan Tadeusz" Museum were in 41.33 percent of cases engaging the participants in some form of activity. The largest number was addressed to adults and took the form of adult workshops. Their signature "Nobility workshops" talked about various aspects of life of the Polish nobility. Creative writing workshops or sign language poetry workshops, a poetry slam and a poetry evening referred mostly to literature, rather than history. There were also several concerts and films run at the museum during the analyzed period. There were significantly fewer events addressed directly to children; however, it is important to note that "Pan Tadeusz" Museum was the only museum that has created occasions for parents with small children (under two years old) to visit the institution. The goal of *Muzealniaki* was to bring attention to the fact that museums can be a safe space for children of all ages as well as their parents, who should not be afraid to come to a museum with such a small child. The museum has definitely developed the most diverse and balanced offer. Not only forms of events but also their topics varied greatly and allowed for everyone to find something interesting to them.

In the Depot History Center, engaging events constitute 55.3 percent. Most of them were film screenings with discussions afterward, which is understandable, as the museum has its own in-museum cinema hall. A large part were meetings of different kinds, with the most notable being talks given by witnesses to history in a series called "Witnesses to History Tell a Story." During those meetings, people who took part in oral history projects in the Depot History Center had the opportunity to tell participants about their lives and engage in discussion with the audience. "Meetings with History" is a series of meetings about contemporary history held in English and targeted at pupils and students who temporarily live in the city. There were significantly fewer workshops organized by the Depot History Center, compared to the other museums; however, they were most varied in forms and types of publics engaged. There were several exhibitions that utilized the involvement of not only the local community, but also students. Two of them are especially worthy of notice, as they were developed in collaboration with Public History students at the University of Wrocław. Those were: "I Grew up Here!—Childhood in Lower Silesia through Four Seasons" and "Colors of Information: Posters in Wrocław 1945–2000."

The events designed for children included a morning cartoon screening which featured cartoons from the 1970s and 1980s, a Christmas ornament workshop and events organized in conjunction with the exhibition "Tytus, Romek and A'Tomek," which talked about one of the most popular Polish comic book series. Additionally, the Depot History Center organized a couple of competitions for children as well as for adults. Children's competitions included a "Solidarity Olympiad" (a competition quiz based on the participants' knowledge of the Solidarity trade union of 1980–1981 and its history) and two drawing competitions on a larger series "Paint Me History." The two adult competitions were a competition for an oral history grant and an art competition "But What about Values?" Many events were set up to commemorate the 100th anniversary of Poland's independence—the most notable being "A Hundred 100-year-olds for a Centenary," an oral history project aimed at interviewing a hundred people born before 1922—a task which involved the participation of students. The Depot History Center has also organized Flea Markets, as well as a concert, a special guided tour and Grandmothers' and Grandfathers' Day. The uniqueness of the Depot History Center lies in creating exhibitions that involve the public's participation: the use of outside collections, of the oral history method to create exhibitions, and help from Public History students.

Almost 57 percent of the events organized by the City Museum engaged the audience. Just as in the National Museum, most of those were workshops aimed at children. They presented the history of Wrocław and its culture and revolved around permanent and temporary exhibitions. There were also several occasions for the elderly to visit the museum, a genre of events that rarely appears in the analysis of the other museums, and unique festivals, city tours, activities for teenagers and tours for parents with small children.

Conclusion

On the one hand, the researched museums of the city of Wrocław are full of creativity and work systematically to create and promote their efforts. On the other hand, the diversity of the "engaging" offers leaves a lot to be desired. Once those events are in motion, they are endlessly repeated.

Focusing on the youngest members of the public creates a gap for activities and events for anyone over the age of 12—once the children have matured, they will become part of this orphaned public. They then might realize in horror that they have actively to create their own engaging experience at the museum, because it will not be arranged for them. Senior citizens can also be regarded as a privileged group (perhaps due to the fact that they are perceived to have a lot of free time).

None of the analyzed museums has a consciously diverse, fully considered program that would cater to the public of students. The Depot History Center came the closest—its "Meeting with History" was created in part for students and the format allowed for interaction and connecting with other participants. Other events that could be considered somewhat aimed at students are the poetic slams organized by Pan Tadeusz Museum, however nowhere was it explicitly stated. The lack of any sort of a digital-based event or program catering to the Generation Z portion of the student public was also striking. This began to change during the COVID-19 pandemic, but it is still too early to indicate whether it will remain a permanent trend and how the student-public will respond.

While creating the questionnaire which was the basis of the above analysis, I and my fellow students were not aware of how dramatically scarce the museums' offerings for students were. Now that we know this is so, and looking ahead to the possibility of repeating the same research, some changes to the questionnaire would be helpful in gathering more detailed data. Firstly, it would be preferable to create separate, multiple questions exploring the museum-going habits, instead of the two general ones included in the current questionnaire. Moreover, adding questions directly relating to students' views of museums' offerings and their expectations would be important in gaining more insight into those issues. Especially relevant due to COVID-19 and the inclusion of Gen Z-ers into the student body would be questions relating to digital tools and communications channels, as well as engaging (participatory) practices. There are many possibilities for future research apart from repeating what has been described above—for example, investigating the matter from the perspective of museum professionals, trying to ascertain their approach to students as the museums' public and their views on the findings of this research. It is essential to consider both of those perspectives, as the struggle to stay relevant in the digital-centric, fast-paced world in which history is often used as a tool for profit is clear in the actions undertaken by Wrocław's museums. Students are a public not easily ignored, yet all four analyzed museums seem to do it. Finding out why this happens would be the starting point in making the younger members of the museums' public future enthusiasts, instead of non-visitors.

Notes

1 The proposed definition has sparked a heated discussion. Those opposing it argue that it is overly ideological, too long and detailed, but—most importantly—impossible to apply to most museums in the world.

2 Peter Vergo, introduction to *The New Museology*, ed. Peter Vergo (London: Reaktion Books, 2006), 3.

3 John E. Simmons, *Museums: A History* (Lanham: Rowman & Littlefield, 2016), 213–214.

4 Mathilde Pulh and Rémi Mencarelli, "Web 2.0: Is the Museum–Visitor Relationship Being Redefined?" *International Journal of Arts Management* 18, no. 1 (Fall 2015): 43.

5 Anna Ziębińska-Witek, *Historia w muzeach. Studium ekspozycji Holokaustu* (Lublin: Wydawnictwo UMCS, 2011), 32–33.

6 Pulh and Mencarelli, "Web 2.0," 45–46.

7 In 2018, 79 percent of students in Poland were under the age of 25; PBS. "Społeczne i ekonomiczne warunki życia studentów w Polsce na tle innych krajów europejskich," (Sopot, Warsaw 2018), 26.

8 See, for instance, Pandora L. Kay, Emma Wong, and Michael J. Polonsky, "Marketing Cultural Attractions: Understanding Non-Attendance and Visitation Barriers," *Marketing Intelligence & Planning* 27, no. 6 (2009): 833–854.

9 Richard Prentice, Andrea Davies, and Alison Beeho, "Seeking Generic Motivations for Visiting and Not Visiting Museums and Like Cultural Attractions," *Museum Management and Curatorship* 16, no. 1 (1997): 64.

10 John H. Falk and Lynn D. Dierking, *The Museum Experience Revisited* (London, New York: Routledge, 2016), 62.

11 Marylin Hood, "After 70 Years of Audience Research, What Have We Learned? Who Comes to Museums, Who Does Not, and Why?" *Visitor Studies* 5, no. 1 (1993), 16–27.

12 Aleah Vinick and Rachel Abbott, "How to Design Programs for Millennials," *History News* 70, no. 4 (2015): 4.

13 Ibid., 2.

14 Ibid., 4.

15 "Muzea we Wrocławiu," Tripadvisor, accessed August 14, 2020, https://pl. tripadvisor.com/Attractions-g274812-Activities-c49-Wroclaw_Lower_Silesia_ Province_Southern_Poland.html.

16 "O Muzeum," Muzeum Narodowe we Wrocławiu, accessed August 14, 2020, https://mnwr.pl/oddzialy/muzeum-narodowe/o-muzeum.

17 "O Muzeum," Muzeum Miejskie Wrocławia, accessed August 14, 2020, http://muzeum.miejskie.wroclaw.pl/o-muzeum.

18 "O Muzeum," Muzeum Pana Tadeusza, accessed August 14, 2020, http://muzeumpanatadeusza.ossolineum.pl/pl/o-muzeum.

19 "O Ośrodku," Centrum Historii Zajezdnia, accessed August 14, 2020, https://www.zajezdnia.org/o-osrodku.

20 National Ossoliński Institute is a historic-cultural foundation, publishing house, an archival institute and research center.

21 "O Ośrodku," Centrum Historii Zajezdnia.

22 "Kolekcja," Muzeum Narodowe we Wrocławiu, accessed August 14, 2020, https://mnwr.pl/oddzialy/muzeum-narodowe/kolekcja.

23 Władysław Bartoszewski (February 19, 1922–April 24, 2015)—Polish historian, diplomat, social and political activist, member of the Provisional Committee of Assistance to Jews "Żegota," Auschwitz survivor. Recognized as "Righteous Among the Nations" in 1965.

24 Jan Nowak-Jeziorański (May 15, 1913–January 20, 2005)—Polish journalist and political activist. Member of the Home Army, POW during Second World War, known as "the Courier from Warsaw" for successfully completing several trips between Warsaw and London as a courier for the Home Army High Command. Decorated with the War Order of Virtuti Militari, highest of Polish military orders. In 1952–1976 Nowak was director of the Polish Section of Radio Free Europe in Munich, and upon retirement he actively lobbied in the United States for Poland's liberation from communism.

25 The long May weekend refers to the national holidays of 1 May (International Workers' Day) and 3 May (3 May Constitution Day).

Bibliography

Centrum Historii Zajezdnia. "O Ośrodku." Accessed August 14, 2020. https://www.zajezdnia.org/o-osrodku.

Dzikowska, Joanna. "Wrocław przyjazny młodym? W rankingu tuż za podium." *Gazeta Wyborcza*, September 21, 2018.

Falk, John H., and Lynn D. Dierking. *The Museum Experience Revisited*. London, New York: Routledge, 2016.

Główny Urząd Statystyczny. "Szkolnictwo wyższe w roku akademickim 2018/2019 (wyniki wstępne)." Accessed 10 August 2020. https://stat.gov.pl/obszary-tematyczne/edukacja/edukacja/szkolnictwo-wyzsze-w-roku-akademickim-20182019-wyniki-wstepne, 8,6.html.

Hood, Marylin. "After 70 Years of Audience Research, What Have We Learned? Who Comes to Museums, Who Does Not, and Why?" *Visitor Studies: Theory, Research and Practice* 15 (1993): 16–27. Informal Science.

International Telecommunication Union. "Statistics." Accessed 10 August 2020. https://www.itu.int/en/ITU-D/Statistics/Pages/stat/default.aspx.

Kay, Pandora L., Emma Wong, and Michael J. Polonsky. "Marketing Cultural Attractions: Understanding Non-attendance and Visitation Barriers." *Marketing Intelligence & Planning* 27, no. 6 (2009): 833–854.

Muzeum Miejskie Wrocławia. "O Muzeum." Accessed August 14, 2020. http://muzeum.miejskie.wroclaw.pl/o-muzeum.

Muzeum Narodowe we Wrocławiu. "Kolekcja." Accessed August 14, 2020. https://mnwr.pl/oddzialy/muzeum-narodowe/kolekcja.

Muzeum Narodowe we Wrocławiu. "O Muzeum." Accessed August 14, 2020. https://mnwr.pl/oddzialy/muzeum-narodowe/o-muzeum.

Muzeum Pana Tadeusza. "O Muzeum." Accessed August 14, 2020. http://muzeumpanatadeusza.ossolineum.pl/pl/o-muzeum.

NIMOZ. "Statystyka muzeów. Muzea w 2018 roku." Warsaw, 2019.

PBS. "Społeczne i ekonomiczne warunki życia studentów w Polsce na tle innych krajów europejskich." Sopot, Warsaw 2018.

Prentice, Richard, Andrea Davies, and Alison Beeho. "Seeking Generic Motivations for Visiting and Not Visiting Museums and Like Cultural Attractions." *Museum Management and Curatorship* 16, no. 1 (1997), 45–70.

Pulh, Mathilde, and Rémi Mencarelli. "Web 2.0: Is the Museum–Visitor Relationship Being Redefined?" *International Journal of Arts Management* 18, no. 1 (2015): 43–51.

Simmons, John E. *Museums: A History*. Lanham: Rowman & Littlefield, 2016.

Tripadvisor. "Muzea we Wrocławiu." Accessed 14 August 2020. https://pl.tripadvisor.com/Attractions-g274812-Activities-c49-Wroclaw_Lower_Silesia_Province_Southern_Poland.html.

Urząd Statystyczny we Wrocławiu. "Statystyczne Vademecum Samorządowca 2019. Miasto Wrocław." Wrocław, 2019.

Vergo, Peter, ed. *The New Museology*. London: Reaktion Books, 2006.

Vinick, Aleah, and Rachel Abbott. "How to Design Programs for Millennials." *History News* 70, no. 4 (2015): 1–8.

Ziębińska-Witek, Anna. *Historia w muzeach. Studium ekspozycji Holokaustu*. Lublin: Wydawnictwo UMCS, 2011.

5

ON FIRE, UNDER FIRE

Public Reactions to the Destruction of the Brazilian National Museum

Ricardo Santhiago

In 2008, for four desperate hours, the Cultura Artística theater was consumed by a fire that slowly destroyed the 384 square meter fresco created by the acclaimed Modernist painter Di Cavalcanti. Also damaged were the building's very structure and the costumes for plays being staged at that

FIGURE 5.1   Fire at the main building of the Brazilian National Museum in Rio de Janeiro on September 2, 2018, © Felipe Milanez, public domain.

time. Two years later, one of the world's major collections of living snakes, at the renowned Butantan Institute, suffered the same fate. In 2013, it was the turn of the Latin American Memorial, whose enormous main room, with its fascinating 800 square meter tapestry by Japanese-Brazilian artist Tomie Ohtake, went up in flames. And in 2015, the three floors of the Museum of the Portuguese Language—the first in the world devoted to an idiom, creatively dealing with a challenging immaterial object—were quickly and entirely destroyed. All this in São Paulo, the richest and most developed metropolis in Brazil, and the financial center of all of Latin America.

Fires and correlative accidents, in short, have not been unusual in the recent history of Brazil's museums and other national treasures, but, while these events are not infrequent, strong and abiding public reactions to them are uncommon, with the exception of one recent tragedy that became news throughout the world. A genuine maelstrom, both domestic and international, followed the horrific fire that began on the night of September 2, 2018, at the main building of the Brazilian National Museum, in Rio de Janeiro, Brazil's capital for nearly two centuries.

Intense flames consumed the old palace, located within the municipal park Quinta da Boa Vista, which held more than 400,000 items in its collections (an additional 1,600,000 items remained intact since they were stored in an underground annex and another building). These master collections began in June 1818, following a decree by Dom João VI, a few years before the Proclamation of the Republic. A couple of months after celebrating its 200th anniversary, the Museum saw most of its collection—best described, in fact, as unique—destroyed. Egyptian mummies, remnants of frescoes from Pompeii, sound recordings of lost languages, objects of significance to native peoples—all turned into ashes. A day later, at dawn on September 4, rain helped to extinguish the areas still burning—but it also caused even more damage to whatever items of the museum's collections remained.

There were no human losses; the four security guards assigned to the building managed to escape. But the tally of the final damage is sorrowful and until now has been impossible to enumerate precisely. The ethnographic collection of 42,000 pieces, for example, was almost entirely lost—except for pieces on loan at the time to an exhibition in Brasília. Scholars of indigenous culture consider the loss to be a new genocide, this time a symbolic one, since this thematic collection included documents, language records, medicinal studies not available elsewhere, along with 30,000 material artifacts made by American, Asian, African, and Oceanian indigenous peoples.

In addition to the museological and archival items, the fire consumed the rooms of the museum's graduate program, research laboratories, and the important Francisca Keller Library specialized in anthropology. The building's structure itself was severely damaged, with deep cracks and ruined internal pavements. But apart from its architectural value, the building's historical importance is unmatched. The palace was the residence of the

Portuguese royal family and the stage for unique moments in the history of Brazil, such as the Declaration of Independence, signed by Empress Leopoldina in 1822.

Formerly visited for leisure and knowledge, the Quinta da Boa Vista park became, throughout the month of September, a place for mourning and lamentation. "There will be absolutely nothing left of the National Museum," said the institution's desperate deputy director, Luiz Fernando Dias Duarte, in a TV interview, echoing a generalized feeling.[1] In front of the palace—during and after its burning—teachers, students, researchers, and members of the surrounding community wept for what was permanently lost.

"It's not just as if the British Museum is burning, it's as if Buckingham Palace is too," the British journalist Jonathan Watts stated.[2] Other declarations, however, showed that the suffering over the loss of the National Museum was not unanimous. "It's done, it's on fire, what do you want me to do?," a man said on TV, adding that even though his middle name is "Messias" [Messiah] he "can't do miracles."[3] His first name is Jair, his last name is Bolsonaro, and a few months later he would be elected Brazil's 38th president.

This is an extreme example of the variety of public reactions to the tragedy that befell Brazil and the world. In this chapter, I intend to highlight the complexity of these reactions of various groups of public, which together constitute a case study of how diverse perceptions, reactions, and narratives are elicited by significant public events that affect many sectors of the populace. Collectively, these reactions also provide an unusual opportunity to examine the ways by which a major public history institution commands public attention, and how audiences understand and elaborate its social significance.

History under Fire

Meaningful by itself, the tragedy of the National Museum is also an optimal metaphor of the changing place that history has occupied in Brazil in recent years—both as knowledge and as a wellspring from which one can extract valuable lessons for action in the present and for imagining the future. It is, in fact, impossible to take the event out of a broader context in which humanistic, and especially historical, knowledge is under fire in contemporary Brazil.

The great example of this state of affairs is Jair Bolsonaro, elected president in late 2018, whose term started in 2019. Bolsonaro is widely known for his frequent attacks on knowledge, for his contempt for universities as spaces for the production and circulation of diverse knowledge, and for his alarming negationist public statements. It is not surprising, then, that in the middle of his campaign, when approached by journalists about his proposals for heritage preservation, he dared to pronounce the sentence cited above, nor that, in May 2019, already in office, he would block 20 percent—i.e., 12 of the 55 million Brazilian Reais—of the federal budget allocated for the museum's reconstruction.

Intellectuals claim that the contempt for history and the past began to emerge publicly in June 2013, as part of popular revolts that took to the streets. The anti-institutional and, allegedly, anti-political discourse of these demonstrations was captured by a populist right that then directed attacks toward the left, which was in power at federal and many state and city levels. Until then, the philosopher Vladimir Safatle writes, "support for figures like Jair Bolsonaro, the cult of the military dictatorship, and openly violent speech was marginal,"[4] but thereafter gained ground. Following Dilma Roussef's reelection, in 2014, an alliance between the center-right, the right, and the extreme right—all devoted to defeating the Workers' Party, elected for four consecutive terms and facing public charges of corruption—employed every possible means to discredit the left.

Not surprisingly, intellectuals and public universities have become the prime target of Bolsonaro and his allies. A campaign against these universities (which, in Brazil, are tuition-free and almost entirely publicly funded) unfolded, operating on two levels. At the administrative level, it was argued that public universities consume a high volume of resources, without giving anything back to the society in terms of research, and prevent investments in basic education.[5] At the symbolic level, it would claim that public universities are the most fertile ground for attacking alleged traditional values relating to sex, family, and nation, among others. Social scientists and historians, particularly, would be held responsible for corrupting moral values—values that Jair Bolsonaro claimed he would restore.

This brief contextualization is important in understanding the singularity of the extreme right's reaction toward the fire: they systematically denied historical knowledge itself and its relevance for the present, but after the disaster they posed as great defenders of national heritage. They did not celebrate the fire; on the contrary, they took advantage of it as another reason to attack, both on a political and cultural basis, intellectuals and universities, particularly the one university that, as a federal organism, is directly responsible for the museum.

The National Museum falls under federal jurisdiction. Since 1946, it has been managed by the Federal University of Rio de Janeiro (UFRJ), a large public university created in 1920, which in 2020 has about 4,200 professors, 9,000 staff, and 67,000 students. As with many universities, UFRJ is the body responsible for administering various federal services. Thus, in addition to its five major *campi*, 179 undergraduate, and 345 graduate programs, it is accountable for 43 libraries, a university press, hundreds of laboratories, nine hospitals, and seven museums. The National Museum is one of these, and it competes with each of the other sectors of the university for an ever-smaller budget.

Still, the fire quickly led members of the extreme right to point fingers at UFRJ: it was said to be guilty of not investing sufficiently in the museum, thus bearing responsibility for the lost patrimony. The director of the museum was accused of negligence, for having failed to carry out the necessary renovations that could have prevented the disaster. While these are not literal lies, neither are they true. What these accusations hide is that the fire resulted from a chain of (in)actions, involving consecutive negligence toward a cultural good registered as a National Historical and Artistic Heritage since 1938. Indeed, in July 2020, the final report delivered by the Federal Police did rule out the hypotheses of any criminal action in the fire, and, more important, discarded charges of dereliction on the part of the museum administration.

Commenting on a news item in the newspaper *Folha de S. Paulo*, however, a reader rejects the very content of the piece, and says: "an administration led by a person like the UFRJ president [...], is obviously a disaster of incompetence [...] A university run by a leftist radical [...] will never be any good to itself or to the country."[6] Proclaiming that the fire happened because the UFRJ president had allegedly taken political control over the museum machinery, the reader sides with Bolsonaro, the first to publicly blame the left: "The entire administration is made up of people affiliated with [leftist parties]. That's what political nominations lead to,"[7] he said, neglecting to mention the fact that the entire museum staff is composed of tenured public servants, hired after open, highly competitive selection procedures.

Exposing half-truths, concealing information, distorting arguments— these are some of the underpinnings of the extreme right's reactions toward the museum fire. The museum had been dealing for decades—due to the lack of resources—with the struggle against its "three fundamental challenges: rain, termites, and fire."[8] Various radical right-wing websites, such as *O antagonista* [The antagonist], treated this information as if it were a recent discovery rather than common knowledge, not only never denied by the museum administration, but actually exposed by it in public appearances as a reason to pursue proper funding. The rebellious, inflamed tone of these discourses can tempt one to discredit and ignore them, instead of exposing their weakenesses. These are, however, public opinions with whom historians working at the public arena inescapably deal.

Materializing Publics

The use of the National Museum fire by the extreme right wing to attack, at the same time, the left and the public universities is an important phenomenon that must be noted—but it is only one piece in the larger framework of public reactions to the tragedy. It is not easy to go deeper into the contemporaneous public responses to the event, particularly when this is done *a posteriori*. We are stuck with fragmentary, unsystematic data. And we can count mainly on one ally, the press, which produced reports on the fire and the reactions to it in real time. This is not surprising: the fire was an enormous disaster involving a large historic building, highly visible in the city of Rio de Janeiro. Especially in times of scarcity of hot news, tragedies are a must for media producers.

It is useless to attempt to assess whether the press's purposes in such cases are noble or not, nor to judge the sensational and exploitative character of the coverage. What is undeniable is that, by covering these events for weeks on end, the press carries out a first public writing of history, one designed for immediate consumption, characterized by high velocity, immediacy, fragmentation, and of course framed by the powerful economic interests of the media groups. But such coverage remains an inscription of an event in time, in a way that influences future historical interpretations—as a foundational account. Sonia Meneses has called it a "mediographic operation,"[9] extending to the press the foundational notion of "historiographic operation" created by the French historian Michel de Certeau.

In some sense, the media coverage of the event can be understood as a form of public history—not because it is carried out by professional historians working at the public arena, but because it documents how different publics reacted to an event related to a major public history institution. And that coverage was nothing short of impressive. Naturally, images of the blaze consuming the immense palace were shown over and over. Interviews with politicians, local authorities, museum staff, and fire fighters created the well-known passing-the-buck game, in which every individual or institution blames the other. Within this framework, the fire chief bluntly uttered one of the most absurd phrases in the entire coverage. In a press conference held in front of the ever more harrowing and highly visible flames, he managed to say, "Everything is under control."

One of the most striking of the many aspects of the media response was the marked disparity between the coverage of the tragedy and the coverage of the reconstruction efforts. As usual, after a few weeks the museum disappeared from the news—and all the concern for historic heritage, loudly announced through emotional coverage and endless debates, turned to dust. Mentions of the museum became occasional and limited to reporting whatever was exceptional, as with the survival or recovery of certain items, such as the Bendegó meteorite, some pieces of Karajá dolls, and fragments of the fossil Luzia. This is not uncommon, though, in the relationship the press maintains with most tragedies: what makes a headline becomes, one week later, a short note at the bottom of the page.

It is interesting, however, that in the days and weeks following the fire, the press was firmly dedicated to writing the story of a human tragedy, and not (only) the story of the destruction of a building and numerous objects. The major recent disasters in Brazil that generated trauma and national unrest had very visible victims. The fire in the Kiss nightclub, in 2013, killed 242

persons and injured 680 others—affecting directly or indirectly the inhabitants of the small college town of Santa Maria, in the state of Rio Grande
do Sul. The rupture of tailings dams in the cities of Mariana (2015) and Bru-
madinho (2019), both in the state of Minas Gerais, left hundreds of people
dead and thousands homeless and deprived of the means of survival. The
victims in all of these cases had very identifiable faces and names—which
fed the opportunity for weeks and weeks of sentimental coverage.

At the National Museum, by contrast, the direct victims were inanimate—
but the press, over the month, carried out a conceptual construction that
brought to the scene the face of the human victims; and these coincided
with the different groups the museum had as its public. Whether or not the
media's goal was to add color and drama to objects, attracting a larger audience with compelling personal dramas does not matter so much here; what is
important to notice is that, in its historical narrative, the media clarified the
different publics that benefited from the existence of the National Museum.
And in doing so, the press underscored the institution's local, national, and
international relevance even for those who had never visited it. Instead of an
abstraction, the tragedy became concrete, affecting different communities
of audiences, each shaped by the media's narrative.

Two of those are quite clear. First, the research community, composed of
students and scholars, directly connected to and concerned with the historical and cultural heritage that was lost. This community understood how the
institution was beneficial to the construction and preservation of knowledge.
It is no surprise that academics such as the anthropologist Laura Moutinho
would describe what they saw as "horrific scenes, kindling our torpor, ig-
niting our personal and professional memories, like the flames that roared
without mercy over 200 years of our history."[10] The research community in
a way intensified the reactions of shock and indignation felt by the society
(Brazilian and international) as a whole.

Public statements and open letters, as well as social media posts, were
the most usual outlet for expressing the dismay of these groups. Innocu-
ous in themselves, they hinted at the formation of a solidarity and support
network. International statements would primarily mourn the incalculable
losses. The International Council of Museums (ICOM) talked about a "dark
day for not only Brazilian heritage but also for the world's heritage," and expressed its "belief in the resilience and professionalism of Brazil's museum
professionals,"[11] while the Smithsonian ranked itself among those who "in
Brazil and well beyond [...] have benefited from and appreciated this wonderful museum."[12] The French president, Emmanuel Macron, stated that
"France will put its specialists at the service of the Brazilian people, to help
with reconstruction"—not anticipating that months later an equally devastating fire would damage Paris's Notre Dame Cathedral. In their restraint,
most international manifestations did not reach the heart of the matter, unlike the World Archeological Congress that added, to its expression of shock

and sadness, the comment that it shared "the anger and grief expressed, particularly concerning the way the museum had been treated over many years up to the incident."[13]

In Brazil, a curious phenomenon occurred: many statements were categorized as "repudiation letters," which is a genre of public statement often used to directly oppose the opinions and acts of politicians, policy makers, and prominent members of civil society. Here, they seemed custom-made to respond to the event. Since they could not—of course—repudiate the flames, these "repudiation letters" were reinvented as charges aimed at politicians, expressing disapproval, criticizing "the policies of budget cuts, year after year, with the objective of stinting on public resources in favor of paying the interest on public debt,"[14] denouncing the political choice made by "Michel Temer's illegitimate office" in favor of those cuts,[15] as well as contributing to the "precarization of public institutions."[16] The National Confederation of Educational Facilities Workers adopted an even more emphatic tone, asserting that the blaze

> was a criminal fire. The crime is Constitutional Amendment 95 and the freezing of public investments for 20 years. The crime is the largest museum in Latin America needing to survive on just 300 thousand BRL per each year for the past three years, two-thirds of what should be allocated and much less than a Federal Supreme Court (STF) minister earns in a year. The crime is undermining public universities—including UFRJ, responsible for the National Museum—with the aim of privatizing them. The crime is a government that cuts funds from culture and education.[17]

In a similar spirit, and reacting to the privatizing urge demonstrated by members of the extreme right, the Institute for Brazilian Studies at the University of São Paulo thought it relevant to clarify for the public that "State investments in the preservation of the cultural and scientific heritage, which are proportionally small, are in no way capable of leading the country into budgetary imbalance."[18]

In the heat of the moment, statements like these were read on TV channels and featured in newspapers, but the press managed to encapsulate, in an even more concrete way, the reactions to the fire. It did so by showing that a museum is not an assemblage of a building and its objects. "It's like I'm at a funeral. My feeling is that I lost a close relative," a former student of the museum said, humanizing an institution around which an academic and professional community organized.[19] This community offered some of the most impactful images and testimonials of the coverage: people left their own houses to take chances in rescuing objects, or at least to cry in front of the ruins.[20] Following the huge flames, it was the gatherings of desperate persons, leaning on the protective grids that provided the second most striking image of the event. Equally impressive was the staff's night watch, and their anxiety to enter the building the next day, to find out whether anything had survived.

There was a reason for their anxiety, based on the human tragedy that the press highlighted. The museum's professional team—administrative personnel, professors, students in six graduate programs, researchers—not only lost their place of work, but in many cases the very objects they were devoted to, often for years. Hundreds of people had their daily lives, their routines, and their professional goals entirely suspended—and, in a few cases, interrupted permanently, since offices, laboratories, equipment, personal libraries, and document collections were irretrievably destroyed.

Some of them had to redirect their perspectives to the work of reconstruction of the museum collections. Archaeologists, for example, turned to the painful task of looking for pieces that had, partially or completely, survived the fire and the landslides. "I have students who will make their first excavation here, in the ruins of the palace," said the director of the Egyptology Laboratory.[21] In an article of August 2019, the *Nature* website followed up on the dramas of the research and museology community. The zoologist Paulo Buckup is, among others, the source of touching stories. On the night of the fire, he, his colleagues, and students drove to the museum and removed as many materials from the rear of the building as they could, before the fire got there. What they rescued included 664 types of specimens from the mollusc collection. Buckup also recounts how the internal life at the museum was affected after the fire; a professional community developed into an emotional community, marked by a common trauma. "In the competitive world of academia, scientists tend to hide their emotions, says Buckup, but that is no longer true at the museum," the reporter writes. He adds that the spatial compression itself created new bonds.[22]

Emotions set the tone for this coverage, as well as for the approach of another group of publics made visible by the fire: the population surrounding the Quinta da Boa Vista park, for whom the museum was a reference point both in terms of heritage and daily life—a place that could be visited for free, a frequent destination for local schools, a recreational space for the population of Rio's Northern Zone, especially on the weekends. By rendering visible the suffering and shock of the community, the press ended up doing the museum a great service: it prevented the rise of an understanding of the museum as a useless structure that should indeed be subjected to budget cuts. And, by highlighting the dozens of outreach projects carried out by the staff in partnership with the local community, as well as the touching reactions of many who considered the museum an integral part of the urban landscape they accessed on a daily basis, the media narrative emphasized the different levels on which knowledge, produced and circulated by a museological institution, is able to affect the public, and continues to do so.

Emotions, Arts, and Memories

Standing before cultural goods bequeathed by societies and cultures that preceded us and are interpreted in a museum, or witnessing the destruction of those very goods and places, are quite different experiences—but they can be equally affecting. In Brazil, we are wont to turn to popular culture as a fount that allows us to grasp traces of public perceptions of a person or an event. Folk music and carnival festivities are well established not only as sources of leisure and entertainment, but as *loci* where different social subjects—producers and receptors, often in dialogue—meet each other. These types of art promote a social discussion of relevant contemporary issues. Indeed, the primacy of both as spaces for a broad social dialogue is a legacy of an ongoing national wound, illiteracy.[23]

Grassroot leaders such as Zumbi dos Palmares, a slave liberationist in the seventeenth century, and Lampião, a sort of Robin Hood of the early twentieth century Brazilian northeast, had their stories told in samba schools' parades, as did the history of slavery in Brazil, folk traditions such as *congadas* and *maracatu*, and historical representations of popular neighborhoods. With few exceptions, carnival walkways have been a place to recount history brushed against the grain, as Walter Benjamin would put it.[24] Not surprisingly: carnival is a great festival created by the people and reflecting primarily the leaders, events, and processes that they consider valuable.

It is significant, therefore, that a few months before being consumed by flames, the National Museum was for the second time the theme of a *samba-enredo* (samba-story)—which belies any claim that its existence was largely ignored by the populace. Ten years earlier, in 2008, the samba school Arrastão de Cascadura organized its parade around by a clever samba that would recount the transformation of the royal palace into a museum.[25] In 2018, the famous samba school Imperatriz Leopoldinense took advantage of the museum's bicentenary to present the parade *Uma noite real no Museu Nacional* (*A Royal Night at the National Museum*), watched by almost 7.5 million spectators in addition to the 72,500 seats of the samba avenue parade grounds.[26] Rio's carnival parades, known throughout the world, often concentrate on historical themes as seen through the prism of popular culture. This makes them an important public history enterprise, as many authors such as Ana Maria Mauad have analyzed.[27] In addition to disseminating popular history, they are also occasions that unite thousands of people in a cooperative endeavor, involving public discussions of possible themes, bibliographic research to support the creation of music themes and costumes, debates with historians who work as consultants, and months of rehearsals.

That was before the fire, but popular culture found its own way to convey the public's shock at the tragedy. The seasoned and respected composer Chico César, for example, created *Luzia Negra*, a seven-minute blues-rock piece that honors Luzia—the oldest fossil ever found in the Americas and one of the most important pieces in the National Museum's collection. Within the tragedy of the fire, the nearly total loss of Luzia, who lived 11,500 years ago, gained special symbolic value. She now became the main character in a fine song described by him as "artivism," which draws on a long tradition in which folk and popular music are central to the debate on relevant national issues. And, because of manifestations like this song—created by a respected artist who has about 1,800,000 listeners per month at Spotify—Luzia would also remain alive in the public memory, where Chico César's committed songs wish to intervene.

The same applies to other artists' poems, songs, and literary pieces, which have become the bricks through which members of the public insist on keeping the museum's memory alive. Even a ludic creation can be a memory medium, as two Brazilian publicists, Caio Gandolfi and Diego Ferrit, tried to demonstrate. In early 2019, they entered a LEGO contest with a proposal to produce a model of the National Museum building in the company series. Their project highlighted that "the greatest historical, artistic, cultural and scientific patrimony in Brazil was destroyed by an enormous fire," and explicitly stated that they wished to "leave the National Museum alive in the public imaginary." Should their project be voted for by 10,000 individuals within 500 days, it would then be reviewed by LEGO and considered for an award. In less than five days, half the necessary supporters had been gathered, reaching the required total number in just two months. Subsequently, however, the proposal was turned down by the LEGO team, a suggestive reminder that public involvement very often stumbles upon institutional and commercial barriers. A 13-year-old child was more diligent in overcoming difficulties like this: dismayed by the destruction in the fire of the Throne of Adandozan, from the ancient African kingdom of Dahome, he produced his own replica in papier-maché and varnish, which touched the museum's staff to the point that it was incorporated into the collection of the institution, now housed in the palace's annex.[28]

As folk and popular forms that reinforce the public's experience with the National Museum (or with its absence), Carnival, the song, and the replicas all demonstrate the inscription of this institution in public memory. But, as Lucia Santa Cruz[29] demonstrates, it is also chiseled into memory on an individual level. Cruz analyzed the flood of social media posts following the tragedy and employed the hashtag #MuseuNacionalVive (National Museum Lives), reaching simple and exciting conclusions. Tracking the hashtag, Cruz was able to perceive how intimate were the relationships between a given object—for example, a *panapana*, an object mimicking the flight of butterflies—and different individuals. She also found frequent expressions of guilt and regret by those who had never visited the institution, allusions to childhood moments, accusations against politicians and the UFRJ, and the understanding of the fire as an analogy with the country's current state of affairs. And, because of a change in the way visitors interact with the museum in the last two decades—through extensive documentation of their own visits, with the use of portable and affordable devices—she pointed to a resource that has been used elsewhere to collaboratively rebuild part of the museum's collection: user-produced iconography.

Tears Don't Rebuild

In the last two decades, the National Museum has gone through a gradual process of digitizing its collections, using a variety of high technology devices that go beyond mere photography or 2D scanning and include ultrasonography, modeling, prototyping, and 3D printing. Originally, these would allow, for example, the construction of replicas both for study and for exhibition, while preserving the original in a technical reserve.[30] After the fire, the possibilities of restoring lost pieces based on digital records became crucial and challenging, since they will demand the creation of a new pact between museum and visitors, based on an altered notion of authenticity.[31]

Digital engagement was one of the immediate responses to the museum fire. The National Museum's Inter-wikis Wikiproject was particularly effective in mobilizing the public. In the early days after the disaster, 250 people added texts and images to Wikipedia, and the material started to be curated by a team of more experienced users, leading to a specific project bringing together—under the banner of open, collective knowledge—images produced by users.

On September 4, 2018, the official Wikipedia profile on Twitter announced: "There were over 20 million objects inside the #MuseuNacional. Did you take a photo of any of them? Help us preserve the memories of as many as we can and add them to @wikicommons." The post had 4,500 likes and 5,900 retweets and comments, and prompted a crowdsourced effort that, as of early September 2020, includes 3,961 images. On the project's page, one can access both the digital collections and features such as monitoring loadings, which informs us that the beautiful palace at the Quinta da Boa Vista park is the leader of visualizations. The project also includes the creation of entries pertinent to the museum, while recognizing that "visual memory is now our main heritage."

If fire is understood, ironically, as a "metaphor for the current state of science in the country"—as a group of researchers wrote in *Science*—the wiki effort also can be understood as a metaphor for a number of initiatives that catalyze different publics around the reconstruction of a common cultural good. Digital tours, archeology projects, video documentaries, and the exhibition of pieces rescued are among the works that have been carried out by a staff who—in the face of a social and individual tragedy—did not capitulate. Within their limitations, they try to keep the museum alive, in itself and in the public memory. In July 2020, a group of scientists led by the museum's paleontologist Juliana Sayão baptized the most recent dinosaur fossil discovered in Brazil *Aratasaurus museunacionali*—the first word referring to its natural genus, and the second being a homage to the museum staff, with the full name meaning "the dinosaur born from the National Museum fire."[32]

After the fire, the museum strengthened its presence in social media, taking advantage, for example, of commemorative dates to publicize images of pieces from its collection. Furthermore, it is committed to explaining to the public what a museum does beyond exhibiting, such as by showing informative and compelling videos of its own internal workings. This online presence, however, is not hassle-free. As in other countries currently hit by "cancel culture," in Brazil too there is now controversy about whether and which monuments to the past should be exhibited, and a photo of a statue of Dom Pedro II, posted in June 2020 by the museum director, led to a heated discussion.[33]

Other controversies concern the museum's own decisions—and, interestingly, allow us to glimpse public conceptions and misconceptions about heritage. While one individual asks for an "an architecture competition so that the palace and museum can be remodeled," another argues that it is "unacceptable to modernize the interior style of the palace. Only the structure and security systems should be updated." A third person echoes the last position and urges the director to preserve the "ancient architecture, faithful to the golden times of the empire," and "not to let the imperial palace become a series of lifeless rooms, a modern art gallery." All of them, however, are equally unaware that there are rules and good practices governing each of those decisions. They do not, in any event, govern the opinion of a skeptic, who puts an end to the discussion by saying that "anyway, the restoration won't be done before the 30th century."

Perhaps this is a prudent skepticism—in addition to sarcasm. In January 2020, the public campaign for donations created by the Society of Friends of the National Museum had collected the paltry amount of 680,000 Brazilian Reais, worth about US $170,000 at the time. A network of financial support announced by former president Michel Temer, which would include banks as well as public and private companies, never got off the ground.[34]

It is estimated that 371.8 million Brazilian Reais (about $69 million US dollars, as of June 2020) will be required for the museum's complete reconstruction, which aims to be finished in 2025. That is quite a modest budget in view of the museum's magnitude and the financial allotment for equivalent institutions in other countries. Still, less than half that amount has been secured—37.7 million Reais provided by the federal government, 56.3 million Reais by national congressmen through funds they direct to agendas of personal interest, and 20 million Reais by the Rio de Janeiro city council.

The participation of private companies is negligible. Only the mining company Vale—very eager to recover its public image after monumental environmental disasters severely eroded it—made a donation, in the significant amount of 50 million Reais.[35] In a country with no tradition of public philanthropy, other wealthy companies, large banks, and families with huge fortunes did nothing. But the billionaire Lily Safra sent 88 million Reais for the reconstruction of Notre Dame—an expression of the commitment of Brazilian elites to the preservation of the nation's historical heritage.[36] In September 2020, the museum reconstruction is nothing but uncertain, and the aim of having at least part of the building reopen by 2022—to celebrate the bicentennial of Independence from Portugal—seems more and more remote.

The National Museum fire—one among many tragedies for Brazil's historical and cultural heritage—has not taught us much: less than two years later, a significant natural history collection at the Minas Gerais Federal University was similarly consumed by flames.[37] Lack of investment persists and shows that not even the public dimension of the tragedy makes politicians and large national entrepreneurs commit to preserving Brazil's heritage. Neither indignation nor expressions of pain from these agents—whether genuine or instrumentalized for political and economic purposes—translated into effective contributions. Despite the extensive public interest and concern over the fate of the museum, this tragedy reveals a sad reality that cannot be ignored: wishes and possibilities for having a significant impact on public memory do not always coincide, and this is, and will continue to be, a reality against which public history practices must creatively fight.

Notes

1 Talita Bedinelli and Marina Rossi, "Controlado o incêndio que destruiu o Museu Nacional, a primeira instituição científica da história do país," *El País*, September 3, 2018, https://brasil.elpais.com/brasil/2018/09/03/politica/1535932675_816618.html.

2 Eliane Brum, "O Brasil queimou—e não tinha água para apagar o fogo," *El País*, September 3, 2018, https://brasil.elpais.com/brasil/2018/09/03/opinion/1535975822_774583.html.

3 Fernanda Calgaro, "'Já está feito, já pegou fogo, quer que eu faça o quê?', diz Bolsonaro sobre incêndio no Museu Nacional," *G1*, September 4, 2018, https://g1.globo.com/politica/eleicoes/2018/noticia/2018/09/04/ja-esta-feito-ja-pegou-fogo-quer-que-faca-o-que-diz-bolsonaro-sobre-incendio-no-museu-nacional.ghtml.

4 Vladimir Safatle, *Só mais um esforço* (São Paulo: Três Estrelas, 2017), 55.

5 Nelson Cardoso Amaral, "As universidades federais brasileiras sob ataque do governo Bolsonaro," *Propuesta Educativa* 52, no. 2 (November 2019): 127–138.

6 "PF descarta ação criminosa e omissão de gestores no incêndio do Museu Nacional," *Folha de S.Paulo*, July 6, 2020, https://comentarios1.folha.uol.com.br/comentarios/6141213?skin=folhaonline.

7 "MEC cortou R$ 12 milhões da verba da reconstrução do Museu Nacional," *Hora do povo*, May 29, 2019, https://horadopovo.com.br/mec-cortou-r-12-milhoes-da-verba-da-reconstrucao-do-museu-nacional.

8 Luiz Fernando Dias Duarte, "Museu Nacional: Elogio, lamento, augúrio," *Anuário Antropológico* 44, no. 1 (2019): 20.

9   Sonia Meneses, *Operação midiográfica: O golpe de 1964 e a Folha de S. Paulo* (São Paulo: Intermeios, 2016).

10 Laura Moutinho, "A tragédia do Museu Nacional, a tragédia dos museus," *Revista de Antropologia* 61, no. 3 (2018), https://doi.org/10.11606/2179-0892. ra.2018.153137.

11 "Statement Regarding the Devastating Fire in the National Museum of Brazil," International Council of Museums, last modified September 3, 2018, accessed August 21, 2020, https://icom.museum/en/news/statement-regarding-the-devastating-fire-in-the-national-museum-of-brazil-in-rio-de-janeiro.

12 "Smithsonian Statement on the Fire at the National Museum of Brazil," Smithsonian, September 3, 2018, accessed August 21, 2020, https://www.si.edu/newsdesk/releases/smithsonian-statement-fire-national-museum-brazil.

13 "WAC Statement on the Devastating Fire and Loss of Heritage Housed in the Brazilian National Museum," Worldarch, last modified October 9, 2018, accessed August 21, 2020, https://worldarch.org/blog/wac-statement-on-the-devastating-fire-and-loss-of-heritage-housed-in-the-brazilian-national-museum.

14 "Nota de repúdio aos Governos responsáveis pela destruição do Museu Nacional," *Sindsef-SP*, September 4, 2018, http://www.sindsef-sp.org.br/portal/node/13559.

15 "Nota de repúdio e alerta," ASUFPel, accessed August 21, 2020, http://asufpel.com.br/2018/09/05/nota-de-repudio-2.

16 "Nota de apoio ao Museu Nacional e de repúdio à precarização dos órgãos públicos," Indigenistas Associados, last modified September 4, 2018, accessed August 21, 2020. https://indigenistasassociados.org.br/2018/09/04/nota-de-apoio-ao-museu-nacional-e-de-repudio-a-precarizacao-dos-orgaos-publicos.

17 "Contee publica nota de pesar pelo Museu Nacional: 'não é tragédia, é crime,'" *Sinprominas*, September 3, 2018, http://sinprominas.org.br/noticias/contee-publica-nota-de-pesar-pelo-museu-nacional-nao-e-tragedia-e-crime.

18 "Nota de grande pesar – Museu Nacional da Quinta da Boa Vista," *Jornal da USP*, September 3, 2018, https://jornal.usp.br/atualidades/nota-de-grande-pesar-museu-nacional-da-quinta-da-boa-vista.

19 "Itens mais preciosos do Museu Nacional queimaram, dizem funcionários," *Isto É Dinheiro*, September 3, 2018, https://www.istoedinheiro.com.br/itens-mais-preciosos-do-museu-nacional-queimaram-dizem-funcionarios.

20 Vinicius Lisboa, "Funcionários do Museu Nacional choram ao ver o que sobrou do incêndio," *Agência Brasil*, September 3, 2018, https://agenciabrasil.ebc.com.br/geral/noticia/2018-09/funcionarios-do-museu-nacional-choram-ao-ver-o-que-sobrou-do-incendio.

21 Marcos Pivetta, "Pré-história em pedaços," *Pesquisa Fapesp*, October, 2018, https://revistapesquisa.fapesp.br/pre-historia-em-pedacos.

22 Emiliano Rodriguez Mega, "The Battle to Rebuild Centuries of Science after an Epic Inferno," *Nature*, July 16, 2019, https://www.nature.com/articles/d41586-019-02141-2.

23 Once widespread, only 15 years ago did illiteracy reach still disturbing rates: in 2005, 7 percent of the population were entirely illiterate, and 68 percent were considered to be functionally illiterate. These days, 29 percent of Brazilians are considered to be functionally illiterate.

24 Walter Benjamin, "As teses sobre o conceito de história," in *Magia e técnica, arte e política ensaios sobre literatura e historia da cultura*, Obras escolhidas, vol. 1 (São Paulo: Brasiliense, 1985), 222–232.

25 Regina Dantas, "Quando um museu dá samba: A popularização do Museu Nacional/UFRJ no carnaval carioca," in *Universidade e lugares de memória*, ed. Antonio José Barbosa de Oliveira (Rio de Janeiro: WalPrint, 2008), 127–144.

26 "Ibope atualiza ponto de audiência para 2020," *Meio & Mensagem*, December 20, 2019, https://www.meioemensagem.com.br/home/midia/2019/12/20/ibope-atualiza-valor-do-ponto-de-audiencia-para-2020.html.

27 Ana Maria Mauad, "O Carnaval da História Pública," in *História Pública em Debate: patrimônio, educação e mediações do passado*, ed. Juniele Rabêlo de Almeida and Sonia Meneses (São Paulo: Letra e Voz, 2018), 227–236.

28 Vinicius Lisboa, "Exposição sobre Museu Nacional tem peça refeita por estudante de 13 anos," *UOL*, February 27, 2019, https://entretenimento.uol.com.br/noticias/redacao/2019/02/27/exposicao-sobre-museu-nacional-tem-peca-refeita-por-estudante-de-13-anos.htm.

29 Lucia Santa Cruz, "Muito mais que um museu: Museu Nacional e memórias coletiva," *Museologia e Patrimônio* 12, no. 2 (2019): 10–29.

30 Fernanda Miranda de Vasconcelos Motta and Ronaldo André Rodrigues da Silva, "A adoção de tecnologias digitais na reconstrução do patrimônio: Relato da experiência do Museu Nacional, Brasil," *Informação & Sociedade* 30, no. 2 (2020): 1–16.

31 Benjamin, "A obra de arte," 165–196.

32 Juliana Manso Sayão et al., "The First Theropod Dinosaur (Coelurosauria, Theropoda) from the Base of the Romualdo Formation (Albian), Araripe Basin, Northeast Brazil," *Scientific Reports* 10 (2020): 1–15.

33 A former faculty member at the museum, Marcio Goldman, was one of those who replied. He wrote

> it is sad and shameful to see the director of the institution where I spent 40 years of my life come out to publicly condone slaves and racists, rather than start discussing the removal of this statue from the position of honor in which those who have always benefited from the slavery and structural racism put it,
>
> Facebook, June 28, 2020, accessed August 21, 2020.

34 Guilherme Mazui, "Planalto anuncia 'rede de apoio' com empresas públicas e privadas para reconstrução do Museu Nacional," *G1*, September 3, 2018, https://g1.globo.com/politica/noticia/2018/09/03/planalto-diz-que-conversou-com-empresas-e-entidades-financeiras-sobre-reconstrucao-do-museu-nacional.ghtml.

35 Victor França, "Museu Nacional recebe recursos da Alerj para apoio à reconstrução," *Conexão UFRJ*, August 19, 2020, https://conexao.ufrj.br/2020/08/19/museu-nacional-recebe-recursos-da-alerj-para-apoio-a-reconstrucao/?fbclid=IwAR0wwnwEFeM0Hx73k5JRIrt3HBiCaCQdEyfXsxx5o8xICJisozDzCMwuoiw.

36 "Conheça a brasileira que doou R$ 88 milhões para a reconstrução da Notre Dame," *Último Segundo*, April 18, 2019, https://ultimosegundo.ig.com.br/mundo/2019-04-18/conheca-a-brasileira-que-doou-r-88-milhoes-para-a-reconstrucao-de-notre-dame.html.

37 Cristiane Silva and Edésio Ferreira, "Museu de História Natural da UFMG é atingido por incêndio," *Estado de Minas*, June 15, 2020, https://www.em.com.br/app/noticia/gerais/2020/06/15/interna_gerais,1156619/museu-de-historia-natural-da-ufmg-e-atingido-por-incendio.shtml.

Bibliography

Amaral, Nelson Cardoso. "As universidades federais brasileiras sob ataque do governo Bolsonaro." *Propuesta Educativa* 52, no. 2 (November 2019): 127–138.

ASUFPel. "Nota de repúdio e alerta." Accessed August 21, 2020. http://asufpel.com.br/2018/09/05/nota-de-repudio-2.

Bedinelli, Talita, and Marina Rossi. "Controlado o incêndio que destruiu o Museu Nacional, a primeira instituição científica da história do país." *El País*, September 3, 2018. https://brasil.elpais.com/brasil/2018/09/03/politica/1535932675_816618.html.

Benjamin, Walter. *Magia e técnica, arte e política ensaios sobre literatura e historia da cultura*. Vol. 1 of Obras escolhidas. São Paulo: Brasiliense, 1985.

Brum, Eliane. "O Brasil queimou—e não tinha água para apagar o fogo." *El País*, September 3, 2018. https://brasil.elpais.com/brasil/2018/09/03/opinion/1535975822_774583.html.

Calgaro, Fernanda. "'Já está feito, já pegou fogo, quer que eu faça o quê?', diz Bolsonaro sobre incêndio no Museu Nacional." *G1*, September 4, 2018. https://g1.globo.com/politica/eleicoes/2018/noticia/2018/09/04/ja-esta-feito-ja-pegou-fogo-quer-que-faca-o-que-diz-bolsonaro-sobre-incendio-no-museu-nacional.ghtml.

"Conheça a brasileira que doou R$ 88 milhões para a reconstrução da Notre Dame." *Último Segundo*, April 18, 2019. https://ultimosegundo.ig.com.br/mundo/2019-04-18/conheca-a-brasileira-que-doou-r-88-milhoes-para-a-reconstrucao-de-notre-dame.html.

"Contee publica nota de pesar pelo Museu Nacional: 'não é tragédia, é crime.'" *Sinprominas*, September 3, 2018. http://sinprominas.org.br/noticias/contee-publica-nota-de-pesar-pelo-museu-nacional-nao-e-tragedia-e-crime.

Dantas, Regina. "Quando um museu dá samba: A popularização do Museu Nacional/UFRJ no carnaval carioca." In *Universidade e lugares de memória*, edited by Antonio José Barbosa de Oliveira, 127–144. Rio de Janeiro: WalPrint, 2008.

Duarte, Luiz Fernando Dias. "Museu Nacional: Elogio, lamento, augúrio." *Anuário Antropológico* 44, no. 1 (2019): 13–26.

França, Victor. "Museu Nacional recebe recursos da Alerj para apoio à reconstrução." *Conexão UFRJ*, August 19, 2020. https://conexao.ufrj.br/2020/08/19/museu-nacional-recebe-recursos-da-alerj-para-apoio-a-reconstrucao/?fbclid=IwAR0wwnwEFeM0Hx73k5JRIrt3HBiCaCQdEyfXsxx5o8xICJisozDzCMwu oiw.

Indigenistas Associados. "Nota de apoio ao Museu Nacional e de repúdio à precarização dos órgãos públicos." Last modified September 4, 2018. Accessed August 21, 2020. https://indigenistasassociados.org.br/2018/09/04/nota-de-apoio-ao-museu-nacional-e-de-repudio-a-precarizacao-dos-orgaos-publicos.

International Council of Museums. "Statement Regarding the Devastating Fire in the National Museum of Brazil." Last modified September 3, 2018. Accessed August 21, 2020. https://icom.museum/en/news/statement-regarding-the-devastating-fire-in-the-national-museum-of-brazil-in-rio-de-janeiro.

"Itens mais preciosos do Museu Nacional queimaram, dizem funcionários." *Isto É Dinheiro*, September 3, 2018. https://www.istoedinheiro.com.br/itens-mais-preciosos-do-museu-nacional-queimaram-dizem-funcionarios.

Lisboa, Vinicius. "Exposição sobre Museu Nacional tem peça refeita por estudante de 13 anos." *UOL*, February 27, 2019. https://entretenimento.uol.com.br/noticias/redacao/2019/02/27/exposicao-sobre-museu-nacional-tem-peca-refeita-por-estudante-de-13-anos.htm.

Lisboa, Vinicius. "Funcionários do Museu Nacional choram ao ver o que sobrou do incêndio." *Agência Brasil*, September 3, 2018. https://agenciabrasil.ebc.com.br/geral/noticia/2018-09/funcionarios-do-museu-nacional-choram-ao-ver-o-que-sobrou-do-incendio.

Mauad, Ana Maria. "O Carnaval da História Pública." In *História Pública em Debate: patrimônio, educação e mediações do passado*, edited by Juniele Rabêlo de Almeida and Sonia Meneses, 227–236. São Paulo: Letra e Voz, 2018.

Mazui, Guilherme. "Planalto anuncia 'rede de apoio' com empresas públicas e privadas para reconstrução do Museu Nacional." *G1*, September 3, 2018. https://g1.globo.com/politica/noticia/2018/09/03/planalto-diz-que-conversou-com-empresas-e-entidades-financeiras-sobre-reconstrucao-do-museu-nacional.ghtml.

Mega, Emiliano Rodriguez. "The Battle to Rebuild Centuries of Science after an Epic Inferno." *Nature*, July 16, 2019. https://www.nature.com/articles/d41586-019-02141-2.

Meneses, Sonia. *Operação midiográfica: O golpe de 1964 e a Folha de S. Paulo*. São Paulo: Intermeios, 2016.

Motta, Fernanda Miranda de Vasconcelos, and Ronaldo André Rodrigues da Silva. "A adoção de tecnologias digitais na reconstrução do patrimônio: Relato da experiência do Museu Nacional, Brasil." *Informação & Sociedade* 30, no. 2 (2020): 1–16.

Moutinho, Laura. "A tragédia do Museu Nacional, a tragédia dos museus." *Revista de Antropologia* 61, no. 3 (2018). https://doi.org/10.11606/2179-0892.ra.2018.153137.

"Nota de grande pesar – Museu Nacional da Quinta da Boa Vista." *Jornal da USP*, September 3, 2018. https://jornal.usp.br/atualidades/nota-de-grande-pesar-museu-nacional-da-quinta-da-boa-vista.

"Nota de repúdio aos Governos responsáveis pela destruição do Museu Nacional." *Sindsef-SP*, September 4, 2018. http://www.sindsef-sp.org.br/portal/node/13559.

Pivetta, Marcos. "Pré-história em pedaços." *Pesquisa Fapesp*, October, 2018. https://revistapesquisa.fapesp.br/pre-historia-em-pedacos.

Safatle, Vladimir. *Só mais um esforço*. São Paulo: Três Estrelas, 2017.

Santa Cruz, Lucia. "Muito mais que um museu: Museu Nacional e memórias coletivas." *Museologia e Patrimônio* 12, no. 2 (2019): 10–29.

Sayão, Juliana Manso et al. "The First Theropod Dinosaur (Coelurosauria, Theropoda) from the Base of the Romualdo Formation (Albian), Araripe Basin, Northeast Brazil." *Scientific Reports* 10 (2020): 1–15.

Silva, Cristiane, and Edésio Ferreira. "Museu de História Natural da UFMG é atingido por incêndio." *Estado de Minas*, June 15, 2020. https://www.em.com.br/app/noticia/gerais/2020/06/15/interna_gerais,1156619/museu-de-historia-natural-da-ufmg-e-atingido-por-incendio.shtml.

Smithsonian. "Smithsonian Statement on the Fire at the National Museum of Brazil." Last modified September 3, 2018. Accessed August 21, 2020. https://www.si.edu/newsdesk/releases/smithsonian-statement-fire-national-museum-brazil.

Worldarch. "WAC Statement on the Devastating Fire and Loss of Heritage Housed in the Brazilian National Museum." Last modified October 9, 2018. Accessed August 21, 2020. https://worldarch.org/blog/wac-statement-on-the-devastating-fire-and-loss-of-heritage-housed-in-the-brazilian-national-museum.

PART II

Publics in Commemorations

6

THE PERSISTENCE OF THE VANISHING INDIAN IN THE MASSACHUSETTS MERRIMACK VALLEY

The Passaconaway Monument

Linda S. Thomas

Today, the United States is experiencing a racial reckoning. Black Lives Matter marches and demonstrations have thrust past and present racial injustices into the public eye. Part of this reckoning has involved questioning, rethinking, and in some cases dismantling and replacing public monuments erected to confederate soldiers, buildings named after slaveholders, flags depicting white supremacy, and racist sports team mascots and names.[1] In addition to confederate monuments, across the country, monuments to Christopher Columbus and Junipero Serra have been toppled or defaced by Indigenous communities and their allies.

These national debates about memory and monuments have played out at the state and local level as well. In Massachusetts, at Harvard University, the Law School crest has been redesigned to cease elevating enslavers over the Africans they enslaved.[2] In the city of Boston, African-American activists call for the renaming of the high-traffic Boston tourist site, Faneuil Hall, because Faneuil was a slaveholder and trader.[3] Also in Boston's North End, the Columbus statue was beheaded, and Indigenous groups such as the North American Indian Center of Boston (NAICOB) and the United American Indians of New England (UAINE) have called for the monument and pedestal to be permanently removed.[4]

While the Mississippi state flag has already been redesigned to remove its Confederate theme, in Massachusetts, state legislation passed in late 2020 to establish a commission to study and redesign its state seal and flag which now depicts a generic Native American male with a sword held threateningly over his head, hardly a welcoming and inclusive symbol to Native Americans who live and work in the state.[5]

In the case of Native American, or as they are also called, Indian monuments, why were they initially erected? Scholars Lisa Blee and Jean

FIGURE 6.1 Passaconaway Statue in Lowell, © Linda S. Thomas.

O'Brien, in *Monumental Mobility: The Memory Work of Massasoit*, examined sculptor Cyrus Dallin's famous monument of Indigenous leader Massasoit in Plymouth, Massachusetts, and the process of its design. Local
Wampanoag and Massachusett Indians in the area were ignored and not
consulted in most of the process, although they were invited to the unveiling
becoming part of the spectacle themselves.[6]

Funded by the Improved Order of Red Men (IORM) in 1921, like many other Indian monuments during this era, the statue of Massasoit was erected to symbolize the presence of absence, to demarcate where Native Americans had once been but supposedly were no longer. Andrew Denson comes to similar conclusions about memorials, monuments and heritage sites set up about the Eastern Band of the Cherokee and the Trail of Tears in Georgia. They were in effect erected to commemorate the absence and dispossession of the Cherokee.[7] Monuments were thus part of the mythologizing process of vanishing and replacement, Blee and O'Brien assert. They were physical manifestations of those who had power and those who did not. Those who design and place monuments have the power and authority to do so—the means, the money, the land and location.

With domination comes resistance. Beginning in 1970, in the case of the Massasoit statue, local Wampanoag Indians and the United American Indians of New England re-appropriated and redefined the monument for themselves in their own National Day of Mourning ceremonies which continue to occur every year during the US Thanksgiving holiday.[8]

Scholars of American history, American studies and, most importantly, Native American and Indigenous studies have proliferated new ways of thinking and reanalyzing American history. They have also discussed how monuments, memory and white appropriation of Native American cultural practices contribute to the settler colonial project. Patrick Wolfe argued that settler colonialism's "logic of elimination" must destroy, eliminate and dismantle existing structures. This invasive process is not a one-time event but an ongoing structure that takes different forms. In the case of the United States, the goal of white settlers has been to eliminate Indigenous peoples, but then re-appropriate parts of their culture in order to express "Native-ness" to distinguish and differentiate themselves from their English forebears.[9]

Native American studies scholar and historian Jean O'Brien has described in *Firsting and Lasting: Writing Indians out of Existence in New England*,[10] how writers of local southern New England histories systematically ignored acts and actions by Indigenous peoples, instead focusing on those of European settlers. White colonial settlers were worthy of being written about as the doers, and Native Americans were portrayed as disappearing. O'Brien points out that historians and other scholars helped to propagate a myth of the vanishing Indian. This was part of a "replacement narrative" that sought to justify white settler colonialism. That narrative is not only a written one, in terms of history or literature, but one that can be found elsewhere in "historical monuments and commemoration, relics and ruins, place-names, and in the land itself."[11]

King Philip's War had a profound impact on Native Americans in the Northeast, and memories of the war are propagated in a variety of ways. Christine DeLucia's work on memory after King Philip's War and how its study needs to be place-based through "memoryscapes" illustrates how deeply contested and unfinished memories of the war are and at the same time how uniquely local they are. DeLucia argues that they are still being revised by multiple actors in multiple sites. Some of the multiple Native actors, who DeLucia refers to as Algonquians of the Northeast, include "Massachusetts, Wampanoags, Narragansetts, Niantics, Quinnipiacs, Mohegans, Pequots, Schagticokes, Pocumtucks, Pennacooks, Nipmucs, Penobscots, Abenakis and others."[12] Memories of the war are not static, but change over time and place and represent experiences of violence and trauma, but also of regeneration, resistance, regathering and recovery. Memories have frequently been created for consumption in the form of novels, poetry, plays, monuments, pageants and private property names. We must ask: who is creating and who is consuming? When memorials are created, what is their purpose? Do they represent private and sacred ceremonies of mourning or are they for a larger public? Are they meant to achieve a certain political or propagandistic end? Are they meant to be consumed by a particular public?

The appropriation of Native American history, culture, language and traditions has always been central to American national identity, Native American studies scholar Philip Deloria argues in his groundbreaking work *Playing Indian*. Beginning with the Boston Tea Party, this is how white colonial settlers were able to redefine themselves as distinct from their past European selves. They were able to become American through appropriating Indigenous cultural practices. Throughout the nineteenth and twentieth centuries, the white-male-only Improved Order of Red Men (IORM)[13] and other Indian hobbyist groups were frequently behind many Indian public monument projects and not Native Americans themselves or those in consultation with Native Americans.

As a fraternal organization, the IORM sought to support its members in times of need, but it also portrayed itself as a custodian of the past, preserving "the nation's aboriginal roots."[14] Part of the method of keeping history was by appropriating the names of local tribes and leaders; its own internal structure was named mimicking presumably Native terminology, but a sole, generic American Indian. Deloria quotes one member as saying that the mission of being a Red Man was

> not merely to imitate, but to preserve. When the time comes that the Indian race is extinct, our Order will occupy a place original and unique, growing more interesting as years pass on, and becoming at once, the interpreter of Indian customs and the repository of Indian traditions.[15]

This mimicry also represented an expression of power; a symbolic representation of Indian Removal and the vanishing Indian. Native Americans did not have the legal right to practice their own religions until the American Indian Religious Freedom Act was passed in 1978. Thus, hobbyist and fraternal order appropriation of Native cultural practices when Native people could not engage in those practices themselves was an expression of their dominance and power.

Lowell's Indigenous History

In turning to the case study of Lowell's Passaconaway Monument, it is necessary to briefly review Lowell's Indigenous past. Regrettably, it is beyond the scope of this chapter to engage comprehensively with primary accounts of this period, rather some of the more recent scholarly work will be summarized. In general, historical scholarship on Lowell has tended to emphasize its nineteenth-century role in the industrial revolution as one of the first and largest mill cities that attracted and employed growing immigrant populations. Public historians may be familiar with Lowell as today it represents the first "urban national park of its kind."[16] Conceived of and designed in the late 1970s, the Lowell National Historical Park highlights its labor and immigrant history. It also represents a post-industrial city's use of its own history, heritage and culture to promote tourism and economic revitalization.[17]

The Merrimack River Valley, what is now Lowell, was once inhabited by the Pennacook who gradually lost their lands to English settlers. According to the Lowell Historical Society, the Pennacook revered leader, Passaconaway, "tried to live in peace with the English colonists."[18] Established as a praying town by Rev. John Eliot in 1653, Wamesit was the smallest of the other 13 praying towns, and its establishment as a praying town "aided in Native American dispossession."[19]

Since Native American historical perspectives and sources are often hard to locate, Native American motivations for participating in the praying towns are difficult to establish.[20] Native Americans converted and joined praying towns after the Massachusetts Bay Colony had already waged multiple wars on them. They were already weakened by disease and loss of their lands and perhaps saw Christian praying towns as a potential means of survival.[21] Despite the praying towns essentially making up a reservation system where white colonists exercised dominance, Native Americans within each town maintained their own traditional leadership positions and day-to-day autonomy.

During and after King Philip's War, Wamesit and neighboring Pawtucket were ethnically cleansed. Despite missionary promises, conversion did not protect those in Wamesit.[22] In 1675, white settlers from nearby Chelmsford rounded up from Wamesit, "145 Native men, women and children" who were force-marched to Boston.

> Only a short while after this incident, a group of Chelmsford settlers barged into the Native village and killed a boy and injured several women. Afraid of further attacks, the Wamesit Indians fled into the

forests. Suffering from the cold temperatures and lack of food, they returned to their settlement in December and lobbied the Massachusetts government to provide protection. When the government refused, they fled north to meet up with Wannalancet, leaving several elderly and sick persons behind who were unable to travel. In an act of cruelty, settlers massacred about a half dozen people when they burned down the settlement. Colonists took over the Indians' fields by the spring.

After this, references to Wamesit in the historical record disappeared and "few Native Americans" remained. But the end of Wamesit did not "mean the end of Native life in the greater Lowell area."

Indeed, Native peoples maintained a continuing presence in the Northeast. "Survivors and their descendants continued to inhabit this region," through adapting to their changing environment.[23] King Philip's War was in reality an expression of multitribal resistance to the Puritans' "coercive conversion project."[24] In addition, the scope of the praying towns should not be exaggerated, for

> praying towns never encompassed the entirety, or even majority, of Natives in Southern New England. Roughly seventy Natives lived in each of the old towns, ninety in the new ones, by the 1670s, while large numbers maintained their livelihoods, kinship ties, and sovereignties apart from this system. They did so substantially beyond the sight lines of English observers who documented Native presences and whose writings have formed the foundations of colonial archives.[25]

Contemporary Native American leaders also reference the trauma of the war. Cheryll Toney Holley, current Chief of the Hassanamisco band of the Nipmuc Nation, in her essay entitled "Brief Look at Nipmuc History" discusses King Philip's War and how praying Indians were forcibly removed to Deer Island:

> The Hassanamisco Indians were attacked and carried off by the Nipmucs fighting for freedom in November of 1675. That same month the English fired upon Wamesit, killing innocent women and children. The Wamesits, besieged by both the English and their Nipmuc neighbors, asked the colonial government for protection and were sent to Deer Island as well. Before the end of the war even the praying Indians that spied for and fought on the English side were sent to Deer Island in Boston Harbor as prisoners of the war.[26]

The Wamesit Indians fled toward the French out of fear of being sent to Deer Island.[27] It was northern kin who took the war refugees in. The refugees saw these kin to the north as being more likely to offer protection since the English had failed to protect them.[28]

The English settlers did not just fail to protect, they actively betrayed the Christianized Indians. Indians of the praying towns who surrendered to the English were enslaved and separated from their families, sent as far away as Barbados and Bermuda.[29] Children of those who surrendered were also enslaved, forced into servitude in English homes, separated from their families until they reached twenty-four years of age.[30] These policies of enslavement were not just about labor, however, because ultimately they were enacted to dispossess Indians of their lands.

Historians continue to debate what happened in Wamesit after King Philip's War. While accounts and interpretations remain contested, there is mostly agreement that after the war, most of the Native Americans from the Pennacook Confederacy who populated the praying town of Wamesit were either forced out or they fled.[31]

Passaconaway Statue in Lowell

The *Boston Herald* newspaper in April 1869, in a small announcement, indicated that "strong in numbers in Baltimore, Philadelphia, Washington, and other places South and West," the Improved Order of Red Men (IORM) would soon be introduced in Boston as the Shawmut Tribe.[32] By 1873, the *Herald* reported that "Sagamore Tribe No. 2" would be established in Lynn and its mission was "the relief of its indigent members and their families."[33] Announcements continued to appear weekly, documenting the new "tribes" that were added to the Order in Massachusetts. In July of 1887, the Passaconaway Tribe in Lowell was lauded for having inducted over 200 new members.[34] In November of that same year, the *Boston Globe* reported that "Passaconaway of Lowell is the largest in the jurisdiction, with nearly 400 members."[35] By April 1888, the Lowell chapter reported it had 500 members.[36] The IORM expanded into Lowell at the same time that the city was experiencing unprecedented growth, with increasing numbers of immigrants moving in to work in its mills.

A decade later, in January 1898, the *Lowell Sun* reported that the Passaconaway Tribe would hold a multi-day "trading post" in order to raise funds to erect a monument in Edson Cemetery for members who lacked a burial plot.[37] The monument was dedicated in ceremony in August 1899 by the Passaconaway Tribe of the Red Men. The *Boston Sunday Globe* reported on the event, indicating that participants and others involved included local Red Men tribes, the Red Men National Band, hundreds of interested onlookers, Mayor Crowley, Rev. Bowley Green, Rev. George H. Johnson, Senator Putnam and Representative W.H. I. Hayes. There was a parade through the city streets to the cemetery, music by the band, prayer, the unveiling by a Miss Lizzie Farnham and a statement of gratitude from Mayor Crowley. Boston Past Grand Sachem Augustus P. Calder delivered the principal address where he "congratulated the Lowell tribe on the spirit displayed toward departed members," and Rev. George H. Johnson,

Senator Putnam, Rev. Bowley Green and Representative W.H. I. Hayes also addressed the crowd.[38]

The following day the *Globe* included a large illustration of the 15-foot monument, noting that it had been dedicated the evening prior by the Passaconaway Tribe with assistance from the Miantonomo Tribe, another local IORM tribe.

The dedicatory plaque on the monument reads:

> Chief of the Penacooks
> Great Warrior
> And Friend of the White Man
> Embraced Christianity
> Died at the age of 122
> Known as
> Aspinquid—The Indian Saint
> Property of Improved Order of Red Men of Massachusetts

While the plaque names St. Aspinquid (or St. Aspenquid), it remains unclear if this name refers to the Chief of the Pennacook, Passaconaway, or to another Indian leader said to have lived into his hundreds and have been buried at the summit of Mt. Agamenticus in York, Maine.[39] A poem published in New Hampshire in 1879 by John Albee entitled *St. Aspenquid of Mt. Agamenticus* may have been the inspiration for the plaque nomenclature. The poem begins, "The Indian hero, sorcerer and saint, Known in the land as Passaconaway, And after called the good Saint Aspenquid..."[40]

Illustrating the mimicry of Native terminology described in *Playing Indian*, a 1903 *Lowell Sun* article listed IORM leadership titles as Great Chief of the Great Council (of Massachusetts), Past Great Sachem, Great Keeper of the Wampum, Deputy Great Sachem and additional Chiefs of the tribe. Members were referred to as Braves.[41] A 1910 *Lowell Sun* article listed the additional titles of junior sagamore and guard of the forest.[42]

Throughout the next decade, the Passaconaway Tribe continued to hold weekly meetings and admit new members. From the late 1930s, 1940s and 1950s in the *Lowell Sun*, the only references to be found of the Red Men were in the obituaries when its members began to pass away. When the Lowell tribe "faded out of existence" in 1937, "Frank E. Henry of Boston, executive secretary of the Great Council of the Massachusetts Improved Order of Red Men, and Frank H. Fielding of Methuen, past great sachem of the Massachusetts Council," reported that the "property and statue were deeded to the Great Council of Massachusetts."[43]

Little appeared in the press on the monument itself until 1965 when it was reported as having vanished. Provocatively, the article began: "Chief Passaconaway, one of the few remaining symbols hereabouts of the American Indian—'The Vanishing American'—has vanished."[44] Councils across the state got together when they learned the statue was in disrepair and decided to refurbish it. They removed it to the B and B Sheet Metal Products in Methuen for repair under the purview of the "Saggahew tribe of that community." The role of the IORM and the Passaconaway Tribe in Lowell is described as "perpetuating the legends and traditions of the Indians" after they had vanished. The statue, the author asserted, had for centuries now "gazed at the scene of progress of the white man from his lofty pedestal." Here, the so-called modernity of the white settler is juxtaposed against the anti-modern (and vanished) Indian.

On May 19, 1967, the *Lowell Sun* announced that the Redmen [sic] would hold a rededication ceremony on Sunday for the newly refurbished statue to be rededicated by "members of the IORM, the city government, students of Indian lore and interested citizens."[45] For the past two years, it had been being repaired under the "loyal, unselfish, diligent work by tribal members throughout the state." A multi-tribe, state IORM ceremony would be attended by IORM officials from Jamaica Plain, East Brookfield, Wakefield, Gloucester, Lynn, Boston and Methuen. The ceremony would include "presentation of flags, music, a color guard unit carrying spears, invocation of the great spirit and the placing of a wreath at the feet of the rebuilt statue." The 1967 article recalls that the real Passaconaway "in his abdication speech to his council of warriors gathered around him, counseled" to seek peace with the White Man, saying it was the "command of the Great Spirit and the wish, the last wish of Passaconaway." Even more telling is the article's assertion that

> the White Man has acceded to Passaconaway's peace plea over the years, much more so than his warriors and descendants of three centuries ago, forming tribes and councils, fraternal organizations, perpetuating the legends and traditions of the Indians and honoring the legendary chieftain for whom the tribe was named, and the statue dedicated to him on Aug. 19, 1899.

Apparently then, according to this sentiment, not only did the IORM think of themselves as replacing vanishing Native Americans but surpassing them.

The following Tuesday the *Sun* described the ceremony as impressive and ran a photograph of IORM members seated at the base of the monument with crossed arms wearing full Native regalia, including what appears to be, although the photograph is grainy, Plains Indian warbonnets which are not actually indigenous to the region.[46]

In May 1968, "the Redmen [sic] of Massachusetts" held a dedication and memorial service there which included the participation of "descendants and representatives of various tribes."[47] What would be considered a "descendant" of a tribe—could this have possibly meant the participation of a person of actual Native American descent? Phil Deloria writes that the IORM did not allow Native membership until "1977, when the order finally recognized Indians as potential members."[48] More likely, the term "descendants" here referred to the Daughters of Red Men, which in Lowell had been active in April 1941 through its Minnequa Council #72.[49]

While white men of the IORM were dressing up as Native Americans, at least one Native American leader in Massachusetts protested this activity by introducing by-request legislation to "prohibit the wearing of Indian regalia except by persons whose national origin is at least one-eighth Indian."[50] Chief Lorenzo Jeffers of the Wampanoag Tribe of Gay Head (Aquinnah) introduced with the aid of House Representative John Clark the aforementioned legislation. Across the United States, this was a time of rising Red Power movements. Native Americans across the country, from many tribes, were forming their own organizations and movements to assert their rights and demand changes in US policy, tribal sovereignty, and religious and cultural rights.

In Lowell, during this same time, the 1960s and the 1970s, there was an active Indian hobbyist association, the Greater Lowell Indian Hobbyist Association (GLIHA), whose membership began to include those who claimed Native American heritage. It is not clear what relationship the hobbyist group had with the IORM, although many of their interests and activities overlapped. Native Americans were still portrayed as being of the past and not the present. The *Lowell Sun* articles during this time described a multitude of public educational events including archaeological talks and powwow dances. According to one 1970 article, for members of the GLIHA,

> The making of Indian costumes and the pageantry of Indian dancing has another value, for it is through them that the true primitive arts and culture of our land can be preserved. The Greater Lowell Indian Hobbyists Association is attempting to do this, with a membership of over 50. Their purpose is not to be like Indians, but to enjoy some of their dancing and crafts, modifying them to show the interesting aspects of those days of the past.[51]

In July of that same year, the "GLIHA Research" team authored a two-page spread in the Sunday *Lowell Sun* Magazine entitled "Early History of Lowell."[52] Accompanied by illustrations of archaeological finds and an Indian tomahawk collection, the text recounts the history of Lowell prior to European contact and strongly invokes the myth of the vanishing Indian with the following language:

> A few traces are now left in Lowell of their habitation. An occasional arrow head or other crude implement, dug up while laying the foundations of modern structures, a few traces of the old trench which once separated their lands from those of the white man remind us that we live on historic ground.

Even though the tribes have vanished their memory lives on and is being perpetuated by members of various organizations such as the Great Council Men, the Passaconaway Tribe 32, Improved Order of Red Men, The Greater Lowell Indian and Hobbiest [sic] Association and The New England Indian Hobbiest [sic] Association, to name but a few... we recognize the historic fact that on the soil Lowell now stands, "once lived and loved another race of beings," whose memory we do not wish to see blotted out.

Authored in 1970, this article casts doubt on whether the IORM Passacona-way Tribe had actually ceased its activities in 1937, as had been previously reported in an earlier *Lowell Sun* article. Had the Passaconaway Tribe been operating underground all these years? Or had it reorganized itself? In any case, the authors have claimed that because Native Americans no longer exist in Lowell, the groups listed, including the Passaconaway Tribe of the IORM and their own organization, GLIHA, became therefore the rightful spokespeople and the experts who should be consulted.

In 2009, Director of the Red Men Museum and Library (in Waco, Texas) David Lintz wrote an article about the Passaconaway Statue for its *Red Men Magazine* noting how it again had fallen into disrepair.[53] Recounting the story of Passaconaway, he pointed out discrepancies between history and lore. In his brief article, he noted how Passaconaway "became a chief of the Pennacook, a federation of over a dozen tribes from that area that is now New Hampshire. It is not known whether he became chief by election or he-redity." Lintz pointed out Passaconaway's renowned influence over the Pen-nacook confederacy, his battles with the Mohawk, a war with the Pequots, and claimed that the Pennacooks "did not participate in King Philip's War," saying they had preferred to remain neutral. Recognizing the leader's re-nown as "a friend of the white man" and a Christian convert, Lintz posits that "he may have been, instead, a clever politician who was doing what the times required to keep his dwindling race alive." Lintz admits there is in fact no record of Passaconaway's conversion to Christianity. And, even in 2009, while the Native leader's savviness and pragmatism were lauded, he was still being referred to as a member of "a dwindling race."

Two years later, in 2011, the IORM would again raise funds to refur-bish the statue. This time the efforts came from members Paul Sadowski, a resident of nearby Wilmington, Massachusetts, and "Incohonee or na-tional president of the Improved Order of Red Men" and Robert Shannon, a resident of nearby Tewksbury and "great sachem or state president" of the IORM. They raised $20,000, "hired craftsman Bruce Lang to lead the project" and enlisted the labor of local metal shop students from Greater Lowell Technical High School.[54] The author of the article points out that "neither Sadowski nor Shannon is actually of Native American heritage," but allows Sadowski to explain that they "use Indian terms in respect to the Native Americans."[55] The refurbished monument includes a new plaque from 2010 which reads:

> Great Council of Massachusetts
> Improved Order of Red Men
> This monument was renovated
> By the students from
> "The Metal Fabrication Shop"
> Of Greater Lowell
> Technical High School
> June 6, 2010

Today, the IORM website includes the most recent issues of The *Red Men Magazine* (2019 and 2020) and documents the activism of state and local chapters (which continue to call themselves tribes) across the United States. The website announced that the 129th Great Council Session and the 46th Session of the National Degree of Pocahontas would be held from September 27 to October 2, 2020, at the Grand Hotel & Spa in Ocean City, Maryland. Current active tribes in Massachusetts are listed as follows: Massachusetts Tribe No. 1 (Charlton); Wonewok Tribe No. 83 (Franklin); Nanapashemet Tribe No. 82 (Lynn); Saggahew Tribe No. 60 (Methuen); Nipmuck Tribe No. 131 (Southbridge); Wamscott Tribe No. 39 (Stoneham); and Cromesett Tribe No. 156 (Wareham).[56]

The IORM Passaconaway Tribe's 1899 Passaconaway Monument was a tribute to its own fraternal members marking their ascendance as a white-male-only fraternal organization. Created to memorialize its deceased IORM members, they remain unnamed on the monument. Projecting an essentialized "Native American" devoid of and decontextualized from history, at the same time the monument represents Native Americans as only in the past, as mythical, heroic, generic and male. The plaque on the monument perpetuates the myth that Passaconaway converted to Christianity, acknowledged as myth by the IORM's own museum director in 2009. Unlike the Massasoit monument in Plymouth which has been re-appropriated as a site of gathering for the annual National Day of Mourning, the Passaconaway Statue does not seem to have become a site of gathering for anyone other than the IORM.[57]

Native American monuments are part of the replacement narrative that settler colonialism seeks to impose. And curiously, as Deloria has argued, it is Native names and cultural practices that white settlers have used to define themselves as Americans. The IORM originally appealed to white men at a time of anxiety around increased immigrant influx and economic insecurity. But surprisingly, it has continued to have an appeal, even to the present day in some communities, and this is where more research needs to be done to learn why it persists.

IORM and Indian hobbyist activities can also be interpreted as a form of historical reenactment. Members participated in parades, powwows and other types of ceremonies, many of which were public facing. Their interpretations of history are unreliable, however, since their very mission assumed a vanishing Indian. By accepting the mythology of the vanishing Indian as truth and propagating it, they effectively generated a missing public— Native Americans in the area who could have been consulted or collaborated with but who were assumed not to exist.

Acknowledgments

I would like to thank Prof. Tiya Miles, in whose Spring 2020 history seminar on Slavery and Public History I developed the ideas for this essay, and American Studies PhD candidate Mary McNeil for her careful feedback. As a Harvard University Extension School student, I would like to acknowledge the campus is situated on the traditional and ancestral homelands of the Massachusett and nearby Wampanoag and Nipmuc peoples.

Notes

1 Mitch Landrieu, "Mitch Landrieu's Speech on the Removal of Confederate Monuments in New Orleans," *The New York Times*, May 23, 2017; Les Carpenter, "Washington's NFL Team to Retire Redskins Name, Following Sponsor Pressure and Calls for Change," *The Washington Post*, July 13, 2020.
2 Angie Beeman, "Royall Must Fall: Old and New Battles on the Memory of Slavery in New England," *Sociology of Race and Ethnicity* 5, no. 3 (2019): 326–339; Claire E. Parker, "Law School Committee Recommends Seal Change," *The Harvard Crimson*, March 4, 2016.
3 Katharine Q. Seelye, "Boston Grapples with Faneuil Hall, Named for a Slaveholder," *The New York Times*, June 6, 2018.
4 Sarah Betancourt, "Beheading of Columbus Statue Prompts Discussion," *CommonWealth: Nonprofit Journal of Politics, Ideas & Civic Life*, June 10, 2020, https://commonwealthmagazine.org/arts-and-culture/beheading-of-columbus-statue-prompts-discussion.
5 Nora McGreevy, "Mississippi Voters Approve New Design to Replace Confederate-Themed State Flag," *Smithsonian Magazine*, November 4, 2020, https://www.smithsonianmag.com/smart-news/mississippi-will-replace-its-confederate-themed-state-flag-180976209; Rich Barlow, "It's time to Retire the Offensive Design of the Mass. Flag and Seal," *WBUR*, July 8, 2020, https://www.wbur.org/cognoscenti/2020/07/08/massachusetts-state-flag-rich-barlow. For more information on the state legislation in Massachusetts, see the MA Indigenous Legislative Agenda, accessed September 25, 2020, http://maindigenousagenda.org.
6 Lisa Blee and Jean M. O'Brien, *Monumental Mobility: The Memory Work of Massasoit* (Chapel Hill: University of North Carolina Press, 2019).
7 See Andrew Denson, *Monuments to Absence* (Chapel Hill: University of North Carolina Press, 2017).
8 Blee and O'Brien, *Monumental Mobility*, 133–135; 203–205.
9 Patrick Wolfe, "Settler Colonialism and the Elimination of the Native," *Journal of Genocide Research* 8, no. 4 (December 2006): 387–409.

10 Jean O'Brien, *Firsting and Lasting: Writing Indians out of Existence in New England* (Minneapolis: University of Minnesota Press, 2010).
11 Ibid., 56.
12 Christine DeLucia, *Memory Lands. King Philip's War and the Place of Violence in the Northeast* (New Haven: Yale University Press, 2018), 8.
13 White women could join the Degree of Pocahontas which was the female auxiliary of the Improved Order of Red Men.
14 Philip Deloria, *Playing Indian* (New Haven: Yale University Press, 1998), 65.
15 Ibid., 66, footnote 63; George W. Lindsay, Charles C. Conley, and Charles H. Litchman, *Official History of the Improved Order of Red Men* (Boston: Fraternal Publishing Co., 1893), 618.
16 Lowell National Historical Park, National Park Service, accessed September 25, 2020, https://www.nps.gov/lowe/index.htm.
17 See Cathy Stanton, *The Lowell Experiment* (Amherst: University of Massachusetts Press, 2006).
18 *Lowell: The River City*, Lowell Historical Society (Charleston, Chicago: Arcadia, 2006), 8.
19 Robert Forrant and Christoph Strobel, "Ethnicity in Lowell," Lowell National Historical Park Ethnographic Overview and Assessment, prepared under contract with University of Massachusetts Lowell History Department (Northeast Region Ethnography Program, National Park Service, Boston, MA March 2011), http://library.uml.edu/clh//OH/ETHNO/Ethnicity%20in%20Lowell.pdf, 19.
20 The Massachusetts State Archives holds multiple petitions from the Wamesit Indians dating from 1665 to 1681.
21 Elise M. Brenner, "To Pray or to Be Prey: That Is the Question. Strategies for Cultural Autonomy of Massachusetts Praying Town Indians," *Ethnohistory* 27, no. 2 (Spring 1980): 138.
22 Forrant and Strobel, "Ethnicity in Lowell," 22. All the quotes in this paragraph come from this article.
23 Christine DeLucia, "An 'Indian Fishing Weir' at Musketaquid: Marking Northeastern Indigenous Homelands and Colonial Memoryscapes," *Environmental History* 23, no. 1 (2018): 194.
24 Ibid., 186.
25 DeLucia, *Memory Lands*, 40.
26 Cheryll Toney Holley, "A Brief Look at Nipmuc History," in *Dawnland Voices: An Anthology of Indigenous Writing from New England*, ed. Siobhan Senier (Lincoln: University of Nebraska Press, 2014), 407.
27 Jill Lepore, *The Name of War: King Philip's War and the Origins of American Identity* (New York: Knopf, 1998), 138. She cites correspondence from John Lyne and Numphow to Thomas Henchman, c. November 15, 1675; reprinted in Daniel Gookin and Samuel G. Drake, *An Historical Account of the Doings and Sufferings of the Christian Indians in New England, in the Years 1675, 1676, 1677*, 1836, 483.
28 Lisa Brooks, *Our Beloved Kin* (Yale University Press, 2018), 235–236.
29 Linford Fisher, "'Why Shall Wee Have Peace to Bee Made Slaves': Indian Surrenderers During and After King Philip's War," *Ethnohistory* 64, no. 1 (January 2017): 91–114.
30 Ibid., 99.
31 Additional scholarship on this topic includes Louise Breen, *Daniel Gookin, the Praying Indians, and King Philip's War: A Short History in Documents* (New York: Routledge, 2020); Richard W. Cogley, *John Eliot's Mission to the Indians before King Philip's War* (Cambridge: Harvard University Press, 1999); Linford D. Fisher, "Native Americans, Conversion, and Christian Practice in Colonial New England, 1640–1730," *Harvard Theological Review* 102, no. 1 (2009): 101–124; David Stewart-Smith, "Pennacook-Pawtucket Relations: The Cycles of

Family Alliance on the Merrimack River in the 17th Century," *Papers of the Algonquian Conference* 25 (1994): 445–468.

32 "Improved Order of Red Men," *Boston Herald*, April 28, 1869.

33 "Lynn Items," *Boston Herald*, April 10, 1873, 4.

34 "Improved Order of Red Men," *Boston Herald*, July 3, 1887 (a figure is included that is not decipherable to me; it could be 230 or 250 or 280).

35 "Improved Order of Red Men," *Boston Globe*, November 11, 1887, 9.

36 "Improved Order of Red Men," *Boston Herald*, April 1, 1888, 5.

37 "Passaconaway Tribe of Red Men," *Lowell Sun*, January 25, 1898, 16.

38 "Red Men's Monument, Lowell," *The Lowell Sun*, August 20, 1899, 5.

39 Charles Edward Beals, *Passaconaway in the White Mountains* (Boston: Badger, 1916), 48–49.

40 John Albee, *St. Aspenquid of Mt. Agamenticus: An Indian Idyl* (Portsmouth: Lewis W. Brewster, 1879).

41 "Passaconaway: Red Men Observe Their 17th Anniversary," *Lowell Sun*, January 17, 1903, 1.

42 "The Red Men: Meeting of Passaconaway Red Men Held Last Night," *Lowell Sun*, August 27, 1910, 17.

43 Fred W. Dudley, "Vanished American: Soon to Reappear," *Lowell Sun*, October 10, 1965, 37.

44 Ibid. All the quotes in this paragraph come from this article.

45 Dudley, "Redmen to Rededicate Passaconaway Statue," *Lowell Sun*, May 19, 1967, 10. All the quotes in this paragraph come from this article.

46 *Lowell Sun*, May 23, 1967, 15.

47 "Redmen to Hold Memorial Service for Passaconaway," *Lowell Sun*, May 10, 1968, 11.

48 Deloria, *Playing Indian*, 217, footnote 63.

49 *Lowell Sun*, April 29, 1941, 10.

50 Massachusetts General Court, House of Representatives, House No. 2361, "An Act Regulating the Wearing of Indian Regalia," The Commonwealth of Massachusetts, 1968 House Documents, Massachusetts State Archives, accessed September 25, 2020, https://archives.lib.state.ma.us/bitstream/handle/2452/487759/ocm39986872-1968-HB-2361.pdf?sequence=1&isAllowed=y.

51 Richard P. Cook, "'Indians' Rise to Be Heard," *Lowell Sun*, January 25, 1970, 100.

52 Eugene Kupski et al. (GLIHA Research), "Early History of Lowell," *Lowell Sun*, July 4, 1970, 2–3.

53 David Lintz, "The Statue to Passaconaway," *Red Men Magazine* 33, no. 2 (Summer 2009), 56–60. All the quotes in this paragraph come from this article.

54 Marie Donovan, "Refurbished Statue of Chief Passaconaway Rededicated Sunday in Lowell," *Lowell Sun*, May 20, 2011, https://www.lowellsun.com/2011/05/20/refurbished-statue-of-chief-passaconaway-rededicated-sunday-in-lowell.

55 Donovan, "Refurbished Statue."

56 Massachusetts Tribes, State Great Councils, Improved Order of Red Men, accessed September 25, 2020, http://iorm.online/redmen/state-great-councils.

57 The monument is listed in the Greater Merrimack Valley Convention and Visitors Bureau online guide, using a different spelling of "Pasaqunway" and incorrectly associated with the "lower order of red men" in a section entitled Native American Trail; https://merrimackvalley.org.

Bibliography

Albee, John. *St. Aspenquid of Mt. Agamenticus: An Indian Idyl*. Portsmouth: Lewis W. Brewster, 1879.

Barlow, Rich. "It's time to Retire the Offensive Design of the Mass. Flag and Seal." *WBUR*, July 8, 2020. https://www.wbur.org/cognoscenti/2020/07/08/massachusetts-state-flag-rich-barlow.

Beals, Charles Edward. *Passaconaway in the White Mountains*. Boston: Badger, 1916.

Beeman, Angie. "Royall Must Fall: Old and New Battles on the Memory of Slavery in New England." *Sociology of Race and Ethnicity* 5, no. 3 (2019): 326–339.

Betancourt, Sarah. "Beheading of Columbus Statue Prompts Discussion." *CommonWealth: Nonprofit Journal of Politics, Ideas & Civic Life*, June 10, 2020. https://commonwealthmagazine.org/arts-and-culture/beheading-of-columbus-statue-prompts-discussion.

Blee, Lisa, and Jean M. O'Brien. *Monumental Mobility: The Memory Work of Massasoit*. Chapel Hill: University of North Carolina Press, 2019.

Breen, Louise, and Daniel Gookin. *The Praying Indians, and King Philip's War: A Short History in Documents*. New York: Routledge, 2020.

Brenner, Elise M. "To Pray or to Be Prey: That Is the Question. Strategies for Cultural Autonomy of Massachusetts Praying Town Indians." *Ethnohistory* 27, no. 2 (Spring 1980): 135–152.

Brooks, Lisa. *Our Beloved Kin*. New Haven: Yale University Press, 2018.

Cogley, Richard W. *John Eliot's Mission to the Indians before King Philip's War*. Cambridge: Harvard University Press, 1999.

Deloria, Philip. *Playing Indian*. New Haven: Yale University Press, 1998.

DeLucia, Christine. "An 'Indian Fishing Weir' at Musketaquid: Marking Northeastern Indigenous Homelands and Colonial Memoryscapes." *Environmental History* 23, no. 1 (2018): 184–198.

DeLucia, Christine. *Memory Lands. King Philip's War and the Place of Violence in the Northeast*. New Haven: Yale University Press, 2018.

Denson, Andrew. *Monuments to Absence*. Chapel Hill: University of North Carolina Press, 2017.

Fisher, Linford D. "Native Americans, Conversion, and Christian Practice in Colonial New England, 1640–1730." *Harvard Theological Review* 102, no. 1 (2009): 101–124.

Fisher, Linford D. "'Why Shall Wee Have Peace to Bee Made Slaves': Indian Surrenderers During and After King Philip's War." *Ethnohistory* 64, no. 1 (January 2017): 91–114.

Forrant, Robert, and Christoph Strobel. "Ethnicity in Lowell." Lowell National Historical Park Ethnographic Overview and Assessment. Prepared under contract with University of Massachusetts Lowell History Department. Northeast Region Ethnography Program, National Park Service, Boston, MA March 2011. http://library.uml.edu/clh//OH/ETHNO/Ethnicity%20in%20Lowell.pdf.

Lepore, Jill. *The Name of War: King Philip's War and the Origins of American Identity*. New York: Knopf, 1998.

Lindsay, George W., Charles C. Conley, and Charles H. Litchman. *Official History of the Improved Order of Red Men*. United States: Fraternity Publishing Company, 1893.

Lintz, David. "The Statue to Passaconaway." *Red Men Magazine* 33, no. 2 (Summer 2009): 56–60.

Lowell Historical Society. *Lowell: The River City*. Charleston, Chicago: Arcadia, 2006.

Lowell National Historical Park, National Park Service. Accessed September 25, 2020. https://www.nps.gov/lowe/index.htm.

MA Indigenous Legislative Agenda. Accessed September 25, 2020. http://maindigenousagenda.org.

Massachusetts General Court, House of Representatives. House No. 2361. "An Act Regulating the Wearing of Indian Regalia." The Commonwealth of Massachusetts, 1968. House Documents. Massachusetts State Archives. Accessed September 25, 2020. https://archives.lib.state.ma.us/bitstream/handle/2452/487759/ocm39986872-1968-HB-2361.pdf?sequence=1&isAllowed=y.

Massachusetts Tribes. State Great Councils. Improved Order of Red Men. Accessed September 25, 2020. http://iorm.online/redmen/state-great-councils.

McGreevy, Nora. "Mississippi Voters Approve New Design to Replace Confederate-Themed State Flag." *Smithsonian Magazine*, November 4, 2020. https://www.smithsonianmag.com/smart-news/mississippi-will-replace-its-confederate-themed-state-flag-180976209.

"Native American Trail." Greater Merrimack Valley Convention & Visitors Bureau. Accessed September 25, 2020. https://merrimackvalley.org.

O'Brien, Jean M. *Firsting and Lasting: Writing Indians out of Existence in New England*. Minneapolis: University of Minnesota Press, 2010.

Stanton, Cathy. *The Lowell Experiment*. Amherst: University of Massachusetts Press, 2006.

Stewart-Smith, David. "Pennacook-Pawtucket Relations: The Cycles of Family Alliance on the Merrimack River in the 17th Century." *Papers of the Algonquian Conference* 25 (1994): 445–468.

Toney Holley, Cheryll. "A Brief Look at Nipmuc History." In *Dawnland Voices: An Anthology of Indigenous Writing from New England*, edited by Siobhan Senier, 404–410. Lincoln: University of Nebraska Press, 2014.

Wolfe, Patrick. "Settler Colonialism and the Elimination of the Native." *Journal of Genocide Research* 8, no. 4 (December 2006): 387–409.

Press

Boston Globe, November 11, 1887.

Boston Herald, April 28, 1869; April 10, 1873; July 3, 1887; April 1, 1888.

Lowell Sun, January 25, 1898; August 20, 1899; January 17, 1903; August 27, 1910; April 29, 1941; October 10, 1965; May 19, 1967; May 23, 1967; May 10, 1968; January 25, 1970; July 4, 1970; May 20, 2011.

The Harvard Crimson, March 4, 2016.

The New York Times, May 23, 2017; June 6, 2018.

The Washington Post, July 13, 2020.

7

RETURN TO 1918

The Serbian American Public and First World War Memory at the Centenary

Alexandra Zaremba

In early June of 2018, Serbian American social media feeds were flooded by the Serbian Orthodox Diocese of Eastern America's (SODEA) advertisements for its commemorative event: "The Day the Serbian Flag Flew

FIGURE 7.1 Bishop Irinej Dobrijević addresses the public at the Gala Banquet at the National Press Club during the First World War Centennial Commemoration hosted by the Serbian Orthodox Diocese of Eastern American on July 28, 2018, © Alexandra Zaremba.

Over the White House." Serbian American religious, social, cultural, and political organizations vigorously shared recently created illustrations of the Serbian and American flags proudly flying over the White House on Facebook and across the internet. Together with the event's flyer, the commemoration promised to be an "historic" event that would celebrate the First World War centenary and Serbian-American friendship. However, the centennial committee who named, organized, and circulated the commemoration soon realized that no historical evidence existed to show that the Serbian flag had ever flown over the White House. Despite changing the commemoration to "The National Day of Prayer for Serbia,"—an event verified by a July 1918 proclamation made by acting Secretary of State Robert Lansing on behalf of President Woodrow Wilson[1]—the Serbian American public clung to the image and sentiment of the Serbian and American flags waving together over a great symbol of American power and often continued to call the event by its original name.

This episode of mis-memory that placed false historical knowledge into Serbian-American consciousness articulates the central questions this article addresses: how do institutions and organizations insert forgotten history or new interpretations of history into a public's memory, and what role does that public play in the process?[2] Public history and memory studies scholarship have collectively made the argument that public history and memory, whether constructed from the top-down or the bottom-up, are always imagined to serve the needs of the present.[3] But what does it mean for the past to serve the present? What does this look like, and how does this process work?

Contemporary memory theories are based on rich studies of monuments, memorials, past commemorations, and museums where scholars reach into the past to study how a public relates to histories through their engagement with cultural mediations. Only rarely do they examine and historicize *contemporary* commemorative events and the processes through which the past is reinvented in the image of the present and installed in public consciousness. Aleida Assmann theorized that cultural and political memories are reliant upon and mediated through material symbols and spaces where historical memory is stored, neither actively remembered nor forgotten. She contends that only "specialists" with access to those archives can "activate" this memory through acts of remembrance where historical narratives are repeated and the line between past and present is blurred.[4] While applying Assmann's memory theorizations to the SODEA's First World War Centenary Commemoration proves apt in its articulation of how historical memory is accessed and activated, it also reveals the need to historically, politically, and culturally contextualize these processes and foreground the ways a public influences them, if we are to better understand how they take place.

Using the SODEA's 2018 centenary commemoration as a case study, I revise dominant understandings of cultural memory and offer a more precise definition of what it means for the past to serve the present. I argue that forgotten histories or new interpretations of history can only enter public consciousness under historically, politically, and culturally dependent conditions that are expressly linked to the public being engaged. To garner renewed interest for a neglected past, the history must have new and significant relevance for a public. It must be mobilized through participatory activities that use a vocabulary of images, sounds, rhetoric, and symbolism familiar to that public. This enables the construction of a strong shared memory that individuals can continue to repeat and distribute, thus sustaining that history within their groups' consciousness. Recognizing the individual elements in this process and understanding how they interact to form a cohesive narrative framework demonstrates that reconstructions of the past are not arbitrary nor are they solely contingent on the institution or actor initiating the process. There are specific conditions and actions that "memory entrepreneurs"[5] must consciously consider when reconstructing the past to suit their public.

Serbian Americans were the primary "public" whose interests, reference points, and visual, material, symbolic, and cultural vocabularies determined the SODEA's First World War centenary commemoration. While American political figures participated in the commemoration and might be considered a secondary "public" that the commemoration oriented itself toward, they were primarily included to add legitimacy and prestige to the event. Certainly, the SODEA hoped to create a bond between itself and the US political establishment, but Serbian Americans were the primary public the SODEA formed the commemoration around. By instilling the memory of Serbian-American friendship from 1918 within the Serbian American public, the SODEA strengthened its relationship with Serbian Americans and created a strong living memory and physical archive it can continue to cultivate and politically mobilize in the long-term. Serbs in Serbia and non-Serbian Americans might also be considered "publics" that the commemoration attracted but only marginally so, as evidenced by participants' self-identification, the social, cultural, and digital networks information about the commemoration circulated within, and the commemoration's overt appeal to Serbian Americans' dual character, values, and culture.[6]

Before the Centenary

Political Context as a Precondition

The historical and political moment in which the SODEA hosted the centenary of the First World War and "The National Day of Prayer for Serbia," was a critical precondition for Serbian Americans' positive reception of this forgotten history. Scholars have observed that commemorations tend to occur around significant anniversaries, yet vacillating US-Serbia foreign relations and shifts in Serbian American attitudes suggest that any commemoration emphasizing Serbian-American friendship and shared values was unlikely to occur in the second half of the twentieth century. In 1968, at the 50th anniversary of the First World War and "The National Day of Prayer for Serbia," Serbia was a part of the Yugoslav Federation. The United States and Yugoslavia engaged in trade and other economic and cultural exchange, but maintained a level of mutual political distance given Yugoslavia's socialist orientation. More importantly, Yugoslavia's policy of multinationalism was intended to obscure particular emphasis on any of its states' national history and in the US, the Serbian diaspora had mixed (although predominately negative) response to socialist rule.[7] It is unclear how any institution or actor could have reformulated Serbian-American First World War History for contemporary relevance at that historical moment. Likewise, commemoration of the 75th anniversary would have been untenable during the 1990s conflict given the United States' involvement in the wars of Yugoslavia's dissolution. Serbian Americans' disposition toward the US reached new lows following the US supported 1999 NATO bombing campaign of Serbia and US recognition of Kosovo's independence in 2008.

In the post-Yugoslav era, Serbia has pivoted between Russian and American spheres of influence.[8] However, following the 2016 election, Serbian American attitudes toward the United States have grown more positive in the wake of the Trump administration's encouraging position on Serbia's interests in Kosovo.[9] With the centenary of the First World War, 2018 was the most apt historical and political context for this commemoration. Serbian-American friendship and the "National Day of Prayer for Serbia" became useful and non-contentious history Serbian American institutions and publics could leverage for potential political advantage.

Accessing and Creating Physical Archives

Critical to the Serbian American publics' reception of this forgotten moment of First World War history was the SODEA's position as a trusted institution. It had access to the cultural archive where the history and memory of the First World War Serbian-American cooperation exists.[10] Functioning as the "specialist" Assmann notes in her cultural memory theory, the SODEA had the ability to conduct research necessary for retrieving details on "The National Day of Prayer for Serbia" and Serbian-American First World War relations, the funds necessary to host an elaborate multi-day commemoration, and the profile to elicit cooperation from its churches, US officials, Serbian Americans, and related organizations like the Serbian National Defense Council or the Serbian National Federation. As a hub for Serbian American life, the SODEA not only retrieved and reinterpreted this once obsolete history, but used its network of churches and organizations to market the events and attract participation from a significant number of Serbian Americans.

As Assmann notes, repetition is critical to memory activation for its ability to imply continuity with the past. Because the National Day of Prayer for Serbia was never previously commemorated and was absent from Serbian American consciousness prior to July 2018, the narrative of the First World War the SODEA sought to disseminate amongst the public had to be interpreted in several forms and performed in several venues to resonate deeply with participants. This is why the commemoration was significantly promoted and its activities were stretched over a five-day period. Each commemorative activity, text, performance, symbol, and speech legitimized and informed the other, creating a totalizing framework wherein attendees could not help but leave the event with an understanding of the First World War rooted in a narrative of Serbian-American friendship. This interpretation not only seemed legitimate given the variety of ways in which it was constructed and reinforced, but it left the impression that this had always been the case; this was not a reimagined history, but history as it was.

For this reason, the physical source base the SODEA produced for "The National Day of Prayer for Serbia" was fundamental. While we will later see that this commemoration also created a sort of living archive, the physical archive it left behind is equally crucial. *Televizija Hram*, the television network of the Serbian Orthodox Church, recorded the commemoration and broadcast it on Serbian television in a three-part series on which I draw on in this article. That series remains available on YouTube and accessible to the public, making the SODEA's version of First World War history easily available to Serbian Americans. In addition, multiple event programs were created and distributed with special graphics and letters many participants returned to their home communities with. Perhaps most notable was a program produced for the commemoration's gala which contained a letter by the Centenary Commemoration's chairman Branko Terzić. It confirmed all the usual rhetoric and symbolism used to define the SODEA's interpretation of the Great War throughout the commemoration. It portrayed the United States and Serbia's alliance as something unique, impenetrable, and sacred. Projecting into the future, Terzić also alluded to the SODEA's desire to continue this "historic friendship" and "rich tradition."[11] Along with the living archive, the SODEA constructed through this commemoration, the program containing this letter and similar commemoration paraphernalia became a physical archive available for the public to draw on to reference and maintain this understanding of Serbian-American history and memory. Should the SODEA's version of Great War history fade from living Serbian American memory, future actors could access this physical documentation and bring it back to the fore.

Crafting a Useable Serbian-American Great War Vocabulary

While the context in which the SODEA hosted the "National Day of Prayer for Serbia" centenary commemoration was crucial, the vocabulary of images, sounds, rhetoric, and symbolism it used to attract interest and participation before and during the commemoration were absolutely key. Appealing to Serbian Americans' dual identity, the SODEA successfully highlighted a middle ground of shared values and symbols relevant to contemporary Serbian Americans and the First World War. The SODEA's initial save-the-date graphic first introduced the commemoration's ideals and visual and rhetorical vocabularies. Still containing text for the commemoration's previous title "The Day the Serbian Flag Flew at the White House," this three by five graphic featured what appears to be an American war stamp with an illustration of Serbian soldiers carrying weaponry as women and children cowered behind them. Indicating Serbia's *need* for American support, accompanying text, "Save our Serbian Ally," suggested to viewers that the United States met, or at least showed concern for Serbia's need. The SODEA distributed this image with notice of the commemoration to its clergy through official channels. Clergy were then able to disseminate the image and announcements about the commemoration to their parishioners and associated organizations through their own social networks.

It is unlikely that this illustration originated from the First World War era. Nevertheless, the image and language it used appealed to contemporary Serbian Americans' dual identity by demonstrating American compassion for Serbian interests and playing on both nations' reverence for military service.[12] Images such as this gave viewers the idea that despite their distance from this past, they were experiencing or interacting with it in an authentic way. More than that, by compressing the commemoration's interpretation of the Great War into simple visual narratives, these graphics were easily remediated by the individuals who shared them.

The initial poster that outlined the commemoration's schedule of events likewise participated in the construction of a specific image of Serbian-American relations. Here, a faded backdrop of Serbian soldiers overlaid with images of the White House, Serbian flag, and the Serbian Orthodox Diocesan crest. This composition fostered the idea of an intimate connection between these symbols. However, it also demonstrated both states' national strength. Despite Serbia needing the United States' help as the *save the date* implied, the Serbian soldiers in either image are not depicted as weak or cowardly but brave and noble like their American counterpart; the Serbian military may have been modest and lacked technologically advanced weapons, but their aims were honorable. They wanted to protect their people. Emphasizing those characteristics not only attracted Serbian American interests, but they countered any image of Serbs or what it meant to be Serbian that have endured in the United States following Yugoslavia's dissolution in the 1990s. Herein lies the real appeal these images and posters repeatedly made throughout the commemoration: Serbia and America were strong and they had always been friends and allies. This was not just a statement or narrative about the past, but the present and future.

While the voice articulating this image and narrative is hard to identify, and at times seem produced by some amorphous figure of history, the diocesan crest in the event poster and the continual presence of clergy throughout the commemoration are persistent reminders of where this interpretation of the Great War comes from and how it is disseminated. Both in this announcement and in a separate episcopal act, Bishop Irinej Dobrijević, the leader of the SODEA, called on clergy, parish council members, and Serbian organization representatives to encourage their parishioners and members to attend this "solemn" celebration and "historical jubilee."[13] Consistently stressing the idea of Serbian-American friendship, the SODEA emphasized Serbia's and the United States' shared sacrifice by characterizing the commemoration as an opportunity to remember Serbian Americans who joined both the Serbian Army and later the US Army in the First World War.

These memory agents quickly responded to this call and became accessories to the SODEA's cause. They issued their own statements, announcements, and perhaps most importantly, shared information about the commemoration including the *save the date* and poster on personal and organizational Facebook pages. Individuals and groups participated in highlighting the commemoration's importance and encouraged followers to attend.[14] By making the "National Day of Prayer for Serbia" centenary commemoration's central narrative available through these multilayered images on a platform where content is easily shared, even the most casual user became a participant. By liking and sharing related posts, users helped build the event's online presence and garnered buy-in to the version of Great War history the commemoration sought to elevate. More than a month prior to the event and without even attending it, Serbian Americans already participated in the circulation and embedding of the SODEA's interpretation of the First World War and Serbian-American friendship into Serbian Americans' consciousness.

The National Day of Prayer for Serbia Centenary Commemoration

The "National Day of Prayer for Serbia" centenary commemoration's numerous activities helped to further develop a commemorative language that took numerous forms and was used to craft the SODEA's First World War narrative. If an attendee was not struck or convinced by the images produced for the commemoration, perhaps they connected to a First World War era song. If music did not sufficiently engage attendees, maybe Bishop Irinej Dobrijević's prayer given at the US House of Representatives or the symposium on Serbia and America in the Great War offered a sense of legitimacy to this interpretation of history and commemorative event. Each of these material, rhetorical, or symbolic strategies were intended to engage the public on various levels: the sentimental, the political, the experiential, and the intellectual. While we should examine each of these elements separately, we must also recognize how they were synchronized to produce a larger commemorative "world" where the SODEA's interpretation of the Great War was unquestionable.

To establish a more profound relationship between Serbia and the United States, and to underline the importance of their shared past, the centenary commemoration began with Dobrijević's opening of the US House of Representatives with a prayer. This act suggested that just as the United States prayed for the struggling Serbian nation in 1918, one hundred years later, Serbs now prayed for the United States. This action did not necessarily erase the years of complicated and often contentious relations these two states had in the last century. Instead, it *obscured* the nature of those relations, appearing to casual participants and observers that there was nothing distinct about the present moment that allowed for this prayer and larger commemoration to take place. Dobrijević was accompanied by roughly 30 Serbian American children dressed in traditional Serbian costumes. Some of these children were local to the DC Metro area while others traveled from Philadelphia and New York to attend. Together with leaders of Serbian American organizations like the Serbian National Defense Council and the Serbian National Federation, these children posed with Dobrijević and US Congressmen in both the US Capitol rotunda and floor of the House Chamber. Their presence in these spaces ratified the idea that there was an intimate political and fraternal connection between Serbia and the US, initially raised in the commemoration's advertisements.

In the prayer itself, Dobrijević offered the first of many orations that emphasized sacrifice, honor, freedom, and friendship as the ideals that defined the United States and Serbia's relationship and Great War alliance. Dobrijević asked the "God of Justice" to guide US legislators to write US law in a way that answers the "resounding cry of those who earnestly pledge indivisible liberty and justice for all…"[15] Without directly mentioning Serbia or the First World War, he suggested that Serbs and Americans held a shared regard for freedom and asked US legislators to orient themselves toward Serbia and mutual Serbian-American interests like they had in 1918.

This rhetoric and intimation toward a shared Serbian-American past and joint ideal were repeated in remarks made to commemoration participants at a reception held at the US House Visitor's Center. Deputy Assistant Secretary Laura Cooper spoke on behalf of the Department of Defense. She thanked the Serbian people for their sacrifice during the First World War and recognized the one million plus Serbian lives lost during the Great War. Emphasizing the theme of Serbian sacrifice and a shared past, Senator Ron Johnson too reflected that this commemoration was fitting to remember, "we (Serbia and America) were a strong ally back then, we are strong friends now…"[16] Both statements affirmed the rhetoric employed by the commemoration and SODEA to shape its interpretation of the First World War. And to begin the process of blurring past and present, US Representative Ted Poe gifted a US flag flown over the White House in 1918—a literal symbol of freedom, honor, and sacrifice already engrained in the commemoration's vocabulary of symbols—to Serbian Prime Minister Ana Brnabić. Much like Dobrijević's prayer at the US House of Representatives earlier that morning, this act affirmed that an intimate relationship between the US and Serbia existed that dates back to the First World War.[17]

This reception was photographed and recorded as a part of *Televizija Hram*'s special, and its imagined audiences were both Serbian Americans and Serbs in Serbia. The remarks given here by US dignitaries and this exchange of symbols functionally verified the First World War narrative the SODEA placed forth through this commemoration. Serbian news agencies quickly picked up images recorded at this event, replicating them and expanding viewership. These images and the articles that accompanied them suggested to Serbs in the US and in the homeland that there was basis for a renewed political relationship between Serbia and the United States rooted in the narrative and sentiments of Serbian-American Great War relations that the commemoration promoted.

The perpetuation of this SODEA conceived and contextually lacking Great War history continued into the commemoration's second day during a symposium on Serbia and America in the First World War. To add a certain gravitas and academic validity to the SODEA's Great War narrative, this event was marketed as a scholarly enterprise to add intellectual weight to the commemoration and suggest that this interpretation of Serbian-American friendship during the Great War was supported by research and individuals who were not just Serbian Americans or clergy, but also scholars.

Scholars, however, were only marginally present at this symposium. Its main speakers were still SODEA figures and US officials who did not give academic papers or presentations but continued to give statements on the importance of this shared Serbian-American past. But no real critical scholarly analysis of the Great War was shared. Here again, Dobrijević and other US officials like Assistant Secretary of State for European and Eurasian Affairs A. Wess Mitchell made statements engrained with the overall narrative of Serbian-American sacrifice, honor, freedom, and friendship, with Mitchell remarking how Serbian courage captured President Wilson and Americans' imagination, leading to the 1918 National Day of Prayer.[18] Assistant Secretary Mitchell's remarks, however, pointed to the Centenary Commemoration's fundamental decontextualization of the First World War. Throughout the commemoration, SODEA figures and US officials made statements that referred to aggression against Serbia or Serbian military and civilian causalities without an explanation of the First World War or its causes. Their speeches alluded to Austria-Hungary as an aggressor or occupier that impeded on Serbia's freedom, liberty, and independence, but their discussion of the larger conflict was void of the war's relevant causes including imperial expansion, nationalism, or global power politics. Although Gavrilo Princip and the assassination of Archduke Franz Ferdinand and Duchess Sophia are critical to Serbian and general First World War historiography, they were never mentioned. The question of Serbia's responsibility for the Great War and topics surrounding it were either too antagonistic or simply not useful to the SODEA's interpretation of this history and were thus ignored.

Creating a Living Archive: Key Commemoration Moments

Using and building on the commemoration's vocabulary, two events were key in constructing a strong shared, or "prosthetic memory," among Serbian Americans that helped to cement the SODEA's interpretation of Great War history in their group consciousness. Allison Landsberg defines prosthetic memory as the deeply felt memory of a past event individuals do not live through but instead gain through an immersive and experiential moment of contact.[19] The cultural event and banquet that the SODEA hosted as a part of its "National Day of Prayer for Serbia" centenary commemoration were immersive interactive experiences that constructed prosthetic memory by playing on Serbian Americans' sentiments toward their heritage and including them in the commemorative spectacle. Binding past with present, the SODEA created a living archive within participants who could and did repeat and distribute this new shared memory among Serbian American circles after the commemoration's end.

The first intense moment of contact participants made with the SODEA's version of First World War history and memory occurred during a cultural event. Similar rhetoric, symbolism, and images used throughout the commemoration and its promotion were again deployed. First World War-era Serbian musical arrangements were performed by a local Serbian singing group and a string quartet from the School for Musical Talents from Ćuprija, Serbia also performed. Bishop Irinej Dobrijević awarded a special commendation to Tyler Sparks, a political officer of the State Department who sat on the Serbia desk for an extended period of time. Dobrijević honored Sparks by proclaiming to the crowd "AXIOS, HE IS WORTHY, DOSTOJAN," words typically declared at the ordination of Orthodox clergy. Much like Representative Ted Poe's earlier symbolic offering of the US flag to Serbian Prime Minister Ana Brnabić, Dobrijević offered Sparks a symbol of Serbian Orthodox significance, once again binding Serbian American symbols and values.[20]

Creating a new shared experience among attendees, this event became immersive when Dobrijević told a story as the evening concluded. He elaborated on the imagery of Serbian sacrifice by describing wounded Serbian soldiers and linked them to the United States by describing allied nurses and soldiers caring for them. Dobrijević described how despite their exhaustion and poor condition, Serbian soldiers began to dance a *kolo* (Serbian folk dance) in anticipation of their break through the Salonika front and return home. Suggesting that their dancing continued into the present, he brought their memory to life and brought participants into contact with this memory. He instructed them to close their eyes and to visualize the scene— to imagine the room filled with women from "*our* villages," children in their tattered clothing, wounded soldiers, nurses from Scotland, America, and Australia, and American and French allies. Filling the space with their presence and surrounding participants with this imagery, he suggested that each of these Great War actors had been a part of the commemoration... "as we walk the streets of Washington from one event to another, there is an army following us in their tattered *opanke* (Serbian peasant shoes) so that they might remain with us."[21] This intense, emotionally-raw built environment that bound past and present was a visceral experience for commemoration participants. They were not encouraged to see themselves as Serbian soldiers, women, or children. Nor as allied nurses or troops. Instead, they were pushed to visualize themselves *among* these two groups, thus allowing them to retain their own positions as Serbian Americans and identify simultaneously with both groups. This moment of contact, instilled an experiential knowledge within commemoration participants, supplementing and potentially surpassing any cognitive understanding of the Great War they had acquired by this point.[22] Serbian Americans became tethered to those soldiers, women, and children that Dobrijević described and a strong shared memory based in this sentiment was produced.

Finally, in the formal gala banquet that closed the "National Day of Prayer for Serbia" Centenary Commemoration, the SODEA brought its interpretation of Great War history to life. At the gala, the army that Dobrijević previously invoked actually appeared. Local young Serbian-American men dressed in First World War military uniform posed gallantly in photos with attendees and escorted invited dignitaries to their seats. By taking photos with these "soldiers," participants staged their own reenactments of the scene that Dobrijević set the previous evening. This personification of Serbian soldiers—a central symbol of this commemoration—might seem like an over the top stunt but it served to up the commemoration's ante and literally brought participants into contact with the SODEA's prescribed version of Great War history. By bringing this version of Great War history to life, the SODEA provided attendees with an opportunity to place, record, and preserve themselves within the constructed historical frame. Attendees could act out and reproduce the history and commemoration after its end through photographs taken throughout the event, but especially after this gala.[23]

Conclusion: "Remember World War I Last Year?"[24]

In the weeks following the SODEA's the "National Day of Prayer for Serbia" Centennial Commemoration, images and videos from the five-day event proliferated among Serbian American social media networks. Continuing the earlier process of circulating and embedding the SODEA's interpretation of the Great War into Serbian Americans' consciousness, users renewed their participation in the commemoration and the process of returning this past to the public. Through their actions following the commemoration, participants expanded the commemoration's reach, underscoring its importance for the Serbian American community. While it is difficult to measure the extent to which the SODEA's commemoration successfully returned their interpretation of First World War history to Serbian American consciousness, more than two years after the commemoration, memories and media from the event continue to be shared on social networks. Most telling, however, remain the conversations Serbian Americans have about the commemoration in which they refer to the July 2018 events as "World War I" itself.[25] Their reference to the July 2018 commemoration as the First World War, rather than the events of the actual 1914–1918 global conflict, suggests that Serbian Americans find the SODEA's interpretation of this history authoritative. The history of the Great War and Serbian-American friendship as told through the Centenary Commemoration of "The National Day of Prayer for Serbia," has found fertile soil for continued growth in Serbian American consciousness.

The SODEA's Centenary Commemoration demonstrates the need to foreground the public's role and historically, politically, and socially contextualize commemorative processes used to return or maintain histories in public consciousness. Examining the SODEA's First World War centenary commemoration's key moments and activities, I show that Serbian Americans were the primary public that the commemoration revolved around. The history of Serbian-American friendship epitomized through the SODEA's interpretation of the 1918 "National Day of Prayer for Serbia" resonated with contemporary Serbian Americans due to more amicable post-Yugoslav diplomatic relations between Serbia and the United States. The SODEA mobilized Serbian American participation through its role as a familiar and trusted institution and partnered with parallel memory agents to use images, sounds, rhetoric, and symbolism that appealed to Serbian Americans' dual character, values, norms, and culture. To create the illusion that their interpretation was legitimate and to instill it within Serbian American consciousness, the Great War's narrative as defined by Serbian-American friendship and shared values was constructed through numerous mediums. A US flag or war stamp bolstering support for Serbia, First World War-era Serbian music, the symbology of US dignitaries, and images of Serbian soldiers, each worked together to reinforce and legitimize this narrative. Though symbols like these appeared in various genres of media, taken together, they constructed a framework wherein alternative interpretations of the Great War both seemed illegitimate and unlikely. Continually expanding this framework and immersing commemoration participants in it, the SODEA hosted participatory events that constructed historical continuity and blurred the line between past and present. Serbian Americans not only passively consumed this new interpretation of the Great War, but became a part of a living archive of sorts, transforming into agents of memory able to replicate and share that memory within Serbian American circles before and after the commemoration's end. Centering the mechanisms which "memory entrepreneurs" like the SODEA used to solicit and maintain public participation in their First World War centenary commemoration, I offer an alternative framework for understanding how history gains new relevance within a public's consciousness. These processes are never arbitrary or a-historical, but rather rely on social and political conditions explicitly linked to a public and its interests.

Notes

1 Mere months before the end of the First World War, the United States declared a National Day of Prayer for Serbia. In this proclamation, Lansing described the Serbian people's war effort as noble, valiant, and courageous and described Serbs devastation, but noted that their spirit remained well-preserved along with their love of freedom and determination to "sacrifice everything for liberty and independence." He called upon Americans of all faiths to gather in their assemblies of worship and pray for Serbs; Joseph V. Fuller and Tyler Dennett, eds., *Foreign Relations of the United States, 1918*, vol. 1, Supplement 1, The World War (Washington: Government Printing Office, 1933), Document 827.
2 Here I use public in the singular in an effort to recognize that a homogenized "public memory" is unlikely to exist in any state or society. Rather, all states and societies have several publics with numerous shared memories and interests that often conflict.
3 John E. Bodnar, *Remaking America: Public Memory, Commemoration, and Patriotism in the Twentieth Century* (Princeton: Princeton University Press, 1991); Jonathan Huener, *Auschwitz, Poland, and the Politics of Commemoration, 1949–1979* (Athens: Ohio University Press, 2003); Jay Winter, *Remembering War: The Great War between Memory and History in the Twentieth Century* (New Haven: Yale University Press, 2006); Maria Bucur, *Heroes and Victims: Remembering War in Twentieth Century Romania* (Bloomington: Indiana University Press, 2009).
4 Most well-known of these is Aleida Assmann, "Memory, Individual and Collective," in *The Oxford Handbook of Contextual Political Analysis*, ed. Robert E. Goodin and Charles Tilly (Oxford: Oxford University Press, 2006), 1–17, here 7–8, 12–13; see also Assmann, *Shadows of Trauma: Memory and the Politics of Postwar Identity* (Fordham: Fordham University Press, 2016), 199–201.
5 Elizabeth Jelin defines memory entrepreneurs as "those who seek social recognition and political legitimacy of one [their own] interpretation or narrative of the past, engaged and concerned with maintaining and promoting active and visible social and political attention on their enterprise." See Elizabeth Jelin, *State Repression and the Labors of Memory* (Minnesota: University of Minnesota Press, 2003), 33–34.
6 Note on Sources and Methodology: This article relies on the three-part documentary special produced by Televizija Hram, the television network of the Serbian Orthodox Church, who recorded the event. I do not utilize the TV networks portrayal or interpretation of the event, but rather the commemorative activities, speeches, and settings themselves which I am able to discern by referencing my

own observations of these events. As a commemoration participant-observer, I collected other primary sources like event programs, images, webpages, and videos related to the commemoration as I became aware of them, and recorded my own observations. As a Serbian American, I am intimately familiar with the institutions and vocabularies mobilized through this commemoration which informs my understanding of the specific resonance commemoration symbology and rhetoric had with the larger Serbian American community. Being "plugged into" this community as it were, I was also able to witness and trace the commemoration's development before and after it was held. My dual identity as both a Serbian American and historian allowed me to link the five-day event to its many social media forms, gave me knowledge of community infrastructure, and access to sources that could otherwise be a challenge to find. I thus rely on my position as a Serbian American to inform my scholarly analysis in this article and find it a necessary methodological approach given how I have centered Serbian Americans as the "public" that shaped the SODEA's reinterpretation of the past for the present.

7 This is a challenging claim to make given an absence of studies on the Serbian Americans' disposition toward socialist Yugoslavia and President Josip Broz Tito. However, I make it here based on my own experience growing up in Serbian American communities in the Northeastern and Southern U.S. Those experiences left me with the impression that while some Serbian Americans were neutral to socialist rule, most (particularly following the 1990s) held it quite negatively. Also see Linda A. Bennett, "Washington and Its Serbian Emigres: A Distinctive Blend," *Anthropological Quarterly* 54, no. 2 (1981): 82–88.

8 Dusan Stojanovic, "Defying Russia, Serbia holds military drills with Americans," *Fox News*, November 17, 2017, https://www.foxnews.com/us/defying-russia-serbia-holds-military-drills-with-americans; Andy Eckardt and Vladimir Banic, "Serbia embraces tug of war between NATO and Russia," *NBS News*, November 25, 2017, https://www.nbcnews.com/news/world/serbia-embraces-tug-war-between-nato-russia-n822431; Maja Zivanovic, "Russia Military Deal Deemed 'Good Thing' For Serbia," *Balkan Insight*, April 15, 2018, https://balkaninsight.com/2018/04/05/new-serbian-russian-military-deal-good-thing-04-04-2018/; Zivanovic, "Russia 'Using Serbia to Destroy Europe', Ukraine Ambassador," *Balkan Insight*, November 1, 2017, https://balkaninsight.com/2017/11/01/russia-using-serbia-to-destroy-europe-ukraine-ambassador-10-31-2017; Zivanovic, "Serbia Thanks Russia For Support Over Kosovo," *Balkan Insight*, February 22, 2018, https://balkaninsight.com/2018/02/22/russian-foreign-minister-support-independent-course-of-serbia-02-22-2018.

9 Since the 1990s conflict and especially following Kosovo's independence and international recognition in 2008, relations between Serbia and Kosovo have remained contentious given Serbia's refusal to recognize Kosovo as an independent state. The EU and international leaders have repeated attempts to broker deals between the two states, but with no success. On the Trump administration's attitudes toward Serbia see for example: Emily Tamkin, "Here's Why the US Has Been Cozying Up to Authoritarians in Eastern Europe," *Buzzfeed News*, October 16, 2018, https://www.buzzfeednews.com/article/emilytamkin/russia-hungary-trump-policy-wess-mitchell; "Serbia, US 'paved way for development of partner relations,'" *B92*, July 30, 2018, https://www.b92.net/eng/news/politics.php?yyyy=2018&mm=07&dd=30&nav_id=104740;_Office of the Spokesperson, "Assistant Secretary Mitchell to Travel to Pristina, Skopje, Belgrade, Athens, and Nicosia," US Department of State, March 11, 2018, https://www.state.gov/assistant-secretary-mitchell-to-travel-to-pristina-skopje-belgrade-athens-and-nicosia.

10 The Serbian Orthodox Diocese of Eastern America is one of thirty-five diocese under the jurisdiction of the Serbian Orthodox Patriarchate. Each diocese has

a level of autonomy but ultimately functions under the blessing of the Serbian Orthodox Patriarch and Holy Assembly of Bishops, the highest body of the church.

11 Serbian Orthodox Church Diocese in the USA, World War I Centennial Committee, Gala Banquet Program, July 28, 2018.

12 For more on the veneration of Great War military service in Serbia and Yugoslavia see for example John Paul Newman, "Forging a United Kingdom of Serbs, Croats, and Slovenes: The Legacy of the First World War and the 'Invalid Question,'" in *New Perspectives on Yugoslavia: Key Issues and Controversies*, ed. Dejan Djokic and James Ker-Lindsay (London, New York: Routledge, 2010), 46–61; John Paul Newman, "Times of Death: The Great War and Serbia's Twentieth Century," in *Aftermath: Legacies and Memories of War in Europe, 1918–1945–1989*, ed. Nicholas Martin, Tim Haughton, and Pierre Purseigle (Surrey: Ashgate Publishing, 2014), 25–40; Ismar Dedović and Tea Sindbæk Andersen, "'To Battle, Go Forth All Heroes.' World War I Memory as a Narrative Template in Yugoslavia and Serbia," in *Re-Visiting World War I: Interpretations and Perspectives of the Great Conflict*, ed. Jaroslaw Suchoples and Stephanie James (New York: Peter Lang, 2016) 295–314.

13 "Save the Date! The Day the Serbian Flag Flew at the White House," News Archives, Eastern American Diocese of the Serbian Orthodox, last modified June 9, 2018, accessed March 25, 2019, https://www.easterndiocese.org/news_180610_1.html.

14 "Joint Statement of the Serbian National Defense Council and Serbian National Federation," The Day the Serbian Flag Flew at the White House, Eastern American Diocese of the Serbian Orthodox Church, last modified June 29, 2018, accessed March 25, 2019, https://www.easterndiocese.org/news_180630_1.html; A few examples: Kraljevo Royal Crowns, Facebook, accessed March 26, 2019, https://www.facebook.com/events/1797848826957578; The Day the Serbian Flag Flew Over the White House hosted by St. Luke Serbian Orthodox Church, Facebook, accessed March 26, 2019, https://www.facebook.com/events/184247388914663; Mim Bizic, "The House of Good News," Facebook, accessed March 29, 2019, https://www.facebook.com/thehouseofgoodnews/posts/1826186860761321.

15 "Guest Chaplain: Bishop Irinej, Serbian Orthodox Diocese of Eastern American, New Rochelle, NY Sponsor: Rep. Ted Poe (TX-02)," C-SPAN, July 25, 2018, https://www.c-span.org/video/?c4742044/opening-prayer-wednesday-july-25-2018&fbclid=IwAR0x5GK4qis0WRXMwQYmOF22XPE2OqRQym-DrzAo99-4lkqn3V-_DwjHL-o.

16 Televizija Hram, "Obeležavanje Stogodišnjice Dana Molitve za Srbiju u Vašingtona (1. Epizoda) / Commemoration of the 100th Anniversary of A Day of Prayer for Serbia in Washington (Episode 1)," YouTube, August 22, 2018, https://www.youtube.com/watch?v=L4KkuUI_5T4.

17 Ibid.

18 Televizija Hram. "Obeležavanje Stogodišnjice Dana Molitve za Srbiju u Vašingtona (2. Epizoda)/Commemoration of the 100th Anniversary of A Day of Prayer for Serbia in Washington (Episode 2)." YouTube. August 23, 2018. https://www.youtube.com/watch?time_continue=196&v=bmPE-wuCTnE.

19 Allison Landsberg, *Prosthetic Memory: The Transformation of American Remembrance in the Age of Mass Culture* (New York: Columbia University Press, 2004), 2–8.

20 Televizija Hram, "Obeležavanje Stogodišnjice Dana Molitve za Srbiju u Vašingtona (3. Epizoda)/Commemoration of the 100th Anniversary of A Day of Prayer for Serbia in Washington (Episode 3)," YouTube, August 24, 2018, https://www.youtube.com/watch?v=L4KkuUI_5T4.

21 Televizija Hram "Obeležavanje Stogodišnjice Dana Molitve za Srbiju u Vašingtona (3. Epizoda)/Commemoration of the 100th Anniversary of A Day of Prayer

for Serbia in Washington (Episode 3)," YouTube, August 24, 2018, https://www. youtube.com/watch?v=L4KkuUI_5T4.

22 Allison Landsberg argues that this is a part of how prosthetic memory functions. The experiential mode of learning and understanding has become increasingly important for the acquisition of knowledge and particularly types of knowledge that are not available on a purely cognitive register. I find that for commemorations such as "The National Day of Prayer for Serbia," where a narrative of the Great War was crafted specifically in a Serbian-American spirit, experiential knowledge acquisition was key to instilling this memory in public consciousness. See Landsberg, *Prosthetic Memory*, 33.

23 Televizija Hram, "Obeležavanje Stogodišnjice Dana Molitve za Srbiju u Vašingtona (3. Epizoda)."

24 Interview with Naela El-Hinnaway, July 15, 2019.

25 Ibid.

Bibliography

Assmann, Aleida. "Memory, Individual and Collective." In *The Oxford Handbook of Contextual Political Analysis*, edited by Robert E. Goodin and Charles Tilly, 1–17. Oxford: Oxford University Press, 2006.

Assmann, Aleida. *Shadows of Trauma: Memory and the Politics of Postwar Identity.* Fordham: Fordham University Press, 2016.

Bennett, Linda A. "Washington and Its Serbian Emigres: A Distinctive Blend." *Anthropological Quarterly* 54, no. 2 (1981): 82–88.

Bizic, Mim. "The House of Good News." Facebook. Accessed March 29, 2019. https://www.facebook.com/thehouseofgoodnews/posts/1826186860761321.

Bodnar, John E. *Remaking America: Public Memory, Commemoration, and Patriotism in the Twentieth Century.* Princeton: Princeton University Press, 1991.

Bucur, Maria. *Heroes and Victims: Remembering War in Twentieth Century Romania.* Bloomington: Indiana University Press, 2009.

Dedović, Ismar, and Tea Sindbæk Andersen. "'To Battle, Go Forth All Heroes.' World War I Memory as a Narrative Template in Yugoslavia and Serbia." In *Re-Visiting World War I: Interpretations and Perspectives of the Great Conflict*, edited by Jaroslaw Suchoples and Stephanie James, 295–314. New York: Peter Lang, 2016.

Huener, Jonathan. *Auschwitz, Poland, and the Politics of Commemoration, 1949–1979.* Athens: Ohio University Press, 2003.

Jelin, Elizabeth. *State Repression and the Labors of Memory.* Minnesota: University of Minnesota Press, 2003.

Landsberg, Allison. *Prosthetic Memory: The Transformation of American Remembrance in the Age of Mass Culture.* New York: Columbia University Press, 2004.

Newman, John Paul. "Forging a United Kingdom of Serbs, Croats, and Slovenes: The Legacy of the First World War and the 'Invalid Question.'" In *New Perspectives on Yugoslavia: Key Issues and Controversies*, edited by Dejan Djokic and James Ker-Lindsay, 46–61. London, New York: Routledge, 2010.

Newman, John Paul. "Times of Death: The Great War and Serbia's Twentieth Century." In *Aftermath: Legacies and Memories of War in Europe, 1918–1945–1989*, edited by Nicholas Martin, Tim Haughton, and Pierre Purseigle, 25–40. Surrey: Ashgate Publishing, 2014.

Rieff, David. *In Praise of Forgetting: Historical Memories and Its Ironies.* New Haven: Yale University Press, 2016.

Winter, Jay M. *Remembering War: The Great War between Memory and History in the Twentieth Century.* New Haven: Yale University Press, 2006.

Primary Sources

Eastern American Diocese of the Serbian Orthodox Church. "Joint Statement of the Serbian National Defense Council and Serbian National Federation." Last modified June 29, 2018. Accessed March 25, 2019. https://www.easterndiocese. org/news_180630_1.html.

Eastern American Diocese of the Serbian Orthodox. "Save the Date! The Day the Serbian Flag Flew at the White House." News Archives. Last modified June 9, 2018. Accessed March 25, 2019. https://www.easterndiocese.org/news_180610_1. html.

Eckardt, Andy, and Vladimir Banic. "Serbia Embraces Tug of War between NATO and Russia." *NBS News*, November 25, 2017. https://www.nbcnews.com/news/ world/serbia-embraces-tug-war-between-nato-russia-n822431.

Facebook. Kraljevo Royal Crowns. "A Day of Prayer for Serbia." Accessed March 26, 2019. https://www.facebook.com/events/1797848826957578.

Facebook. St. Luke Serbian Orthodox Church. "The Day the Serbian Flag Flew Over the White House." Accessed March 26, 2019. https://www.facebook.com/ events/184247388914663.

Fuller, Joseph V., and Tyler Dennett, eds. *Foreign Relations of the United States, 1918*. Vol. 1, Supplement 1, The World War. Washington: Government Printing Office, 1933.

"Guest Chaplain: Bishop Irinej, Serbian Orthodox Diocese of Eastern American, New Rochelle, NY Sponsor: Rep. Ted Poe (TX-02)." C-SPAN, July 25, 2018. https:// www.c-span.org/video/?c4742044/opening-prayer-wednesday-july-25-2018& f b c l i d = I w A R 0 x 5 G K 4 q i s 0 W R X M w Q Y m O F 2 2 X P E 2 O q R Q y m - DrzAo99-4lkqn3V-_DwjHL-o.

Office of the Spokesperson. "Assistant Secretary Mitchell to Travel to Pristina, Skopje, Belgrade, Athens, and Nicosia." US Department of State, March 11, 2018. https://www.state.gov/assistant-secretary-mitchell-to-travel-to-pristina-skopje-belgrade-athens-and-nicosia.

"Serbia, US 'Paved Way for Development of Partner Relations.'" *B92*, July 30, 2018. https://www.b92.net/eng/news/politics.php?yyyy=2018&mm=07&dd=30& nav_id=104740.

Serbian Orthodox Church Diocese in the USA, World War I Centennial Committee, Gala Banquet Program, July 28, 2018.

Stojanovic, Dusan. "Defying Russia, Serbia Holds Military Drills with Americans." *Fox News*, November 17, 2017. https://www.foxnews.com/us/defying-russia-serbia-holds-military-drills-with-americans.

Tamkin, Emily. "Here's Why the US Has Been Cozying Up to Authoritarians in Eastern Europe." *Buzzfeed News*, October 16, 2018. https://www.buzzfeednews. com/article/emilytamkin/russia-hungary-trump-policy-wess-mitchell.

Televizija Hram. "Obeležavanje Stogodišnjice Dana Molitve za Srbiju u Vašingtona (1. Epizoda) / Commemoration of the 100th Anniversary of a Day of Prayer for Serbia in Washington (Episode 1)." YouTube, August 22, 2018. https://www. youtube.com/watch?v=L4KkuUI_5T4.

Televizija Hram. "Obeležavanje Stogodišnjice Dana Molitve za Srbiju u Vasšingtona (2. Epizoda)/Commemoration of the 100th Anniversary of a Day of Prayer for Serbia in Washington (Episode 2)." YouTube, August 23, 2018. https://www. youtube.com/watch?time_continue=196&v=bmPE-wuCTnE.

Televizija Hram. "Obeležavanje Stogodišnjice Dana Molitve za Srbiju u Vašingtona (3. Epizoda)/Commemoration of the 100th Anniversary of a Day of Prayer for Serbia in Washington (Episode 3)." YouTube, August 24, 2018. https://www.youtube.com/watch?v=L4KkuUI_5T4.

Zivanovic, Maja. "Russia 'Using Serbia to Destroy Europe', Ukraine Ambassador." *Balkan Insight*, November 1, 2017. https://balkaninsight.com/2017/11/01/russia-using-serbia-to-destroy-europe-ukraine-ambassador-10-31-2017.

Zivanovic, Maja. "Russia Military Deal Deemed 'Good Thing' For Serbia." *Balkan Insight*, April 15, 2018. https://balkaninsight.com/2018/04/05/new-serbian-russian-military-deal-good-thing-04-04-2018.

Zivanovic, Maja. "Serbia Thanks Russia for Support over Kosovo." *Balkan Insight*, February 22, 2018. https://balkaninsight.com/2018/02/22/russian-foreign-minister-support-independent-course-of-serbia-02-22-2018.

8

THE ROLE OF THE PUBLIC IN SHAPING NEW COLLECTIVE MEMORY(IES)

The Irish Public and Their Representation of History during and after the Irish Civil War of 1922–1923

Caitlin White

The town of Nenagh in North Tipperary has been chosen as a microstudy through which we might examine the role of the Irish public outside of the capital city and seat of central government of Dublin in shaping representations of history and a collective memory in the aftermath of what has been termed by historians as the "Revolutionary Decade."[1] Drawing on theories of memory and commemoration, this chapter will present the public history erected in the town and consider contesting narratives, how representative they might be of the wider public in the Irish Free State and the significance of the debates surrounding conflicting narratives in the public sphere.

In the five years following the overwhelming success of the republican Sinn Féin party in the 1918 General Election, Ireland had been partitioned into two jurisdictions, fought a War of Independence that brought the British government to the negotiating table and experienced sectarian violence and a civil war. The Irish Civil War, fought mainly in the Irish Free State, was between former comrades, neighbors, families and friends over the terms of the Anglo-Irish Treaty of 1921. Broadly, it was between two opposing sides, the pro-Treaty Cumann na nGaedheal government and their supporters, backed by the National Army, and the anti-Treaty Sinn Féin party, backed by the Irish Republican Army (IRA). By May 1923, the 26-county Irish Free State was consolidated by the IRA's admission of defeat by the order from Chief of Staff Frank Aiken to dump arms. The two Irish states established in this period were founded and divided along established political affiliations, social identities and religious beliefs. Simplified versions of identity caused conflict and division in both states and contributed to violence and discrimination throughout the twentieth, and into the twenty-first, century on the island of Ireland.

The publics that both perpetuated and absorbed these myths were ordinary people engaging in education, local government, agriculture and

FIGURE 8.1   War Memorial Cross, Nenagh (1928) in May 2020 © Caitlin White.

trade. They were both receptors and effectors of their collective social identities, participating in public history processes that had been established since the eighteenth and nineteenth centuries. The nineteenth century in particular had seen an unprecedented monument boom throughout Europe coinciding with the rise of nationalism and the concept of the nation-state. In Ireland, this manifested in the erection of upward of 40 monuments between 1870 and 1914 of men who had either practiced or preached armed resistance to British rule.[2] While public history is a term we associate with modern historiographical thinking, having been coined and defined by Robert Kelley in California in the 1970s, evidence of public history practice can be found throughout history in societies all over the world.[3] In relation to social memory and public history processes in Nenagh in this period, monuments provided a popular platform for history engagement and collective identity expression.

Prior to the reforms introduced in the Local Government (Ireland) Act 1898 jurisdictions were administered by prominent local landowners and gentry. The democratic election of representatives to local government was a recent development and was far more representative of the local populations than the previous administrative system. In the case of the public space in Nenagh, it is often these local representatives (Urban District Councillors, UDCs) who reveal some of the nuances of discourse and debates happening within the community. While not representative of every individual, their role granted them status as a democratically elected curator or gatekeeper of the collective identity of the community in a broader sense. Private committees were established to erect and fund these monuments and, in many cases, claim to possess the true knowledge of what the wider public really want, but it is the debates and discussions between the private committees and public representatives, and even among the public representatives themselves, alongside opinions expressed in local media that we shall use to consider the public's relationship to the shape their history was taking. None of the monuments erected in Nenagh were state-led initiatives.[4] These monuments were all community initiatives, some of which received support and approval from the local Urban District Council and some which did not.

As Ian McBride notes, "what we remember or forget…has as much to do with external constraints, imposed by our social and cultural surroundings, as with what happens in the frontal lobes of our brains."[5] It is the process of creating these cultural surroundings that will be used to examine the public's role in articulating their past in the town of Nenagh.

The Memorial to Denis Carey

Monuments in the urban center of Nenagh began to be planned, funded and erected very soon after partition. In one case, a memorial to Denis Carey, a young IRA volunteer killed in a reprisal attack by British forces in November 1920, was erected in the uncertain and tense atmosphere of a country on the brink of civil war.[6] On June 25, 1922, three days before the Free State government fired on the anti-Treaty forces holding the Four Courts in Dublin, an action that signalled the beginning of the civil war, a memorial was unveiled on Ashe Road, Nenagh, honoring Carey.[7]

The memorial is made of Irish limestone inscribed in the old Irish script and reads:

> I ndíl chuimhne Dhonnachadha uí Chiardha, a dunmharbhuigheadh le Gallaibh an 26adh Mí na Shamhna 1920. Ar son na hÉireann d'éag

sé. ["In Loving Memory of Denis Carey, murdered by foreigners on 26 November 1920. He died for Ireland."]

The choice of language for the memorial was appropriate, as Carey had been actively involved with the local branch of the Gaelic League known as the Nenagh Literary Institute. The Gaelic League, founded by Douglas Hyde in 1893, was (and still is) a social organization founded to promote the Irish language, literature and Gaelic culture.[8] The choice of language for the monument also serves as an identity marker to indicate that his memory belonged to the group of people in the locality who considered themselves Gaels.

The wording is surrounded by decorative Celtic crosses and knots and features a plain cruciform in the center of the bordering. It forms part of the adjoining wall and is placed on the spot that Carey was believed to have been shot on November 24, 1920.[9] The unveiling ceremony was led by a local priest, Fr. Patrick O'Halloran, who (in Irish first, then in English) urged people in remembrance of the tragic death of a young man to come together and forget their differences in an apparent reference to the gang rape of Mrs. Harriet Biggs, the Protestant wife of a member of a well-known landed military family, which had been committed in the locality only nine days previous on 16 June. A particularly violent attack, Mrs. Biggs suffered a mental breakdown and was later institutionalized.[10] Fr. O'Halloran's admonishments were seemingly in vain as that summer there were multiple attacks in North Tipperary by men on the local Protestant population, a number of them involving sexual harassment of women including one on the 75-year-old Mrs. McKenna in Roscrea in August 1922.[11]

The monument features the Christogram containing the letters "IHS" surrounded by shamrocks. "IHS" is an abbreviated form of the Greek word for Jesus and this particular Christogram is present on both monuments financed by the Literary Institute in this period.[12] The strong links with religion do not end at the design of the monument, but permeate all aspects, visual and symbolic. This infusion of Irishness, Celticness and Catholicism as one and the same is a common articulation of Irish identity in the twentieth century among those who remained in Ireland and the Irish diaspora.[13]

In 1922, Fr. O'Halloran's speech at the unveiling of the monument heroicized the young martyr Carey, declaring that the spot in which the plaque is placed is a sacred, holy place "for it has drunk the blood of one who died for Ireland."[14] In so highlighting the connection between the place that blood was spilled and the holiness and sacredness of that act, Fr. O'Halloran associated Carey with images of Christ and his sacrifice. As a figure of authority among the Catholic community, which made up 94.5 percent of the population of Co. Tipperary in the 1911 census, he undoubtedly had a great deal of influence over his parishioners and their ideas of collective identity.[15]

The Nenagh Great War Memorial

People self-identify as belonging to one of many available imagined communities. Benedict Anderson introduced this concept and argued that whole nations and states belong to one particular community or another simply because they imagine themselves to be so.[16] In states with upheaval and huge change citizens require more than a vague awareness of their own identity, Anthony D. Smith argues that concrete manifestations of self are necessary to make tangible sense of a communal identity, and thus, in both Irish states we see a huge surge in the erection of monuments to the heroes of the newly created states.[17] These concrete manifestations of identity aim to cultivate imagined, collective identities among citizens of the community, but they also served as tangible territorial markers for an identity group.

As noted by Guy Beiner in his research on social forgetting in Ulster, changes made to monuments or statues, or their erasure, as well as the erection or planning of them, can indicate a perception of social identity within a community.[18] In an attempt to fully understand the role that the public had in employing public history practices as part of social identity processes in this period, we must consider any changes made to monuments, any changes made in the planning process and any monuments removed from public space. These monuments do not only represent a past, but their very presence in the public space epitomizes the values and priorities of the present. The Nenagh Great War Memorial and debates surrounding its erection indicate how conscious of wider public perception the Nenagh UDCs were in this period.

The War Memorial Cross was unveiled on November 11 (Armistice Day), 1928, outside the ex-servicemen's hut on Ashe Road, less than 200 m from the Denis Carey monument.[19] Ex-servicemen's huts were buildings in many towns and cities across the country established for the social and recreational use of British Army veterans. The monument is a limestone cross, 16 feet high and is adorned with Celtic-style artwork.[20] The inscription reads "1914–1918 At the going down of the sun and in the morning we will remember them," a quote from Laurence Binyon's popular poem, *For the Fallen*. Published in September 1914, the poem came to symbolize remembrance of all the war dead by November 1918 and by 1928 was a popular choice for monuments commemorating the war dead throughout the British Empire. An appropriate tone for a war memorial, the use of this poem subtly promotes a fluid British aspect to Irish identity and links war remembrance with the words of an English poet.

The cross resembles an ancient high cross, a feature of early Christian Ireland, with reliefs of Celtic knots and Irish greyhounds, motifs also seen on the Carey monument. The design of the cross, made locally with local limestone, visually connects remembrance of the First World War with what was perceived to be Ireland's Golden Age from which many in the arts and crafts movement during the Gaelic Revival took inspiration. In making this connection, the committee behind the Nenagh Great War Memorial Cross were promoting their proud Celtic identity alongside lines from an English poet's pen to commemorate men who died as Irishmen and British subjects. The tensions that are often referred to when speaking of Irish identity in this period are united in this expression of the complex facets of social identity.

The very center of the cruciform features the Christogram "IHS" in a Celtic style. While this symbol had been used by the Roman Catholic community on the monument to Denis Carey, it is a Christian rather than a Catholic symbol and is used by a variety of denominations. The symbol, being used again in relation to the First World War and by a committee led by the Church of Ireland Minister Rev. McDowell, reaffirms the importance of religion to the communal identity. The individual names of those who lost their lives were not initially inscribed on the monument, but the committee specified that this would be done once they had collected all the names of the fallen and did attempt to collect these after the erection of the cross through notices in local papers.[21] Gerard Dooley's research on Nenagh estimates that between 51 and 66 men from the town itself were killed and that approximately 45 percent of Nenagh's available males, 20 percent of Nenagh's overall population, served in the war.[22] Ultimately, the names were never inscribed and instead the memorial featured a simple inscription dedicating the memorial to "those of Nenagh and district who fell in the Great War 1914–1918."

The unveiling ceremony was attended by approximately 600 people; the *Nenagh Guardian* later attributed the bad weather to what was considered a poor turnout. The ceremony consisted of a parade of ex-servicemen accompanied by the Nenagh Brass and Reed Band and the Ex-Servicemen's Fife and Drum Band from the memorial cross on Ashe Road to the Roman Catholic and Church of Ireland churches (which stand side by side) where services were observed simultaneously, followed by a united march back to the memorial cross and an observation of two minutes silence.[23] The simultaneous remembrance services being observed in both of the local churches suggest cooperation between the two and indicate that, at least among some war veterans, there was a sense of unity. The monument was unveiled by the Dowager Lady Dunalley who had lost her son in the war and whose late husband had been influential in the North Tipperary recruitment drive.[24] The Dunalleys were local landed gentry who were not known for being benevolent or generous landlords and whose house was burned in 1922 during the Irish Civil War.[25] While the majority of ex-servicemen from Nenagh were laborers rather than tenant farmers, it is possible that the presence of a Dunalley as the guest of honor to unveil the monument may have alienated some war veterans in the community.

Mr. E. Heeney on behalf of the committee originally requested space in the town's main thoroughfare of Banba Square for the memorial to the dead of the First World War, but the site was refused by the Nenagh UDC in

May 1928 on the grounds that it would be an insult to "their own dead," in a sweeping statement rejecting the young men from the town and district who were killed in the trenches.[26] The decision of the Council was not made without discussion and debate, and a number of ideas were put forward to reconcile the erection of the Nenagh Great War Memorial with the nationalist feeling of the town. In their refusal of the site of Banba Square for the erection of a memorial to the dead of the war, the Nenagh UDCs were very conscious of their role in the construction of Nenagh's narrative. Councillor Flannery stated that while he believed that the rank and file were sincere in their motivations to honor dead comrades and acknowledged that they had "every right" to do so, he was suspicious of the motivations of those driving the project and who applied for the public site in the square. He declared that the memorial would become a "rallying point for the forces of Imperialism" not only in Nenagh, but in every town in Ireland where this kind of monument was proposed. Flannery appealed to the Council to consider the matter as a public body rather than individuals and suggested that a monument granted permission to be erected on public grounds by local authorities could "claim to be regarded as a national one."[27] To grant the permission of a public site for such a monument might leave the actions and sentiments of the council—and by extension the community—open to misinterpretation. In agreement, Councillor Gill added that in a few years there may not be prayers for the dead at the base of the proposed monument, but instead "you would hear the strains of the British National Anthem."[28] Only the week before, some Councillors had suggested erecting a memorial to those who died for Irish independence and those who died in the First World War side by side, but after consideration the resolution to refuse the site of Banba Square for the erection of a monument to the war dead was unanimously passed.[29] The ideology behind the Great War Memorial and the implications of what supporting it would insinuate, but importantly not the individuals honoring of the fallen soldiers, would have been too great "an outrage on the national feelings of the town."[30]

North Tipperary Republican Monument

It is evident from the contemporary newspaper sources reporting on the contents of the meeting of the Urban District Council that the Councillors saw themselves as the gatekeepers or curators of the community's identity. They treated their roles as curators with earnest pride and were conscious of the image of the locality as perceived through their public history. The men who answered the call to enlist in the British Army in 1914, many who were nationalists who fought "for a dream born in a herdsman's shed," could not be commemorated at the expense of the reputation and honor of the locality.[31] P. Ryan (Lacken), a member of the North Tipperary Republican Monument Committee, told the Nenagh UDC in 1928 that they had a decision to make, a decision "between the men who died in the Great War and those who laid down their lives for the Irish Republic."[32] There was little room for complex nuances of collective identity expression in the public sphere of Nenagh.

The Nenagh UDC's awareness of the consequences of monuments they chose to support or otherwise adds another dimension to the erection of the North Tipperary Republican Monument. Henri Lefebvre considers space as a form of capital and analyzes how, particularly in urban centers, urban forms are made not only of physical materials but out of meanings, language and symbols.[33] Continuing with Lefebvre's thinking on the use of space Fran Tonkiss develops this concept further and asserts that "urban space is both the object of political agency and its medium."[34] The control of public space, in any community, is one of the most visible ways of exercising power. This was triumphantly exercised by North Tipperary Republican Committee on August 23, 1931, when the North Tipperary Republican Monument was unveiled on the exact spot the Nenagh Great War Memorial Committee had requested for a monument to the dead of the First World War. The years 1930 and 1931 had seen a huge rise in membership of the IRA, according to Brian Hanley. He also asserts that in the period 1926–1936, the IRA was not engaged in any military campaign, and so one of the main activities members engaged in was organizing and participating in commemorative events.[35] The organization had an ability to "mobilize numbers beyond its immediate membership in displays of support for its politics," which may help to explain the huge support the North Tipperary Republican Monument received when recorded strengths for Tipperary IRA were declining.[36]

The monument was unveiled to crowds of approximately 5,000 people following a procession of a further 1,000.[37] They were accompanied by the Nenagh Brass and Reed Band and when the procession reached Banba Square a decade of the Rosary was said in Irish, reinforcing the narrative of Gaelic Irishness as intrinsically Catholic. The monument, inscribed in Irish only, again using the Irish language as a political identity marker, states that it is dedicated to the people of North Tipperary from 1916 onward who gave their lives for the Irish Republic. This monument does not include the soldiers of the Irish Free State's National Army who died during the civil war, only members of the anti-treaty, anti-government side who remained with the IRA. This approach concurs with Anne Dolan's observation that in the aftermath of the civil war "the republicans maintained their rebel air" and their sense of martyrdom.[38] The freestanding monument is in the Romanesque style and sits on a plinth in the town's main thoroughfare. It was accompanied by a sculpture of an Irish Volunteer (who became known locally as Jamesy) to commemorate the soldiers who sacrificed their lives. The monument's prominent position ensures that it dominates the public space and is a central feature of the landscape of the town.

Planning for the monument began relatively soon after the ceasefire that ended the Irish Civil War. After a little over two years since the IRA laid down their arms permission was sought by the Sinn Féin Executive of North Tipperary from the Nenagh UDC to erect a monument in the square to "those who lost their lives in [...] the struggle for independence."[39] Permission was granted from the Nenagh UDC with seemingly little opposition, with the Chairman adding that it would be "an ornament to the locality."[40] What is unclear when the permission was sought for this monument is the extent to which the Councillors knew about the message it would later convey. If any debate over the ideology of the monument was had at the Council Meeting, it was certainly not reported on in the usually detailed and descriptive *Nenagh Guardian*.[41] It is important to note that while the Nenagh UDC granted the space for the monument, it did not contribute to the fundraising efforts in an official capacity. Through dances, GAA games, flag days and private donations chronicled and advertised in the local press the North Tipperary Republican Monument Committee raised the pounds, shillings and pence required to erect their monument to the dead. In this sense, it is one of the many local monuments described by Dolan of being far more significant and meaningful to local communities than the grand gestures in Dublin.[42]

It should also be noted that in December 1921, the Nenagh UDC voted to urge their county representatives to accept the terms of the Treaty, "agreed on by the duly appointed plenipotentiaries of Dáil Éireann."[43] Tipperary's representatives were split on the Treaty, with three voting against it and only one who supported the terms of the agreement.[44] After violent upheavals in various forms since 1914, many people were weary of violence and wanted no part in further conflict.[45] In analyzing the economic situation in the aftermath of the conflict, Gavin Foster noted that concerns about personal economic security were on the minds of many aging revolutionaries—it had been six years since the Easter Rising and almost a decade since the establishment of the Irish Volunteers.[46] Minute Book 7 of the Nenagh UDC illustrates the impact that extreme violence had on the local community, with frequent votes of condolence passed in this period.[47] It is clear that people desired a return to normality, even if that meant accepting a treaty containing terms disagreeable to their principles.

On the day of the unveiling, an eminent anti-Treaty figure, Frank Ryan, was invited to address the crowd and officiate the unveiling of the monument. At this point, Ryan was a well-known leading IRA figure, described by his biographer Fearghal McGarry as a man who "saw physical force as not only necessary but morally superior to other forms of struggle."[48] An avid Irish language speaker and member of the Gaelic League, he was critical of those who entered parliament to negotiate greater freedom for Ireland and believed that a return to the gun would be preferable. McGarry notes that Ryan was opposed to sectarianism and the influence of the Catholic

Church on the state. While republicans cited the provocative display of British imperialism as the reason for their opposition, McGarry notes that it is evident from Ryan's speeches that an intolerance of a non-republican identity was intrinsic to his opposition.[49] He became editor of *An Phoblacht* (the republican newspaper) in 1929 and was targeted as part of the Cumann na nGaedheal government's crackdown on IRA members and their activities in the early 1930s. At the time of his appearance in Nenagh, he had recently been released from prison where he had been held for printing seditious material in *An Phoblacht* and would be arrested a few months later in December 1931 for his membership of the IRA.[50]

"Ryan's popularity was also partly due to the fact that he was invariably the most bloodthirsty speaker at any meeting," and in Nenagh he did not disappoint.[51] Delivering his speech first in Irish, then in English, he asserted that the people of Nenagh "have the right spirit in you, and that you know by raising a monument you have done a good thing." However, in line with the message of the monument, Ryan went on to say: "You have not done enough. There is one monument which you in conjunction with the people of Ireland must raise—the one and only fitting monument you can raise—an independent and undivided Irish Republic," which was met with applause.[52] The monument, he believed, should not only be a source of inspiration for those present, but also a source of shame. It was to serve as a reminder that they were "living still in the slavery which brave men died rather than endure."[53] His criticism extended to the policies of the Free State government which he believed was the cause for the mass emigration of young people from the state. His incendiary speech was typical of Ryan's speeches in this period. The opening of the monument was mentioned in multiple local and national newspapers all reporting on the content of Ryan's oration.[54]

The choice of Ryan as the guest of honor was in itself a political act and indicates that even among communities in Nenagh who were commemorating the very same people, the treaty split was manifesting in the public space. Ryan did not speak of tolerance or reconciliation in the same vein as Fr. O'Halloran, but gave voice to a more radical republican identity which was finding expression during this period through the establishment and growth of the Fianna Fáil party, the Republican Party, which went on to secure electoral victory the following year in the 1932 general election.

Discussion

The monuments in Nenagh and the controversies, or lack thereof, that surrounded them give an indication to the identities wished to be expressed by local communities and groups, or at least by the most dominant communities and groups in the area. It is clear from all three monuments that the people of Nenagh, through committees and local representatives, took a proactive role in shaping their public space, and in engaging with public history practices in monumental form. It is evident that the life of a monument is not static; they are public expressions of collective identity, which is fluid and can undergo huge transformations within a short space of time. They represent the remembrance of past events or people of perceived significance.

The focus in all communities throughout this period was on remembrance. This is a theme that can be seen throughout Europe in the aftermath of the First World War, and the Irish Free State was no different. In Nenagh, the focus was not on the dead of the war, but on those who had died in the fight for Irish freedom.

The monuments erected in Nenagh are indicative of a community of different ideologies and identities. Perhaps most revealing in the analysis of all three monuments is the debate among the Nenagh UDC on the decision not to grant public space to the monument of the First World War. The acceptance of the desire to honor the dead conflicted with an increasing rejection in the Free State of the ceremonies associated with the erection of monuments to or commemorations of the war and the Union Jack flags, poppies and renditions of "God Save The King" that accompanied it.[55] These suspicions were not entirely unfounded, as tension about the pro-British triumphalism surrounding commemorations of the war increased throughout the 1920s and in November 1930 Chief Superintendent David Neligan complained on behalf of the Garda Síochána (the police keeping force of the Irish Free State and the present-day state of Ireland) that the Armistice Day parade was "a definite Imperialistic display, and not a commemoration to the war dead."[56] These tensions were even reflected in national government, with Minister for Justice Kevin O'Higgins opposed to the proposed location for a Memorial Park to the First World War on the grounds of its proximity to the seat of government; "This state," he argued, "has particular origins, and particular roots, and we should not suggest either to ourselves or to people coming here amongst us that it has any other roots."[57] The Nenagh UDC agreed to decline the request to grant either a public space or the moral support that was sought for this monument, disassociating themselves with the narrative of the fallen soldiers.[58]

What is notable about their action is how this decision was made by a council that included men who had served and lost family in the British Army during the First World War. John Tierney, a councillor on the Nenagh UDC in this period, had himself served in the British Army during the Great War and lost a younger brother, Michael, in action in March 1915.[59] His son Martin died in 1923 after complications from prolonged hunger strike while imprisoned in the Curragh by Free State forces during the Irish Civil War, the same forces his other son, John, joined at the outbreak of civil war.[60] Statistically, Tierney could not have been alone in the community at having connections with what would later seem to be conflicting narratives. Brian Walker notes that "official attitudes were ambivalent but generally tolerant in the 1920s" toward commemoration of the First World War, but public opinion became increasingly opposed to commemorative ceremonies and monuments as the decade progressed into the 1930s.[61] As a result of this increasing disassociation, the narrative of the Irishman who enlisted in the British Army was not given the public space for consideration and expression in the Irish Free State. We cannot presume to understand what, if any, effect this rejection of narrative had on individuals within the community. The rejection of this narrative starkly contrasts with the more widely accepted and projected nationalist and republican identities in the Irish Free State and highlights the tensions playing out within communities for control of the collective identity.

Cecile Sachs Olsen observed that creations in an urban space do not necessarily exist primarily to create communal agreement.[62] These monuments or statues could be erected to reaffirm the supremacy of one community in a divided society and to belittle, intimidate or erase the identity of other communities present. In the case of Nenagh, the variety of communities expressing themselves in the public space in such quick succession indicates that they each sought recognition and a display of authority within their sphere. Like the prospectors in the Californian gold rush of the nineteenth century, communities competed to stake their claim on a visual presence for their identity. The public space was a commodity which they all sought to exert ownership over. In less than a decade, the urban landscape of the town had been altered in light of the changing political situation to reflect the local community. These collective identities had greater freedom here than in Dublin, where they were expressed through state-led statutory and subversive destruction of symbols of imperialism.[63]

While these case studies of narratives and counter-narratives reveal an analysis of the evolution of identities in this period in areas outside of Dublin and allow for a nuanced and detailed understanding of the complexities of identity expression during this period, they also offer a deeper understanding of these publics and societies. They offer us a glimpse into what the new citizens of the Irish Free State sought to define themselves by and how they attempted to shape the narrative of the story of this period in their own public space. The hope epitomized in the Denis Carey Memorial hints at another future that might have been, that was possible at a point in time. The deterioration of this hope of reconciliation and the rejection of imperialist, unionist identities in the new, proud Irish Free State is evident in the attitudes of the Nenagh UDC in refusing a site or support for a monument to the Great War. Finally, the erection of the North Tipperary Republican Monument in 1931, in the most prominent position of all three, indicated a strong republican community in the area in ideology if not in physical strength. The remainder of the decade saw no further monuments erected, but the commemorative events and the spectacles that accompanied them demonstrate that the identities expressed in this period were solidified and performed in the public space through intense ritualization and displays of devotion.

Conclusion

Globally, monuments continue to play a role in the performance of identities, from Nenagh to Nanjing. They provoke debate and controversy, and publics in 2021 are as concerned with the identity or message projected through a monument as much as those in 1922, 1928 or 1931 were. While people are temporary, a monument offers a sense of permanency, of certain remembrance. Through the erection of monuments, a community attempts to exert control over how the story will be remembered and re-told. While the monuments themselves remain as they were, the society around them is constantly evolving and what was once revered runs the risk of being rejected. Through the alteration, removal or destruction of these monuments, we are reminded that the publics in the present are as much receptors and effectors of their collective social identities as the publics who campaigned, fundraised, lobbied and erected them.

Notes

1 This decade spans roughly from the signing of the Ulster Solemn League and Covenant in 1912 to the end of the Irish Civil War in 1923 and is currently being commemorated as part of the Decade of Centenaries program.
2 Ian McBride, "Memory and National Identity in Modern Ireland," in *History and Memory in Modern Ireland*, ed. Ian McBride (Cambridge: Cambridge University Press, 2001), 30.
3 Thomas Cauvin, "The Rise of Public History: An International Perspective," *Historia Critica* 68 (2018): 3–26.
4 Anne Dolan, *Commemorating the Irish Civil War: History and Memory, 1923–2000* (Cambridge: Cambridge University Press, 2003); Yvonne Whelan, *Reinventing Modern Dublin: Streetscape, Iconography and the Politics of Identity* (Dublin: University College Dublin Press, 2003).
5 McBride, "Memory and National Identity," 6.
6 John Dorney, *The Civil War in Dublin: The Fight for the Irish Capital 1922–1924* (Dublin: Merrion Press 2017).
7 "Unveiling of Denis Carey Memorial," *Nenagh News and Tipperary Vindicator*, July 1, 1922. The press analyzed in this chapter is accessible at Irish Newspaper Archive, accessed March 5, 2021, https://www.irishnewsarchive.com.
8 "The Gaelic League Annual Report," 1894, in *The Handbook of the Irish Revival*, ed. Declan Kiberd and Patrick J. Mathews (Notre Dame: University of Notre Dame Press, 2015), 88–89.
9 "Unveiling of Denis Carey Memorial," *Nenagh News and Tipperary Vindicator*, July 1, 1922.
10 "The Dromineer Outrage," *The Nenagh Guardian*, August 5, 1922.
11 CO 762/137/6, The National Archives, Dublin 2.
12 The other monument erected at Knigh Cross, Tipperary, is to the memory of Thomas and John O'Brien, also members of the Nenagh Literary Institute, who were bayoneted by British Forces on November 5, 1920, see Sean Hogan, *The Black and Tans in North Tipperary* (Dublin: Untold Stories, 2013), 277.
13 Brian M. Walker, *Irish History Matters: Politics, Identity and Commemoration* (Dublin: The History Press Ireland, 2019).
14 "Unveiling of Denis Carey Memorial," *Nenagh News and Tipperary Vindicator*, July 1, 1922.

15 William E. Vaughan and André J. Fitzpatrick, *Irish Historical Statistics: Population 1821–1971* (Dublin: Royal Irish Academy, 1978), 67.
16 Benedict Anderson, *Imagined Communities: Reflections on the Origins and Spread of Nationalism* (London: Verso, 1983), 6.
17 Anthony Smith, *National Identity* (London: Penguin Books, 1991).
18 Guy Beiner, *Forgetful Remembrance: Social Forgetting and a Vernacular Historiography of a Rebellion in Ulster* (Oxford: Oxford University Press, 2018).
19 "Remembrance Day in Nenagh—Memorial Unveiled," *The Nenagh Guardian*, November 17, 1928.
20 "Cross Unveiled at Nenagh," *Cork Examiner*, November 12, 1928.
21 "Nenagh War Memorial," *The Nenagh Guardian*, April 20, 1929.
22 Gerard Dooley, *Nenagh 1914–21*, 28–29.
23 "Remembrance Day in Nenagh."
24 Dooley, *Nenagh 1914–21*, 30–32.
25 James Gleeson from Cloughjordan said: "The old Lord Dunalley or the present Lord Dunalley's father is said to have been a very cruel landlord and would not give his tenants permission to keep as much as a goat or kid in the house and when they had a big fire down he ordered them to have it put out, and the people were often perished." Recorded by Josie Gleeson in 1938 as part of the Schools' Folklore Project. UCD National Folklore Collection, The Schools' Collection, Volume 0533, Dublin 4, 157.
26 "Great War Victims," *The Nenagh Guardian*, May 12, 1928.
27 "Memorial for Nenagh—Application for Site Refused," *The Nenagh Guardian*, May 5, 1928.
28 Ibid.
29 "Two Memorials," *The Nationalist*, May 2, 1928.
30 "Memorial for Nenagh."
31 Lines written by Irish nationalist soldier Tom Kettle in his poem "To My Daughter Betty," in which he describes his motivations for enlisting in the British Army as being linked to his Catholic faith.
32 "Two Memorials," *The Nationalist*, May 2, 1928.
33 Henri Lefebvre, *The Production of Space* (New Jersey: Wiley, 1974); Fran Tonkiss, *Space, the City and Social Theory: Social Relations and Urban Forms* (Cambridge: Polity, 2015).
34 Tonkiss, *Space, the City and Social Theory*, 63.
35 Brian Hanley, *The IRA, 1926–36* (Dublin: Four Courts Press, 2002), 14, 50.
36 Ibid., 16.
37 "North Tipperary Republican Memorial Unveiling Ceremony at Nenagh," *The Nenagh Guardian*, August 29, 1931.
38 Dolan, *Commemorating the Irish Civil War*, 123.
39 Minutes of Proceedings of Monthly Meeting of the Nenagh Urban District Council, June 3, 1925, Nenagh Urban District Council Minute Book 7, Nenagh Municipal Council Archives, Nenagh, Co. Tipperary.
40 "Memory of the Dead," *The Nenagh Guardian*, June 6, 1925.
41 Ibid.
42 Dolan, *Commemorating the Irish Civil War*, 138.
43 Minutes of Proceedings of Monthly Meeting of the Nenagh Urban District Council, December 30, 1921, Nenagh Urban District Council Minute Book 7, Nenagh Municipal Council Archives, Nenagh, Co. Tipperary.
44 "How the People Voted," *Freeman's Journal*, June 28, 1922.
45 In his interview given to the Bureau of Military History, Pádraig Ó Catháin estimated that approximately half of the Carlow Brigade remained neutral in the Anglo-Irish Treaty split. Himself, he admits to not being for the treaty but at the same time not participating in the civil war; Bureau of Military History, BMH.WS1572 – Pádraig Ó Catháin, https://www.militaryarchives.ie/collections/

online-collections/bureau-of-military-history-1913-1921/.com. This is corrobo-
rated by Nan Nolan's account in which she remembers how many who did not
want the Treaty would not take sides in the conflict, suggesting an understandable desire to return to normality; ibid., BMH.WS1747 – Nan Nolan.
46 Gavin Foster, *The Irish Civil War and Society: Politics, Class and Society* (London: Palgrave Macmillan, 2015), 172.
47 Nenagh Urban District Council Minute Book 7, Nenagh Municipal Council
Archives, Nenagh, Co. Tipperary.
48 Fearghal McGarry, *Frank Ryan* (Dublin: UCD Press, 2010), 13.
49 McGarry, *Frank Ryan*, 16–17.
50 "Arrest Leads to Street Scene—Mr. Frank Ryan Again Taken into Custody,"
The Irish Press, December 9, 1931.
51 McGarry, *Frank Ryan*, 18.
52 "North Tipp Republican Memorial," *The Nenagh Guardian*, August 29, 1931.
53 Ibid.
54 "Nenagh Ceremony," *The Evening Herald*, August 24, 1931; "Unveiled," *Irish
Independent*, August 24, 1931; "Memory of Irish Republicans," *Donegal Democrat*, August 29, 1931.
55 Hanley, *The IRA, 1926–36*, 71–72.
56 Correspondence from Chief Supt David Neligan to Secretary, Dept of Justice,
November 11, 1930, DJ 8/684, The National Archives, Dublin 2.
57 "Private Business – Merrion Square (Dublin) Bill, 1927. Seanad Resolution,"
Dáil Éireann Debate–Tuesday 29 March 1927, vol. 19, no. 5, https://www.
oireachtas.ie/en/debates.
58 "Great War Victims," *The Nationalist*, May 12, 1928.
59 Michael's death recorded in Tom and Ruth Burnell, *The Tipperary War Dead*
(Dublin: Nonsuch Publishing, 2008), 328.
60 "Shooting in Nenagh," *Nenagh News*, August 12, 1922.
61 Walker, *Irish History Matters*, 83.
62 Cecile Sachs Olsen, "Urban Space and the Politics of Socially Engaged Art,"
Progress in Human Geography 43, no. 6 (December 2019): 985–1000.
63 Whelan, *Reinventing Modern Dublin*, 159.

Bibliography

Anderson, Benedict. *Imagined Communities: Reflections on the Origins and Spread
of Nationalism*. London: Verso, 1983.
Beiner, Guy. *Forgetful Remembrance: Social Forgetting and a Vernacular Historiog-
raphy of a Rebellion in Ulster*. Oxford: Oxford University Press, 2018.
Burnell, Tom, and Ruth Burnell. *The Tipperary War Dead: A History of the Casual-
ties of the First World War*. Dublin: Nonsuch Publishing, 2008.
Cauvin, Thomas. "The Rise of Public History: An International Perspective." *His-
toria Critica* 68 (2018): 3–26.
Dolan, Anne. *Commemorating the Irish Civil War: History and Memory, 1923–2000*.
Cambridge: Cambridge University Press, 2003.
Dooley, Gerard. *Nenagh, 1914–21: Years of Crises*. Dublin: Four Courts Press, 2015.
Dorney, John. *The Civil War in Dublin: The fight for the Irish Capital 1922–1924*.
Dublin: Merrion Press, 2017.
Foster, Gavin M. *The Irish Civil War and Society: Politics, Class and Society*. Lon-
don: Palgrave Macmillan, 2015.
Hanley, Brian. *The IRA, 1926–36*. Dublin: Four Courts Press, 2002.
Hogan, Sean. *The Black and Tans in North Tipperary*. Dublin: Untold Stories, 2013.

Kiberd, Declan, and Patrick J. Mathews, eds. *The Handbook of the Irish Revival.* Notre Dame: University of Notre Dame Press, 2015.

Lefebvre, Henri. *The Production of Space.* Hoboken: Wiley, 1974.

McBride, Ian, ed. *History and Memory in Modern Ireland.* Cambridge: Cambridge University Press, 2001.

McGarry, Fearghal. *Frank Ryan.* Dublin: UCD Press, 2010.

Sachs Olsen, Cecile. "Urban Space and the Politics of Socially Engaged Art." *Progress in Human Geography* 43, no. 6 (December 2019): 985–1000.

Smith, Anthony. *National Identity.* London: Penguin Books, 1991.

Tonkiss, Fran. *Space, the City and Social Theory: Social Relations and Urban Forms.* Cambridge: Polity, 2015.

Vaughan, William Edward, and André Jude Fitzpatrick, eds. *Irish Historical Statistics: Population 1821–1971.* Dublin: Royal Irish Academy, 1978.

Walker, Brian M. *Irish History Matters: Politics, Identity and Commemoration.* Dublin: The History Press Ireland, 2019.

Whelan, Yvonne. *Reinventing Modern Dublin: Streetscape, Iconography and the Politics of Identity.* Dublin: University College Dublin Press, 2003.

Press

Cork Examiner, November 12, 1928.

Donegal Democrat, August 29, 1931.

Freeman's Journal, June 28, 1922.

Irish Independent, August 24, 1931.

Nenagh News and Tipperary Vindicator, July 1, 1922.

Nenagh News, August 12, 1922.

The Evening Herald, August 24, 1931.

The Irish Press, December 9, 1931.

The Nationalist, May 2, 1928; May 12, 1928.

The Nenagh Guardian, August 5, 1922; June 6, 1925; November 17, 1928; April 20, 1929; May 5, 1928; May 12, 1928; August 29, 1931.

Archives

Bureau of Military History, Military Archives. Accessed March 5, 2021. https://www.militaryarchives.ie/collections/online-collections/bureau-of-military-history-1913-1921.

CO 762/137/6 and DJ 8/684. National Archives of Ireland. Dublin 2.

Dáil Éireann Debates. Accessed March 5, 2021. https://www.oireachtas.ie/en/debates

National Folklore Collection, UCD. Volume 0533. Dublin 4.

Nenagh Urban District Council Minute Book 7. Nenagh Municipal Council Archives, Nenagh, Co. Tipperary.

9

THE ROLE OF DISTINCT PUBLICS IN FRAMING AND RE-FRAMING THE IMAGES OF HISTORICAL FIGURES. A STUDY ON THE PUBLICS REMEMBERING EDITH STEIN

Ewa Woźniak-Wawrzyniak

Edith Stein's Autobiography and Her Biographies

Edith Stein—a German citizen from a Jewish family of Breslau; a nun and a philosopher; a Holocaust victim and a Catholic saint—remains a figure central to multiple communities. This chapter draws fundamentally on three texts biographic in nature. The first is Edith Stein's autobiography,

FIGURE 9.1 Edith Stein Stumbling Stone in Cologne, Germany, © asthenop, public domain.

Life in a Jewish Family: Edith Stein, completed immediately before she joined the Carmelite Order in 1933.[1] At the time, this was Edith Stein's last opportunity to address the public, because by then she had been barred, by the Third Reich's anti-Semitic policies, from lecturing, teaching in school settings and publishing her work. Therefore, one of her spiritual mentors suggested that she describe a typical Jewish family, to rebut the decade's false propaganda besmearing the Jewish race. Stein agreed. She penned a family history, starting with that of her great-grandparents and ending with a joyous memory of receiving her doctoral degree in 1916. Her narrative also contains selected information about events up to 1920. Although Stein had intended to complete the book, she initially failed to do so. Later, she added sections about her entry into the Carmelite Order in Cologne. This autobiographical narrative is written ex post, in retrospect and as such susceptible to distortions caused by the extended time perspective and the re-vision of events through the lens of subsequent developments.[2] The surviving members of Stein's family attempted to offer corrections in the years that followed.

The second source is the first official biography of Stein, authored by Sister Teresia Renata Posselt, titled *Edith Stein: The Life of a Philosopher and Carmelite*, first published in 1948.[3] Posselt, a fellow nun of Stein's, wrote the biographical sketch about Stein at the request of the authorities of the Carmelite Order in the Dutch city of Echt. Posselt used Stein's autobiographical work cited supra, Stein's correspondence as well as recollections of persons who had known Stein. She also gathered information about the Stein sisters' journey to the German Nazi concentration camp Auschwitz-Birkenau; and she undertook to reconstruct the last hours of their lives, prior to their death in a gas chamber. In effect, the last pages of this work are fiction, aiming to somehow "complete" the biography of Edith Stein. This biography has been widely popular and repeatedly re-published, despite numerous confirmed errors and over-readings of selected themes of Stein's life.

The third source is Susanne Batzdorff's *Aunt Edith: The Jewish Heritage of a Catholic Saint*.[4] Batzdorff is Stein's niece, who paints Stein's persona against the background of the same family which Stein herself had critically depicted in great detail. She thereby takes to task both Stein's autobiography and her first biography. Speaking for all members of the extensive Stein clan, Batzdorff describes her aunt as a full-blooded human being, countering the hagiographic bend of Posselt's writing. She recounts the Jewish history in Breslau, shares family stories and memorializes additional Steins who perished in the Holocaust. She also comments on the inter-faith and international discourse about Stein which originated in the 1960s and inspired her beatification. Lastly, she reports from Stein's beatification process and ceremonies (of 1987) and her canonization (of 1998).

These three works have shaped the global memory about Edith Stein. Additional important texts include the sermons of Pope John Paul II given during Stein's beatification and canonization ceremonies that can be treated as de facto statements of the Catholic Church's official position regarding this saint, a position impacting the multi-million Catholic community all over the globe. While analyzing Stein's autobiography, I also rely on the published volumes of her correspondence.[5]

The Life of Edith Stein

Edith Stein was born on October 12, 1891, in Breslau, as daughter of Auguste and Siegfried Stein, who were Orthodox Jewish. Her parents had previously lived in Gleiwitz and Lublinitz and were lumber traders. In Breslau, Edith's mother, Auguste, took over the business after her husband's passing in 1893. Due to the mother's business engagements, the older daughters took care of the younger children. Edith had six siblings, but was particularly attached to her younger sister Erna. Until age 15, Edith studied at Victoria School in Breslau, but left in 1906 to move to Hamburg, to help the older sister Elsa with her children. At that time, Edith abandoned Orthodox Jewish religious practices, in part due to Elsa's own religious indifference and to the weakened observance of Jewish traditions by the Stein siblings at home. Edith's mother remained the sole person among the Steins deeply engaged in Orthodox Jewish life.

In 1911, Edith Stein began her studies at Breslau University. She chose to focus on the German language, history and philosophy. She also attended lectures in psychology given by William Stern. In 1913, after philosophy became her main focus, Stein transferred to Gottingen University, where she joined the philosophy seminars of Edmund Husserl, the founder of phenomenology. Gathered around Husserl was a circle of thinkers who would build on his contributions. In 1914, World War I interrupted Stein's studies with Husserl. She spent the war years as a Red Cross nurse in Moravian Hranice; then as a teacher in her own alma mater Victoria School. At that time, she was also working on her doctoral dissertation titled *On the Problem of Empathy*, which Stein defended *summa cum laude* in 1916.

Stein spent the following years in Breslau, conducting her own seminar in phenomenology and on the concept of empathy. At that time, Stein's interest in Catholicism increased, to such a point that in 1920 she experienced a spiritual epiphany after reading the biography of Saint Teresa of Avila. Stein spent two years preparing to receive baptism and confirmation. In 1923, already a Catholic, she gave up philosophy and accepted the position of a teacher at the St. Magdalen School in Speyer, which was run by the Dominican order. For the next ten years, she taught there, while also studying the work of St. Thomas Aquinas and intensely corresponding with Husserl.

After leaving her teaching position in Speyer, Stein again devoted herself to philosophy. She also translated Aquinas' writings titled *De veritate* into German. Starting in 1933, the Third Reich started removing Jews from all public offices and institutions. Stein too was forced to resign from her position at the Institute of Scientific Pedagogy of Münster, but after taking her first steps to be accepted to the Carmelite nun's order in Cologne. Persuaded by her spiritual mentor, she then began to write her family history. She also wrote a letter to Pope Pius XI, in which she asked him to voice protest against the worsening situation of the Jews in Germany.

Upon entering the convent of Carmelite Sisters, during her 1934 veiling ceremony, Edith Stein took the name Teresa Benedicta of the Cross. She made her eternal vows four years later. Stein's mother Auguste died in 1936. After Auguste's death, Edith's sister Rosa was also baptized, after secretly practicing Catholic rites for some time.

As dangers from the Nazi regime multiplied, in 1938, the convent's authorities decided to move the sisters from Cologne to the Dutch city of Echt. In Echt, Edith Stein wrote her final work, *The Science of the Cross.* Four years later, Dutch bishops issued a pastoral letter opposing deportations of Dutch Jews to the German Nazi concentration camps. In revenge, the Nazis performed around 700 arrests of Jews who had converted to Christianity. A safe hiding place was not timely found for Edith and Rosa, so they too were arrested on August 2, 1942. After brief stays in transitional camps, the sisters were transported to Auschwitz-Birkenau, where they died in a gas chamber, most likely on August 9, 1942.

The Publics

In attempting to identify the communities that shaped the image of Edith Stein in global public memory and culture, the following questions can be asked: what groups was Edith Stein connected to in her lifetime? After her death, who set out to advance awareness of her figure and who strove to show that her life could be a source of inspiration? What groups engaged in discourse about this figure? What groups accepted the values Edith Stein espoused as guides for action?

Edith Stein self-defined during her lifetime, and her self-definition allows for easier identification of some of the groups invested in her legacy. For example, in a short bio attached to her doctoral dissertation, Stein introduces herself as follows: "I was born in Breslau on October 12, 1891. I am a Prussian citizen and a Jew."[6] She is therefore a Breslauer (and a Silesian), a German/Prussian and a Jew. And these three communities—the people of Wrocław (formerly Breslau), the Germans and the Jews—all commemorate her figure today. The subsequent changes in Stein's life—converting to Catholicism and entering a Carmelite Order—identify another invested group: members of the Roman Catholic faith.

The three communities—or publics—so identified turn out to have broad boundaries. Among members of the Catholic faith are both ethnic Germans and Poles; Carmelite brothers and sisters and lay Catholics. Jews include both Israelis and members of the global Jewish diaspora, and also Jewish persons who converted to other faiths. Among the people of Wrocław are also afficionados of Silesia's German history, such as those from The House of Edith Stein museum in Lubliniec (formerly Lublinitz) and inhabitants of the town of Gliwice (formerly Gleiwitz), where the Stein family once resided.

We observe that certain groups treated Stein like a saint: a model of virtues and a symbol of values. Other groups strove to commemorate thoughts about Stein in the minds and memories of subsequent generations and undertook the labor of continually reminding those generations about the vicissitudes of her life. Others still treat the facts of Stein's life and sainthood as interesting "information" to be shared with the multitudes.[7]

The Catholics: Canonization

Chronologically, the first steps toward commemorating Edith Stein's legacy were efforts to establish what fate Stein and her sister met after their arrest in 1942. The sisters were taken from the monastery in Echt. After no news of their fate reached family members over a prolonged time, the family initiated an investigation. In 1945, Herman van Breda, OFM, Director of the Husserl-Archive, initiated steps to locate the manuscripts of Stein's works, taken by her fellow sisters during their evacuation from Echt. After the manuscripts were found in Herkenbosch, work began on publication, which occurred in 1950.[8] The editing and preparation for the printing press were done by Lucie Gelber, the archivist from Husserl-Archive, and by Barefoot Carmeline monk Romeaus Leuven.

The search for Edith and Rosa lasted almost a decade and officially ended in 1951, when the Red Cross confirmed what The Dutch State Newsletter had reported about the deaths of women in Auschwitz-Birkenau on August 9, 1942. During that time, the first biographies of Stein were being developed. In 1946, after receiving numerous inquiries about Stein's fate, the Carmelite Order published a brief biographical sketch of which 100,000 copies were distributed. This caused another inflow of information from persons who concluded that Stein was noteworthy, memorable, a model of virtues. An effort to collect incoming recollections about Stein was initiated, to yield inter alia the account of one Dr. Lenig, the lone survivor of a stay at the transitional camp in Amersfoort, where Stein was also detained. Moreover, in 1947, a short bio was published in the Vatican's journal *L'Osservatore Romano*. Although it misstated the date of Stein's death, it was reprinted by Catholic publications around the world.[9]

Facing the growing interest in Stein's philosophical and spiritual legacy, the Carmelite Order elected to publish the first brief biography of its sister. The collection of letters and memoirs, edited by Sister Teresia Renata Posselt in 1948, caused an influx of more recollections from persons who had met the Stein sisters on their way to the concentration camp. One contribution of this book is that, based on the submitted reports and recollections, it reconstructs the route by which the Stein sisters traveled to the concentration camp and identifies their stopover camps, such as Amersfoort and Westerbork.

Notably, Sister Posselt's biography for years was the sole source of information about Stein accessible to Catholic readers. This biography is designed to enhance and strengthen the veneration cult of Edith Stein, with an eye to her imminent beatification. Consistent with this goal, the author first liberally cites Stein's autobiographical *Life in a Jewish Family*; then addresses the submitted testimonials; then nearly reverses the meaning of Stein's words in her autobiography by casting her life's events as steps toward conversion to Catholicism, joining a convent, and martyrdom in a concentration camp. Such an interpretation, by a person steeped in Catholic spirituality and surveying the world from its perspective, has caused distortions in the picture of Stein's life. This is especially visible in the depiction of the Stein family and their home—Jewish through and through—and of the family's reaction to Stein's conversion. As described by Sister Posselt, the Steins are intolerant people with a rigidly orthodox faith, from which Stein's devotional search would sprout.[10]

Stein's life is here presented in the complex, pathos-laden language of theologians. The result is an image of a saint, one who—in the discourse of Catholic spirituality—incorporates such high virtues as wisdom, a love of truth, humility and love for fellow brethren. The same sanctification effect arises from the beatification and canonization processes. The German Catholic community set out to initiate and implement the veneration of Edith Stein. Subsequent biographical studies and published volumes would only strengthen the claim of Stein's sainthood, as it was being embraced by more and more Catholics around the world. Fascinated with the legacy of their compatriot, German Catholics organized their activism around several institutions, of which the central one is the Edith Stein Archive (Edith-Stein-Archiv zu Köln) attached to the Carmelite convent of Mary of Peace in Cologne. In the Dominican convent in Speyer, Stein's former room has been transformed into a museum. Since 1944, the German Edith Stein Society is also associated with the convent. The Society integrates smaller groups interested in Stein. Additional institutions devoted to Stein as a German saint are located in Lambrecht and Tübingen.

Preparations for Stein's beatification and canonization crucially strengthened her worship and veneration. But the standard process of presenting Stein as a candidate to be elevated to the Catholic altars took some unexpected turns when an international controversy erupted about the circumstances of her death. Stein was the first Jewish individual to be canonized based on the heroic nature of her virtues, but she could not meet certain required criteria. A candidate for beatification must have proof of a miracle performed through his/her intercession, a grave to which faithful pilgrims could travel and relics. As someone who perished in a concentration camp, Edith Stein had no grave and left no relics, as her personal effects were lost in a fire in the Echt monastery. To avoid a delay in the beatification process, in 1983, the German bishops petitioned Pope John Paul II to declare Stein's death a martyrdom: motivated by the Nazi's vengeance for the Dutch bishops' letter of July 27, 1942, and thus martyrdom for Stein's Catholic faith and the Church. The Pope accepted this solution and in 1984 initiated the beatification process, causing unease in Jewish communities worldwide.[11] The fundamental question was whether Edith Stein died because of her Jewish blood or because of her Catholic faith. According to the Jews, Stein was one of many millions of Holocaust victims, so emphasizing her uniqueness tarnished the memory of the remaining men and women who perished in concentration camps. Challenged was also the Catholics' failure to address its Church's activities during the Nazi regime and World War II. But despite protests against elevating Stein to the level of martyrdom, beatification proceeded and was finalized in 1987. Over a decade later, Stein was canonized and another year later she was pronounced a patron of Europe, alongside Saint Bridget of Sweden and Saint Catherine of Siena.

Pope John Paul II gave homilies during both the beatification and the canonization ceremonies. Aware of the resentment and doubts which the Jews felt at the Catholics' controversial interpretation of Stein's death, he labored to reconcile the discrepant interpretations. He stated that Stein had died as a daughter of her people, to sacrifice herself for them in the name of her chosen faith. He emphasized that Stein had felt as a Jew even after converting, citing her admission that she felt connected with Jesus not only spiritually, but also by ties of blood. This reconciliation effort was visible in the canonization homily, where John Paul II affirmed that the Stein sisters had been deported to Auschwitz-Birkenau precisely because they were Jewish. Notably, the Pope, although providing clarifying explanation, resorted to a language steeped in theological thought. He imparts to Stein's figure numerous Christian, biblical characteristics, thereby strengthening a mythical image of Edith Stein—a German philosopher of Jewish extraction who experienced the grace of Catholic conversion.[12] The most controversial matter is thus Edith Stein's conversion, which Catholics cast as the event completing and crowning Stein's life. The Pope's words about this new saint solidified this perception and formalized her public veneration, which previously had been shaped mostly by German Catholics.[13]

The Jews: Commemoration

Those surviving members of the Stein family (they are: sister Erna Biberstein and her family; brother Arno Stein and his family; sister Elsa Gordon with her family; and nephew Gerhard Stein), who had managed to emigrate from Breslau initiated searches for their relatives immediately after the war ended. The news of Edith's and Rosa's arrest reached their sister Erna Biberstein only in 1945 and came from the Carmelite Sisters of Echt. By that time, the truth about the cruelties of the Nazi German concentration camps was becoming more widely known. The Bibersteins slowly lost hope that they could find their relatives. On March 13, 1947, the Jewish Council of Rotterdam officially announced that no living person returned from the contingent in which Edith and Rosa had been transported.

In the year that followed, Erna Biberstein assisted the archivists at the Husserl-Archive and the Carmelite Order by sending, from the United States, copies of documents, photographs and information useful in publishing Stein's further works. She was also required to take position on legal matters related to her sister's testament, including the clause forbidding the publication of Stein's autobiography in her siblings' lifetimes. Ultimately, *Life in a Jewish Family: Edith Stein* was published in 1965, forcing Stein's relatives to face Stein's highly critical and painfully honest account, which evoked a whole range of emotions. Erna Biberstein agreed to publish an abridged version of the work. With other family members, she excluded the most controversial sections discussing family secrets. A complete version of the book appeared in 1985.

Familiarity with Edith Stein's autobiography forced the Stein family to revise their relationship with the famed relative. Suzanne Batzdorff remembers that her mother Erna extensively corresponded about Stein and that the surviving Steins—in memoirs written for their children, essays and newspaper articles—corrected multiple claims made in Stein's autobiography.[14] Another time difficult for the Stein family was Edith's beatification, but especially the Catholic interpretation of her death as Stein's martyrdom for the Catholic faith and Church. Many relatives had mixed feelings and disagreements. Among others, Ernst Ludwig Biberstein concluded that Edith Stein never wished or elected to die and always hoped to be saved.[15]

Casting Stein's death as martyrdom in the name of her Catholic faith and the Catholic Church stirred indignation among the Jewish communities. The Catholic Church, after the completion of the Second Vatican Council in 1965, by beatifying Stein wished to accomplish its ecumenical goals of rapprochement with members of the Judaic faith. But from the Jewish perspective, the beatification was a glaring exploitation and co-option of the tragedy that had befallen millions of people of Jewish blood. One important question in the Stein controversy became: how is the Holocaust interpreted? How is it discussed in writing, and how is it memorialized? Of special importance turned out to be the same challenges which would preoccupy historians in the 1980s: of giving up the elaborately metaphorical descriptive style in favor of the most spare, honest narrative about the Annihilation, while striving to eliminate bias. After all, Edith Stein was a Holocaust victim, just as her sisters and brother, a niece and some six million of other Jewish people. Stein's elevation to Catholic altars drew variant Jewish reactions.

For some, including Gerhard Stein, the son of Edith's oldest brother, she could be the universal symbol of the Jewish race annihilated in the Holocaust. Others—including Suzanne Batzdorff—doubted that a person who renounced Judaism and accepted Catholicism could be such a symbol.[16] Stein's beatification and canonization were met with protests. Immediately prior to the beatification, Pope John Paul II received representatives from Jewish communities who voiced their concerns about beatifying Stein. In 1998, Efraim Zuroff, head of the Simon Wiesenthal Center, stated that canonization was a "very public slap in the face of the Jewish community," and that "the pope is sending an extremely negative message to the Jewish community, that in the eyes of the Catholic church the best Jews are those that convert to Catholicism."[17] Numerous commentators assert that Edith Stein's elevation to Catholic altars serves to cover up the Catholic Church's passive posture regarding the Jews' extermination in World War II. Batzdorff cites her aunt's (Edith Stein's) notes expressing disappointment at Pius XI's failure to respond to her letter sent in 1933. In that letter, Stein asked Pius XI to publish an encyclical condemning European anti-Semitism. She received no response.[18] Over five decades later, the issue of Catholic responsibility for anti-Semitism has remained unresolved, despite conciliatory gestures on the part of the Catholic Church.

Voices prepared to reflect upon the Jewish legacy of this Catholic saint do emerge. One California newspaper published this opinion piece: "What do we Jews care about Edith Stein? Not much right now."[19] Stein's autobiography can be an informative source for the Jews, likely to deter some assimilated intellectuals from Judaism. In the early decades of the twentieth century, Judaism may have appeared to become only part of history and tradition, progressively ossified, un-inspiring and anti-humanist. It is noteworthy that the author of this opinion piece uses Edith Stein as an opportunity to evaluate the condition of Judaism, both in Stein's time and while he writes. He asks whether Stein would have converted to Catholicism if she had had the opportunity to encounter modern Judaism, which creates space for self-fulfillment of passionate creatives and of women desiring lives not centered on marriage and family. On the other hand, Suzanne Batzdorff concludes that her aunt's figure particularly inspires converts, as illustrated by the work of the Edith Stein Guild, which supports individuals post-conversion and fosters Catholic-Jewish dialogue.[20] She also emphasizes that her aunt rightly inspires ecumenical efforts, because she had demonstrated the capacity to form deep, honest friendships across national and faith divides.

For the Stein family, the process of "grappling" with the figure of the aunt has strengthened their familial ties. After reading the autobiography, the family performed a critical analysis of the work and discovered the importance of their own recollections. Those recollections serve not only to reveal "another side" of the story, but also to present Stein's figure *not* in the pathos-imbued, mythical light preferred by the Catholic Church. The family's task is to do the "labor of reminding" about who Edith Stein had been as a person experienced through direct contact.

We begin to note the many domains in which a historical figure functions in the public sphere. The two groups identified supra both aspire to present Stein in their chosen light: one as a heroic persona, a martyr saint exemplifying their value system; the other as one of millions of nameless victims, murdered only for their blood origins, sanctified by the fact of joining a host of those who perished. In memorializing the Holocaust, the Jews are also memorializing Edith Stein. Her relationship with Judaism can also depict how that faith was perceived by some Jewish intellectuals in the early twentieth century.

The People of Wrocław: Promulgation

In her native city, the awareness and memory of Edith Stein have taken a long time to emerge. Her life story was initially forgotten, as were the stories of other German inhabitants of Breslau. Breslau's sizeable Jewish commune—with its rich history and multi-century tradition—had seized to exist; the city had been emptied of people who would remember Edith Stein, her family and countless others. The radical population exchange, which occurred as a result of Josef Stalin's decree about Breslau's inclusion within Poland's boundaries (to become Wrocław), effected discontinuity and a cultural rupture. Germans and German Jews were replaced by Poles arriving from all parts of the land and the world. The aggressively anti-German policies of the Polish communist authorities hoped to erase every trace of a German past of Wrocław and accomplish "re-polonization."

It is not easy to establish who in Wrocław first became interested in Edith Stein's figure. Sławomir Kowalewski, cofounder of the Edith Stein Society, believes that a biography of Stein, probably the one penned by Sister Tersia Renata Posselt, was brought to Wrocław by Władysław Czapliński, professor of history at the University of Wrocław, in the early 1950s. Polish Catholic press articles began to appear about Stein's Wrocław roots. Interest in Stein as a Wrocław citizen increased after 1962, once the pre-beatification informational process began.

Notably, at that time, first attempts were made to achieve rapprochement between the Poles and the Germans, although rapprochement appeared near-impossible after the events of World War II and the Federal German Republic's failure to recognize Poland's state boundary on the Odra-and-Nysa rivers (established by Stalin). Many German Christians made pilgrimages to the sites of German atrocities in Poland and lobbied internally for reconciliation with Poland and for recognition of its western border.[21]

The Polish initiative was the "Pastoral Letter of the Polish Bishops to their German Brothers" published on November 15, 1965. Its pages summarize several centuries of Polish-German relations, including both the deaths of millions of Poles during World War II and the mass removal of German citizens from newly Polish Silesia.[22] The Letter was penned by Bishop Bolesław Kominek, who would become the Archbishop of Wrocław. His excellent command of German may have further promulgated the memory of Edith Stein in Wrocław. This may have occurred during the informational session held by the Wrocław Club of Catholic Intelligentsia in 1968. The opening Mass was said by Bishop Kominek, with the intention of Stein's imminent beatification. Prominent intellectuals lectured at the session, including Rev. Józef Tischner and Sister Janina Immaculata Adamska, a Carmelite nun from Poznań who later translated Stein's works into Polish.[23]

The only Pole who personally knew Edith Stein was Roman Ingarden, a Polish philosopher, who received his doctorate under Edmund Husserl in 1918 and who corresponded with Stein. He reverently preserved a packet of her letters, especially during World War II. In 1968, at the request of the Krakow Archbishop Karol Wojtyła (future Pope John Paul II), Ingarden gave a lecture titled "About the Philosophical Studies of Edith Stein,"[24] whose text reached Wrocław as well. In 1985, Paweł Taranczewski,[25] a member of the reading public, wrote a letter to *Tygodnik Powszechny* (*The Catholic Weekly*). Strongly impressed by the lecture reprinted in the Catholic monthly journal *Znak* (*Sign*), Taranczewski visited the Steins' home at 38 Nowowiejska Street in Wrocław. He found that the building housed the Training Center of the Cinematography Department of the Ministry of Culture and Art. He inquired about the value of placing a commemorative plaque on the wall of the building, as well as organizing a museum and an archive of mementos of Edith Stein.

A breakthrough in the evolution of Edith Stein's public memory in Wrocław was Karol Wojtyła's elevation to papacy in 1978. Wojtyła had personal interest not only in the biography and spirituality of Stein, but also in her studies in phenomenology. This personal interest manifested as a desire to commemorate her. He considered Stein an individual exceptional in the history of the Jews and Germans, and also the Poles—especially the Poles of Wrocław. During his first pilgrimage to Poland, John Paul II visited the German Nazi concentration camp in Auschwitz-Birkenau. On June 7, 1979, during a homily and a Mass held at the camp, he named two persons who had perished there: Father Maksymilian Kolbe and Sister Teresa Benedicta of the Cross: "...to the world Edith Stein, a philosopher by profession, a brilliant student of Husserl's, who became a luminary of contemporary German philosophy, but who derived from a Jewish family residing in Wrocław..."[26] The homily was reprinted by all major press outlets and Catholic periodicals of more local reach, thereby promulgating the knowledge of Stein's Wrocław roots.

A more lively interest in Stein developed in her hometown in 1987, during her beatification. Only at that time do we observe intentional activism by groups organized around the memory of her life and the values she espoused. One such group coalesced around the parish of Saint Michael the Archangel, whose rector, Father Jerzy Witek, held services and said masses commemorating Edith Stein. The parish is located around the church which Stein herself attended. Stein's house, which stands nearby at Nowowiejska Street, understandably drew the parishioners' interest. In 1989, when grassroots organizations were allowed to register and operate, Father Witek— assisted by the Warsaw historian Sławomir Kowalewski—filed an application to register, in Wrocław, the Association of the Blessed Edith Stein. The parish was approached by a group of students of the University of Wrocław, who wished to register a similar society, and who were informed by the registering authorities that registration efforts had already been initiated.

The two groups offered two distinct perspectives on Edith Stein. The parishioners hoped to promulgate and preserve the Wrocław legacy of Stein, and to present her intellectual accomplishments to the general public. The students hoped to find a figure who represented the unbroken connection between Wrocław's historical past and its current days. They saw Stein as an element of Breslau's German history, not a saint or clergy person. Eventually, the two groups merged and formed The Wrocław Society of Edith Stein.[27] The Society considered Stein as an appropriate patron of institutions promoting Polish-German relations.[28]

The significance given to Stein by Polish-formed institutions impacts the Polish public's understanding of her figure. Emphasized is her ability to form friendships bridging divides, her drive to understand the truth completely and her desire to understand the conduct of other people. The goal of preserving Edith Stein's legacy in Poland goes hand in hand with respect for the historical past of the lands incorporated within the Polish borders after World War II. This may go counter to the earlier effort at "re-polonizing" Wrocław and the "Western and Northern Territories" undertaken by the communist authorities. By imparting significance and meaning to Stein's figure, Polish institutions indirectly endorse that the history of these lands is shared and that both Poles and Germans must bear the burdens of meaningfully, rationally discussing this fact.

The people of Wrocław are uniquely well-positioned to experience and sense a symbolic connection with their compatriot, in such locales meaningful to Stein as her childhood home, the University, the church and the other addresses she lived at. Through and in those locales, Stein becomes familiar, a compatriot who had spent her childhood in the same city, walked the same streets, lived in a house nearby and studied at the same institutions. One might venture to say that such commemoration and promulgation of Stein is one more stage in "domesticating the city," albeit symbolic. It reintegrates such preceding stages as arrival in the ruined city in 1945, its slow re-construction and the setting up of its Polish institutions. After the city's physical space is secured, the time comes to forge a sense of identification with this locale, and nothing helps develop such identification better than engagement with local history.

The Publics' Imprint on the Image of Edith Stein

Studying the processes of remembering Edith Stein reveals that various publics' views of history overlap and that the groups uniquely strive to shape views of history. A discussion about Stein—especially in the context of Catholic-Jewish relations—occasions a recognition of her exceptionality and re-ignites old disagreements. Was the Catholic project of creating a veneration cult of Stein aimed only at honoring her virtues? Or did it seek to attract larger numbers of Jews to the Catholic Church, treating Christianity as a natural complement of Judaism? No simple answer exists. Members of Jewish communities certainly perceived Stein's canonization as the latter. Catholics saw her elevation to their altars as proof that members of their Church—Polish and German—respect Judaism and its people and strive for ecumenical dialogue.

In addressing Stein, the Jews do not form new narratives about her, but rather dialogize with the Catholic one. They see Stein as a doubly lost individual: first upon her conversion to Catholicism (which they consider apostasy) and then again upon her canonization. The Jewish public appears to dynamically react against enshrining Stein within the walls of Catholic mythical thinking. When the Jewish community's understanding of its foundational events, such as the Holocaust, is re-cast in ways disparaging the victims, defensive reactions follow. This is exemplified by interpreting Stein's canonization as an attempt at Christianizing the Holocaust, by casting Catholics as equally persecuted to the Jews. By rejecting the Catholic story of Stein's life, the Jews defend the foundations of their Jewish identity, which Stein apparently rejected. But they honor her as one of millions of Holocaust victims, as well as a noted philosopher. Stein's family contend with a still different picture of Stein. As consecutive generations include people of various faiths, they appreciate their aunt's many friendships with non-Jews. But the family continues to re-interpret Stein's life in an effort to keep alive an authentic memory picture observed by historical witnesses, such as Susanne Batzdorff. At one time, the Steins needed to correct distortions in the widely promulgated picture of Stein, including those regarding the family's religious life or the décor of their home. But their aunt's history still serves them. The making of a family history strengthens their ties and promotes healing, especially for such far-flung people as the Steins.

The people of Wrocław play a significant role in memorializing the figure of Stein. By promulgating information about her, they preserve the history of the German city of Breslau. They help forge a more universal identity of the city, inserting Stein into the canon of figures crucial to the city's both

German and Polish history. They accept Stein as a person well-suited to symbolically oversee the renewal and growth of Polish-German relations.

Lastly, noteworthy is the crucial role of feelings in interpreting the past by the respective publics, feelings understood as a psychological state reflecting one's relationship to events, the surrounding world and oneself. Various societal groups (the nonprofessional ones) invest with feelings selected motifs which allow them to better comprehend history. Edith Stein's figure is thereby emotionally variegated, multifaceted. The Catholic perspective on Stein is joyfully celebratory: her life was fulfilled upon canonization; her suffering so ennobling that she ascended to the Catholic altars. The Jewish perspective taps into the feelings of grief and pain, as experienced by the victims of the Holocaust. It also channels ire, both about Stein's conversion and about its Catholic recasting as glorious. The family history fashioned by the Steins is tinged with feelings of nostalgia, fondness and familiarity, which connect the family more closely to the people of Wrocław who promulgate Stein's memory in their home city. The public of Wrocław also taps into the feelings of familiarity and congeniality.

At first sight, the person and legacy of Edith Stein do not appear to be remarkable. But a closer look at the history of the forming and shaping of her images in the public memories of groups and communities exposes a difficult discourse about one person's significance to various publics, filled with attempts at rapprochement, understanding and agreement, often unresolved and ongoing. It illustrates how a history of an individual person can be interpreted and used by various publics that themselves act as public historians who aim at reaching even wider publics with their interpretations and messages of that person's significance and historical role.

Translated from Polish by Urszula Tempska

Notes

1 Edith Stein, *Aus dem Leben einer jüdischen Familie: das Leben Edith Steins: Kindheit und Jugend* (Louvain: Nauwelaerts; Freiburg: Herder, 1965); for the English edition, see *Life in a Jewish Family: Her Unfinished Autobiographical Account* (Washington: ICS, 1986).
2 Jerzy Maternicki, "Materiały autobiograficzne i ich rola w badaniach historiograficznych," in *Biografistyka we współczesnych badaniach historycznych*, ed. Jolanta Kolbuszewska and Rafał Stobiecki (Łódź: Wydawnictwo Uniwersytetu Łódzkiego, 2017), 71.
3 Teresia Renata Posselt, *Edith Stein Schwester Teresia Benedicta a cruce; Philosophin u. Karmelitin* (Nürnberg: Glock u. Lutz, 1948); for latest English edition, see *Edith Stein: The Life of a Philosopher and Carmelite*, ed. Susanne M. Batzdorff, Josephine Koeppel and John Sullivan (Washington: ICS. 2005).
4 Susanne Batzdorff, *Aunt Edith: The Jewish Heritage of a Catholic Saint* (Springfield: Templegate, 1998).
5 Stein, *Self-Portrait in Letters 1916–1942* (Washington: ICS Publications, 1993).
6 Stein, *On the Problem of Empathy* (Washington: ICS, 1989).

7 On the controversies between Christians and Jews in relation to Edith Stein, see Waltraud Herbstrith, *Never Forget: Christian and Jewish Perspectives on Edith Stein* (Washington: ICS, 1998).
8 Stein's manuscripts were published as *Edith Steins Werke* in the years 1950–2010.
9 Posselt, *Edith Stein: The Life of a Philosopher*, 223–231.
10 Ibid., 3–63.
11 Kenneth L. Woodward, *Making Saints: How the Catholic Church Determines Who Becomes a Saint, Who Doesn't, and Why* (New York: Simon & Schuster, 1990), 138–144.
12 John Paul II, "Homily for Beatification of Edith Stein," May 1, 1987, accessed November 30, 2020, http://www.christianunity.va/content/unitacristiani/en/commissione-per-i-rapporti-religiosi-con-l-ebraismo/atti-commemorativi/pope-john-paul-ii/1987-homily-for-beatification-of-edith-stein.html; John Paul II, "Homily for the Canonization of Edith Stein," August 9, 1998, accessed November 30, 2020, http://www.vatican.va/content/john-paul-ii/en/homilies/1998/documents/hf_jp-ii_hom_11101998_stein.html.
13 John Paul II, "Motu proprio," October 1, 1999, accessed November 30, 2020, http://www.vatican.va/content/john-paul-ii/en/motu_proprio/documents/hf_jp-ii_motu-proprio_01101999_co-patronesses-europe.html.
14 Batzdorff, *Aunt Edith*, 170–175.
15 Ibid., 205.
16 Batzdorff, *Aunt Edith*, 204.
17 J. Correspondent, "Sainthood for Jewish Born Nun Troubles Some Jews," *The Jewish News of Northern California*, October 16, 1998, https://www.jweekly.com/1998/10/16/sainthood-for-jewish-born-nun-troubles-some-jews.
18 Batzdorff, *Aunt Edith*, 198.
19 J. Correspondent, "Jews Can Actually Learn from Edith Stein's Example," *The Jewish News of Northern California*, October 16, 1998, https://www.jweekly.com/1998/10/16/jews-can-actually-learn-from-edith-stein-s-example.
20 Batzdorff, *Aunt Edith*, 208.
21 Jarosław Kłaczkow, "Memorandum Rady Kościoła Ewangelickiego w Niemczech 'Sytuacja wypędzonych a stosunek narodu niemieckiego do jego sąsiadów wschodnich': reakcje w Europie i w Polsce w świetle polskiej dokumentacji," *Dzieje Najnowsze* 38, no. 4 (April 2006): 166.
22 Wojciech Kucharski, "Jak powstało orędzie biskupów polskich do biskupów niemieckich z 18 listopada 1965 roku," *Pamięć i Sprawiedliwość* 34, no. 2 (2019): 504.
23 Józef Puciłowski, "Edyta Stein," *Więź* 122, no. 6 (1968): 135–139.
24 Roman Ingarden, "O badaniach filozoficznych Edyty Stein," in Stein, *O zagadnieniu wczucia* (Cracow: Znak, 1988), appendix.
25 Paweł Taranczewski, "O pamięć Edith Stein. Listy do redakcji," *Tygodnik Powszechny* 39, no. 16 (1985): 6.
26 John Paul II, "Homily in Auschwitz-Birkenau," June 7, 1979, accessed November 30, 2020, http://www.vatican.va/content/john-paul-ii/en/homilies/1979/documents/hf_jp-ii_hom_19790607_polonia-brzezinka.html.
27 Danuta Skraba and Jerzy Witek, "Geneza Towarzystwa im. Edyty Stein we Wrocławiu," *Kwartalnik TES – Pismo Towarzystwa im. Edyty Stein* 25–29, no. 2–3 (2009): 3.
28 Wojciech Hann, "Towarzystwo im. Edyty Stein we Wrocławiu," in *Szukając prawdy. Edyta Stein w kulturze polskiej*, ed. Anita Czarniecka-Stefańska (Wrocław: Wydawnictwo Uniwersytetu Wrocławskiego, 1998), 127–128.

Bibliography

Batzdorff, Susanne. *Aunt Edith: The Jewish Heritage of a Catholic Saint*. Springfield: Templegate, 1998.

Correspondent, J. "Jews Can Actually Learn from Edith Stein's Example." *The Jewish News of Northern California*, October 16, 1998. https://www.jweekly.com/1998/10/16/jews-can-actually-learn-from-edith-stein-s-example.

Correspondent, J. "Sainthood for Jewish Born Nun Troubles Some Jews." *The Jewish News of Northern California*. October 16, 1998. https://www.jweekly.com/1998/10/16/sainthood-for-jewish-born-nun-troubles-some-jews.

Hann, Wojciech. "Towarzystwo im. Edyty Stein we Wrocławiu." In *Szukając prawdy. Edyta Stein w kulturze polskiej*, edited by Anita Czarniecka-Stefańska, 127–130. Wrocław: Wydawnictwo Uniwersytetu Wrocławskiego, 1998.

Herbstrith, Waltraud. *Never Forget: Christian and Jewish Perspectives on Edith Stein*. Washington: ICS, 1998.

Ingarden, Roman. "O badaniach filozoficznych Edyty Stein." In Edyta Stein, *O zagadnieniu wczucia*, appendix. Cracow: Znak, 1988.

John Paul II. "Homily in Auschwitz-Birkenau." June 7, 1979. Accessed November 30, 2020. http://www.vatican.va/content/john-paul-ii/en/homilies/1979/documents/hf_jp-ii_hom_19790607_polonia-brzezinka.html.

John Paul II. "Homily for Beatification of Edith Stein." May 1, 1987. Accessed November 30, 2020. http://www.christianunity.va/content/unitacristiani/en/commissione-per-i-rapporti-religiosi-con-l-ebraismo/atti-commemorativi/pope-john-paul-ii/1987-homily-for-beatification-of-edith-stein.html.

John Paul II. "Homily for the Canonization of Edith Stein." August 9, 1998. Accessed November 30, 2020. http://www.vatican.va/content/john-paul-ii/en/homilies/1998/documents/hf_jp-ii_hom_11101998_stein.html.

John Paul II. "Motu proprio." October 1, 1999. Accessed November 30, 2020. http://www.vatican.va/content/john-paul-ii/en/motu_proprio/documents/hf_jp-ii_motu-proprio_01101999_co-patronesses-europe.html.

Kłaczkow, Jarosław. "Memorandum Rady Kościoła Ewangelickiego w Niemczech 'Sytuacja wypędzonych a stosunek narodu niemieckiego do jego sąsiadów wschodnich': reakcje w Europie i w Polsce w świetle polskiej dokumentacji." *Dzieje Najnowsze* 38, no. 4 (April 2006): 165–178.

Kucharski, Wojciech. "Jak powstało orędzie biskupów polskich do biskupów niemieckich z 18 listopada 1965 roku." *Pamięć i Sprawiedliwość* 34, no. 2 (2019): 502–522.

Maternicki, Jerzy. "Materiały autobiograficzne i ich rola w badaniach historiograficznych." In *Biografistyka we współczesnych badaniach historycznych*, edited by Jolanta Kolbuszewska and Rafał Stobiecki, 69–90. Łódź: Wydawnictwo Uniwersytetu Łódzkiego, 2017.

Posselt, Teresia Renata. *Edith Stein Schwester Teresia Benedicta a Cruce; Philosophin u. Karmelitin*. Nürnberg: Glock u. Lutz, 1948.

Posselt, Teresia Renata. *Edith Stein: The Life of a Philosopher and Carmelite*. Edited by Susanne Batzdorff, Josephine Koeppel, and John Sullivan. Washington: ICS Publications, 2005.

Puciłowski, Józef. "Edyta Stein." *Więź* 122, no. 6 (1968): 135–139.

Skraba, Danuta, and Jerzy Witek. "Geneza Towarzystwa im. Edyty Stein we Wrocławiu." *Kwartalnik TES – Pismo Towarzystwa im. Edyty Stein* 25–29, no. 2–3 (2009): 3.

Stein, Edith. *Aus dem Leben einer jüdischen Familie: das Leben Edith Steins: Kindheit und Jugend.* Louvain: Nauwelaerts; Freiburg: Herder, 1965.

Stein, Edith. *Life in a Jewish Family: Her Unfinished Autobiographical Account.* Washington: ICS, 1986.

Stein, Edith. *On the Problem of Empathy: The Collected Works of Edith Stein.* Washington: ICS, 1989.

Stein, Edith. *Self-Portrait in Letters 1916–1942.* Washington: ICS Publications, 1993.

Taranczewski, Paweł. "O pamięć Edith Stein. Listy do redakcji." *Tygodnik Powszechny* 39, no. 16 (1985): 6.

Woodward, Kenneth L. *Making Saints: How the Catholic Church Determines Who Becomes a Saint, Who Doesn't, and Why.* New York: Simon & Schuster, 1990.

PART III
Digital Publics

10

RESEARCHING THE PUBLIC(S) THROUGH INTERNET READERS' COMMENTS

Case Study of the Cursed Soldiers in Northeastern Poland[1]

Dorota Choińska

The virtual space no longer represents just a fraction or a prosthesis of human life but rather its integral part. As Will Douglas Heaven has written in the context of the 2020 Covid-19 pandemic: "Our internet connection has become an umbilical to the outside world. We now depend on it to do our jobs, to go to school, and to see other people. It is our primary source of entertainment."[2] Someday, a significant part of knowledge about human

FIGURE 10.1 Monument to Cursed Soldiers in Rzeszów, Poland, © Lowdown, public domain.

activity might be accessible almost exclusively through the digital riches. Social media profiles, blogs, e-mails, internet forums, online ads, and streaming platforms might become—if they survive—primary sources for the future historians.

The internet, however, is still a relatively new domain in historical research. Doubtless, it is indispensable for both "classical" and public historians to connect with their audiences and diffuse knowledge. This article, however, explores the online sphere not as a historian's tool for communication but rather as a research field in its own right. I will use an example of a research project based on internet comments in which I examined the memory and commemoration of the anti-communist fighters in post-war Poland.

An online-based study—as any other—has its limitations. First of all, one cannot assume that the behavior exhibited or declared by the users in the virtual sphere truly represents their attitudes in "real" life. The anonymity of the online communities' members also prevented me from identifying them with precise, flesh-and-blood persons. This is why this study focuses on the information and its circulation in the digital world rather than on the offline behaviors of a particular group of people.

Commemoration of the Post-war Resistance in Poland

After 1944, the territory of Poland was controlled by the Soviet Union and the subordinated communist authorities. Marching towards Berlin, the Red Army detained the Polish soldiers who revealed themselves in the fight against the remaining German troops. The NKVD, along with the Polish institutions of the new communist regime, started purges among the underground leaders. The Polish Committee of National Liberation, a new government controlled from Moscow, was established in Lublin on July 22, 1944. It ousted the legitimate Polish representation exiled in London from international recognition.[3]

For many Poles, this situation felt like yet another form of occupation. The Polish government exiled in London dissolved the resistance, headed by the Home Army, as lacking probabilities of success, but some resistance fighters decided to continue the underground struggle. They formed relatively small groups, engaging the local authorities in guerilla warfare in spite of the unfavorable international situation and the overwhelming enemy forces. For many years after the Second World War, the communist apparatus led meticulous actions to decimate the remaining armed opponents. The last one, Józef Franczak, *nom de guerre* "Lalek," was killed in 1963.[4]

Communist propaganda presented the Cursed Soldiers as "forest gangs" and attributed to them the worst qualities of ruthless criminals.[5] When their rebellion was eventually suppressed, they were condemned to oblivion by the communist regime. It was only after the political transformation of 1989 that the interest of scholars and the general public in the post-war anti-communist fighters—dubbed "the Cursed soldiers"—could blossom. However, the long-awaited historical investigation not only uncovered the glorious deeds of the Polish soldiers, but also brought to light the less honorable examples of their activity, somehow confirming the image imposed by the communist propaganda. Among the accusations against the underground fighters were brutal killings of civilians, often representatives of the national minorities, traditionally deemed as unfavorable towards the Polish cause.

The number of commemorative activities concerning the Cursed Soldiers has been steadily growing over the past 30 years. At first, they were mainly local initiatives inspired by simple amateurs interested in history or small groups of professional researchers. Their determined efforts brought the history of the post-war resistance to the general consciousness of Poles. Finally, in 2011, March 1 was officially announced by the Polish parliament as the National Remembrance Day of the Cursed Soldiers.[6] Since then, many events have been organized around this date, both on national and regional levels.

The aim of my research was to deconstruct the public's reactions to a variety of commemorative initiatives. I decided to narrow down the geographical scope of the study to the region of Podlasie in northeastern Poland—firstly, due to the fact that the anti-communist resistance was exceptionally numerous and active there, and secondly because it was driven not only by the determination to liberate the country from the Soviet occupation but also by the tensions between the Polish/Catholic majority and the Belorussian/Orthodox minority inhabiting the region.

The articles from the digital versions of the regional newspapers, *Kurier Poranny* and *Gazeta Współczesna*,[7] the two most popular titles at the time of my study,[8] were a source of information on current commemorative events and their impact on local communities. Moreover, the two platforms offered the possibility of commenting on the published pieces. Some of them attracted much attention and the online readers' remarks proliferated. It allowed me to gather a large amount of data quickly.

Methodology

In designing my study, I took a cue from the accomplishments of sociology (e.g., Mann and Stewart;[9] Fielding, Lee and Blank,[10] and Hughes[11]). Initially, sociologists mainly used online sources for data triangulation. Its purpose was to complete the more traditional methodologies with the analysis of the persons' conduct on the internet.[12] The researchers have noticed, though, that online behavior does not necessarily coincide with the patterns that the users followed in real life. In consequence, analyses of the virtual sphere offer the social sciences a distinct research field, allowing the examination of previously studied cultures from an utterly new perspective. Thanks to the online-based approach, behaviors that formerly did not exist or could not be investigated with the help of traditional tools can now be observed and described.[13]

Regarding the analysis of the internet comments, I also turned to a methodology from the social sciences, Barney G. Glaser's and Anselm L. Strauss's "grounded theory."[14] It encourages the researcher to reject any *a priori* hypotheses in order to create a theory based exclusively on the thorough and meticulous study of the gathered data. I began with the analysis of a limited sample of internet comments[15] and soon discerned the principal themes brought up by the contributors. I started describing the internet users' opinions and ideas using the etiquettes ("codes" according to Glaser and Strauss), in a manner that would be the most precise and exhaustive. I treated each comment as an open questionnaire in which the interviewee had independently decided on the subject and the number of questions that they agreed to answer. Each post was a means to broaden, complete, or confirm the previous observations. I regularly monitored the applied categories in order to gradually adapt and refine them. When I noticed that the further analysis did not convey new findings, I assumed that the state described by Glaser and Strauss as the "theoretical saturation" of data was achieved and that I could conclude the research.[16]

Eventually, 1,161 online comments were gathered that commented on 16 different articles from the local newspapers published between 2013 and 2018. I tried to identify as many different forms of commemoration as possible, in order to describe the public's reaction to a wide range of activities. The choice of articles was also dictated by the number of replies they gathered. As a result, the acts that provoked the biggest interest of the internet community fell in the scope of my research. Among them were events such as street names' changes, marches, creation of a mural, and new monuments.

Internet Public—Definition and Characteristics

Unless one intends to analyze large sets of digital data—the so-called "big data"—which require more advanced computing skills,[17] the study of internet content may seem an easy task. A research project based on online comments does not require any particular tools, just a computer and an internet connection.[18] There are, however, a number of factors one ought to consider when engaging in a qualitative analysis of the virtual sphere. One of them is the internet public.

Anonymous

Anonymity is probably one of the most popular associations linked with the internet. It becomes, however, less and less accurate with the contemporary increase of digital surveillance. As Deborah Lupton argues, "The internet now knows where you live. It also knows who you are, and many things about not only you but your friends and followers on your digital social networks."[19]

It seems equally true, though, that the researcher often might be unable to determine and verify even the very basic demographical data of their online "interviewees."[20] This was the case in my study, where, apart from nicknames, no information about the authors of the analyzed comments was publicly available. And, even if they voluntarily provided information about their age, origin, profession, sex or religious beliefs, it would be reckless to take those statements at face value.[21]

One might even argue that since the internet users are a group of unidentified, unrelated people, we should not treat them as a public at all. Moreover, if one cannot determine even the basic characteristic traits of the study sample, then the research cannot be considered credible or representative.[22]

While it is difficult to refute this doubt, I would like to highlight that the aim of internet-based research as I describe it is not to study the tangible people sitting in front of the computer screens or the social group they form but rather the information and its circulation in the virtual sphere. I was not aiming to investigate who infused the given internet forum with particular ideas, nor their motivation and purpose. My goal was to track the messages disseminated via the digital platforms, regardless of their source and authenticity, and the reactions they provoked among the members of the online community.

The veracity of the interviewees' statements is equally uncertain in case of more traditional strategies of data collection, such as surveys, face to face interviews, and focus groups. They might allow us to verify the basic demographic information about the respondents, but the accuracy between the statements declared in the presence of a researcher and their actual behavior remains questionable. The "intangible" internet setting merely highlights this doubt.[23]

An identified result of the virtual anonymity, however, is the phenomenon dubbed "the online disinhibition effect."[24] When the internet users' faces are not visible and their personal details remain hidden, they might feel like they do not have to care about social norms or restraints that are difficult to ignore in real life.[25] The internet, through the anonymity it gives, encourages people to speak openly about even the most controversial matters and to assert opinions which they might have never uttered publicly offline. Which of these two sides reflects a more "true" way of the thinking of the internet public(s) requires further inquiry.[26]

Pluralist

In an earlier part of this publication, David Dean argued that, in order to practice public history successfully, it is crucial to distinguish between many different groups of addressees with various expectations and needs.

Following Joss Hands' line of thinking that "we do not have a single internet anymore, but rather a multiplicity of distinct platforms,"[27] I believe that it is equally true to speak not of one, global internet public, but rather of many different publics or online communities.

Robert Plant understands this term as "a collective group of entities, individuals or organizations that come together either temporarily or permanently through an electronic medium to interact in a common problem or interest space."[28] The readers of the digital versions of the local newspapers from my study are indeed an example of an online community, an impermanent assemblage of individuals who gather on the virtual platforms to read about or discuss a particular matter. Moreover, they do not constitute a monolith themselves. They may also represent a potentially unlimited variety of backgrounds, creating a mosaic of opinions, ideas, and beliefs.

Spontaneous

The participants of the virtual discussions are theoretically allowed unlimited time to "pause" the stream of messages. Before replying, they can reflect on the statement to which they are going to respond, carefully formulate their thoughts, and even double-check their answer.[29] It is hard to determine how many internet users actually take advantage of the asynchronous nature of the online exchange. But, as Suler observes, instead of altering their instinctive reaction, they rather express it with more assurance, in a meticulously chosen set of words.[30]

Another take on the spontaneity of an internet audience refers to the factor encouraging their reactions. In the case of my online-based study, I neither triggered nor moderated the exchange of opinions on the commemoration of the Cursed Soldiers. The internet users initiated the stream of messages on their own, replying to information provided by a journalist in the article. The gathered material was thus an intuitive, natural expression of the human activity in the global network,[31] which I consider its important value.

Interactive

The digital forum which I chose as the setting of my research is an example of a virtual platform where the internet users can create content, share it, and interact. It may be, however, challenging to unravel the structure of their communication. The contributors can either react directly to the information provided in the news article or its particular excerpts, reply to another commentator's message, or even post a seemingly unrelated note that stands out from the rest of the exchange. Although it is indispensable to comprehend the flow of the comments and its meaning, it can be time-consuming or even impossible to achieve.[32]

Engaged

Only a fraction of all internet users actually share their input in the global network. Up to 90 percent of online communities' members are "noncontributing" and "resource-taking"—so-called "lurkers."[33] The fervent commitment of the minority might suggest that everybody is equally interested in the given subject, which might be just a false impression. When it comes to my study, for instance, a report published in 2017 by a Polish opinion polling institute, CBOS, showed that only 55 percent of the interviewed Poles had ever heard of the Cursed Soldiers.[34]

Although passive, these readers still constitute the internet public(s). They read the opinions of the most engaged contributors and are impacted by their points of view, even though they might not fully adhere to them. Moreover, since the internet eliminates the boundaries of authority present in the offline world,[35] the other contributors seem more like "peers" than superior experts. Just as in various peer-learning strategies, where the participation of an equal companion in the learning process makes acquiring knowledge more effective, the equal online contributors may exert considerable influence on the consciousness of internet public(s) in general.

On the other hand, the devotion of the active users might also result in "online firestorms": outbreaks of negative, aggressive, and hateful comments.[36] Although some participants could have a justifiable reason for venting their anger and demonstrating indignation over certain situations, the "firestorming" is often used by trollers and bots to manipulate the discussion, polarize the online community, and do harm to its members.

A troller is an internet user who, disguised as a truly engaged participant of the virtual interaction, intends to create confusion and antagonism and make fun of others.[37] The bots, on the other hand, are "software applications that perform automated tasks over the internet."[38] They were introduced as neutral aids replacing the human workforce, executing repetitive, mechanical tasks, but soon they started to be used in malicious cyberattacks.[39] It is sometimes possible to verify the metadata indicating the activity of such online provocateurs, e.g. their IP address and the regularity with which they publish their remarks. There are also techniques that internet users may apply to identify them and prevent the discussion from deviating from its substance and polite tone.[40]

Regardless of the source of a firestorm, it might entangle the interaction of the users who fervently reply to each other's comments. Secondly, as happened in a few cases of firestorms I witnessed during my study, the users, instead of sharing their opinions on a given commemorative event or a historical fact, started to attack each other's alleged political views, religious beliefs, or even their families' status. Although it was not pleasant to observe such an outbreak of incivility, it did point me towards the values and issues which trigger strong reactions in the online community.

Hypertextual

In his bestselling book *The Shallows*, Nicholas Carr enumerates four important qualities of the contemporary global network: interactivity, hyperlink-
ing, searchability, and multimedia.[41]

Many comments from the internet forum that I studied were packed with
references to other websites, videos, or pictures. The members of the online
community also pasted entire chunks of quotes into their posts. This manner of constructing one's feedback might pose a dilemma for a researcher
on how to interpret its meaning. Barbara Cyrek suggests that hyperlinks
should be classified as a distinct category of the analyzed data.[42] I assumed,
however, that the message they conveyed was an extension of the user's
opinion unless they stated otherwise. I, therefore, labeled such inputs according to the judgments they delivered. It is nevertheless true that the same
text, image, or song shared by an internet user might hold utterly distinct
associations for other participants of the online discussion.

(Occasionally) Ill-mannered

The internet users posting their comments on an online forum can seem like
a lowbrow target for academic research. The virtual environment is often
associated with verbal aggression and vulgar language. This idea seems particularly applicable to the spaces where users remain anonymous. Arthur
Santana found that around 53 percent of the comments published by unidentified contributors on news websites contained examples of uncivil behavior,
in comparison to approximately 29 percent of the nonanonymous posts.[43]

Moreover, users are not always capable or willing to write their insights
in a correct manner. They often ignore the rules of grammar, spelling, and
punctuation. Longer messages can also be poorly structured, missing the
logical composition reflecting the progression of thoughts. They may be
difficult to decipher, not only for the researcher but also for the rest of the
online community.[44]

Other Issues to Consider

Data Fluctuation

The amount of internet data and its content may frequently change. An
online comment can be edited by the author or deleted by the administra-
tors of the website if it has infringed its terms of use.[45] The digital resources
to which comments refer may also direct us to inactive, "rotten" links.

In mid-2019, both *Kurier Poranny* and *Gazeta Współczesna* changed their
interface and the rules of moderation for publishing posts. Suddenly, many
backdated comments appeared, and others, especially those that contained

hyperlinks, vanished. The modification was introduced when I was about to finish my research and I was not able to update my results. Luckily, I had saved all the data on my computer and I was able to complete the analysis.[46]

Ethics

It is the researchers' choice as to whether they inform the targeted community that their online utterances are being used as the basis of a scientific analysis. Some practitioners claim that if the users post the information on a website whose access does not require any permissions nor identification, then such data can always be considered public and available for study. Others stress that even if the data is not confidential but discloses personal or intimate details, its contributors should be aware of their use for scientific purposes.[47] Moreover, Dariusz Jemielniak suggests that if the utterances are only available to the members of a particular, restrained-access group, the researcher should always anonymize them to prevent their authors from being recognized.[48]

The internet also gives researchers the ability to go undercover easily. They can join a conversation to evoke the users' reactions to a particular subject. I believe that if one intervenes directly in an online discussion in order to obtain information or opinion from its participants, one should inform them about the purpose of the exchange.

It was not the case of my study, though. I did not participate in the conversations nor influenced them in any other way. Moreover, the online forum I investigated was openly accessible, and the users were identified exclusively by nicknames. In the large majority, they did not disclose any sensitive data either. Therefore, I did not judge it necessary to ask anybody for permission for using their utterances (nor was it possible to track their authors), and I did not need to anonymize their messages.

Questions a Researcher Could Pose to the Internet Public

How Does the Internet Public Interpret the Historical Events?

The study demonstrated that the internet users' views on the historical issues in question are strongly divided.[49] It allowed me to confirm the online presence of a conflict of two collective memories related to this part of the regional history. Following the thought of Anna Moroz, to distinguish these sides of the dispute, almost equal in the number of their participants on the internet forum, I used the names "the memory of the heroes" and "the memory of the victims."[50]

The adherents of the first one fervently praise the courage and honor of the Cursed Soldiers, who boldly defied the overwhelming communist forces and struggled for Polish independence. Their supporters call them heroes,

Patriots (with a capital "P"), unforgiving towards the enemies but just and righteous. The Belorussian inhabitants of the region, on the other hand, are portrayed as traitors and Soviet collaborators. According to this group of internet users, they were forming anti-Polish political and paramilitary organizations, joining the communist institutions of repression, and actively persecuting their Polish neighbors. As such, they deserved to be eliminated by the anti-communist fighters.

The other side of the conflict, however, vehemently condemns the deeds of the post-war resistance militants. Their opponents perceive them as merciless assassins, lawless thieves, and, overall, criminals. They were killing innocent civilians, children, elderly people, and even pregnant women, who could not have been engaged in any anti-Polish hostility, and surely not in armed action. These users accuse the Cursed Soldiers of the genocide of the Belorussian minority, whose only fault was to be born as non-Poles.

What Do They Think about the Commemorative Initiatives?

Eighty-three percent of the users commenting on the regional commemorative events judge them negatively. Even the contributors who generally perceive the Cursed Soldiers as national heroes are upset to see some controversial historical figures placed on a pedestal. Moreover, the internet users believe that the commemorative activities only served to polarize the local community. The Memory Marches are the most contested form of celebration because of their provocative and aggressive tone. One user even called them "the marches of hatred." The other *lieux de mémoire*,[51] such as the mural painted in Białystok and the monument resembling a tombstone erected in the neighboring town of Supraśl, are criticized for their poor aesthetic value.

Other internet users, although inferior in number, do appreciate the commemorative acts. They believe that they rekindle the memory of the national heroes and promote the most relevant values: courage, honor, and sacrifice for the motherland. Moreover, they remind the inhabitants of the region that Podlasie is a part of Poland, and as such, it will cherish above all the memory of the Polish heroes.

There are also 8 (out of 159) comments whose authors consider the commemoration of the past events a waste of time and money. They claim that there are other, down-to-earth, and truly relevant problems, such as the development of the regional infrastructure and aid to the impoverished. These issues should be put on the front burner both by the local authorities and the residents.

What Do They Think about the Organizers, Participants, and Other Parties Involved in the Commemorations?

The opinions on the organizers and the participants of the commemorative events are also divided. Their supporters see them as contemporary patriots who promote honorable historical figures and traditional values. The majority of the internet users, however, accuse them of attempting to create national heroes out of mere criminals. They affirm that the people who treat the Cursed Soldiers as their idols do not even have the necessary knowledge to assess their deeds correctly. Furthermore, the online contributors see the majority of the celebrations' participants as bullies and hooligans connected to far-right organizations. They even call them neo-Nazis and compare them to the fascist groups of the pre-war period. They should feel ashamed of taking part in these initiatives, just as their potential sponsors and endorsers.

On the other side of the spectrum, there are the opponents of the commemorative activities, e.g., politicians who stood up against naming the municipal streets after the anti-communist fighters and unidentified culprits who several times devastated the mural in Białystok. The majority (67 percent) of the comments referring to them are against such acts. The internet users describe them as provocations and call their participants "red" and "communists." According to the online contributors, those opponents are unable to create anything on their own but can only destroy the effects of someone else's work. They—and not the organizers of the commemorative events—are the ones who disrupt the order and the serenity of the local residents. Other members of the virtual community praise the contenders against the Cursed Soldiers' commemoration for their openly exhibited disapproval. They are excused for destroying the painting and the monument, which were offensive and hideous. The internet users also encourage future protests—even though some of their forms are indeed illicit.

What Factors Are Influencing the Internet Users' Reactions?

Thirty-eight comments contain claims that the Belorussian/Orthodox minority in the region is generally privileged on economic, social, and religious grounds. Its representatives occupy the highest seats in the local government and manage many local enterprises, although they are not competent and skilled enough to exercise such power. Thanks to this, the Belorussian/Orthodox inhabitants supposedly have more career opportunities and are financially better off. The Orthodox Church is also said to hold a favored position in the region, which makes the Catholic neighbors feel inferior and intimidated.

Another factor may be the potentially perilous domination of the "strangers" who maintain cultural, religious, linguistic, and political ties with the countries east of Poland. Some participants of the online discussion have no doubts that the members of the Belorussian minority do not consider themselves Polish and that they would not defend the Polish borders if the necessity arose.

There were also 13 internet users who did not agree with those allegations. However, the mere presence of such claims suggests that the conflict of collective memories about the post-war anti-communist resistance might have a hidden meaning. It is no longer "just" a matter of different interpretations of the past events but also the contemporary tensions between the Polish/Catholic and Belorussian/Orthodox residents. The historical thorny issues may only be a catalyst for the outbreak of animosity.

Where Does the Internet Public Get Knowledge From?

Last but not least, the internet comments give us some insight into the sources that the online users consulted to gather knowledge and justify their opinions on the given subject. In the case of my research, the sources could be traced via the links shared by the contributors in their messages or the quotations they pasted. They mostly referred to opinion articles (27 percent of comments making use of external references) and the results of investigations conducted on behalf of the Institute of the National Remembrance (IPN), a public institution dedicated to examining the crimes committed by the totalitarian powers of the twentieth century against Polish nationals and citizens (also 27 percent). The accounts of the witnesses to the historical events or the "heirs" of their history (e.g., their descendants) held third place (with 19 percent). Court rulings (7 percent) and scholarly articles (6 percent) were less popular.

It does not necessarily mean, though, that the internet users are well read and well informed on the discussed topic. I was frequently under the impression that their feedback was based on the cherry-picking of facts aiming to confirm their own theories, whatever they were. It is very curious, however, to observe how different sources are endorsed or refuted depending on their stance in the conflict of memory.

Internet Public—Creator or Recipient?

Jay Rosen, in his manifesto "The People Formerly Known as the Audience," contemplates "a shift in power" between the recipients and the producers of contemporary media.[52] The former audiences, passive and malleable, deprived of will or effective means to influence the channels of communication, have become a thing of the past. In the era of Web 2.0, the flow of information no longer depends exclusively on the designers or owners of multimedia platforms. The end users, through their everyday choices and actions, can now actively take part in creating the digital content.

Just as they are both guests and hosts of the online space, the "writing readers"[53] of the online magazines are also both recipients and creators of historical, collective memory. This term, *mémoire collective*, was introduced by the early twentieth-century French sociologist Maurice Halbwachs. He noticed that the memory of each individual is influenced by various social and cultural contexts.[54] He assumed that the two kinds of remembering (and forgetting), the individual and the collective memory, are intertwined and influence each other.

The main factor supporting this symbiosis is the communication between the members of a given community. The acts of communication do not necessarily signify a verbal exchange of information but can also imply the non-linguistic, symbolic rituals passed from generation to generation.[55] First of all, they allow the community to impart its assumptions about the past to each of its members. Secondly, the individuals' contributions allow them to verify or modify the shape of the group's memory.[56]

I perceive the comments from the analyzed online discussions as such acts of communication. They allow the users, on one hand, to (re)build the collective memory of the (digital) community and on the other, to draw from each other's feedback. In this sense, the internet public is both a recipient and a creator of the historical memory.

Conclusion

Thanks to the internet's extensive reach, the online comments have become a widespread, although often overlooked, element of public history. The virtual publics take an active part in shaping collective memory, both as recipients and creators of the digital content. The online comments, with their power to influence the other users' views, can be treated as one of the many narrations on the past. They may draw on, replace, complete, or criticize other, more or less official and formal discourses about history. They allow us to research not only communities' historical consciousness and potential conflicts within them, but also their objects of interest and the sources of knowledge. The added value for public historians is two-fold: the study of internet users not only broadens our understanding of the public(s), but also facilitates the implementation of history-related endeavors, defining the target groups and choosing effective means to engage them in history-related activities.

Notes

1 This article is based on my master's thesis: Dorota Choińska, "Upamiętnienie Żołnierzy Wyklętych na Białostocczyźnie w kontekście konfliktu pamięci zbiorowych oczami internautów" (Master's thesis, University of Wrocław, 2019).
2 Will Douglas Heaven, "Why the Coronavirus Lockdown Is Making the Internet Stronger than Ever," *MIT Technology Review*, accessed July 22, 2020, https://www.technologyreview.com/2020/04/07/998552/why-the-coronavirus-lockdown-is-making-the-internet-better-than-ever.
3 Norman Davies, *God's Playground. A History of Poland*, vol. 2 (London: Clarendon Press, 1981), 472, 556–558.
4 Sławomir Poleszak and Rafał Wnuk, "Zarys dziejów polskiego podziemia niepodległościowego 1944–1956," in *Atlas polskiego podziemia niepodległościowego 1944–1956*, ed. Rafał Wnuk (Warsaw, Lublin: Instytut Pamięci Narodowej, 2007), XXII, XXXIII.

5 Jerzy Kułak, *Rozstrzelany oddział. Monografia 3 Wileńskiej Brygady NZW. Białostocczyzna 1945–1946* (Białystok, 2007), 6.

6 Marta Kurkowska-Budzan, "Coming Out of the Woods: How Partisans of the Polish Anti-Communist Underground Adapted to Civilian Life," in *Continued Violence and Troublesome Pasts: Post-War Europe between the Victors after the Second World War*, ed. Ville Kivimäki and Petri Karonen (Helsinki: Finnish Literature Society, 2017), 44.

7 See Primary Sources in the Bibliography.

8 Michał Kurdupski, "Wszystkie tygodniki lokalne na minusie w maju, *Tygodnik Zamojski* najchętniej kupowany," accessed July 14, 2020, https://www.wirtualnemedia.pl/artykul/sprzedaz-tygodnikow-lokalnych-maj-2018-roku-tygodnik-zamojski.

9 Chris Mann and Fiona Stewart, *Internet Communication and Qualitative Research: A Handbook for Researching Online* (London: SAGE, 2000).

10 Nigel G. Fielding, Raymond M. Lee, and Grant Blank, *The SAGE Handbook of Online Research Methods* (London: SAGE, 2008).

11 Jason Hughes, ed., *SAGE Library of Research Methods: SAGE Internet Research Methods* (London: SAGE, 2012).

12 Beata Cyrek, "Problem fluktuacji danych w badaniach prowadzonych w cyberprzestrzeni – casus komentarzy internetowych," *Zeszyty Naukowe Towarzystwa Doktorantów UJ*, no. 20 (2018): 177.

13 Dariusz Jemielniak, "Netnografia, czyli etnografia wirtualna – nowa forma badań etnograficznych," *Prakseologia*, no. 154 (2013): 98–99; Annette N. Markham, "Internet Communication as a Tool for Qualitative Research," in *Qualitative Research. Theory, Method and Practice*, ed. David Silverman (London: SAGE, 2004), 95.

14 Barney G. Glaser and Anselm L. Strauss, *The Discovery of Grounded Theory. Strategies for Qualitative Research* (New York: Aldine de Gruyter, 1967).

15 David Silverman, *Interpreting Qualitative Data: A Guide to Principles of Qualitative Research* (London: SAGE, 2011), 58.

16 Glaser and Strauss, *The Discovery of Grounded Theory*, 69–70.

17 Deborah Lupton, *Digital Sociology* (London, New York: Routledge, 2015), 45.

18 Cyrek, "Problem fluktuacji danych," 181.

19 Lupton, *Digital Sociology*, 168–169.

20 Cyrek, "Problem fluktuacji danych," 181.

21 Krzysztof Jurek, "Badania społeczne w internecie. Wirtualna etnografia w teorii i praktyce," *Nauka i Szkolnictwo Wyższe*, no. 1/41 (2013): 93.

22 Piotr Cichocki, Tomasz Jędrkiewicz, and Robert Zydel, "Etnografia Wirtualna," in *Badania Jakościowe. Metody i Narzędzia*, ed. Dariusz Jemielniak, vol. 2 (Warsaw: Wydawnictwo Naukowe PWN, 2012), 215.

23 Markham, "Internet Communication," 103.

24 John Suler, "The Online Disinhibition Effect," *Cyberpsychology & Behavior* 7, no. 3 (2004): 321.

25 Markham, "Internet Communication," 102.

26 Suler, "The Online Disinhibition Effect," 325.

27 Joss Hands, "Introduction: Politics, Power and 'Platformativity,'" *Culture Machine* 14 (2013): 1.

28 Robert Plant, "Online Communities," *Technology in Society*, 26, no. 1 (2004): 54.

29 Markham, "Internet Communication," 104.

30 Suler, "The Online Disinhibition Effect," 323.

31 Cyrek, "Problem fluktuacji danych," 181.

32 Ibid., 179.

33 Blair Nonnecke and Jenny Preece, "Lurker Demographics: Counting the Silent," in *Proceedings of the SIGCHI Conference on Human Factors in Computing Systems – CHI '00* (The Hague: ACM Press, 2000), 73.

34 Michał Feliksiak and Antoni Głowacki, "Polskie podziemie antykomunistyczne w pamięci Polaków" (CBOS, 2017), 2.

35 Suler, "The Online Disinhibition Effect," 324.

36 Leonie Rösner and Nicole C. Krämer, "Verbal Venting in the Social Web: Effects of Anonymity and Group Norms on Aggressive Language Use in Online Comments," *Social Media+Society* (July–September 2016): 1.

37 Claire Hardaker, "Trolling in Asynchronous Computer-Mediated Communication: From User Discussions to Academic Definitions," *Journal of Politeness Research* 6, no. 2 (2010): 237.

38 Amr Awadallah, Sajjit Thampy and Daniel Ferrante, "System and Method for Detecting Internet Bots," United States Patent, US008433785B2, issued 2013.

39 Ken Dunham and Jim Melnick, *Malicious Bots: An Inside Look into the Cyber-Criminal Underground of the Internet* (Boca Raton: CRC Press, 2008), 1.

40 Vann Vicente, "What Is an Internet Troll? (And How to Handle Trolls)," How-To Geek, accessed July 18, 2020, https://www.howtogeek.com/465416/what-is-an-internet-troll-and-how-to-handle-trolls.

41 Nicholas Carr, *The Shallows. What the Internet Is Doing to Our Brains* (New York, London: W. W. Norton & Company, 2010).

42 Cyrek, "Problem fluktuacji danych," 180.

43 Arthur D. Santana, "Virtuous or Vitriolic: The Effect of Anonymity on Civility in Online Newspaper Reader Comment Boards," *Journalism Practice*, 8, no.1 (2014): 27.

44 Cyrek, "Problem fluktuacji danych," 180.

45 Beata Cyrek, "Media społecznościowe – nowa przestrzeń nauki," *Kognitywistyka i Media w Edukacji*, no. 2 (2016): 47.

46 A more universal response to the threat of disappearance of the online content is web archiving. One of the most recognized organizations dedicated to this activity is the Internet Archive, a non-profit established in 1996. Its creators' aim is to build "a digital library of internet sites and other cultural artifacts in digital form"; see "About IA," Internet Archive, accessed July 22, 2020, https://archive.org/about. It currently contains more than twenty years of web history accessible through a search engine called Wayback Machine. Although not all web resources are stored there (as in the case of my comments), it can be an important tool allowing the retrieval of seemingly lost digital data.

47 Lupton, *Digital Sociology*, 63.

48 Jemielniak, "Netnografia," 109–110.

49 A study of internet forums dedicated to contemporary Polish movies about the Cursed Soldiers gave very similar outcomes. Maciej Białous, "Dyskurs użytkowników filmowych portali internetowych wobec konfliktów pamięci zbiorowych we współczesnej Polsce," in *Historia wizualna w działaniu. Studia i szkice z badań nad filmem historycznym*, ed. Dorota Skotarczak, Joanna Szczutkowska, and Piotr Kurpiewski (Poznań: Uniwersytet im. Adama Mickiewicza, 2020), 9–23.

50 Anna Moroz, *Między pamięcią a historią. Konflikt pamięci zbiorowych Polaków i Białorusinów na przykładzie postaci Romualda Rajsa* (Warsaw: Instytut Pamięci Narodowej, 2016).

51 See Pierre Nora, "From *Lieux de mémoire* to Realms of Memory," in *Realms of Memory: Rethinking the French Past*, ed. Pierre Nora, vol. 1 (New York: Columbia University Press, 1996), XVII.

52 Jay Rosen, "The People Formerly Known as the Audience," in *The Social Media Reader*, ed. Michael Mandiberg (New York, London: New York University Press, 2012), 13.

53 Ibid.

54 Maurice Halbwachs, *On Collective Memory*, trans. Lewis A. Coser (Chicago: University of Chicago Press, 1992), 172.

55 Aleida Assmann, "Cztery formy pamięci," trans. Karolina Sidowska, in *Między historią a pamięcią. Antologia*, ed. Magdalena Saryusz-Wolska (Warsaw: Wydawnictwo Uniwersytetu Warszawskiego, 2013), 49 [from German original: "Vier Formen des Gedächtnisses," *Erwägen, Wissen, Ethik* 13, no. 2 (2002): 183–190].

56 Jacek Nowak, *Społeczne reguły pamiętania. Antropologia pamięci zbiorowej* (Cracow: NOMOS, 2011), 13.

Bibliography

Primary Sources

"1 marca – Narodowy Dzień Pamięci Żołnierzy Wyklętych – program." *Kurier Poranny*, February 28, 2013. https://poranny.pl/1-marca-narodowy-dzien-pamieci-zolnierzy-wykletych-program/ar/5518212.

"III Marsz Pamięci Żołnierzy Wyklętych w Hajnówce 2018. Policja użyła siły (zdjęcia, wideo)." *Gazeta Współczesna* February 24, 2018. https://wspolczesna.pl/iii-marsz-pamieci-zolnierzy-wykletych-w-hajnowce-2018-policja-uzyla-sily-zdjecia-wideo/ar/12959380.

"Białystok. Marsz Pamięci Żołnierzy Wyklętych." *Kurier Poranny*, March 1, 2016. https://poranny.pl/bialystok-marsz-pamieci-zolnierzy-wykletych-zdjecia-wideo/ar/9454323.

"Białostocki Marsz Uczczenia Pamięci Żołnierzy Wyklętych." *Kurier Poranny*, March 1, 2017. https://poranny.pl/bialostocki-marsz-uczczenia-pamieci-zolnierzy-wykletych-zdjecia/ar/11840675.

"Debata o Marszu Żołnierzy Wyklętych w Hajnówce." *Gazeta Współczesna*, March 12, 2017. https://wspolczesna.pl/debata-o-marszu-zolnierzy-wykletych-w-hajnowce-wideo/ar/11876886.

"Dzień Pamięci Żołnierzy Wyklętych w Białymstoku. Białostoczanie pamiętali. Odsłonięcie pomnika 'Inki' oraz marsz Młodzieży Wszechpolskiej." *Kurier Poranny*, March 1, 2018. https://poranny.pl/dzien-pamieci-zolnierzy-wykletych-w-bialymstoku-bialostoczanie-pamietali-odsloniecie-pomnika-inki-oraz-marsz-mlodziezy/ar/12973820.

"Hajnówka: I Marsz Pamięci Żołnierzy Wyklętych 27.02.2016." *Kurier Poranny*, February 27, 2016. http://www.poranny.pl/wiadomosci/hajnowka/a/hajnowka-i-marsz-pamieci-zolnierzy-wykletych-27022016-zdjecia-wideo, 9443997.

Januszkiewicz, Julita. "Żołnierze wyklęci upamiętnieni przez czarny granitowy pomnik tuż przy plaży w Supraślu. Mieszkańcy: Wygląda jak nagrobek na cmentarzu." *Kurier Poranny*, March 27, 2018. https://poranny.pl/zolnierze-wykleci-upamietnieni-przez-czarny-granitowy-pomnik-tuz-przy-plazy-w-supraslu-mieszkancy-wyglada-jak-nagrobek-na/ar/13044770#material-komentarze.

Mikulicz, Tomasz. "Będzie rondo Żołnierzy Wyklętych. Po wielu sporach." *Kurier Poranny*, September 22, 2014. http://www.poranny.pl/wiadomosci/bialystok/art/4922183,bedzie-rondo-zolnierzy-wykletych-po-wielu-sporach-wideo, id, t.html.

Mikulicz, Tomasz. "Ulica Łupaszki w Białymstoku. Partia Razem przeciwko Łupaszce: Bohater? To zbrodniarz." *Kurier Poranny*, April 24, 2018. http://www.poranny.pl/polityka/a/ulica-lupaszki-w-bialymstoku-partia-razem-przeciwko-lupaszce-bohater-to-zbrodniarz-wideo, 13125206.

"Młodzież Wszechpolska przygotowała mural w Białymstoku poświęcony Żołnierzom Wyklętym." *Kurier Poranny*, October 30, 2016. http://www.poranny.pl/wiadomosci/bialystok/a/mlodziez-wszechpolska-przygotowala-mural-w-bialymstoku-poswiecony-zolnierzom-wykletym zdjecia, 11202480.

"Młodzież Wszechpolska musiała odnowić mural Żołnierze Wyklęci. Ktoś go zniszczył." *Kurier Poranny*, November 9, 2016. http://www.poranny.pl/wiadomosci/bialystok/a/mlodziez-wszechpolska-musiala-odnowic-mural-zolnierze-wykleci-ktos-go-zniszczyl-zdjecia, 11439880.

Paszkowska, Katarzyna. "W Grajewie powstanie pomnik Żołnierzy Wyklętych?" *Gazeta Współczesna*, May 6, 2017. https://wspolczesna.pl/w-grajewie-powstanie-pomnik-zolnierzy-wykletych/ar/12037322.

"Poświętne. Pomnik żołnierzy wyklętych zdewastowany. Zamazany Bury. Policja już prowadzi dochodzenie." *Kurier Poranny*, August 3, 2018. https://poranny.pl/poswietne-pomnik-zolnierzy-wykletych-zdewastowany-zamazany-bury-policja-juz-prowadzi-dochodzenie/ar/13387960.

Sawczenko, Agata. "III Hajnowski Marsz Pamięci Żołnierzy Wyklętych. Policja zatrzymała sześć osób." *Kurier Poranny*, February 24, 2018. https://poranny.pl/iii-hajnowski-marsz-pamieci-zolnierzy-wykletych-policja-zatrzymala-szesc-osob-zdjecia-wideo/ar/12959544.

Zdanowicz, Andrzej. "II Hajnowski Marsz Pamięci Żołnierzy Wyklętych. Wojna na krzyki. I już po marszu." *Kurier Poranny*, February 26, 2017. https://poranny.pl/ii-hajnowski-marsz-pamieci-zolnierzy-wykletych-wojna-na-krzyki-i-juz-po-marszu-zdjecia-wideo/ar/11830434.

Literature

Assmann, Aleida. "Cztery formy pamięci." Translated by Karolina Sidowska. In *Między historią a pamięcią. Antologia*, edited by Magdalena Saryusz-Wolska, 39–57. Warsaw: Wydawnictwo Uniwersytetu Warszawskiego, 2013.

Awadallah, Amr, Sajjit Thampy, and Daniel Ferrante. *System and Method for Detecting Internet Bots*. United States Patent. US008433785B2, issued 2013.

Białous, Maciej. "Dyskurs użytkowników filmowych portali internetowych wobec konfliktów pamięci zbiorowych we współczesnej Polsce." In *Historia wizualna w działaniu. Studia i szkice z badań nad filmem historycznym*, edited by Dorota Skotarczak, Joanna Szczutkowska, and Piotr Kurpiewski, 9–23. Poznań: Uniwersytet im. Adama Mickiewicza, 2020.

Carr, Nicholas. *The Shallows. What the Internet Is Doing to Our Brains*. New York, London: W. W. Norton & Company, 2010.

Christensson, Per. "Hyperlink." TechTerms. Accessed July 19, 2020. https://techterms.com/definition/hyperlink.

Cichocki, Piotr, Tomasz Jędrkiewicz, and Robert Zydel. "Etnografia Wirtualna." In *Badania Jakościowe. Metody i Narzędzia*, edited by Dariusz Jemielniak, 203–220. Vol. 2. Warsaw: Wydawnictwo Naukowe PWN, 2012.

Cyrek, Beata. "Media społecznościowe – nowa przestrzeń nauki." *Kognitywistyka i Media w Edukacji*, no. 2 (2016): 45–56.

Cyrek, Beata. "Problem fluktuacji danych w badaniach prowadzonych w cyberprzestrzeni – casus komentarzy internetowych." *Zeszyty Naukowe Towarzystwa Doktorantów UJ*, no. 20 (2018): 175–191.

Davies, Norman. *God's Playground. A History of Poland.* Vol. 2. London: Clarendon Press, 1981.

Dunham, Ken, and Jim Melnick. *Malicious Bots: An Inside Look into the Cyber-Criminal Underground of the Internet.* Boca Raton: CRC Press, 2008.

Feliksiak, Michał, and Antoni Głowacki. "Polskie podziemie antykomunistyczne w pamięci Polaków." CBOS, 2017.

Fielding, Nigel G., Raymond M. Lee, and Grant Blank. *The SAGE Handbook of Online Research Methods.* London: SAGE, 2008.

Glaser, Barney G., and Anselm L. Strauss. *The Discovery of Grounded Theory. Strategies for Qualitative Research.* New York: Aldine de Gruyter, 1967.

Halbwachs, Maurice. *On Collective Memory.* Translated by Lewis A. Coser. Chicago: University of Chicago Press, 1992.

Hands, Joss. "Introduction: Politics, Power and 'Platformativity.'" *Culture Machine* 14 (2013): 1–9.

Hardaker, Claire. "Trolling in Asynchronous Computer-Mediated Communication: From User Discussions to Academic Definitions." *Journal of Politeness Research* 6, no. 2 (2010): 215–242.

Heaven, Will Douglas. "Why the Coronavirus Lockdown Is Making the Internet Stronger than Ever." *MIT Technology Review.* Accessed July 22, 2020. https://www.technologyreview.com/2020/04/07/998552/why-the-coronavirus-lockdown-is-making-the-internet-better-than-ever.

Hughes, Jason, ed. *SAGE Library of Research Methods: SAGE Internet Research Methods.* London: SAGE, 2012.

Internet Archive. "About IA." Accessed July 22, 2020. https://archive.org/about.

Jemielniak, Dariusz. "Netnografia, czyli etnografia wirtualna – nowa forma badań etnograficznych." *Prakseologia*, no. 154 (2013): 97–116.

Jurek, Krzysztof. "Badania społeczne w internecie. Wirtualna etnografia w teorii i praktyce." *Nauka i Szkolnictwo Wyższe*, no. 1/41 (2013): 86–99.

Kułak, Jerzy. *Rozstrzelany oddział. Monografia 3 Wileńskiej Brygady NZW. Białostocczyzna 1945–1946.* Białystok, 2007.

Kurdupski, Michał. "Wszystkie tygodniki lokalne na minusie w maju, *Tygodnik Zamojski* najchętniej kupowany." Accessed July 14, 2020. https://www.wirtualnemedia.pl/artykul/sprzedaz-tygodnikow-lokalnych-maj-2018-roku-tygodnik-zamojski.

Kurkowska-Budzan, Marta. "Coming Out of the Woods: How Partisans of the Polish Anti-Communist Underground Adapted to Civilian Life." In *Continued Violence and Troublesome Pasts: Post-War Europe between the Victors after the Second World War*, edited by Ville Kivimäki and Petri Karonen, 44–59. Helsinki: Finnish Literature Society, 2017.

Lupton, Deborah. *Digital Sociology.* London, New York: Routledge, 2015.

Mann, Chris, and Fiona Stewart. *Internet Communication and Qualitative Research: A Handbook for Researching Online.* London: SAGE, 2000.

Markham, Annette N. "Internet Communication as a Tool for Qualitative Research." In *Qualitative Research. Theory, Method and Practice*, edited by David Silverman, 95–124. London: SAGE, 2004.

Moroz, Anna. *Między pamięcią a historią. Konflikt pamięci zbiorowych Polaków i Białorusinów na przykładzie postaci Romualda Rajsa.* Warsaw: Instytut Pamięci Narodowej, 2016.

Nonnecke, Blair, and Jenny Preece. "Lurker Demographics: Counting the Silent." In *Proceedings of the SIGCHI Conference on Human Factors in Computing Systems – CHI '00*, 73–80. The Hague: ACM Press, 2000.

Nora, Pierre. "From *Lieux de mémoire* to Realms of Memory." In *Realms of Memory: Rethinking the French Past*, edited by Pierre Nora, XV–XXIV. Vol. 1. New York: Columbia University Press, 1996.

Nowak, Jacek. *Społeczne reguły pamiętania. Antropologia pamięci zbiorowej.* Cracow: "NOMOS," 2011.

Plant, Robert. "Online Communities." *Technology in Society* 26, no. 1 (2004): 51–65.

Poleszak, Sławomir, and Rafał Wnuk. "Zarys dziejów polskiego podziemia niepodległościowego 1944–1956." In *Atlas polskiego podziemia niepodległościowego 1944–1956*, edited by Rafał Wnuk, XXII–XXXIV. Warsaw, Lublin: Instytut Pamięci Narodowej, 2007.

Rosen, Jay. "The People Formerly Known as the Audience." In *The Social Media Reader*, edited by Michael Mandiberg, 13–16. New York, London: New York University Press, 2012.

Rösner, Leonie, and Nicole C. Krämer. "Verbal Venting in the Social Web: Effects of Anonymity and Group Norms on Aggressive Language Use in Online Comments." *Social Media+Society* (July–September 2016): 1–13.

Santana, Arthur D. "Virtuous or Vitriolic: The Effect of Anonymity on Civility in Online Newspaper Reader Comment Boards." *Journalism Practice* 8, no. 1 (2014): 18–33.

Silverman, David. *Interpreting Qualitative Data: A Guide to Principles of Qualitative Research.* London: SAGE, 2011.

Suler, John. "The Online Disinhibition Effect." *Cyberpsychology & Behavior* 7, no. 3 (2004): 321–326.

Vicente, Vann. "What Is an Internet Troll? (And How to Handle Trolls)." How-To Geek. Accessed July 18, 2020. https://www.howtogeek.com/465416/what-is-an-internet-troll-and-how-to-handle-trolls.

11

VIDEO-GAMERS AS RECIPIENTS AND CREATORS OF PUBLIC HISTORY

Let's Play Videos as Public History

Jakub Šindelář

Public history that deals with digital media is similar to nondigital public history projects concerned with the three fundamental variants of the publics' involvement with history: history *for, with*, and *by* the publics. Public history in the digital sphere can benefit from greater ease of access and interactivity. Digital projects can also exist simultaneously in various languages

FIGURE 11.1 Indie Arcade hosted by the Smithsonian American Art Museum, Washington, DC, in 2016, © S Pakhrin, public domain.

and can be easily complemented with connected support material. Furthermore, to cite Jerome De Groot, the user-generated media content of Web 2.0 allows us to "seemingly conceptually and materially circumvent the historical professional and appear to engage with the past in a more direct fashion."[1]

Video games are a widely popular medium through which the publics around the world get in contact with history. The creators of historical video games have been referred to as developer-historians[2] and public historians.[3] Jeremiah McCall praised the unique capacity of historical video games for players to "take an active role in simulating the past." He further claims that games that accurately simulate historical processes encourage reflection on them and on the position of historical agents.[4]

Even games that only represent a specific historical event or period can have great educational potential.[5] Anderson has argued that the game *Valiant Hearts*, which is the case studied in this chapter, in some aspects works as a kind of interactive museum.[6] Even nonhistorical video games (those that do not explicitly claim to represent history) have been shown to reference and offer meaningful perspectives on real historical events like the Second World War and the Holocaust.[7]

The reception of the historical content of video games remains a relatively underresearched issue. Pötzsch and Šisler have examined how students interpret video games and argue that serious historical video games can "facilitate metahistorical reflections and critical inquiries."[8] Video games are not consumed in a vacuum but in ecosystems of other types of cultural practices around them.[9] Souvik Mukherjee suggested that looking at paratexts that are spurred around video games can facilitate their reception analysis.[10] Let's Play videos are popular videos where people record themselves while playing and commenting on video games. First examples of this practice are hard to trace but generally date to around 2004 and the term is regarded to have been coined in late 2005.[11] Stephanie de Smale analyzed how Let's Play videos on a game inspired by the Siege of Sarajevo during the Yugoslavian Wars play a role in how interpretations of and ways of remembering this historical event circulate among the public.[12]

This chapter will examine how the historical game *Valiant Hearts: The Great War* and the Let's Play video production around it function as a multimedia public history event linked to the centenary of the First World War.

The Game *Valiant Hearts* as History for the Public

The game *Valiant Hearts: The Great War* (*Soldats Inconnus: Mémoire de la Grande Guerre*[13] in the French original) was developed by the *Ubisoft Montpellier* for the occasion of the centenary of the First World War in cooperation with *Mission Centenaire*,[14] the French umbrella institution for the war's national hundred-year anniversary commemoration efforts. Here, we can see that popular media like video games that might previously have been ignored or rejected outright as possible vectors of historical representations have become officially sanctioned by a national public institution.

While all historical video games connect with their historical setting and often try to avoid appearing at least too glaringly historically inaccurate, video game designers approach this with varying importance.[15] The context in which *Valiant Hearts* was created meant that not doing serious historical research was less of an option. The game is a work of fiction, but the story is inspired by real letters sent during the war. The developer diaries indicate that the authors at *Ubisoft* also worked with the French historian Alexandre Lafon who supervised the pedagogical mission at *Mission Centenaire*.[16] While the cooperation might have presented some design limitations for a commercial video game, it assured that the game *Valiant Hearts* received the *Mission Centenaire Label*, which provides some level of historical legitimacy which may have, in turn, helped the marketing of the game.

Released in June 2014, *Valiant Hearts* achieved both critical acclaim[17] and commercial success. In less than two years it had sold over 2.5 million copies worldwide,[18] making it the bestselling World-War-I video game up to that point.[19] Based on these figures,[20] it can be considered a successful public history project—*for the public* because it managed to reach so many. This unprecedented level of success was all the more striking, considering the very lack of games set in this time period compared to the Second World War.[21]

International Perspective and Marginalized Groups

Valiant Hearts is a puzzle adventure video game for a single player where one alternates between the control of multiple characters. The story of the game focuses exclusively on the Western Front.[22] Chronologically, it starts at the outbreak of hostilities between France and Germany in August 1914 and ends over a year before the Armistice of November 11, 1918.[23] The diversity of the playable characters from multiple nationalities and previously marginalized groups shows the conflict from multiple perspectives. All the characters controlled by the player have their individual backstories, but they also manage to represent the nameless masses of the First World War through their common-folk appearance and the fact that their facial features, most prominently their eyes, remain hidden as is the case for all non-children characters in the game.[24]

The older French farmer-turned-soldier Emile is arguably the main character. He lives in Saint-Mihiel, a part of the mixed French-German population of the region Lorraine. The German perspective is represented by Karl, Emile's son-in-law. As a German citizen living in France when the war begins, Karl is deported and ends up separated from his wife and child while fighting in the German army. The desire to get back to his family, torn apart by the war, is a major part of the story and clearly resonates with the political and historical narrative of Franco-German reconciliation that has been dominant in Europe after the end of World War II.

The only non-European character controlled in the game is Freddy, an African-American volunteer in the French Foreign Legion. The choice to include this character might have been to make the game more relatable to the American public, where the First World War is commemorated less than in Europe. The game also includes nonplayable characters of other nationalities and ethnic groups such as the Indian and Canadian soldiers of the British Empire or the French Moroccan Division.

Anna is the only playable female character. As a Belgian veterinary student, she is also the only civilian. She is portrayed as a very emancipated and competent woman—repairing a broken car, using it to drive French soldiers to the front, and not flinching before an amputation of a wounded soldier's leg. Other civilian characters, including children, are present in the game and the war's impact on their lives is well seen, which is not often the case as game designers are expected to create an enjoyable play experience.[25]

Valiant Hearts shows the war mainly from the Entente perspective, but the German soldiers are not portrayed as the enemy. The only real main villains of the story are the war itself and the character of a German general Baron von Dorf, who symbolizes the inhumane leadership of the commanders of World War I and the abuse of science for the building of more deadly weapons.

Besides the human characters, the player characters can also issue commands to a dog named Walt that often accompanies them. Walt is treated in a friendly manner by both sides of the conflict, highlighting the absurdity that humans cannot get along with each other. People from opposite sides sometimes help each other in the game. For instance, Emile's character cooperates with a German soldier when they both get stuck in a caved-in tunnel. Anna treats the wounded irrespective of their nationality—including a German soldier.

Externalized Killing and the Anti-War Narrative

Valiant Hearts does not shy away from showing the grimness and horror of the war. While the graphics are inspired by comic books, it is in no way appropriate for the very young. It does not go as far as to show the bloodiest details of soldiers blown to bits, but it does show deformed bodies and bloodied and wounded soldiers. The gravity of violence escalates, and toward the end of the game, the background of the battlefield is covered with bloody piles of dead bodies.

Interestingly, the player is never the cause of people dying. Most of the time, the gameplay activities include overcoming obstacles and solving puzzles. Sometimes one has to hit enemy characters and render them unconscious, but they never die. Even in the parts where grenades are in use or a tank is controlled, the game shows that the player did not kill anyone. Enemy soldiers quite comically run away from explosions, and when a plane is shot down, the pilot jumps out with a parachute.

This inability to kill is part of the anti-war narrative of *Valiant Hearts*. The game removed any opportunities to get any sort of enjoyment from killing, which is usually a key component of war games. The war is depicted as a terrible phenomenon, accompanied with killing on an unimaginable scale. Some of the war's bloodiest battles are visited, and the greater context is explained by the narration, as for the Battle of Verdun:

> Meanwhile, the Battle for Verdun only grew longer and bloodier. The death toll was staggering—70,000 per month, almost one Frenchman and one German every minute, and it went on for ten months, day and night.

The only exception to the inability to kill anyone appears toward the end of the game. As Emile, the player takes part in the Nivell Offensive and sees more and more fellow soldiers dying. At one point, the commanding officer ends up throwing his men to certain death with no chance of success. The situation has to be resolved by Emile hitting the officer, killing him in the process. At the very end of the game, Emile is tried and executed for mutiny. As one of those executed by his own army, Emile represents a controversial category of the war victims—traitors to some for failing to support their country, but martyrs to others for resisting the insane destruction.

There are also other ways in which *Valiant Hearts* reinforces the anti-war framing of the historical narrative. The game includes a mini-encyclopedia with 56 entries about historical facts that get unlocked by playing through the game and 119 collectible items. When picked up, each collectible unlocks an entry related to the object. *Valiant Hearts* provides opportunities to learn and tries to spark the player's curiosity without aggressively stressing specific themes and historical facts over others.[26] Each entry consists of a single paragraph and an illustration or a colored photo from the documentary series *Apocalypse: World War I*.[27] Some of the entries add further information concerning the hardships people experienced during the war and its consequences. Reading the encyclopedia and gathering collectibles is in no way necessary for the completion of the game. It is up to the players' choice how much time (if any) they spend going through them. They can also spend different amounts of time on specific levels of the game. So, even though *Valiant Hearts* is a linear game and the player cannot change, for example, the ending of the story, this does not mean that players remain pure recipients—the game does not play itself. Thanks to the interactive nature of the medium, it can be said that the historical narratives and representations present in *Valiant Hearts* get activated, completed, and realized only with the input of players.

Let's Play Videos as History *with* and *by* the Public

Let's Play videos, or just Let's Plays are a fairly new popular genre of video-gaming videos that can be found on the video-sharing platforms YouTube and Twitch (a live streaming platform launched in 2011, dedicated to video-game content). They offer access to recorded experiences of interaction and consumption of historical video games and historical narratives' reception (or lack thereof). They are further a vector of massive remediation of *Valiant Hearts* that helps it engage the public beyond its players. With Let's Play videos counting millions of views in total, it can even be argued that the public interacts with *Valiant Hearts* in a similar amount by watching these videos as by directly playing the game.

This part will analyze a sample of YouTube Let's Play videos in English, French, and German that cover the very end of *Valiant Hearts*. The selection was made to include the most popular videos with the most views and comments in order to cover those that have the greatest potential influence and those that offer rich data for analysis. Focusing only on a specific part of the game allows for a deeper and more meaningful analysis examining multiple videos in different languages. The end of the game has been chosen because it is a climactic point for the game's anti-war narrative, and as an ending, it encourages Let's Players (those who make Let's Play videos) to reflect on the game as a whole. As the game level demands only a little gameplay action from the player, no action at all during the final credits, this allows Let's Players to develop uninterrupted chains of thought and reflections—more so than during any other part of the game. Furthermore, the ending is overall the most discussed part of the Let's Play video series and contains the greatest number of comments by the audience.

In total, 12 Let's Play video YouTube channels have been used for the analysis. Four channels each from the English-,[28] French-[29] and German-speaking[30] communities. Besides English which can be considered as the lingua franca, French and German represent the two main belligerent sides of the First World War. The videos were transcribed using a model proposed by Daniel Recktenwald[31] with a spreadsheet with separate columns for timestamps, in-game events and narration, Let's Player verbal and non-verbal expressions. The comments were analyzed using YouTube *Comment Suite*,[32] a free software that allows one to download and organize comments from YouTube videos.

All but one of the analyzed videos[33] were uploaded to YouTube quite shortly following the release of *Valiant Hearts*—either in the summer of 2014 (seven), later that year in autumn (two), or in the first half of 2015 (two). This chronology suggests that the consumption of *Valiant Hearts* and its remediation by Let's Players can be connected to the First World War centenary commemorations going on at that time.

Reevaluation of History through Shared Sadness?

As mentioned in the previous part, at the end of the game, Emile's character is executed because he participated in a mutiny at the *Chemin des Dames* offensive. Emile was sentenced to death by a firing squad after assaulting his commanding officer and causing his death. The final part of the game consists of Emile walking up to his execution while reading out the last letter to his daughter Marie:

> Dearest Marie, As the war ends for me, I have no regrets. I've seen too much horror. I hope fate has been more merciful to you.

Emile explains he did not wish to kill his officer and blames the war as a reason why people lost their sanity and started killing each other:

> This letter is my last. I've been found guilty by a military court for a death of an officer. It was not my intention to kill him. WAR MAKES MEN MAD.

While Emile expresses his conviction that he fulfilled his patriotic duty, he feels he has failed because he (mistakenly) believes his son-in-law Karl has died:

> Though I failed Karl, I know my sacrifice has not been in vain. I fought for my country and my liberty. My honor is assured.

The ending provokes without exception a very strong emotional reaction of sadness on the part of Let's Players:

> YOGCAST Kim: And there you have it. Valiant Hearts the Great War... Well, we all knew it was gonna make us cry. I just couldn't figure out how.
>
> ExVSK: NOON! Ca peut PAS finir ainsii. Ca peut PAS...noon. Ca peut PAS finir ainsii, PUTAIIN...Ahh, mon DIEUU. Oh, je vous le jure, j'ai larmes aux yeux là. Ohhh, là là. Prrff. Je reste bouche BÉE lá, honnêtement
>
> ... Putain, mais c'est ultra triste comme fin, quoi? C'est... Pfff. C'est ignoble. C'est ignoble comme fin, sérieux.[34]

Most of the Let's Players seem taken aback by the emotions and often struggle to find words.

> Gronkh: Es passiert selten ... Dass man am Ende eines Let's Plays tatsächlich sprachlos ist. Abgesen davon ... dass man ein Kloß im Hals hat.[35]

> Jesse Cox: I was gonna say something there... But I got TOTALLY chocked up. HOLY crap. This ending was SOO sad I just went on like... the most wild emotional rollercoaster. HOLY crap.

For those that include a camera-shot on their head, the sorrow is clearly visible on their faces. The emotional impact is also recognizable in non-verbal expressions like crying, sobbing, and the overall change in the tone of voice. Some of the Let's Players limit their final commentary on the personal tragedy of Emile's situation and on the praise of *Valiant Hearts* as a good game worth buying. In each of the language groups, there were Let's Players who did not go beyond these two topics and did not comment on more general themes strongly present in the narratives of *Valiant Hearts* like the lived experience of the First World War and critique of war.

It could be argued that these Let's Players who do not comment on the historical aspects of *Valiant Hearts* play mainly for the ludic aspect. This category of video-gamers may be compared to the museum-goers who do not particularly care for history as such but enjoy the activity of museum-going in general.[36]

For some, the tragic story of Emile's demise leads to reevaluating their relation to history in general and to how relevant they consider it. The most striking example is that of the Let's Player Cryaotic:

> Growing up I never really... cared about history... I always thought it was stupid and boring and uninteresting. You know I... I always cared about you know the future and all the cool technology that will come from it. I didn't really... EVER... even THINK about... all the SHIT people used to go through... all the shit that people still go through... to this day.

Similarly, in her commentary, Let's Player YOGCAST Kim confesses her previous lack of historical knowledge and mentions how *Valiant Hearts* served as a source to learn about the First World War. Furthermore, she credits the game for motivating her to learn about the topic from other written sources. This new knowledge influenced the creation of her video as she timed her final video for July 28, 2014, the day the war started.

> YOGCAST Kim: If I had timed this right then today it's July 28... And like I said when I first started this... I uhm, I didn't know too much about World War I. Apart from what I was taught distantly when I was at school. And certainly I think this has been a fantastic game in educating me as to what happened and it has encouraged me to read up more.

Comments across the languages also suggest the audience members are in agreement that *Valiant Hearts* helped them learn about the First World War and that it could be a better way to deal with history than traditional school education and textbooks:

> youtoubecommenter1: Yep, I'm crying my eyes out. I also learned so much more about WW1.[37]
>
> youtoubecommenter2: Ich muss ja nicht erwähnen, wie gut das Spiel die Geschichte rüberbringt, wie ein Schulbuch es nie könnte.[38]
>
> youtoubecommenter3: Si cela permet dans ce cas-ci de monter aux plus jeunes ou ados qui n'aiment pas le cours d'histoire (même si le jeu n'entre pas dans les détails) l'intention y est.[39]
>
> youtoubecommenter4: I definitely learned way more about WWI from this game than I did back in high school.[40]

Examples like these testify to the success of *Valiant Hearts* as public history for the public. The game clearly managed to connect with audiences that would not be receptive to history in more traditional formats. Positive experience with public history through video games can be a gateway for further interest in history in other forms of representation.

Duty to Remember that "War Sucks"

Following Emile's death, there is a scene showing a hill full of crosses and the grave of Emile surrounded by Karl, Marie, and the dog Walt. The game's narrator at this moment talks about our obligation to remember those who died:

> Even though their bodies have long since returned to dust, their sacrifice... still lives on. We must strive to cherish their memory and never... forget.

This theme of the duty to remember is picked up and reiterated by multiple Let's Players:

> Funeral Play: Mais c'est vraiment atroce et comme il a dit on n'a pas le droit d'OUBLIER....Ce qui s'est passé.[41]
>
> Gronkh: Nutze den Tag und sei jeden Tag—vielleicht nicht jeden Tag—aber vergiss nicht ab und zu auch ein kleines dankbar zu sein.[42]

The narrative of duty to remember the horrors of war is reinforced by the initiative of Let's Players to appeal actively to their audience. This anti-war narrative is then spread with the help of the public—Let's Players and their audience.

The way Let's Players talk about the war at the end of the game leaves no doubt how negatively they view it. They denounce its stupidity and serious dark nature and simply say it "sucks:"

Jacksepticeye: Because these wars, as I said... War sucks. War sucks a big load of ass!

Cryaotic: War sucks...war is one of the... darkest fucking things... That man has... MADE.

ExVSK: Après tout on déconne pas avec la guerre, heh? On peut pas déconner avec la guerre. On peut pas. Non, on peut pas... La guerre c'est pas jolie à voire... Ça montre aussi des mauvais coté de la guerre ce jeu. Parce que oui, la guerre... Elle n'est pas que come dans le Call of Duty, heh? Dans Call of Duty en général tout finit bien. Et vous touez tout le monde.[43]

Let's Play video comments are like internet forums—a place for potential historical discussions.[44] That being said, historical arguments or discussions are not prevalent in the selected sample. A good example from a different part of *Valiant Hearts*[45] is a comment thread with over 90 replies that debates the German responsibility for WWI.

youtoubecommenter5: Also ich find das Spiel echt gut, nur find ich es doof, dass die Deutschen wieder als die Bösen dargestellt werden, obwohl die Deutschen nicht für den ersten Weltkrieg verantwortlich waren. Aber nichts desto trotz ist es ein gutes Spiel.

Reply by youtoubecommenter6: Wer war denn verantwortlich für den 1. WK?[46]

Different Publics and Meanings

Let's Player reactions show that *Valiant Hearts* has varying meanings for different publics. The French public understandably notices and interprets more intensely the irony that Emile is executed by his own country:

Funeral Play: Ahh... je suis encore prisonnier. Ouais... allez ah, oh làlà... Après toutes ces années de service. Tout ça parce que je n'avais pas envie de mourir... Je me suis rebellé contre une stratégie STUPIDE. Je me fais emprisonné par mes-mon PROPRE pays, ça va être ATROCE.[47]

The French commentators as well highlight the fact that Emile is executed by his own (and also their own) country:

youtoubecommenter7: Se sacrifie pour son pays... Tuer par son pays... D: c'est tous simplement horrible...[48]

youtoubecommenter8,[49] youtoubecommenter9:[50] Prêt à mourir pour son pays, tué par son pays.

youtoubecommenter10: J'ai rempli mon devoir, j'ai tenu mon rang pour la France. Et dire que c'est elle qui te tue...[51]

The same French Let's Player also shows empathy for the German side of the war in line with the narrative of Franco-German reconciliation.

> Funeral Play: Je pense que du ce même du coté des Allemands il y doit avoir des trucs comme ça. Même si voilà ils sont considérés comme les méchants, parce que comme on dit c'est des vainquers qui écrivent l'histoire. Ahhh, mais... bon mais c'est eux qui ont attaqué... Apparament blablabla, on s'en fout.[52]

The German Let's Player Gronkh does not refer to the French side of the war and does not really discuss the First World War. Instead, he denounces the very concept of war:

> Sondern vor allen Dingen was zu mir persönliche ich weiss nicht was was jetzt dir am moistens aufgefallen ist oder meisten was ich am meisten beeinflusst, hat bei mir ist einfach... Mir persönlich wird hier diese Sinnlosigkeit des Krieges einfach aufgezeigt.
>
> ...
>
> Diese vollkommen die Idiotie irgendwann die ja nicht mal Verzweiflung ist sondern einfach nur Dummheit. Ich verstehe es einfach nicht.[53]

German comments on the ending of *Valiant Hearts* follow a similar line. They do not mention Germany's role in World War I and argue that war is never justified.

> youtoubecommenter11: Jetzt sollte jeder wissen... KRIEG IST NICHT DIE LÖSUNG, FÜR NICHTS![54]
>
> youtoubecommenter12: Warum Menschen auch heute noch in den Krieg ziehen wollen verstehe ich nicht—und werde es NIE verstehen.[55]
>
> youtoubecommenter13: Auch wenn Kriege heute anders ablaufen als damals: Jeder Tote ist einer zu viel und aus Krieg entwächst nur Leid und Tod.[56]
>
> youtoubecommenter14: Liebe Leute ich hoffe das Spiel und andere medieninhalte haben euch sensibilisiert, Krieg ist immer die schlechteste Lösung auf Gottes Erden![57]

Similar historical narratives would be more problematic in the French context, for example, where the national narratives at least partially focus on the soldiers' sacrifice in defense of France.

Most Let's Players and their audience members who express themselves in comments seem to find something relevant for their local context. This seems to be stimulated by the diversity of perspectives across borders and nationalities that *Valiant Hearts* presents. This diversity is positively high-lighted by one British Let's Player:

> YOGCAST Kim: What I appreciate is that it represented as many na-tions as it could and it represented as many troops from different parts of world like Canada or Morocco and India.

The Thin Line between History with and by the Public

The Let's Players, through their performance,[58] take on an even more active role in the forming of public history. With Let's Play videos, they become the main creators of a remediated experience. It might seem that Let's Players only use existing material, but the input of their gameplay and commentary results in the creation of something distinct and new. There is no clear line where Let's Players act as recipients and where they are creators. Even the reading out of the in-game encyclopedia, which could be viewed as a prime example of history with the public where the Let's Player only provides his voice for the game's narratives, is not as clear as it might seem.

In a different part of the game, an Irish Let's Player reacts to the entry about women's emancipation during World War I in a way where his per-spective and interpretation overshadow the original text:

> Jacksepticeye: "The Home Front...Women took on traditional male jobs, some even held positions of responsibility." They were ahead of their time... in a war. "This new role changed their status in society, and in the wake of the war, women over 30 years old were given the vote."... Given the right to vote... I think. That's actually COOL! So because of WAR, and all the men were gone... like sexism... took a step forward! That's WEIRD! It's WEIRD that it took war to be able to do that. "The Women Institute held its first meeting in 1915, with the aim of encouraging women to become more involved in food produc-tion during the war, and the movement flourished..." That's, that's all what we have to do these days... to bring up feminism. Just start a war apparently. Don't take that seriously, Jesus![59]

While generally rather short, some comments of Let's Play video viewers can be quite extensive yet attract attention for the perceived added value they bring, as shown by the following comment:

> youtoubecommenter15: Jack, I have a penchant for history, so allow me to share some of my knowledge with you. This game is based in World War I. The game is titled, "The Great War" because that was what people called WWI before the dawn of WWII...[60]

This sample from a comment that is originally over 600 words long provides historical insight on the First as well as the Second World War that is appreciated by other viewers. This is visible at the number of likes (484) and replies (145), many of which explicitly praise and admire the commenter's "historical knowledge." Furthermore, the Let's Player who filmed the original video acknowledges it and underlines its usefulness to other viewers and himself as well:

> Jacksepticeye: @youtoubecommenter16 SO MUCH KNOWL-
> EDGE!!!! thanks though, not just for me but for others in the comments too :D.[61]

This appreciation and praise by the Let's Player definitely raises credibility of the comment, thus further reinforcing the authority it may obtain from other audience members. There seems to be some kind of "peer review" process in the evaluation of comments that try to present historical facts and insight. Other long comments that are not written in an understandable manner and do not bring information relevant for the audience get downvoted and do not appear as visible.

Conclusion: Recipient-Creator Continuum in Let's Play Videos

Valiant Hearts can be considered a kind of multifaceted multimedia public history event that culminated from the game's release until 2015, where the dominant number of sales of the game and Let's Play videos occurred. It has been a very successful project, as it has managed to reach millions of people both directly and indirectly through Let's Play videos.

The analysis of the game itself confirms that it is focused on the presentation of the public experiences from the past. Research on Let's Play videos, on its part, provides insights into the interactions of the game with its public or, more precisely, with different publics.

It proves that not only game developers bear some professional characteristics of public historians but Let's Players, too. Some of them, just as other public historians, profit from generating public interest in the past. Like museum exhibitions, Let's Players who create and perform in these videos for a living are pragmatically concerned with the popularity of the content they create, but their success is not measured only in financial terms.

The reaction examples show the potential of *Valiant Hearts* and other well-crafted historical video games to reach people who might reject more traditional forms of history in books, public exhibitions, etc. With their capacity to reach those who might be dissuaded only by the very mentioning of words like history or historical, video games as public history can be a unique asset to engage new publics actively. As shown in the example, a positive experience with a historical video game can be a gateway for further historical interest.

Moreover, Let's Play videos present a case where the shared authority between professionals, products, and the public is visible. These videos always build on the history for the public embedded in *Valiant Hearts* with the anti-war narrative, international perspective, and focus on marginalized groups. Let's Players as creators and players, however, not only "deliver" the games rich in historical content provided by the game developers but add their own perspective and emphasis that influences the experience of their audience (who can be called "second generation public" of *Valiant Hearts*). Here, we can see the *with* the public and *by* the public part of public history.

Moreover, not only the creators of Let's Play videos but also their audiences can, through their comments, achieve positions of historical authority—in relation to other audience members and even the Let's Players. The situation is not clear-cut, and rather than a dichotomy, the recipient–creator relation often resembles that of a continuum. Let's Players and audience members in the comments can bring their own topics and interpretations of history, potentially sparking online discussion on both the past itself and its interpretation(s).

The public's interaction with historical video games can be considered in two wider contexts: firstly, in the context of cultural practices of play that are spurred around historical video games where Let's Play videos with tens or hundreds of thousands of views and hundreds or thousands of comments constitute a major way that video-gamers interact indirectly with this historical medium; and secondly in the wider context of public history events in other forms—here represented by the First World War centenary commemorative efforts in various countries. *Valiant Hearts* itself is an example of a project sanctioned by the French umbrella institution *Mission Centenaire*.

Across the three examined language groups, the anti-war narratives present in the game appear to have positively resonated with the public. A comparison of themes and narratives that favor the French compared to the German-speaking communities showed specific local contexts with different publics that interact with history in *Valiant Hearts* and the impact of different pre-understanding or historical cultures probably constructed in their families, schools, and other communities. Further research might look at more language groups and communities that are also non-European or analyze the comments section across the whole game.

Valiant Hearts can be considered a uniquely successful case of public history through video games, but the observations may be also applied to other historical video games and Let's Play videos around them.

Notes

1 Jerome De Groot, *Consuming History: Historians and Heritage in Contemporary Popular Culture* (London: Routledge, 2016).
2 Adam Chapman, *Digital Games as History: How Videogames Represent the Past and Offer Access to Historical Practice* (New York, London: Routledge, 2016).
3 Joanna Wojdon, "Public Historians and their Professional Identity," *Public History Weekly* 8, no. 4 (2020), https://public-history-weekly.degruyter.com/8-2020-4/public-historians-videogames.
4 Jeremiah McCall, "Video Games," in *A Companion to Public History*, ed. David Dean (London: John Wiley & Sons, 2018), 405–416.
5 Farzan Baradaran Rahimi et al., "A Game Design Plot: Exploring the Educational Potentials of History-Based Video Games," *IEEE Transactions on Games* 12, no. 3 (2019): 1–10.
6 Sky LaRell Anderson, "The Interactive Museum: Video Games as History Lessons through Lore and Affective Design," *E-Learning and Digital Media* 16, no. 3 (2019): 177–195.
7 Johannes Koski, "Reflections of History: Representations of the Second World War in Valkyria Chronicles," *Rethinking History* 21, no. 3 (2017): 396–414.
8 Holger Pötzsch and Vít Šisler, "Playing Cultural Memory: Framing History in Call of Duty: Black Ops and Czechoslovakia 38−89: Assassination," *Games and Culture* 14, no. 1 (2019): 3–25.
9 Kerstin Radde-Antweiler, Michael Waltmathe, and Xenia Zeiler, "Video Gaming, Let's Plays, and Religion: The Relevance of Researching Gamevironments," *Gamevironments* 1 (2014): 1–36.
10 Souvik Mukherjee, *Video Games and Storytelling: Reading Games and Playing Books* (Houndmills, Basingstoke: Palgrave Macmillan, 2015).
11 Patrick Klepek, "Who Invented Let's Play Videos," Kotaku, last modified May 6, 2015, accessed September 15, 2020, https://kotaku.com/who-invented-lets-play-videos-1702390484.
12 Stephanie de Smale, "Ludic Memory Networks: Following Translations and Circulations of War Memory in Digital Popular Culture" (PhD diss., Utrecht University, 2019), https://www.narcis.nl/publication/RecordID/oai%3Adspace.library.uu.nl%3A1874%2F384896.
13 "Unknown Soldiers: Memory of the Great War."
14 "The Centenary Partnership Program," Mission Centenaire 14–18, accessed September 14, 2020, https://www.centenaire.org/en/la-mission/centenary-partnership-program.
15 McCall, "Video Games," 406–407.
16 Ubisoft, "Valiant Hearts Developer Diary 3: History [US]," YouTube, June 19, 2014, https://youtu.be/PlbO70XuZcA.
17 It won the "Best narrative" and the "Games for change" categories at the 2014 Game Awards; "2014 Recap: Winners," *The Game Awards*, accessed September 14, 2020, https://thegameawards.com/history/2014-2.
18 Dean Takahashi, "Valiant Hearts Creator Cooks up Lost in Harmony for His Next Game," VentureBeat, last modified September 17, 2015, accessed September 14, 2020, https://venturebeat.com/2015/09/16/valiant-hearts-creator-cooks-up-lost-in-harmony-for-his-next-game.
19 Later surpassed by *Battlefield 1* by EA DICE, released in 2016 that sold well over ten million copies.
20 The real size impact has been greatly amplified by Let's Play videos with even greater reach as will be discussed further in this chapter.
21 The question of why video games avoided the the First World War setting has been explored and explained by multiple scholars: Adam Chapman, "It's Hard to Play in the Trenches: World War I, Collective Memory and Videogames,"

Game Studies 16, no. 2 (2016), http://gamestudies.org/1602/articles/chapman; Chris Kempshall, *The First World War in Computer Games* (New York: Palgrave Macmillan, 2015).

22 The limitation on the Western Front is common for most video games related to World War I; Kempshall, *The First World War in Computer Games*, 40.

23 Ubisoft, "Valiant Hearts Developer Diary."

24 Kempshall, "Pixel Lions – the Image of the Soldier in First World War Computer Games," *Historical Journal of Film, Radio and Television* 35, no. 4 (2015): 656–672.

25 Holger Pötzsch, "Selective Realism: Filtering Experiences of War and Violence in First- and Third-Person Shooters," *Games and Culture* 12, no. 2 (2017): 156–178.

26 Anderson, "The Interactive Museum," 192–193.

27 Daniel Costelle and Isabelle Clarke, dirs., *Apocalypse: The First World War* (France: CC&C and Ideacom International, 2014).

28 Cryaotic, "Cry Plays: Valiant Hearts [P9] [Final]," YouTube, October 16, 2014, https://youtu.be/KEU4Op2Z0v8; Jacksepticeye, "A TEARFUL GOODBYE | Valiant Hearts: The Great War (END)," YouTube, June 6, 2015, https://youtu.be/iU10cgzfJHY; Jesse Cox, "Valiant Hearts [The End] – Never Forget...," YouTube, July 29, 2014, https://youtu.be/5BxzZfoGhhs and YOGSCAST Kim, "Valiant Hearts: The Great War – War's End (#15)," YouTube, July 28, 2014, https://youtu.be/q3eX2joS2q4.

29 Aypierre, "Soldats Inconnus – Ep 11," YouTube, August 4, 2014, https://youtu.be/IhHmBhBrIzI; ExVSK, "Soldats Inconnus – Mémoires De La Grande Guerre Ending," YouTube, July 1, 2014, https://youtu.be/NAkIK4cK86E; Funeral Play, "Soldats Inconnus: Playthrough #08 / Ending," YouTube, June 28, 2014, https://youtu.be/GknY0Cz9bXY and Seaside, "Une gameuse sur Soldats inconnus / épisode 19/ 'Cette FIN......' [FR/PS4]," YouTube, November 9, 2014, https://youtu.be/om2W4hJtS3U.

30 Beam, "Let's Play Valiant Hearts The Great War #020 Das Ende (Gameplay German Deutsch)," YouTube, July 11, 2014, https://youtu.be/J0UfPbPRBBU; DannyJesden, "ICH WAR KURZ VORM WEINEN !!! | Valiant Hearts (Part 8 ENDE)," YouTube, June 18, 2018, https://youtu.be/6ZRKo0tZxrY; Gronkh, "VALIANT HEARTS [HD+] #020 – Keine Reue (ENDE) ★ Let's Play Valiant Hearts," YouTube, July 9, 2014, https://youtu.be/gZZvK5S8VN4 and K Y Y R A, "[Valiant Hearts] Das Ende | #22," YouTube, February 2, 2015, https://youtu.be/I4UTQDE2vHE.

31 Daniel Recktenwald, "Toward a Transcription and Analysis of Live Streaming on Twitch," *Journal of Pragmatics* 115 (2017): 68–81.

32 Mattwright324, "youtube-comment-suite," GitHub, accessed August 28, 2020, https://github.com/mattwright324/youtube-comment-suite.

33 DannyJesden's video, uploaded in 2018, was included for the significant number of views and comments in the language group.

34 "NOO! It CANNOT end that way. It CANNOT... noo. It CANNOT end like this, FUCK... Ahh, my GOD. Oh I swear to you I have tears in my eyes. Ohhh-là-là. Prrff. I remain stupefied, honestly... Damn, but it's ultrasad as an ending, what? This is... Pfff. It is despicable. It is horrible as an ending, seriously."

35 "It seldom happens... That one is actually speechless at the end of a Let's Play. Apart from when you have a lump in your throat."

36 See Chapter 4 by Marta Kopiniak in this volume for details on the types of the museums' public.

37 YOGSCAST Kim, "Valiant Hearts: The Great War." All the names of YouTube commenters were anonymized by the author.

38 "Needless to say, how well the game conveys the story like a schoolbook never could." Gronkh's video.

39 "If it allows in this case to reach the youngest or teenagers who do not like the history lesson (even if the game does not go into details) the intention is there." Funeral Play's video.

40 Jacksepticeye, "A TEARFUL GOODBYE."

41 "But it's really atrocious and as he said we have no right to FORGET... what happened."

42 "Enjoy your day and be every day—maybe not every day but don't forget to be thankful a little every now and then."

43 "After all, you don't mess around with war, huh? We can't mess around with the war. We can't. No, we can't... The war is not pretty pretty to look at... This game also shows the bad side of the war. Because yes, the war... It is not like in Call of Duty, heh? In Call of Duty in general everything ends well. And you kill everyone." *Call of Duty* is a war-game shooter.

44 McCall, "Video Games," 410–413.

45 Gronkh, "VALIANT HEARTS [HD+] #002 – Freddy ★ Let's Play Valiant Hearts," YouTube, June 24, 2014, https://youtu.be/XW7GFPlLD48.

46 "I think the game is really good, but I think it's stupid that the Germans are portrayed as the bad guys again, even though the Germans weren't responsible for the First World War. Still, it's a good game
Reply: Then who was responsible for WWI?" Ibid.

47 "Ahh... I'm still a prisoner. yeah... come on ah, oh-là-là... after all these years of service. All because I didn't want to die... I rebelled against a STUPID strategy. I'm getting jailed by my-my OWN country, it's gonna be ATROCIOUS."

48 "He sacrifices himself for his country...... Killed by his country... D: it's all just horrible..." Aypierre, "Soldats Inconnus – Ep 11."

49 Ibid.

50 ExVSK, "Soldats Inconnus."

51 "I fulfilled my duty, I held my rank for France. And to think that it is she who is killing you..." Ibid.

52 "I think that even on the side of the Germans there must be things like that. Even if they are considered the bad guys, because as they say it's the winners who write history. Ahhh, but... well... but it is they who attacked... Apparently blah blah blah, who cares."

53 "But above all, what to me personally, I don't know what, what you noticed most. What impacted me the most is simply... For me personally is how it pointed out this senselessness of war... This complete idiocy at some point, which isn't even desperation but just stupidity. I just don't understand it."

54 "Now everyone should know... WAR IS NOT THE SOLUTION, FOR ANY-THING!" Beam, "Let's Play Valiant Hearts."

55 "I don't understand why people still want to go to war today—and will NEVER understand." Ibid.

56 "Even if wars run differently today than they did back then: every death is one too many and only suffering and death grow out of the war." Gronkh, "VAL-IANT HEARTS [HD+] #020 – Keine Reue."

57 "Dear people, I hope the game and other media content made you aware that war is always the worst solution on God's Earth!" Beam, "Let's Play Valiant Hearts."

58 Josef Nguyen argues Let's Player reactions are not authentic and are perfor-mances of specific playing personalities; Josef Nguyen, "Performing as Video Game Players in Let's Plays," *Transformative Works and Cultures* 22 (2016), https://dx.doi.org/10.3983/twc.2016.0698.

59 Jacksepticeye, "BLOW YOU WITH MY ORGAN | Valiant Hearts: The Great War #3," YouTube, May 4, 2015, https://youtu.be/O6l2jADVIP0.

60 Ibid.

61 Ibid.

Bibliography

Anderson, Sky LaRell. "The Interactive Museum: Video Games as History Lessons through Lore and Affective Design." *E-Learning and Digital Media* 16, no. 3 (2019): 177–195.

Baradaran Rahimi, Farzan, Beaumie Kim, Richard M. Levy, and Jeffrey E. Boyd. "A Game Design Plot: Exploring the Educational Potentials of History-Based Video Games." *IEEE Transactions on Games* 12, no. 3 (2019): 1–10.

Chapman, Adam. "It's Hard to Play in the Trenches: World War I, Collective Memory and Videogames." *Game Studies* 16, no. 2 (2016). http://gamestudies.org/1602/articles/chapman.

Chapman, Adam. *Digital Games as History: How Videogames Represent the Past and Offer Access to Historical Practice.* New York, London: Routledge, 2016.

Costelle, Daniel, and Isabelle Clarke, dirs. *Apocalypse: The First World War.* France: CC&C and Ideacom International, 2014.

Groot, Jerome de. *Consuming History: Historians and Heritage in Contemporary Popular Culture.* London: Routledge, 2016.

Kempshall, Chris. "Pixel Lions – the Image of the Soldier in First World War Computer Games." *Historical Journal of Film, Radio and Television* 35, no. 4 (2015): 656–672.

Kempshall, Chris. *The First World War in Computer Games.* New York: Palgrave Macmillan, 2015.

Klepek, Patrick. "Who Invented Let's Play Videos." Kotaku. Last modified May 6, 2015. Accessed September 15, 2020. https://kotaku.com/who-invented-lets-play-videos-1702390484.

Koski, Johannes. "Reflections of History: Representations of the Second World War in Valkyria Chronicles." *Rethinking History* 21, no. 3 (2017): 396–414.

McCall, Jeremiah. "Video Games as Participatory Public History." In *A Companion to Public History,* edited by David Dean. London: John Wiley & Sons, 2018.

Mission Centenaire 14–18. "The Centenary Partnership Program." Accessed September 14, 2020. https://www.centenaire.org/en/la-mission/centenary-partnership-program.

Mukherjee, Souvik. *Video Games and Storytelling: Reading Games and Playing Books.* Houndmills, Basingstoke: Palgrave Macmillan, 2015.

Nguyen, Josef. "Performing as Video Game Players in Let's Plays." *Transformative Works and Cultures* 22 (2016). https://dx.doi.org/10.3983/twc.2016.0698.

Pötzsch, Holger, and Vít Šisler. "Playing Cultural Memory: Framing History in Call of Duty: Black Ops and Czechoslovakia 38–89: Assassination." *Games and Culture* 14, no. 1 (2019): 3–25.

Pötzsch, Holger. "Selective Realism: Filtering Experiences of War and Violence in First- and Third-Person Shooters." *Games and Culture* 12, no. 2 (2017): 156–178.

Radde-Antweiler, Kerstin, Michael Waltmathe, and Xenia Zeiler. "Video Gaming, Let's Plays, and Religion: The Relevance of Researching Gamevironments." *Gamevironments* 1 (2014): 1–36.

Recktenwald, Daniel. "Toward a Transcription and Analysis of Live Streaming on Twitch." *Journal of Pragmatics* 115 (2017): 68–81.

Smale, Stephanie de. "Ludic Memory Networks: Following Translations and Circulations of War Memory in Digital Popular Culture." PhD diss., Utrecht University, 2019. https://www.narcis.nl/publication/RecordID/oai%3Adspace.library.uu.nl%3A1874%2F384896.

Takahashi, Dean. "Valiant Hearts Creator Cooks up Lost in Harmony for His Next Game." VentureBeat. Last modified September 17, 2015. Accessed September 14, 2020.   https://venturebeat.com/2015/09/16/valiant-hearts-creator-cooks-up-lost-in-harmony-for-his-next-game.

Wojdon, Joanna. "Public Historians and their Professional Identity." *Public History Weekly* 8, no. 4 (2020). https://public-history-weekly.degruyter.com/8-2020-4/public-historians-videogames.

Videos

Aypierre. "Soldats Inconnus – Ep 11." YouTube. August 4, 2014. https://youtu.be/IhHmBhBrIzI.

Beam. "Let's Play Valiant Hearts The Great War #020 Das Ende (Gameplay German Deutsch)." YouTube. July 11, 2014. https://youtu.be/J0UfPbPRBBU.

Cryaotic. "Cry Plays: Valiant Hearts [P9] [Final]." YouTube. October 16, 2014. https://youtu.be/KEU4Op2Z0v8.

DannyJesden. "ICH WAR KURZ VORM WEINEN!!! | Valiant Hearts (Part 8 ENDE)." YouTube. June 18, 2018. https://youtu.be/6ZRKo0tZxrY.

ExVSK. "Soldats Inconnus – Mémoires De La Grande Guerre Ending." YouTube. July 1, 2014. https://youtu.be/NAkIK4cK86E.

Funeral Play. "Soldats Inconnus: Playthrough #08 / Ending." YouTube. June 28, 2014. https://youtu.be/GknY0Cz9bXY.

Gronkh. "VALIANT HEARTS [HD+] #002 – Freddy ★ Let's Play Valiant Hearts." YouTube. June 24, 2014. https://youtu.be/XW7GFPlLD48.

Gronkh. "VALIANT HEARTS [HD+] #020 – Keine Reue (ENDE) ★ Let's Play Valiant Hearts." YouTube. July 9, 2014. https://youtu.be/gZZvK5S8VN4.

Jacksepticeye. "A TEARFUL GOODBYE | Valiant Hearts: The Great War (END)." YouTube. June 6, 2015. https://youtu.be/iU10cgzfJHY.

Jacksepticeye. "BLOW YOU WITH MY ORGAN | Valiant Hearts: The Great War #3." YouTube. May 4, 2015. https://youtu.be/O6l2jADVIP0.

Jesse Cox. "Valiant Hearts [The End] – Never Forget…" YouTube. July 29, 2014. https://youtu.be/5BxzZfoGhhs.

K Y Y R A. "[Valiant Hearts] Das Ende | #22." YouTube. 2 February 2, 2015. https://youtu.be/I4UTQDE2vHE.

Seaside. "Une gameuse sur Soldats inconnus / épisode 19/ 'Cette FIN……' [FR/PS4]." YouTube. November 9, 2014. https://youtu.be/om2W4hJtS3U.

Ubisoft. "Valiant Hearts Developer Diary 3: History [US]." YouTube. June 19, 2014. https://youtu.be/PlbO70XuZcA.

YOGSCAST Kim. "Valiant Hearts: The Great War – War's End (#15)." YouTube, July 28, 2014. https://youtu.be/q3eX2joS2q4.

12

THE USERS OF TRIPADVISOR AS THE PUBLIC(S) OF PUBLIC HISTORY

Case Study of the Hiroshima Peace Memorial Museum

Agata Moskwa

According to the established definition of public history, the following types of publics can be identified: audience (*for* the public), participants (*with* the public), activists (*by* the public), and public as a subject (*about* the public).[1] It is reasonable to conclude that a significant proportion of the historical tourist attractions (especially the older ones) is audience-oriented and targeted at history-consumers in order to increase access to the past and to

FIGURE 12.1 Hiroshima Peace Memorial Park (the HPMM is a part of it), © BriYYZ, public domain.

convey an appropriate narrative in accordance with the "mission" of the facility. However, a sort of revolution in the public's approach has made the audience more active and ready to take a critical approach to the presented narratives, sometimes even questioning the "received" message. The manifestation of these transformations of the public can be vividly observed on the Tripadvisor portal.

Research Area

The Medium

Tripadvisor is one of the largest internet platforms that allow users to add information and opinions about hotels, restaurants, or other tourist attractions. According to Tripadvisor itself, the site is the largest travel platform in the world, generating over 463 million unique visitors per month and containing more than 859 million reviews of 8.6 million objects and services.[2] The reviews and rankings posted therein impact the choices made by potential customers and tourists.[3] Due to its form and range, Tripadvisor seems to be a fairly reliable source concerning opinions on tourism-related issues.

Reviews published on Tripadvisor concern various types of facilities and services and can be accessed by practically every internet user, including travelers, competitors, and researchers. Thanks to the nature of the service, the opinions of respondents on history-related objects can also be used in public history as a laboratory for research on the public.

Due to the enormous volume of material concerning the reception of memorial sites related to the nuclear bomb explosion in Japan on Tripadvisor, I decided to analyze in detail only one object, which served as a representation of the entire complex in Hiroshima. Given its substantive, symbolic, and media value, I chose the Peace Memorial Museum as the most suitable facility for this purpose.

According to Tripadvisor, the Hiroshima Peace Memorial Museum (HPMM) is the third (out of 290) best-rated attraction in Hiroshima.[4] At the same time, the museum has the highest number of reviews. It is also the most popular of all Peace Memorial Museums in Japan (with a total of about 50). Annually, the HPMM is visited by more than one million visitors, according to the report of the city of Hiroshima for the year 2017. In addition, the museum is a place of remembrance which, in addition to its commemorative function, also has an educational purpose and is thus able to address audiences on many levels of consciousness.

Hiroshima is the place where a tremendous human tragedy took place, which is permanently inscribed on the pages of history. It is apparent that this place has become a place of remembrance both in topographical and commemorative contexts. It is worth noting, however, that this place may have different interpretations in the international and Japanese contexts, but due to the fact that only English-speaking comments were analyzed, this paper focuses on the international aspect.

The Object

It may be considered that Hiroshima has become a symbol of tragedy due to the policy of the city authorities, who have decided to combine the tourist appeal of the area with a commemorative function.[5] However, the narrative accompanying Hiroshima as a Peace Memorial City[6] is interpreted in two ways due to the exposition of the victimage.[7]

Benedict Giamo in his accurate, but also extremely critical, article on HPMM has included a detailed description of the exhibition along with the accompanying interpretation of an almost pathetic promotion of peace.[8] Giamo also criticizes the museum in the context of public history as an object that does not carry historical consciousness but only protects and preserves established beliefs and ultimately leads to mass ignorance of the visitors. However, it should be stressed that Giamo's observations as well as the following research concern the description of the HPMM before modernizations were undertaken, which is also a valuable starting point for future studies.

The HPMM consists of two buildings: the main and the eastern one. Since 1994, both buildings have become one museum object. The eastern building was renovated from August 2014 to April 2017, while the main building was renovated from April 2017 to April 2019. Parts of the exhibition during the renovation were moved to whichever building was open to the public.[9] The exhibition contains illustrative maps and photographs, as well as mementos of the victims, which in many cases tell the stories of individuals. The individual segments of the exhibition cover both the immediate and long-term effects of the explosion (the main part of the exhibition); one section is devoted to the history of Hiroshima (before and after the bombing), and an entire section is devoted to the history of nuclear weapons and Hiroshima's contribution to world peace. Information about the entire exhibition is available on the museum's website in English.[10] In addition to basic information on opening hours, ticket prices, and instructions on how to access the museum, it also has the abovementioned detailed exhibition plan, a PDF leaflet in 12 language versions, information on available lectures or seminars, and a link to the HPMM library database with online access to some of the films and photos.

Research Topics and Possibilities

An undeniable advantage of using the already existing opinions of internet users, such as reviews posted on the Tripadvisor website, is the fact that they were not adjusted to a specific theory and were not evoked by the researcher. Moreover, the source material is constantly expanding but also archived, allowing any study to be repeated and the outcomes of analyses to be compared.

Thanks to the visitors' reviews, a vast amount of information can be obtained, from basic information about the museum as an institution (the content of the exhibition, events, opening hours, etc.), through interpretations of the museum's narrative, to information about the public itself. The most interesting aspects of my focus are: what means does the Museum use to influence its public? Does the public engage and, if so, how? What message does the public receive? Is it coherent and complete? Is there room for reflection or criticism? And, above all, who is the public of the HPMM.

Methodology

The analysis was conducted on the English-language reviews published on a Tripadvisor subpage dedicated to the HPMM. The opinions in English were used due to the international nature of the language. Such an approach has allowed me to analyze the largest number of comments of all language categories and has enabled the assessment of representatives of many nationalities who were able to get acquainted with the content of exhibitions in the HPMM for foreign visitors.

Reviews posted on Tripadvisor are available without the requirement of creating an account on the site, but to express an opinion about a tourist attraction, hotel, or restaurant, registration on the site is necessary (it can be also accessed via a Facebook profile or a Google account). Due to the requirement of creating an account, opinions are not fully anonymous. However, due to the specific nature of the internet medium, one cannot be certain that the data included in the user profile are authentic. When viewing reviews, the following information about the user posting the review is available: user name, location, gender, age-range, and Tripadvisor experience—date of joining Tripadvisor, interests by portal category, number of cities visited, number of photos posted, and the number of reviews with ratings. Data such as location, age, and gender need not be disclosed. It is also possible to look at the user's profile, where all the reviews and photos posted by the user are available. The reviews themselves are posted on the website of the tourist destination/hotel/food facilities and are categorized according to the language in which they are written. It is also possible to filter the reviews according to the rating, the period of the year in which they were posted, and the type of "traveler" (family, couple, business trip, etc.). Each review can be supplemented with photos.

Research material such as reviews published on the Tripadvisor portal is a suitable source for analysis due to its functioning in virtual space as a spontaneous and natural need to express one's opinion by a user who has visited a particular tourist attraction. It is worth noting that nowadays an account on a social networking site is often considered a "must" in business, both as a form of contact with the customer and as an advertisement.[11] This may lead to certain abuses in the context of "requested" opinions, which are in fact camouflaged advertising, but I am of the opinion that in the case of this study, potential manipulations should not be given particular consideration due to the general character of the researched object. In addition, Tripadvisor takes pride in its care to present only unbiased opinions, as seen in the publication of Content Transparency Report[12] which "details never-before-shared insight into Tripadvisor's moderation process for reviews and the advanced techniques it uses to fight fraud."[13]

In the first phase of the analysis, 3,287 opinions on the HPMM were collected. They were published on the Tripadvisor website between August 23, 2005 (the first entry for this museum) and April 31, 2018. Due to the immense amount of material to be analyzed, the statistics were calculated on the basis of the reviews posted on the website in the months with the highest rate of interest, i.e. in April 2016 and 2017, as well as in October 2016. It is worth noting that, according to the Hiroshima Peace Memorial's Report, the yearly number of foreign visitors to the facility exceeds 300,000 people (in 2015—338,891; in 2019—522,781).[14]

According to the grounded theory,the gathered reviews were examined without any prior hypotheses.[15] This provided the possibility to determine the topics and trends that recurred in reviews, which in turn allowed further in-depth analysis to be more effective. The recognition of recurring trends in reviews has led to establishing a list of issues mentioned by the public, which I categorized in the following way:

- Must see/recommended — did the reviewer consider the HPMM to be a recommended tourist destination? If so, did she/he specify the audience?
  - For politicians—that is, for people who have a direct influence on the political situation and thus the future;
  - For people visiting Japan or Hiroshima—interpreted as a recommendation for people who are already in Japan for tourist purposes;
  - For each/unspecified recipient—interpreted as a recommendation for any person. Sometimes commentators stressed that the Museum should be visited by everyone to appreciate the value of peace in the world.
- Emotions during the visit—mentioned emotions or emotional terms that accompanied the service user during his/her visit to the HPMM.
- Information about the exhibition—did the service user include information about the Museum or the exhibition in his/her statement? If so, what type of information was it?
  - Description of the exhibition—information about the exhibition itself, e.g., what can be found in the exhibition (souvenirs, photographs, films, witness accounts, drastic photographs, etc.);
  - Opinion about the exhibition—a subjective opinion related to the content of the exhibition;

- Practical information—any information related to the functioning of the Museum, e.g., ticket prices, warning about the closure of part of the museum due to renovation, warning about queues, etc.
- Referring to other memorial sites—has there been a comparison or have different memorial sites been mentioned? If so, what were these places?
  - In Hiroshima/Nagasaki—any other memorials related to the atomic bomb explosion?
  - Outside Japan—places of remembrance which, for example, refer to the subject of the extermination of people.
- Commentary on the use of the atomic bomb in Japan—did the user of the portal in any way refer to the event the consequences of which were presented in the Museum?
- Appeal/reference to the concept of peace—has the commentator noticed (consciously or unconsciously) the message of the founders of the entire Peace Memorial City?
- Reference to current events or political situation—did the commentator mention current events (if so, which ones?) and associate them with the atomic bombing?

Upon this brief analysis, it becomes evident that the public perceives the Peace Memorial Museum on various levels—as a tourist destination (one of the places to visit during the trip), a museum (an institution that collects artifacts and shares its collection), a facility that commemorates historical events, an educational center that teaches about history, an object that evokes emotions and induces reflection, or as a monument carrying the message of peace. Only a deeper examination allows us to determine which of the mentioned functions of the HPMM reached the visitors most effectively.

The Public

Due to the information provided by the users, it is not possible to determine the gender or age of the visitors, and even the origin of the traveler is not always available. Among the visitors posting a review about the Museum, only about 20 percent of users declared their place of residence to be other than the United Kingdom, the USA, Australia, or Canada. As for "the company" of the traveler who visited the object, most reviewers of the HPMM came with a partner (49.5 percent) or with family (18.8 percent).

The Public as Tourists

Recommendations

Tripadvisor is a tourist portal and the reviews placed there usually contain information that reflects visitors' feelings about their experience. The overall rating for the HPMM is 4.5/5, whereas many as 72 percent of the reviews are 5/5 (the rest: 22 percent—4/5, 4 percent—3/5, 1 percent—2/5, 1 percent—1/5).

First of all, when analyzing the reviews taking into account the tourist aspect, I focused on the recommendation of the HPMM to other users. As keywords, in addition to direct recommendation of the object, I considered terms such as "must-see" and "must-visit." The percentage of reviews considering the HPMM as a sort of "obligatory" place is nearly 35 percent.

Recommendations for the HPMM usually did not have a specific addressee or contained a message that each person should visit the facility at least once. The repetitiveness of the Museum's recommendations for visitors to Japan or Hiroshima itself was also noticeable. In these reviews, there were even "persuasions" targeted at prospective tourists to include a trip to Hiroshima in their plans: "If you are in Tokyo and have time for a day trip to Hiroshima, I strongly recommend you go." (April 4, 2017, tripadvisoruser1,[16] United States).

Moreover, there are several reviews (2 percent), where a visit to the HPMM is recommended for politicians. One of the users stated: "I wish we could take Kim Jong-un, Donald Trump, Vladimir Putin, and Bashar al-Assad and require them to take the tour and then sit down together and resolve their differences." (April 22, 2017, tripadvisoruser2, United States).

Description of the Exhibition and Useful Information

Other content referring to the tourist character of the Museum included in the reviews is the actual description of the exhibition and practical information related to the facility. Thirty-nine percent of the reviews contained a description of the exhibition, and 49 percent of the reviews included useful information for prospective visitors.

A considerable amount of information contained in the reviews can also be found on the website of the HPMM,[17] e.g., ticket entrance prices, the possibility of renting an audio guide, access to the facility, and warning about closing part of the exhibition due to renovation work. Despite the fact that the HPMM was updating and publishing all the information on the website, the reviews show that the visitors were surprised by the closure of one of the premises for the period of renovation. Further information in the reviews concerning the unavailability of parts of the exhibition was possibly intended to reassure prospective visitors that despite the closure of parts of the exhibition, the Museum continues to operate and offer interesting content: "Half the museum was closed for renovation, but there is still sufficient exhibits that provide graphic evidence of the personal experiences of the survivors." (April 21, 2016, tripadvisoruser3, Australia).

In numerous reviews, there is also additional relevant information for prospective visitors concerning visiting times. Some reviewers indicated how long they devoted to visiting the Museum. One of them noted:

> Because we did linger in a few places and watched short clips and as I said read every display, it took us 3 hours to comfortably to [sic] cover the Museum (I believe the East Building was closed for renovation so it may take longer when this reopens).
>
> *(April 23, 2017, tripadvisoruser4, Great Britain)*

One may also read advice on the amount of time needed during the trip to the museum ("You can do the tour in one hour, but allow two for plenty of time.") (April 28, 2017, tripadvisoruser5, United Kingdom). In addition, a large number of reviews included information about the large volume of visitors and suggestions on how to avoid crowds during the tour: "Avoid the crowds by going early in the morning or before closing (you need about 2 hours)." (April 18, 2017, tripadvisoruser6, Slovenia).

The content of the reviews on the Tripadvisor portal enables us to determine which elements of the exhibition "spoke" to the public. The majority of users mentioned the objects that were most memorable, such as a model of the city, melted bottles or tiles, lunch boxes, remnants of clothes, or a human shadow on the stairs. The touching stories of the survivors occur repeatedly in the reviews; however, the most frequently recalled part of the exhibition is that which presents objects belonging to children and short stories about the owners:

> The next section, in which guides wander around talking to attendees and explaining things, are a number of glass cases, each showing a personal item (tattered school uniform, books and sewing kits), which each belonged to a child if [sic] Hiroshima. The recount tells a little bit about what happened to the child and how the belongings ended up back with the family (usually if the child returned home before passing away).
>
> *(October 5, 2016, tripadvisoruser7, Australia)*

The users frequently warn about the drastic content at the exhibition: "There were also many gruesome photos of the victims both dead and the survivors." (October 9, 2016, tripadvisoruser8, United Kingdom). Several reviews also included information about exceptional events in the museum, such as a multimedia presentation conducted by the daughter of one of the survivors or a guided tour by an English-speaking volunteer.

The Public's "Memory"

Opinions

A significant part of the reviews was of a personal nature where the users shared their experiences and thoughts and, therefore, explicitly expressed their opinion on the Museum and its exhibition. The reviews containing a clear opinion about the exhibition constituted more than 75 percent of all the reviews.

Among the neutral expressions, the term "informative" is the most popular and can be found in about 8 percent of reviews, e.g., "Very informative and well laid out. Easy to move around and view all artifacts." (October 28, 2016, tripadvisoruser9, Australia) and "Impressive, stunning, and very informative. The exhibitions are really well done." (April 11, 2017, tripadvisoruser10, United Kingdom).

Many emotional terms were used to evaluate the Museum and they appeared in 73 percent of the users' reviews. The adjectives that were frequently used were: "terrible," "haunting," "harrowing" (in 11.5 percent of the comments); "moving," "touching," "emotional" (50.5 percent); "thought-provoking," "confronting" (20.5 percent); "sad," "depressing" (22 percent); "powerful," "impactful," "unforgettable" (17 percent); "sobering," "eye-opening" (12 percent); "humble," "respectful" (7.5 percent). Lastly, terms similar to "somber" or "grim" appeared in 8.5 percent of the reviews.

The complexity of emotions accompanying visitors to the museum can be evidenced by the reviews themselves:

> A very moving experience, well presented and pulls no punches. Thought provoking and somewhere everyone should visit. Understated and somber.
>
> *(October 23, 2016, tripadvisoruser11, United Kingdom)*

> Somber and educational. Everyone should visit at least once. A roller-coaster of emotions that will change the way you think about life, human survival, war, and even the world. My 13-year-old brother's outlook on life and war changed a lot, as did mine.
>
> *(April 7, 2016, tripadvisoruser12, not mentioned)*

> The horrors of nuclear war are well brought home in this museum. It is a stark reminder of man's inhumanity to his fellow humans. The displays tell a powerful and poignant story. An unforgettable experience.
>
> *(April 28, 2017, tripadvisoruser13, Australia)*

My wife grew up in Hiroshima and visited the museum at various times for school. I was a little surprised when she said: 'I don't feel like going right now, you go.' She explained that the museum is wonderful but so impactful for her that it requires some time afterwards to process it all. After my visit several months ago, I totally agree. I find myself thinking about it on occasion still. A sobering experience. So—there are a lot of facts and information shared with few details spared. I think it's fine well enough for families and kids to see, but some of the displays are shocking. Really very interesting and important to share and remind generations of WWII.

(April 22, 2016, tripadvisoruser14, United States)

The "Memory Carrier"

The reviews taken into consideration in this study show that the HPMM fulfills its function as a place of remembrance. The terms related to memory or remembrance can be found in more than 10 percent of the reviews.

Reference to Other Memory Sites

Due to the similar subject matter of memorial sites in Hiroshima and Nagasaki, it is natural for the public to associate the two sites. The reference to other memorials related to the nuclear bomb explosion in Japan appeared in over 23 percent of the reviews.

However, among Tripadvisor users, there were also more experienced recipients, who referred in their reviews to memorials other than Japanese ones (less than 2 percent of reviews). These memorials include the United States Holocaust Memorial Museum in Washington, D.C., the National Museum in Seoul, and the Korean War Memorial, Dachau, as well as the Holocaust Memorial museums in general and museums established at the sites of the former concentration camps. This may indicate some kind of greater history/remembrance sensibility among the public of the Museum or testify to the development of the so-called "dark tourism".

Historical Aspect

Some reviewers have made general reference to the historical knowledge received at school and the fact that direct contact with history (at the memorial site) is significantly more powerful, e.g.,

> This is an absolute must-visit if you are in Hiroshima, to really understand the gravity of what happened here in 1945 [...] The exhibits are informative and interesting, and even those who studied the WW2 history in school will find it interesting and will learn something.
>
> *(April 23, 2017, tripadvisoruser15, not mentioned)*

No history books could ever prepare you for this visit. Emotional and profound. Our group were fortunate to have had a guide whose mother, a nurse, arrived in Hiroshima three days following the bombing to help the dying and injured.

(October 28, 2016, tripadvisoruser16, Australia)

At this point, however, it should be noted that the Japanese activity in World War II did not go unnoticed by the public. The reviews on Tripadvisor concerning the HPMM provide content accusing the creators of the Museum's exhibition of not showing the Japanese warfare in a broader perspective and highlighting the facts that led to the atomic bombs being dropped on Hiroshima and Nagasaki, e.g.

This museum sometimes overstates the importance of Hiroshima in the entire spectrum of horrible things that happened in WWII. For example many more people were lost in Tokyo from the conventional bombing that preceded Hiroshima. The museum very much understates the reason why there was a war, and why the US was bombing Japan.

(April 17, 2017, tripadvisoruser17, United States)

To a large extent, however, even if the reviewer noted that there was no historical background before the atomic bombs were dropped, it was accepted as a chosen concept of the creators, e.g.,

There are a number of reviews on here that lament over the fact that this museum does not focus on contrition or regret on Japan's part for their involvement in World War Two. Make no mistake: this is not a museum about the war, nor is it a museum about the political or international influences of war. It is purely about the atomic bomb in Hiroshima and you could say that its purpose is really to educate about this awful arm and hope to prevent its use in the future... Do not come here looking for a political agenda or for some sort of *mea culpa* approach to the war. Come here to witness a country's position on a warfare that we should all know a lot more about.

(April 17, 2016, tripadvisoruser18, Australia)

Some users also noticed that although the part of the exhibition devoted to the reasons why the atomic bombs were dropped is missing, there is also a lack of blame for the United States, e.g. "One of the biggest catastrophes of History explained. Expect to see the brutality of a defining event in human history. Be prepared to read and hear about great suffering. Victims are mentioned by name and age but there is no blame. Just the facts." (April 15, 2016, tripadvisoruser19, United Kingdom) or "Interestingly, there is no particular anti-USA sentiment in the presentation of the material that I could see. It's more 'matter-of-fact'—the bomb was dropped and this is what happened." (April 20, 2016, tripadvisoruser20, Australia).

Reference to Current Events or Political Context

The reviews also referred to the present day. Apart from comparisons of photographs after the atomic bomb explosion with the current appearance of Hiroshima, there are many references to current events or the political situation. The percentage of references to contemporary times is above 5 percent.

These statistics could have been influenced by the visits of international politicians connected with the G7 meeting of Foreign Ministers (April 10–11, 2016) and the visit of President Barack Obama on May 27, 2016, as users directly referred to these events in their reviews, e.g. "We were there a day after the G-7 visit. I agree with John Kerry; leaders of every country should visit." (April 20, 2016, tripadvisoruser21, United States).

The international visits of the authorities were also discussed in the context of the memorial pictures and peace-related news that are presented in the Museum. One of the users wrote: "… kind of sickening to see pictures of US & Russian presidents who have visited & promised the campaign to put an end to nuclear weapons, while actually doing nothing about it." (April 13, 2017, tripadvisoruser22, United Kingdom). This commentary invokes another aspect discussed in reviews—the movement promoted in the Museum for complete nuclear disarmament, which leads to a further function of the Museum.

The Public as Recipients of the Museum's Message

Hiroshima itself has been named the *Peace Memorial City* (under the 219th article of "Hiroshima Peace Memorial City Construction Law," established on August 6, 1949), which clearly indicates a deep connection with the idea of peace, and which is further enhanced by the numerous facilities in the Peace Memorial Park complex (the HPPM is a part of it). The exhibition covers such topics as peace and the dangers of nuclear weapons and highlights the importance of undertaking efforts to disarm the global nuclear arsenal. Despite the quite obvious message, it is worthwhile to analyze the reviews from the Tripadvisor portal and see if the appeal was heard. The users' references to the idea of peace appeared in more than 30 percent of the reviews.

The way of addressing the idea of peace in reviews can be divided into two categories, which are sometimes supplemented by thoughts on the future of the world. The first category is the wish that tragedies such as the atomic bombing never happen again, in the name of the slogan "No more Hiroshimas": "…should have enough of an impact on you to not want this to happen EVER again, regardless of the politics that led to this. All life is precious." (April 23, 2016, tripadvisoruser23, Australia).

The second category is the reference to the dangers of nuclear weapons or a call to stop amassing nuclear arsenals, e.g. "This museum is a reminder of what a nuclear weapon can do. It is something we all should learn from history." (April 24, 2017, tripadvisoruser24, United States).

Conclusion

The quantitative analysis presented in this paper clearly demonstrates that a significant part of the reviews contains very similar elements and that recurring trends can easily be noticed. The analyzed samples turned out to be a useful tool in deconstructing the narrative and its impact on the visitors.

The HPMM conveys its message primarily through the language of emotion. The evoked emotions bind the public to the memorial site and, in a way, instill a certain message—in this case, it is an appeal for peace and a warning against the danger of nuclear weapons. The main medium that the visitors have noticed are the relics and vivid pictures, accompanied by moving "private" stories, often the ones of the children. This combination must have an impact on the recipient and is the main way in which the HPMM engages its public. The educational function of the HPMM cannot be denied: it is clearly conveyed by the content of the exhibition, as the visitors agree, but the vast majority of posted opinions contain descriptions of emotions.

Furthermore, the museum's message is strengthened by the cohesion of the entire Hiroshima Peace Memorial Park complex, which is also noticed by the public. Many of the visitors mention a very clear appeal for peace and nuclear abolition (which is even literally included in the name of the Hiroshima's complex). This message is not questioned by the public; however, some of the visitors stress the insufficiency of the narrative (e.g., lack of information about the reasons for using nuclear weapons against Hiroshima) and openly criticize the HPMM narrative.

The comments posted on Tripadvisor show that the HPMM's public is primarily an audience that passively consumes the narrative presented. It should be additionally emphasized that a vast part of the audience probably did not even publish their opinion about the HPMM, so the fact of making an effort to describe one's experience of the HPMM on a portal like Tripadvisor should already be considered a form of activity of the public. Even the simplest posts that recommend (or discourage) visiting the HPMM can have an impact on potential visitors. A more detailed analysis of the reviews has revealed a greater involvement of a small part of the public. Some took on the role of the museum staff and provided practical details, tips and tricks to potential visitors. Some made their choice of the exhibition highlights. And some made elaborate comments referring to the political situation in the world, mentioning other memorial sites (unrelated to the atomic bomb explosion), and most of all—the criticism of the narrative in the HPMM.

Thanks to the public's engagement, Tripadvisor not only reflects how the public perceives a history-related tourist attraction and its public history-related activities, but it also is instrumental in shaping their perception by other public(s), becoming itself a tool or form of public history. More detailed research on the profile of this most active part of the public could bring insights on who is actually doing the public history "from below."

Notes

1 Barbara Franco, "Public History and Memory: A Museum Perspective," *The Public Historian* 19, no. 2 (1997): 66.
2 Tripadvisor, accessed August 8, 2020, https://tripadvisor.mediaroom.com/caen-about-us.
3 Susan V. Scott and Wanda J. Orlikowski, "Entanglements in Practise: Performing Anonymity Through Social Media," *MIS Quarterly* 38, no. 3 (September 2014): 873–893; Catheryn Khoo-Lattimore and Erdogan Haktan Ekiz, "Power in Praise: Exploring Online Compliments on Luxury Hotels in Malaysia," *Tourism and Hospitality Research* 14, no. 3 (July 2014): 152–159.
4 The first best-rated attraction is the Atomic Bomb Dome and the second–Hiroshima Peace Memorial Park (Hiroshima Peace Memorial Museum is part of Hiroshima Peace Memorial Park); Tripadvisor, accessed July 26, 2020, https://www.tripadvisor.com/Attractions-g298561-Activities-a_allAttractions.true-Hiroshima_Hiroshima_Prefecture_Chugoku.html.
5 Huong T. Bui, Kaori Yoshida, and Timothy Lee, "Heritage Landscapes of Hiroshima and Nagasaki," *Heritage and Tourism: Places, Imageries and the Digital Age*, ed. Linde Egberts and Maria D. Alvarez (Amsterdam: Amsterdam University Press, 2018), 55–75.
6 Under the 219th article of the Hiroshima Peace Memorial City Construction Law (August 6, 1949), Hiroshima was established as the Peace Memorial City.
7 Bui, Yoshida, and Lee, "Heritage Landscapes"; Yuki Miyamoto, *Beyond the Mushroom Cloud: Commemoration, Religion, and Responsibility after Hiroshima* (New York: Fordham University Press, 2012), 47–77.
8 Benedict Giamo, "The Myth of the Vanquished: The Hiroshima Peace Memorial Museum," *American Quarterly* 55, no. 4 (December, 2003): 703–728.
9 Hiroshima Peace Memorial Museum, "Museum History," accessed September 13, 2020, http://hpmmuseum.jp/modules/info/index.php?action=PageView&page_id=67&-lang=eng.
10 Hiroshima Peace Memorial Museum, accessed August 8, 2020, http://hpmmuseum.jp.
11 Dina Mayzlin, Yaniv Dover, and Judith Chevalier, "Promotional Reviews: An Empirical Investigation of Online Review Manipulation," *The American Economic Review* 104, no. 8 (August 2014): 2421–2455.
12 2019 Tripadvisor Transparency Report, Tripadvisor, https://www.tripadvisor.com/TripAdvisorInsights/wp-content/uploads/2019/09/2147_PR_Content_Transparency_Report_6SEP19_US.pdf.
13 Introduction to Content Transparency Report, Tripadvisor, https://www.tripadvisor.com/TripAdvisorInsights/w5144.
14 Report of the number of visitors to Hiroshima Peace Memorial Museum, https://www.city.hiroshima.lg.jp/uploaded/attachment/112306.pdf.
15 See David Silverman, *Interpreting Qualitative Data: A Guide to Principles of Qualitative Research* (London: SAGE, 2011). Chapter 10 by Dorota Choińska in this volume presents the grounded theory in more detail.

16 All quotations contained in the paper are from the "Reviews" section of the Tripadvisor subpage of the Peace Museum website, accessed April 21, 2020, https://www.tripadvisor.com/Attraction_Review-g298561-d320360-Reviews-Hiroshima_Peace_Memorial_Museum-Hiroshima_Hiroshima_Prefecture_Chugoku.html. All the usernames were anonymized by the author.

17 Hiroshima Peace Memorial Museum, accessed August 8, 2020, http://hpmmuseum.jp.

Bibliography

Bui, Huong T., Kaori Yoshida, and Timothy Lee. "Heritage Landscapes of Hiroshima and Nagasaki." In *Heritage and Tourism: Places, Imageries and the Digital Age*, edited by Linde Egberts and Maria D. Alvarez. Amsterdam: Amsterdam University Press, 2018.

Franco, Barbara. "Public History and Memory: A Museum Perspective." *The Public Historian* 19, no. 2 (1997): 65–67.

Giamo, Benedict. "The Myth of the Vanquished: The Hiroshima Peace Memorial Museum." *American Quarterly* 55, no. 4 (December, 2003): 703–728.

Hiroshima Peace Memorial Museum. Accessed September 13, 2020. https://hpmmuseum.jp.

Hiroshima Peace Memorial Museum. "Museum History." Accessed September 13, 2020. http://hpmmuseum.jp/modules/info/index.php?action=PageView&page_id=67&lang=eng.

Hiroshima Peace Memorial Museum. Tripadvisor. Accessed July 26, 2020. https://www.tripadvisor.com/Attraction_Review-g298561-d320360-Reviews-Hiroshima_Peace_Memorial_Museum-Hiroshima_Hiroshima_Prefecture_Chugoku.html.

Khoo-Lattimore, Catheryn, and Erdogan Haktan Ekiz. "Power in Praise: Exploring Online Compliments on Luxury Hotels in Malaysia." *Tourism and Hospitality Research* 14, no. 3 (July 2014): 152–159.

Mayzlin, Dina, Yaniv Dover, and Judith Chevalier. "Promotional Reviews: An Empirical Investigation of Online Review Manipulation." *The American Economic Review* 104, no. 8 (August 2014): 2421–2455.

Miyamoto, Yuki. *Beyond the Mushroom Cloud: Commemoration, Religion, and Responsibility after Hiroshima*. New York: Fordham University Press, 2012.

Report of the number of visitors to Hiroshima Peace Memorial Museum. https://www.city.hiroshima.lg.jp/uploaded/attachment/112306.pdf.

Scott, Susan V., and Wanda J. Orlikowski. "Entanglements in Practise: Performing Anonymity Through Social Media." *MIS Quarterly* 38, no. 3 (September 2014): 873–893.

Silverman, David. *Interpreting Qualitative Data: A Guide to Principles of Qualitative Research*. London: SAGE, 2011.

Tripadvisor. 2019 Tripadvisor Review Transparency Report. https://www.tripadvisor.com/TripadvisorInsights/wp-content/uploads/2019/09/2147_PR_Content_Transparency_Report_6SEP19_US.pdf.

Tripadvisor. Introduction to Content Transparency Report. https://www.tripadvisor.com/TripAdvisorInsights/w5144.

13

THE PUBLIC OF A PUBLIC HISTORY WEBSITE—NOTES FROM THE FIELD

Tihana Kušter

In my final year of graduate study, one professor said that the main problem of current historiography is that historians do not read their colleagues' works outside of their field of study. Two years later, this problem was the main catalyst of a website I started to develop. I called it Povcast, a combination of two words *povijest* ("history" in Croatian) and "podcast" (which would become only one type of media shared by this website).

Two years after launching the website, Facebook page and YouTube channel, Povcast is sharing article reviews of new books and scholarly papers, works of young experts from the humanities, as well as promoting good-quality YouTube channels and events, and publishing creative materials (games, exercises, e-books, videos) for teaching history in elementary schools and high schools.[1] Although anyone can access the content, the targeted public of our website are historians and history teachers by profession or training, history enthusiasts, and other specialists in the humanities (art history, archaeology, philosophy, literature). One and a half years after launching the website, it has had around 4,000 views and 2,500 visitors per month, an 8 percent bounce rate and a two-minute average session duration. With overall around 170 published articles by 11 authors, the website has an approximate frequency of publishing two articles per week. It is most active on Facebook where it has around 4,600 followers.

Instead of behaving like a one-sided authority that is mostly sharing encyclopedic knowledge and historical facts, Povcast is first and foremost an open platform that emphasizes the sharing of historiographical facts, interpretations and arguments that are open to criticism. Emphasizing published content as someone's interpretations instead of sharing it as historical fact is not common in Croatian society—not even in all parts of higher education let alone in high school or primary education. Since focusing

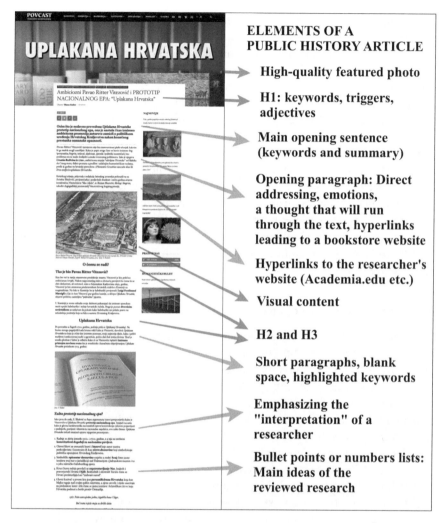

FIGURE 13.1 Elements of a Public History Article, © Tihana Kušter.[2]

on facts instead of interpretations and arguments cannot encourage critical thinking, that kind of long-lasting climate along with the political burden of recent history has resulted in a public that tends to be interested only in limited history topics, often approaching them with their political agenda. That climate has also harmed the status of history as a discipline proceeding from the opinion that history is purposeless.[3] Such an attitude of the intended public poses certain challenges to the history-related website developer.

Before starting a public history website, one has to master certain skills necessary for maintaining a website and producing content. One must have basic knowledge about content writing and visual design, blog tools, publishing platforms and *content management system* (CMS) such as Word-press.org, video and photo editing software like *Adobe Premiere* or *Final Cut Pro X* or social media platforms like Facebook (Business and Page Manager), Instagram, Twitter and YouTube.[4] Yet, technologies evolve and the trends in visual design that are necessary for editing a public history website change even more rapidly. Among younger generations of public historians, those skills are usually quickly mastered. Web content writing is another skill, crucial whether one is launching a private blog, website, publishing articles on different news websites, writing scripts for audio or video podcasts or just sharing news about his or her research on social media. It also changes but does so a bit more slowly. While academic writing is, rightly, much taught in traditional history programs, mastering a writing skill that is greatly different from it can be quite difficult for historians. Its main challenge is achieving a balance between educating the public (in both historical contents and historiographical approaches) and getting the public's attention.

Addressing the Public's Needs

With the rise of Google, smartphones and marketing-oriented social media platforms, digital marketing has become a field that has prospered greatly in the last 15 years. A very simple and broad definition of digital marketing is: a field that uses digital media to stimulate people to like something or someone and buy something or engage with someone (companies, products or people). It is used in commerce, the entertainment industry, politics, and recently in culture and science. Companies can sell products, politicians can win elections, entertainers can get their audience and public historians can promote their field, work and research using digital marketing.

The largest advantage of digital marketing is a wide possibility of analytics. By using analytical and statistical tools such as Google Analytics and Google Search console on our history website, we can know exactly which topics, articles and authors are most read, what the age, gender and interests of our public are, for how long, when and where our public reads our article, how much our public is interested in reading more than one article, etc. Most importantly, by changing sections of our content, we can also test to see which methods in making history content are most successful in achieving goals among our public. For example, when publishing a public history content, one can test which elements of visual content or headline work better than others (e.g., colorful or monochrome featured photographs, visuals with more, less or no text, shorter or longer headlines).

Digital marketing includes, among others, knowledge and skills in search engine optimization (SEO), search engine marketing (SEM), content writing, copywriting, web design, social media marketing, optimization and management. Although the field is vast and digital public historians can learn from every above-mentioned subfield, this chapter focuses on content writing. This skill is most needed in the practice of doing public history, whether for writing web articles or making scripts for video or audio podcasts.

Content Writing

During the first episode of the new International Federation for Public History's video series *Public History with…* (June 2020), viewers had a chance to hear the experience of well-known public historian Suzannah Lipscomb.[5] When talking about the skills she finds necessary for a public historian, she mentioned speaking in front of the camera and writing. While behaving in front of the camera might sound difficult for a historian with only traditional education, writing is a skill that is well known to every historian, as traditional history is based on the written word.

Yet, Lipscomb stated that learning how to write was one of the first skills she had to overcome when writing scripts and doing other public history work. The general necessity to change the way historians write was recognized in public history literature.[6] Among the published essays, Thomas Harbison and Luke Waltzer highlighted six useful characteristics (active, social, open, media-rich, metacognitive, immersive) they considered as the most important when implementing the pedagogical project that encouraged web writing among students.[7] Alex Sayf Cummings and Jonathan Jarrett discussed the benefits and drawbacks of blogging, which they call informal online writing, rightly asking if such kind of writing can be scholarship.[8] Nowadays, it is questionable if we should be using the term informal when describing public history web writing. Informal presupposes that something is without exact form. Although web writing need not be as complex and formal in style as academic writing, today's public history web writing (be it video or audio, or a written text) must be just as well planned, organized, responsible and accurate, with carefully selected references as in academic writing, and with a form and elements that suit the web environment and the public we address. Whatever one's web writing style becomes, it must not be taken lightly as something one can write in half an hour during the lunchtime break. Web writing must be well planned, organized and even more carefully edited afterward. The following advice on writing public history for the web is based on literature and experience from managing Povcast website.[9]

Writing a Story

Even the most complex interpretations can be written as a more or less good story. To do that, historians should force themselves to get away from their well-established ivory tower of academic and encyclopedic writing. Below, there are two examples of an opening paragraph of my article about a recent publication.

> Pavao Ritter Vitezović was a Croatian erudite and scholar who was born in 1652 in Senj and died in 1713 in Wien. During his lifetime he was a historian, linguist, publisher, diplomat, poet, and political theorist, and because of all his work historians usually call him a polyhistor. Among his most famous works are *Kronika aliti spomen vsega svieta vikov (1696)*, *Lexicon Lattino-Illyricum* and *Croatia Rediviva* published in the year 1700. Historians and literary theorists interpreted *Croatia Rediviva* as an ambitious utopia of "revived Croatia" from the Baltic to the Black Sea. However, *Plorantis Croatiae saecula duo* or *Two Centuries of Weeping Croatia*, another important work of Vitezović that is still not well known in past and present academic circles, was only translated last year.

We can also write like this:

> Pavao Ritter Vitezović was probably not the introverted, timid scholar you might imagine him to be. As the list of everything he was is exhaustive (historian, linguist, publisher, diplomat, poet, and political theorist), we can without a doubt call him a polyhistor. While his *Croatia Rediviva* from 1700, an ambitious utopia of "revived Croatia" from the Baltic to the Black Sea, is well known in academic circles, *Plorantis Croatiae saecula duo* or *Two Centuries of Weeping Croatia* was only translated into Croatian last year.[10]

The first paragraph is still not as complex and formal in style as academic writing, and it contains almost the same amount of information as the second one. One might say it resembles the encyclopedic writing we tend to see in public history web writing. But, why is the second version preferable? There are many correct ways to write an opening sentence. Instead of well-known facts and a sequence of synonyms, we can start with addressing the public directly, with emotions, and with a thought that will run through the entire text. It is hard for historians to accept that, but if dates, places of birth and any other facts do not contribute to the point of the story, they are irrelevant. Our public knows approximately where the actor lived. Mentioning only one year is usually enough to place the actor at the correct time. The purpose of the website article is not to give encyclopedic knowledge that can easily be found on Wikipedia (which also tends to develop stories rather than provide raw "encyclopedic" data, especially in the longer entries). Other changes in the paragraph are a result of playing with word order and erasing unnecessary and repetitive words. Instead of 9 lines and 125 words, we got 6 lines and 85 words with the same amount of relevant information but in a content that is more likely to convince the public to read further.

Simple Writing

In *The Elements of Academic Style: Writing for the Humanities*, Eric Hayot, a professor of comparative literature, has argued that "in order to succeed as an academic writer," "you will need to master a professional discourse."[11] However, the very same text where he stated this is written in a compelling, personal, non-academic style without jargon or complex words. After all, Hayot is a literature professor. Writing for the web might be the same as writing a how-to-write manual. We should be thinking about the needs, abilities and expectations of our public when writing an article for them. Even if our public is highly educated, they are busy and the digital revolution has accustomed them to getting information quickly. They will not be spending their time on something that is written in a needlessly complex way. Some might disagree with Eric Hayot who thinks that expanding vocabulary and learning new words and synonyms is a great daily exercise necessary for any academic writer. They might say that for analog publications, it is also advisable to write more plainly simply because reading digital content is already affecting the way we read analog content. But for writing digital content, simple writing is of utmost importance.

Avoiding jargon is, however, the easy part. Unfortunately for writers, it is far harder to write about complex ideas plainly and simply than the other way around. To do so, we have to make an extra effort to transform (!) what we have already written or read in academic texts into interesting content. This transformed content has to be suitable for a public that is not necessarily specialized in the topic, and it has to be readable anytime, anywhere on the web.

Readability Score

When I was in college, professors used to warn us not to leave too much blank space when writing assignments. It would be deceiving, they said, as though we had written more than we had. Although this rule might be necessary for indolent students who have to be sharply disciplined at the beginning of their studies, it is one of the rules that are invalid for web writing. First, the students' main (or even only) audience were their professors, who were accustomed to understanding complex texts. Based on a readability test developed in 1975 for the US Navy by Rudolf Flesch, a strong advocate of plain writing, and J. Peter Kincaid, these complex texts have a low Flesch–Kincaid score (0–30) which means they are harder to understand by those who are not university graduates.[12] Second, analog publications (books, journals) can usually tolerate more words than web articles. Third, blank space is expensive in analog publications.

When writing for the web, one discovers a consequence of the digital and visual revolution: the importance of a readability check defined by syllables, paragraph and sentence length.[13] It is based on the Flesch–Kincaid theory according to which our mind and eyes focus on successive points (punctuation marks and new paragraphs) when reading. Those points allow us to comprehend easily what we have just read.[14] To make the text more readable, words and sentences should be shorter and paragraphs must be divided by headings and subheadings. For example, the most common rule is that the interval between subheadings should not be larger than 250–300 words. Reading from the screen then becomes easier for visually impaired people as well as for those who tend to scan longer texts before reading them entirely.[15] Analytics and search engine optimization show us that sites with good readability scores have better session duration and Google search rank. In other words, our public reads more of the article if the article has a better readability score. They, already altered by the digital revolution, are used to reading articles with shorter sentences and paragraphs divided by headings, blank space and subheadings.

Needless to say, because we were taught to write differently, all of my older articles as well as many articles of authors on our and other websites have very poor readability checks. The result is devastating. We are among the few agile Millennial historians with a strong awareness of the necessity to publish online. At the same time, we produce articles that even we cannot read.

Redundant Words

Another way to improve not only style but readability checks is by eliminating redundant words. While there are many examples of frequently used redundant words, the ones I most often notice in public history writing are transition words and adverbs.

When writing an academic text, we are encouraged to use transition words such as however, also, in sum, in short, nevertheless, therefore, in conclusion or ultimately.[16] Most of the time they are unnecessary. They might even distract the reader from the important part of the sentence. By simply deleting these words and not changing anything else, our text becomes clearer. We were also taught to use adverbs to augment the meaning. If the adverb does not change the meaning, it is unnecessary. Instead of augmenting words with adverbs, it is shorter and preferable to use a synonym with a stronger meaning. By deleting unnecessary words, we get shorter sentences which contribute to a better readability check.[17]

Making Headlines

The 80/20 percent rule about headlines says that approximately eight out of ten people are going to read our headline but only two of them will click on the article.[18] An even lower percentage of them are going to read the entire article. If we want our public to read our history web content, composing a good headline is crucial.

There are many web articles about writing a good headline but not all are suitable for writing history-related content on the web or addressing our public. Neil Patel, bestselling author and one of the most influential people in digital marketing, recommends using clickbait when writing a headline,[19] though some marketing experts disagree with him.[20] Clickbait has gained negative connotations as standing for a content that makes the public believe the content of the article is better than it actually is. That kind of practice can have a long-term negative impact on our public. After all, merely getting clicks should not be the goal of any public history website.[21]

Instead of recycling common forms of clickbait to which the public is already becoming immune, it is preferable to use triggers. Unlike clickbait that tends to make the public feel tricked or used, triggers in headlines must treat the public with respect and must stand behind good quality article content. At the beginning of Povcast, I was trying to promote a publication about the making of premodern public administration. My first version of the title was exactly: "Making of Premodern Administration." One might hardly think of a more unexciting topic on first sight than "public administration." Then, I tried to find triggers or the most interesting parts of the article. In the publication I was promoting, the author explains how the making of premodern public administration also meant that the Habsburg monarchy was trying to cope with corruption and conflict of interests. Since both terms are burning issues in Croatia, I incorporated them into the headline. The second version was: "Making of Premodern Administration: Corruption and Conflict of Interests." Finally, if those words are triggers, it is advisable to put them in the first place in the headline: "Corruption and Conflict of Interests: Making of Premodern Administration." Despite a seemingly unexciting topic, this article was one of the most readable ones at the time it was published.

Other than finding triggers, some advice on creating a better headline in digital marketing can be also useful in public history web writing.[22] Headlines should contain keywords to improve ranking on search engines, and the optimal length should be under ten words. Shorter headlines containing only three to four words do not tell enough about the content of the article and are not eye-catching for the public, while more than about ten words in a headline are not going to be shown on Google Search. Using adjectives, especially ones that are surprising, tends to attract the public to the article. The headline "Ambitious Pavao Ritter Vitezović and Prototype of National Epic: 'Weeping Croatia'" would work better than the same headline without the word "ambitious." Using urgency when writing a headline is the hardest advice to follow if we want to avoid false, fake-news, disrespectful, clickbait headlines. This is especially true for writing public history web content. Unlike politics, commerce or medicine, history is rarely urgent because it has already happened and, in most cases, it does not have a direct ability to save lives or help our public to become wealthier. But in some cases, it is possible to include some element of urgency. For example, how to improve the headline "Public History with Prof. Suzannah Lipscomb: IFPH discussion"? We keep keywords ("Public history with...", "Suzannah Lipscomb"), add an urgent element in the beginning and include adjectives. The preferable headline would be: "LIVE DISCUSSION with outstanding Suzannah Lipscomb: Public History with..."

Educating a Public Accustomed to Positivistic and Politicized History

In addition to finding proper ways to address a public that has been transformed by the digital and visual revolution, when editing a public history website questions might arise on how to address the public affected by special circumstances in the national historiography and society.

Focusing on facts instead of interpretations was interconnected with the great influence of ideology and politics on the history curriculum in the last 50 years. The oldest generations alive today were taught history in the communist Yugoslavia and their children or grandchildren were taught by a completely different history curriculum during the 1990s. During that time, the history curriculum rightly had to be reformed, but it was also excessively influenced by national mythologization. On the other hand, students in the early 2000s were taught a softened version of that ideologization with a new prevailing approach—Europeanization.[23]

The historiographical and political burden of Croatia has resulted in a limitation of relevant public history topics. Although as Jerome de Groot has noted, certain history topics (the Second World War, military history, Egyptology, Empire) tend to be more popular than others, a problem arises when relevant public history topics are exclusively ones that tend to be controversial and political.[24] In particular, confronting and coping with the socio-historical inheritance of Ustashas and Partisans is the topic that is most present in any type of (social) media. It is not only that it causes the strongest reaction in historiographically observed, mostly low-quality, discussions but it is even being used in the political debates preceding the parliamentary and presidential elections. Such a situation with an absence of public space for other public history topics can only emphasize a widespread public opinion that history is an overly politicized discipline that only causes discord in society. Fortunately, no matter how long they have lasted, controversies do have a shelf life and their effect diminishes over time.

To encourage thematic diversity, the public of Povcast can examine the content based on entrenched categorization according either to historical periods (Antique, Medieval, Early Modern, Modern and Postmodern) or to historical (sub)disciplines (e.g., Archaeology, Economic History and

Eco-history, Political, Legal and Military History, Cultural and Social History, Art, Literature, Science, Historical Imagology, History of Religion, Digital History). Although authors write according to their affinities, this categorization not only promotes writing about different periods from the aspect of different historical (sub)disciplines but it also shows the diversity of all that historical discipline is. Since it was not so long ago when the Croatian History curriculum taught only about wars, the disintegration and emergence of states, rulers, and political affairs, widespread public opinion continued to perceive political history as the only "real" history we should care and learn about.

At the end of the long-awaited curriculum reform in Croatia, completed in 2019, the History curriculum was submitted to modifications that caused division both within the Croatian historiographical community and in media and society. Controversial debates that took place around a new History Curriculum are a vivid indicator of heterogeneity of historiographical profession in Croatia which manifests itself at all levels of society.[25]

Besides the politicization of certain topics, an even more important issue of one of the versions of the proposal is the paradigm that enables that politicization. In the Statement of the Department of History of the Faculty of Philosophy in Zagreb on the second version of the Proposal of the History Curriculum, sent for public consultation in February 2019, historians stated that:

> The proposal does not take into account the basic theoretical, methodological, and conceptual propositions of modern historical discipline. This is shown in the non-recognition of the epistemological difference between the past historical reality (historical fact) and its historiographical interpretation and presentation (historiographical fact).[26]

In their opinion, the proposal has "a normative and prescriptive character," which "prevents the development of historical and critical thinking." According to the Statement, "the term 'historical story' (instead of 'historical narrative') should be replaced by the concept of 'historical interpretation.'" That should be implemented in any historiographical text, "whether professional historiography or historical textbooks."[27] When writing for Povcast, I developed practical methods to affirm the concept of historical interpretation and emphasize historical arguments that are prone to the public's criticism. When writing and editing, I tend to integrate the term "interpretation," often not only inside the text but also in highlighted subheadings which are immediately visible when skimming and scanning the article. Although the advice is to transform the academic research into a more or less good story, the author of the historical interpretation should always be kept within that story as a corresponding actor who is not only mentioned often throughout the text but also as someone whose personal websites are linked through the content. In that way, the reader gets a clearer sense that the content they have read is not an indisputable historical fact but a product of interpretation with clearly stated arguments of a live and accessible person whose works, biography and contacts can be easily accessed through hyperlinks.

Situation Unimaginable Ten Years Ago…

The idea of creating a public history website as a platform that can replace numerous dispersed blogs and projects emerged as just one way of doing public history online. Yet, nowadays, ideas become obsolete faster than ever before. Public historians must, on the one hand, adapt to the trends they encounter, and on the other hand, reflect on them. Whether they are writing articles, publishing on social media, or producing audio and video podcasts, content writing is the most basic skill for doing public history. Copy-pasting academic text from analog publications and publishing or performing it online without any modifications is less effective not only because of the environment where they are sharing but also because of the new generations of public they are addressing, and their specific needs. The preferred strategy is to write not simplified but simply, keeping in mind all the advice provided to us by the rich field of digital marketing, content writing and copywriting. However, in order to avoid clickbaiting or writing poor quality content just for the sake of publishing more frequently, it is always desirable to remind yourself that it is better to gain fewer readers that consume and understand the whole content rather than gain a large public that tends to click on the article and exit right away after a few seconds.

A situation unimaginable ten years ago comes clearly to my mind: my two-year-old boy was trying to use a newly bought large TV screen as if it was a touchscreen smartphone. As amusing as it was to see how his brain interchanged the possibilities of different technologies, some of you reading this might already have a large touchscreen TV in your home. It is not only that we have changed, but our public and public that is still maturing is changing even more rapidly. Lamentations about how ways of the past were better will not make any difference. It is our obligation to address forthcoming generations in a way that they would understand us most effectively.

Notes

1 Povcast, accessed August 15, 2020, https://povcast.hr.
2 Based on Tihana Kušter, "Ambiciozni Pavao Ritter Vitezović i PROTOTIP NACIONALNOG EPA *Uplakana Hrvatska*," *Povcast*, April 23, 2020, https://povcast.hr/ambiciozni-pavao-ritter-vitezovic-i-prototip-nacionalnog-epa-uplakana-hrvatska.
3 During the last reform of school curriculum (in 2019), the Ministry of Science, Education and Schooling presented a plan to remove history, biology and

geography from the educational curricula of four professions; L.R. Piše, "Divjak: 'Nismo ukinuli povijest, geografiju i biologiju, samo smo napravili novi kurikulum,'" *Dnevnik*, September 27, 2018, https://dnevnik.hr/vijesti/hrvatska/ministrica-blazenka-divjak-dualno-obrazovanje-odgovara-na-potrebe-trzista-rada-nismo-ukinuli-povijest---532275.html; Željko Godeč, "OPASNI EKSPERIMENT DR. DIVJAK Šest obrazovnih stručnjaka za Globus analizira reformu koja iz strukovnih škola izbacuje povijest, zemljopis, biologiju," *Jutarnji*, November 10, 2018, https://www.jutarnji.hr/globus/politika/opasni-eksperiment-dr-divjak-sest-obrazovnih-strucnjaka-za-globus-analizira-reformu-koja-iz-strukovnih-skola-izbacuje-povijest-zemljopis-biologiju-8042129.

4 Photo editing software Adobe Photoshop or free ones, Canva and PhotoScape, can be used for editing all visual content published on websites. Interesting, high-quality, creative and eye-catching visual content is one of the most important elements that determine short-term and long-term reach primarily on social media and afterward on websites. Video editing software such as Adobe Premiere or Final Cut Pro X is necessary for editing video contents that can be published on YouTube, Facebook, Instagram or other social media.

5 "Public History with Suzannah Lipscomb," IFPH Public History, Vimeo, June 4, 2020, https://vimeo.com/425785493.

6 Jack Dougherty and Tennyson O'Donnell, ed., *Web Writing: Why and How for Liberal Arts Teaching and Learning* (Ann Arbor: University of Michigan Press; London: Trinity College ePress edition, 2014); Thomas Cauvin, *Public History. A Textbook of Practice* (London: Routledge, 2016); Jack Dougherty and Kristen Nawrotzki, ed. *Writing History in the Digital Age* (Ann Arbor: University of Michigan Press, 2013).

7 Thomas Harbison and Luke Waltzer, "Toward Teaching the Introductory History Course, Digitally," in *Writing History in the Digital Age*, 177–199.

8 Alex Sayf Cummings and Jonathan Jarrett, "Only Typing? Informal Writing, Blogging, and the Academy," in *Writing History in the Digital Age*, 426–448.

9 See Ann Handley, *Everybody Writes. Your Go-To Guide to Ridiculously Good Content* (New York: Wiley, 2014); Janice (Ginny) Redish, *Letting Go of the Words. Writing Web Content that Works*, 2nd ed. (San Francisco: Morgan Kaufmann, 2012); Lynda Felder, *Writing for the Web. Creating Compelling Web Content Using Words, Pictures and Sound* (Berkeley: New Riders, 2012).

10 Kušter, "Ambiciozni Pavao Ritter Vitezović."

11 Eric Hayot, *The Elements of Academic Style. Writing for the Humanities* (New York: Columbia University Press, 2014), 390–393.

12 Handley, *Everybody Writes*, 80–81.

13 See more about readability check in Handley, *Everybody Writes*, 80–81; Jono Alderson, "SEO Basics How to Use Headings on Your Site," *Yoast* (blog), accessed June 3, 2020, https://yoast.com/how-to-use-headings-on-your-site; Marieke Van de Rakt, "Paragraph Length Check: Why and How to Write Shorter Paragraphs," *Yoast* (blog), accessed June 3, 2020, https://yoast.com/paragraph-length-check.

14 Handley, *Everybody Writes*, 80–81.

15 See more about headings and subheadings distribution in Alderson, "SEO Basics How to Use Headings"; about scanning text, shorter sentences and paragraphs: Redish, *Letting Go of the Words*, 47–48, 470–483.

16 Hayot, *The Elements of Academic Style*, 244–245.

17 Handley, *Everybody Writes*, 98–99.

18 See more about 20/80 rule in writing headlines in Rick Barron, "The 80/20 Rule of Headlines," *Digital Doughnut*, November 5, 2019, https://www.digitaldoughnut.com/articles/2019/september/the-80-20-rule-of-headlines.

19 See more in Neil Patel, "Why Clickbait Works (And Why You Should Do More of It)," *Neilpatel* (blog), accessed June 5, 2020, https://neilpatel.com/blog/why-clickbait-works.

20 Ann Gynn, "Clickbait Content: Is It Good or Bad?" Content Marketing Institute, last modified July 7, 2020, accessed July 12, 2020, https://contentmarketinginstitute.com/2018/12/practice-content-clickbait.

21 The goal should be having, as much as possible, devoted readers that will consume the whole article and take targeted actions (read, watch or buy the publications or content we are promoting, share its ideas, spread the interpretations, etc.). Instead of taking account of page views primarily, we can test some of these goals in Google Analytics by checking our bounce rate, average session duration and the number of clicks on the links we are incorporating into the article. "A bounce is a single-page session on your site. In Analytics, a bounce is calculated specifically as a session that triggers only a single request to the Analytics server, such as when a user opens a single page on your site and then exits without triggering any other requests to the Analytics server during that session"; see "Bounce Rate," Google Analytics Help, accessed June 5, 2020, https://support.google.com/analytics/answer/1009409?hl=en. See more about the lack of comments and preferable goals of public history website or blog in Jack Dougherty, "Public Writing and Student Privacy," in *Web Writing: Why and How for Liberal Arts Teaching and Learning*, ed. Jack Dougherty and Tennyson O'Donnell (Ann Arbor: University of Michigan Press; London: Trinity College ePress edition, 2014), 300–306.

22 See, for instance, Patel, "How to Write Headlines People Can't Help but Click [Formulas Inside]," *Neilpatel* (blog), accessed June 5, 2020, https://neilpatel.com/blog/write-irresistible-headlines.

23 See Ana Tomljenović, "Slika Hrvata u srpskim i Srba u hrvatskim udžbenicima za osnovnu školu," *Povijest u nastavi* 10, no. 19 (2012): 1–32; Nikolina Jurković, *Prikaz vladara X. i XI. stoljeća u hrvatskim udžebinicama povijesti od početka 20. stoljeća do danas* (Master's thesis, University of Zagreb, 2018); Valentina Krušelj, *Prikaz zrinsko-frankopanske urote u hrvatskim udžbenicima povijesti od 1918. do danas* (Master's thesis, University of Zagreb, 2018).

24 Jerome De Groot, *Consuming History: Historians and Heritage in Contemporary Popular Culture* (London: Routledge, 2008), 31.

25 For more, see Dora Kršul, "Filozofski fakultet traži povlačenje kurikuluma povijesti!" *Srednja*, February 19, 2019, https://www.srednja.hr/zbornica/filozofski-fakultet-trazi-povlacenje-kurikuluma-povijesti; Kršul, "S Filozofskog oštre kritike na kurikulum povijesti: Vraća nas u 20., čak i u 19. stoljeće!" *Srednja*, February 21, 2019, https://www.srednja.hr/zbornica/s-filozofskog-ostre-kritike-kurikulum-povijesti-vraca-nas-20-cak-19-stoljece; Kršul, "Nastavlja se agonija kurikuluma povijesti: Ministrica ga opet poslala u javnu raspravu," *Srednja*, February 9, 2019, https://www.srednja.hr/novosti/nastavlja-se-agonija-kurikuluma-povijesti-ministrica-ga-opet-poslala-javnu-raspravu.

26 After Kršul, "Filozofski fakultet."

27 Ibid.

Bibliography

Alderson, Jono. "SEO basics How to use headings on your site." *Yoast* (blog) Accessed June 3, 2020. https://yoast.com/how-to-use-headings-on-your-site.

Barron, Rick. "The 80/20 Rule of Headlines." *Digital Doughnut*, November 5, 2019. https://www.digitaldoughnut.com/articles/2019/september/the-80-20-rule-of-headlines.

Cauvin, Thomas. *Public History. A Textbook of Practice*. London: Routledge, 2016.

Cummings, Alex Sayf, and Jonathan Jarrett. "Only Typing? Informal Writing, Blogging, and the Academy." In *Writing History in the Digital Age*, edited by

Jack Dougherty and Kristen Nawrotzki, 426–448. Ann Arbor: University of Michigan Press, 2013.

De Groot, Jerome. *Consuming History: Historians and Heritage in Contemporary Popular Culture.* London: Routledge, 2008.

Dougherty, Jack. "Public Writing and Student Privacy." In *Web Writing: Why and How for Liberal Arts Teaching and Learning*, edited by Jack Dougherty and Tennyson O'Donnell, 290–316. Ann Arbor: University of Michigan Press; London: Trinity College ePress edition, 2014.

Dougherty, Jack, and Kristen Nawrotzki, eds. *Writing History in the Digital Age.* Ann Arbor: University of Michigan Press, 2013.

Felder, Lynda. *Writing for the Web. Creating Compelling Web Content Using Words, Pictures and Sound.* Berkeley: New Riders, 2012.

Godeč, Željko, "OPASNI EKSPERIMENT DR. DIVJAK Šest obrazovnih stručnjaka za Globus analizira reformu koja iz strukovnih škola izbacuje povijest, zemljopis, biologiju." *Jutarnji*, November 10, 2018. https://www.jutarnji.hr/globus/politika/opasni-eksperiment-dr-divjak-sest-obrazovnih-strucnjaka-za-globus-analizira-reformu-koja-iz-strukovnih-skola-izbacuje-povijest-zemljopis-biologiju-8042129.

Google Analytics Help, "Bounce Rate." Accessed June 5, 2020. https://support.google.com/analytics/answer/1009409?hl=en.

Gynn, Ann. "Clickbait Content: Is It Good or Bad?" Content Marketing Institute. Last modified July 7, 2020. Accessed July 12, 2020. https://contentmarketinginstitute.com/2018/12/practice-content-clickbait.

Handley, Ann. *Everybody Writes. Your Go-To Guide to Ridiculously Good Content.* New York: Wiley, 2014.

Harbison, Thomas, and Luke Waltzer. "Toward Teaching the Introductory History Course, Digitally." In *Writing History in the Digital Age*, edited by Jack Dougherty and Kristen Nawrotzki, 177'–199. Ann Arbor: University of Michigan Press, 2013.

Hayot, Eric. *The Elements of Academic Style. Writing for the Humanities.* New York: Columbia University Press, 2014.

IFPH Public History. "Public History with Suzannah Lipscomb." Vimeo, June 4, 2020. https://vimeo.com/425785493.

Jurković, Nikolina. *Prikaz vladara X. i XI. stoljeća u hrvatskim udžebinicama povijesti od početka 20. stoljeća do danas.* Master's thesis, University of Zagreb, 2018.

Kršul, Dora. "Filozofski fakultet traži povlačenje kurikuluma povijesti!" *Srednja*, February 19, 2019. https://www.srednja.hr/zbornica/filozofski-fakultet-trazi-povlacenje-kurikuluma-povijesti.

Kršul, Dora. "Nastavlja se agonija kurikuluma povijesti: Ministrica ga opet poslala u javnu raspravu." *Srednja*, February 9, 2019. https://www.srednja.hr/novosti/nastavlja-se-agonija-kurikuluma-povijesti-ministrica-ga-opet-poslala-javnu-raspravu.

Kršul, Dora. "S Filozofskog oštre kritike na kurikulum povijesti: Vraća nas u 20., čak i u 19. stoljeće!" *Srednja*, February 21, 2019. https://www.srednja.hr/zbornica/s-filozofskog-ostre-kritike-kurikulum-povijesti-vraca-nas-20-cak-19-stoljece.

Krušelj, Valentina. *Prikaz zrinsko-frankopanske urote u hrvatskim udžbenicima povijesti od 1918. do danas.* Master's thesis, University of Zagreb, 2018.

Kušter, Tihana. "Ambiciozni Pavao Ritter Vitezović i PROTOTIP NACIONALNOG EPA: *Uplakana Hrvatska.*" *Povcast*, April 23, 2020. https://povcast.hr/ambiciozni-pavao-ritter-vitezovic-i-prototip-nacionalnog-epa-uplakana-hrvatska.

Patel, Neil. "Why Clickbait Works (And Why You Should Do More of It)." *Neilpatel* (blog). Accessed June 5, 2020. https://neilpatel.com/blog/why-clickbait-works.

Patel, Neil. "How to Write Headlines People Can't Help but Click [Formulas Inside]." *Neilpatel* (blog). Accessed June 5, 2020. https://neilpatel.com/blog/write-irresistible-headlines.

Piše, L.R. "Divjak: 'Nismo ukinuli povijest, geografiju i biologiju, samo smo napravili novi kurikulum.'" *Dnevnik*, September 27, 2018. https://dnevnik.hr/vijesti/hrvatska/ministrica-blazenka-divjak-dualno-obrazovanje-odgovara-na-potrebe-trzista-rada-nismo-ukinuli-povijest---532275.html.

Redish, Janice (Ginny). *Letting Go of the Words. Writing Web Content that Works.* 2nd ed. San Francisco: Morgan Kaufmann, 2012.

Tomljenović, Ana. "Slika Hrvata u srpskim i Srba u hrvatskim udžbenicima za osnovnu školu." *Povijest u nastavi* 10, no. 19 (2012): 1–32.

Van de Rakt, Marieke. "Paragraph Length Check: Why and How to Write Shorter Paragraphs." *Yoast* (blog). Accessed June 3, 2020. https://yoast.com/paragraph-length-check.

PART IV

Publics in Public History Research

14

DIGITAL ORAL HISTORY AND THE ETHICAL DILEMMAS OF DEALING WITH THREE KINDS OF PUBLIC IN PUBLIC HISTORY

Sugandha Agarwal

In the last two decades, new digital technologies have opened up a wide range of possibilities for listening to diverse stories, curating narratives and disseminating audio and video interviews.[1] Housed in digital archives and libraries supported by repository and content management systems, these stories can be accessed by both scholars and the general public. Haskins has singled out the growing memorialization projects or public digital memorials and archives on the internet, attributing their rise to increasingly available digital tools for both creating and disseminating oral histories.[2] However, this online memorialization or the creation of "digital memory" by public institutions cannot be separated from the exploitative political economy of doing such work. In her research on the production of testimony in South Africa, Monica Eileen Patterson argues that while testimonies can be a powerful form of protest, the context within which such work is done and by whom is equally important. She asserts that the numerous journalists, researchers and authors who have written and published extensively about the former apartheid state of South Africa benefit disproportionately from capitalizing on others' stories to advance their own careers. Critical of big public archives, she calls this unequal exchange of stories of suffering as "the political economy of extraction."[3] Robin Ruth Linden has similarly referred to this commodification of memories as the "remembrance industry" because it highlights "the inherently politico-economic nature of the work of remembering, documenting, and commemorating."[4]

According to Anna Sheftel and Stacey Zembrzycki, the recent shift to digital memorialization has only led to further commodification of peoples' intimate histories.[5] They describe the digital world as a "competitive private industry, which thrives on selling us products and commodifying everything from how we communicate with our loved ones, to how we read the news

FIGURE 14.1 1947 © Trilok Singh Artist, public domain.

and absorb information, and even how we make decisions."[6] Owing to the internet's transactional nature, uploading oral histories online, by archives, for instance, inevitably means hiring advertisers for publicity, mining data and selling personal information to advertising agencies.[7]

Sheftel and Zembrzycki have also pointed to methodological concerns that emerge with online recording, editing and dissemination of oral histories. They are particularly critical of techniques of indexing and clipping that distort the interview, fragmenting it into "manageable" and searchable clips to extract information. Researchers fail to listen for details such as the organization of narrative, silences and the use of language. By prioritizing the usability and utility of these stories, such practices fail to account for the complexity of life stories.[8]

[margin handwriting: How is this any different than say, using a letter of a personal journal to present a historical narrative) historical story?]

Oral historians are also critical of the traditional ways of measuring audience engagement with oral histories online.[9] Steve Cohen argues that tools such as hit and view counters fail to give a qualitative measure of how people engage with testimonies online. Therefore, it is unclear if visitors are able to make meaningful connections between themselves and the stories they hear. Cohen argues for the need to formulate "new ways of accessing oral histories" that anticipate why people would value oral histories and relate to them.[10] Sheftel and Zembrzycki have also questioned the heterogeneity of online audiences in terms of class and economic status. They highlight the issue of digital divide, arguing how marginalized communities are excluded from online spaces.[11] At the same time, researchers have also questioned unrestricted public access to oral histories, citing the loss of control over dissemination and representation of their narrators' voices.[12]

The aforementioned issues outline how the creation of public digital archives poses myriad challenges to its primary stakeholders: the oral historians, the interviewees and the audience. For oral historians, the slow and steady practice of listening to stories is reduced to extracting and categorizing information. Narrators' testimonies are hacked down into "digestible" clips to be used as promotional material for financial gain. Audiences are allowed limited access to disjointed and manufactured narratives that they can flip through without meaningful engagement.

[margin handwriting: What are you talking about?]

Informed by these debates on the relationship between digital oral history and public archives, this chapter examines some of the technological, methodological and ethical concerns of working with testimony in online spaces. I conduct a critical analysis of the "1947 Partition Archive"—an open-access digital repository of oral testimonies of Partition survivors collected by volunteers around the world and housed by the Stanford University Library. "Partition" here refers to the 1947 division of the Indian subcontinent into the independent nation-states of India and Pakistan. It was marked by the eruption of large-scale violence between Hindus and Muslims as communal politics between the two communities reached its peak. It resulted in the displacement of 15 million people and the death of two million.[13]

My analysis focuses on the entanglement of digital archives with three kinds of public: the interviewer, the interviewee and the audience. I argue how the "apolitical" Archive,[14] focused entirely on amassing personal testimonies, fails to engage with the complexities of Partition politics, and instead presents a passive narrative of survivors' experiences that is detached from the larger sociopolitical context of the time. Its research process offers little to no space for ethical considerations and fails to include its narrators in the co-production of knowledge. The objective of this chapter is to highlight that in order to engage with stories in the digital age, public archives need to rethink the ways in which narratives are produced and circulated. Further, it highlights their responsibility toward interviewers, narrators and audiences in ensuring collaboration, transparency, reflexivity and shared authority during the research process.

[handwritten margin note: Is the point to be the end to be all history all be all history project?]

Preparing the Interviewer: Examining the 1947 Partition Archive's Oral History Workshop

The 1947 Partition Archive is an open-access public digital repository of oral testimonies collected by volunteers and housed by the Stanford University Library. It was established and registered in 2011 by Dr. Guneeta Singh Bhalla as a nonprofit organization in Berkeley, California.[15] Over the years, it has formed a network of "600 volunteer 'citizen historians' who have devoted an estimated 60,000 hours in volunteer labor towards recording stories."[16] The archive also has a small paid staff that is supported by interns and more than 150 story scholars who also conduct oral histories.

The volunteers associated with the 1947 Partition Archive can be potentially from anywhere in the world and they self-select the individuals they want to interview. While the archive does not offer a sustained reflection on its research methodology, training and interview process, it briefly summarizes what is expected from the interview.[17]

The archive offers a mandatory, online two-hour workshop or webinar that anyone can preregister for, with date and time slots available in Pacific Standard Time.[18] As part of their training, the volunteers are given a "Citizen Historian Training Packet" or a detailed guide with instructions on reaching out to participants, setting up equipment and collecting stories.[19] Volunteers are also provided with two questionnaires or interview field packets—separate for those who migrated during the Partition and those who did not.[20] Other documents include a release form, a post-interview questionnaire and an information card that is left with the interviewees.[21] Interviewers are also required to submit a summary of the interview along with the video file. Completing the workshop and reviewing all the documents, especially the training packet, are mandatory steps to qualify as a "citizen historian" for the archive.[22]

As part of my analysis of the archive's training and interviewing process, I took their two-hour online oral history workshop on September 28, 2019.

An examination of the workshop reveals the archive's treatment of its citizen historians in terms of the training and resources they receive. The workshop began with the coordinator, Rumaila, introducing herself as joining the workshop on behalf of the 1947 Partition Archive. No other essential information was provided about her educational qualifications or prior training, or even her position within the archive. Following a quick round of introductions, it became clear that a number of the workshop participants were students and individuals from different parts of India and Pakistan wanting to interview Partition survivors within their own families. It should be noted that all of the communication was done in English, even though some of the participants struggled to speak the language.

The session began with a brief introduction to the archive and outlined the purpose of the workshop. Discussing the extent of Partition violence, the coordinator compared it to the historical events of Holocaust and Hiroshima, highlighting their extensive systematic documentation within history. She stated that there had been no similar record-keeping of the Partition until 2010 when the archive started its work. However, this appears to be a gross oversight since several oral history projects with survivors of Partition have been conducted throughout the 1990s and late 2000s.[23] Workshop participants were then redirected to a nine-part BBC documentary on YouTube and a list of books for further context on the Partition.

Referring to the pre-interview phone call, the workshop coordinator described it as a way to "break the ice."[24] She framed it as an opportunity to explain to the interviewees what the process entails and decide on a time and place to meet with the interviewee. Moving on to the interview encounter, she advised the citizen historians to "make a human connection"[25] with their interviewees within the first 15–20 minutes, preferably before setting up the camera gear. What such a connection would entail is not elaborated on. Rather, the oral historians are ambiguously urged to "let the person see that you care about him or her."[26] In their own oral history work, Sheftel and Zembrzycki have highlighted the importance of establishing trust and building a relationship with narrators by using the in-person pre-interviews as an opportunity to explain the project to the interviewee and address the process of informed consent.[27]

A significant portion of the workshop time was allotted to the logistics of the interview process. Participants were told to procure their own equipment including a digital video recorder, microphone, tripod, extra batteries, digital still camera, headphones, laptop and extra recording media. The archive does not provide its citizen historians with any equipment, studio space or hands-on support in acquiring and using technical equipment. The emphasis is on capturing high-quality footage and sound with focus on specific camera angles, light, background and noise reduction. Citizen historians were told to be mindful of not including the room or its elements in the portrait photos they captured to ensure that viewers are not "distracted" by these "unnecessary"[28] additions. In isolating the participants from their surroundings, the archive fails to account for the complexity of people's lives—how intimate personal histories are deeply entangled and shaped by mundane routines and objects. The rooms and spaces that the narrators decorate and occupy give us an insight into their everyday lives and can be instrumental in documenting fuller life stories.

According to Larson, there are two aspects of the interview that remain largely undocumented in its digital and audio forms: "the specific context of the oral history event itself, which [...] falls more in the personal than political realm; and the larger cultural context, which tends more to the political."[29] Larson therefore emphasizes the need for sufficiently and richly contextualizing audio/video narratives that are circulated digitally, in terms of both their immediate context and the larger political landscape. Tony Kushner further advises oral historians to refer to a range of other sources while doing narrative research such as diaries, letters, memories and photographs "to reveal the complex layers of memories in the construction of [one's] life story."[30] This allows in the creation of rich, multidimensional and contextualized narratives.

Additionally, the workshop coordinator strongly discouraged the presence of family members or any engagement with them during the interview. They are explicitly forbidden from sitting next to the narrator, not even for emotional or moral support. The training packet also outlines the following:

> If there are other observers and people in the room, avoid eye contact with them, as this usually tempts them to speak up and interrupt the interview. It is best to NOT engage anyone other than the interviewee. Make this clear to everyone before the interview.[31]

According to the archive, this is done to ensure that the focus remains on the interviewee. However, this again poses the question: what aspects of the story are omitted by removing the interviewee from their familial context? As Urvashi Butalia stated in her oral history project, Partition was a familial experience for a number of survivors which is why many of her interviews turned into collective narrations where each member added to the story in their own way. She further notes that interjections made by family members were not only useful sources of information, but they also offered unique insights into the family dynamic within which the interviewee existed and formulated their views. It also shaped how they remember and recount the past. To detach them from this context then is to tell an incomplete story.[32]

The workshop coordinator also urged the citizen historians to look for "possible B-roll opportunities" which could include a 10-minute footage of the participant "doing something casual,"[33] perhaps showcasing a talent or skill such as singing or pottery. Asking survivors of genocide who have experienced immeasurable trauma to "perform" for the camera reduces their narratives to spectacles made for consumption and entertainment. Additionally, workshop participants were told to refrain from filming anything that did not have the interviewee in the frame—footage of the participant's street, for example, or any footage of the interviewer was discouraged. In fact, the interviewers are urged to make themselves "as invisible as possible" both during the interview and on any kind of film. Interviewers are advised to "keep their moral judgements out of the interview."[34] Rather despotically, they are also forbidden from coughing, sneezing and making encouraging sounds to preserve the superior quality of the video footage.

In addition to being silenced on film, the interviewers are given little to no space to offer their own reflections, or talk about their personal experiences, hesitations or doubts with regard to the interview process. A section for biographies of team members, interns and story scholars is also missing. Such a complete erasure of the interviewer's presence from the interview—a shared encounter between the two subjects—robs the oral historian of the opportunity to be reflexive and analyze their own feelings and observations. Valuable insights on how the interviewer's thoughts, ideas, background and personal views shaped the interview encounter are also lost. Sheftel and Zembrzycki, in their testimonial work with survivors of war and genocide, have emphasized the importance of the interviewer's involvement in the oral history process.[35] They stress the significance of a genuine exchange of details and experiences between the two parties to establish a friendly rapport as one would do in any other budding relationship.[36] A shared history and culture between the interviewer and the interviewee also helps in deepening the dialogue, making it possible for some respondents to tell their very difficult stories for the first time.[37]

Workshop participants were also told to remain "objective" during the interview. They were instructed to "focus on the strengths" of their interviewer if the conversation took an emotional turn. While they were not allowed to "deviate from the topic" to make their interviewees feel better, they could complement their interviewees by saying "you are very strong" to keep their "morale" up.[38] Anthropologist Liisa Malkki has argued that one should simply listen "without pretensions to being authenticating experts, investigators, or inquisitors who ask hard questions" by adopting "a caring form of vigilance."[39] Redirecting the interviewee to focus on the "positive" when they are narrating their experiences, could not only undermine the severity of their trauma, but also interrupt a potential moment of grieving.

The archive also fails to provide any meaningful tools to compensate its citizen historians either emotionally, physically or monetarily. It is important to note that while citizen historians are essentially volunteers, they are neither provided with technical assistance or equipment nor financially remunerated for hours of labor. There is no shared studio space or office for them to debrief or exchange feedback. The archive also fails to provide them with adequate counseling measures, needed especially if the stories shared are particularly intense.

Approaching the Interviewee: Listening Deeply

The archive claims to have amassed "8000 memories" (or testimonies) across "400+ cities in 12 countries" till date, with the goal of reaching "10,000 families" by 2020.[40] Of these testimonies, 50 interviews, conducted with both men and women, are currently publicly accessible via the Stanford Library Archive.[41] In this section, I examine two publicly available interviews with women survivors to understand the archive's interactions with its narrators. These include Sushiri Motilal's (79 years old) interview conducted by Zain Alam on November 13, 2013, in Lucknow,[42] India, and Leela Mamtani's (87 years old) interview conducted by Prakhar Joshi in New Delhi, India, on January 29, 2014.[43] I selected these interviews based on the following criteria: they include experiences of both migrant and non-migrant women, are in Hindi language and were conducted in India. It should be noted that both interviewers identify as men whereas both interviewees are women.

In his interview, Alam strictly follows the questionnaire and begins by asking questions about Sushiri's family history. However, these questions are too open-ended and unstructured, causing the interviewee to give abrupt, confused responses. This can be observed in the following transcript:

Z: "Do you know anything about your family history?"
S: "What kind of family?"
Z: "Like..." (trails off, possibly trying to think of a specific term)
S: "My father?"
Z: "What your father or grandfather or great-grandfather used to do, their traditions, their traits..."[44]

Sushiri then goes on to give a standard narration of the city in which her father lived and the job he was employed in until his retirement. The interviewer fails to engage her by asking follow-up questions. Instead, he mutters, "and [...] do you know if you have any family history [...] can you trace your great-grandfather, his grandfather and so on..."[45] Sushiri simply shakes her head in refusal and says "no." In merely following the script and asking Sushiri to remember and recite her entire family history, the interviewer misses the opportunity to ask inquisitive questions that would draw meaningful responses from the interviewee. As Sheftel and Zembrzycki also discovered in their interviews with Holocaust survivors, interviewees tend to give a "factual, narrative recitation" of their experiences because that is what they anticipate the interviewer to be looking for in the interview.[46] However, unlike the archive, Sheftel and Zembrzycki learned to adapt their methodology after sensing a pattern in the interviews they conducted. While interviews would often begin with formal recitations of memories, they listened carefully for cues regarding what might be important to the interviewees and used that to deepen their conversations.[47]

In talking to oft-interviewed Holocaust survivors about what they defined as "real interviews," Henry Greenspan and Sidney Bolkosky discovered that interviewees valued it when narrators were able to find a rhythm.[48] In "asking the right thing at the right time,"[49] interviewers exhibit sensitivity, attentiveness and prior knowledge. This was visibly lacking in both of the archive's interviews. In case of Joshi's interview with Mrs. Mamtani, he failed to follow a coherent narrative and, instead, jumped from one question to another. In one instance, when Mrs. Mamtani is talking about her passion for singing—and how, as a TV and radio artist, her songs and interviews are often broadcast internationally—the narrator abruptly switches the conversation to her village, despite her being clearly keen on discussing her singing career. In another instance, Joshi interrupts a mundane discussion about her schooling to casually ask if the women in her village were "oppressed, dominant or free."[50] She laughs and responds, "...my elder sisters weren't allowed to go out without covering their head nor were they allowed to talk to strangers."[51] In creating neat categories for women to fit in, Joshi erases the complexities and ambiguities surrounding the ways in which women occupy space in the world. He also fails to ask Leela about how she felt about these restrictions. Anderson and others have argued that "if we want to know how women feel about their lives, we have to allow them to talk about their feelings as well as activities."[52] We have to ask them how certain events made them feel and what meaning they hold for them.[53] In imposing his own questions and perspectives in the interview, Joshi misses the opportunity to learn about the Partition from Leela's standpoint.

Calling an interview a collaborative effort, Greenspan and Bolkosky assert that "a testimony that is simply given by one side, and gathered up by the other, need not entail any collaboration at all. It is more like a speech delivered to an assembly of one—'an interviewer.'"[54] Such a one-sided "interview" resembles an "interrogation" aimed at collecting data rather than a shared engagement between two individuals.[55] It fails to offer us an insight into the interviewer's thoughts, experiences and emotions that both inform and influence the interview encounter. This lack of contextualization became clear to me as I listened to Alam's interview with Mrs. Sushiri. For instance, at one point during the interview, an off-camera male voice, most likely a family member, can be heard telling her to "speak loudly" to which she responds with a mumbled "okay." She is also seen pausing the interview briefly to talk to the house-help, asking them to set up food. Sounds of food being prepared and cooked are also audible in the background. What does it mean, for Sushiri's story to be framed and positioned against the sound of a pressure cooker's whistle? What does her immediate agreement to "speak loudly," on the insistence of presumably her husband, imply? According to Anderson and others, "interviews can also tell us how women felt about what they did and can interpret the personal meaning and value of particular activities"[56] but only if we listen to them deeply. "Deep listening," a key principle of the methodology used by the multimedia Montreal Life Stories[57] project, involves "listening for meanings, not just facts, and listening in such a way that prompts more profound reflection from the interviewee."[58] By failing to meaningfully situate Mrs. Sushiri's testimony in the context of her positionality as a woman, Joshi fails to listen deeply.

According to Larson, in order to win the trust of a community, researchers have to go beyond their own disciplinary needs to "see what the project participants hope to get out of their involvement."[59] She recommends a stance of ongoing involvement with the communities being researched by inviting their inputs on the interpretation, presentation and contextualization of the project. This would help researchers understand how people would like to be represented and what holds meaning for them.[60] Michael Frisch has referred to this process of co-creating knowledge with narrators as sharing authority.[61] The 1947 Partition Archive, however, fails to meaningfully involve its participants in determining how they would like to be represented. A standard fact-checking e-mail is sent to the interviewers to go over the accuracy of the material shared. They are not, however, allowed to view the final video or make any suggestions or recommendations before it is uploaded online. The archive also fails to provide its narrators with any counseling services or other similar resources that offer emotional support to cope with the traumatic nature of their testimonies.

Facing the Audience: The Importance of Contextualization

Within collaborative research, it is imperative that researchers monitor and reflect ethically on their research practices.[62] While the archive does require its interviewers to write a 1- to 2-page "interview summary" with a section reserved for "interviewer's background/personal reflection," neither of the two summaries[63] include any personal information on the interviewer. Rather, they read more like blurbs designed to enhance accessibility for viewers who may be combing through the interviews. Following this, I inspected the online Google Form for submitting the "Interview Summary."[64] It became clear that while this is framed as a space for the citizen historians to share their own experience of the interview, the guidelines explicitly require the interviewers to fill out "half to two pages" simply summarizing the interview. Interviewers are left with little space to elaborate on their personal reflections and thoughts about the interview. Further, the section comes with the following warning: "THIS WILL BE A PUBLIC SUMMARY. CHOOSE WORDS CAREFULLY,"[65] thus clearly wanting the interviewers to censor themselves for the public. This further points to the archive's emphasis on curating narratives for public consumption at the cost of erasing the interviewer's presence completely.

The lack of critical observations and commentary from the interviewer becomes palpable in Mrs. Mamtani's interview. While constantly asserting that Hindus and Muslims had amicable relations in her village pre-Partition,

Leela remarks that Muslims were "illiterate" and worked primarily as manual workers and drivers for landowners (her father also belonged to the landowning class). Here, neither does she seem to be aware of her own animosity toward Muslims nor does she acknowledge the obvious communal class difference between Hindus and Muslims, accepting it as what was normal for the time. When asked if both Hindus and Muslims participated in the freedom rallies organized by the Indian National Congress, she answered, "our Hindu women used to participate, not Muslim women,"[66] alluding to the varying levels of education between the two religious groups. A close reading of these statements reveals Leela's concealed hostility toward Muslims. However, nowhere in her interview or the interview summary is this acknowledged or highlighted. Had her testimony been contextualized within the growing religious animosity of the time, it could have led to a bigger conversation about the negative biases harbored by Hindus against Muslims in pre-independence India.

More importantly, however, it should be noted that Leela's response, in part, may have been shaped by how she perceived the interviewer and the wider audience on the internet. DeSouza and others have argued that power relations between the interviewer and the interviewee often compel the narrators to respond in ways that might earn them the researcher's "approval." They might also present a persona for the perceived audience by exaggerating or concealing certain parts of the story to appear "likable."[67] Therefore, a critical interrogation of why narrators say certain things in relation to their circumstances is essential for audiences to grasp the complete meaning of the narratives being presented. In alienating survivors' narratives, the archive robs its audiences of a fuller, richer history of the Partition.

According to Deepra Dandekar, significant methodological differences exist between public archives and oral histories that are personally recorded by researchers.[68] She argues that subaltern feminist research favors a relationship between the researchers and research participants in order to create "a layered and empathetic narrative, produced outside the domain of power relations."[69] However, she observes that this method seems to have been reversed in the 1947 Partition Archive with it "being the first public oral history archive of its kind that defocusses from the interviewer and the relationship between interviewer and respondent."[70]

As seen above, the lack of a relationship between the interviewer and the interviewee can easily translate into the loss of reflexivity on the interviewer's part. This has resulted in the creation of video stories and summaries that are highly curated, censored and individualized. The archive's narration of the Partition is, therefore, "apolitical"[71] and isolated from the larger landscape of communal violence in post-colonial India.[72] By reimagining the Partition as unique from other instances of violence, the archive abdicates any responsibility of highlighting the state's role in instigating violence. More importantly, however, in freezing the Partition as an isolated event in the past, the archive enables its audience to "collectively project their anger and despair away from the present instances of collective violence."[73] It gives them the license to "objectively" and publicly discuss the chilling mass violence, death and displacement that accompanied India's independence without having to interrogate the historical continuity of religious violence in India. This also brings into speculation the nature of audience engagement and the importance of qualitative measures to ascertain how audiences assign meanings to testimonies. Finally, a question worth asking is: who are these narratives created for and to what end? It sheds light on concerns such as those voiced by Kaur who argues that the archive's individualized narratives can be easily co-opted by the fundamentalist governments of India and Pakistan for "nationalist deployment, as part of renewed history-writing endeavors."[74]

Conclusion

This chapter reveals the entanglement of the 1947 Partition Archive—an open-access digital repository of "memories"—with three kinds of public: the interviewer, the interviewee and the audience. It examines the archive's research ideologies and methodologies to reveal a lack of collaboration, reflexivity and shared authority between the three stakeholders in the research process. However, it is important to note that an archive such as the 1947 Partition Archive, while it can be critiqued for its flawed research methodologies and skewed interview process, is inevitably entangled in a process of gathering testimonies and expanding in scale and size. Due to a lack of social history resources on the Partition, the "methodologically imperfect"[75] oral histories curated by the 1947 Partition Archive constitute an important resource for researchers interested in the fields of migration, oral history, memory and violence.[76] However, we can learn about Partition from the archive only if we critically situate the oral narratives within their political and historical contexts. The idea then, perhaps, is to find ways to carefully listen to and meaningfully engage with these stories and honor its narrators who exhibit unfathomable courage in revealing intimate details about their lives. This also opens up questions for future researchers about exploring ethical forms of creating digital history as well as examining the politics of archiving when it comes to public institutions.

Notes

1 Douglas A. Boyd and Mary A. Larson, introduction to *Oral History and Digital Humanities: Voice, Access, and Engagement*, ed. Mary Larson and Douglas A. Boyd (New York: Palgrave Macmillan, 2014), 4–5.
2 Ekaterina Haskins, "Between Archive and Participation: Public Memory in a Digital Age," *Rhetoric Society Quarterly* 37, no. 4 (2007), 402.
3 Monica Eileen Patterson, "The Ethical Murk of Using Testimony in Oral Historical Research in South Africa," in *Oral History off the Record*, ed. Stacey Zembrzycki and Anna Sheftel (New York: Palgrave Macmillan, 2013), 215.

4 Robin Ruth Linden, "Reflections on 'Bearing Witness,'" in *Making Stories, Making Selves: Feminist Reflections on the Holocaust* (Columbus: The Ohio State University Press, 1993), 73.

5 Anna Sheftel and Stacey Zembrzycki, "Slowing Down to Listen in the Digital Age: How New Technology Is Changing Oral History Practice," *The Oral History Review* 44, no. 1 (2017): 94–112.

6 Ibid., 109.

7 Ibid.

8 Ibid., 101–102.

9 Steve Cohen, "Shifting Questions: New Paradigms for Oral History in a Digital World," *The Oral History Review* 40, no. 1 (2013): 154–167; Sheftel and Zembrzycki, "Slowing Down to Listen," 94–112.

10 Cohen, "Shifting Questions: New Paradigms," 160–163.

11 Sheftel and Zembrzycki, "Slowing Down to Listen," 107.

12 Sherna Berger Gluck, "From California to Kufr Nameh and Back: Reflections on 40 Years of Feminist Oral History," in *Oral History off the Record*, ed. Stacey Zembrzycki and Anna Sheftel (New York: Palgrave Macmillan, 2013), 25–42.

13 Gyanendra Pandey, "Community and Violence: Recalling Partition," *Economic and Political Weekly* 32, no. 32 (1997): 2037–2045.

14 In this chapter, I refer to the "1947 Partition Archive" as the "archive."

15 "Mission: About Us," The 1947 Partition Archive, accessed May 1, 2019, https://in.1947partitionarchive.org/our_team.

16 Ibid.

17 "The Interview Process: Share a Story," The 1947 Partition Archive, accessed May 1, 2019, https://in.1947partitionarchive.org/interview_process.

18 "Collect Stories: Get Involved," The 1947 Partition Archive, accessed May 1, 2019, https://in.1947partitionarchive.org/collect_stories.

19 "Citizen Historian Training Packet," The 1947 Partition Archive, www.1947partitionarchive.org/sites/default/files/Citizen_Historian_training_packet_March_2019.pdf.

20 See "Interview Field Packet" [with questionnaire for migrants] and "Interview Field Packet" [with questionnaire for non-migrants], The 1947 Partition Archive, www.1947partitionarchive.org/Oral_History_Documents. "Migrants" here refer to those who crossed the border from India to reach Pakistan and "non-migrants" to those who were displaced within India.

21 See release form, post-interview questionnaire and the Archive Information Card "Oral history documents," The 1947 Partition Archive, accessed May 1, 2019, www.1947partitionarchive.org/Oral_History_Documents.

22 "Collect Stories: Get Involved," The 1947 Partition Archive, accessed May 1, 2019, https://in.1947partitionarchive.org/collect_stories.

23 Examples of these include 1998 oral histories by Kamla Bhasin and Ritu Menon with women survivors of the Partition as well as Urvashi Butalia's 2002 testimonial work; Ritu Menon and Kamla Bhasin, *Borders & Boundaries: Women in India's Partition* (New Delhi: Kali for Women, 1998); Urvashi Butalia, *The Other Side of Silence: Voices from the Partition of India* (Durham: Duke University Press, 2000).

24 Oral History Workshop, organized online by the 1947 Partition Archive, September 28, 2019.

25 Ibid.

26 "Citizen Historian Training Packet," 7.

27 Sheftel and Zembrzycki, "Slowing Down to Listen," 196.

28 Oral History Workshop.

29 Mary A. Larson, "The Medium Is Political and the Message Is Personal: Feminist Oral Histories Online," in *Beyond Women's Words*, ed. Katrina Srigley, Stacey Zembrzycki, and Franca Iacovetta (New York: Routledge, 2018), 324–329.

30 Tony Kushner, "Holocaust Testimony, Ethics, and the Problem of Representation," *Poetics Today* 27, no. 2 (2006): 275–295.
31 "Citizen Historian Training Packet," 11.
32 Butalia, *The Other Side of Silence*, 88–89.
33 Oral History Workshop.
34 Ibid.
35 Sheftel and Zembrzycki, "Only Human: A Reflection on the Ethical and Methodological Challenges of Working with 'Difficult' Stories," *The Oral History Review* 37, no. 2 (2010): 200.
36 Ibid., 194.
37 Ibid., 72.
38 Oral History Workshop.
39 Liisa Malkki, "News and Culture: Transitory Phenomena and the Fieldwork Tradition," in *Anthropological Locations: Boundaries and Grounds of a Field Science*, ed. James Ferguson and Akhil Gupta (Berkeley: University of California Press, 1997), 7.
40 "Home," The 1947 Partition Archive, accessed May 1, 2019, https://in.1947partitionarchive.org.
41 See "The 1947 Partition Archive," Stanford Library Archive, accessed May 1, 2019, https://exhibits.stanford.edu/1947-partition.
42 "Sushiri Motilal's interview and summary (conducted by Zain Alam): The 1947 Partition Archive," Stanford Library Archive, Lucknow, November 13, 2013, accessed May 1, 2019, https://exhibits.stanford.edu/1947-partition/catalog/pq164zk2305.
43 "Leela Mamtani's interview and summary (conducted by Prakhar Joshi): The 1947 Partition Archive," Stanford Library Archive, New Delhi, January 29, 2014, accessed May 1, 2019, https://purl.stanford.edu/cc041bc4311.
44 Sushiri Motilal's interview.
45 Ibid.
46 Sheftel and Zembrzycki, "Only Human," 200.
47 Ibid.
48 Henry Greenspan and Sidney Bolkosky, "When Is an Interview an Interview? Notes from Listening to Holocaust Survivors," *Poetics Today* 27, no. 2 (2006): 431–449.
49 Ibid., 441.
50 "Leela Mamtani's interview."
51 Ibid.
52 Kathryn Anderson, Susan Armitage, Dana Jack, and Judith Wittner, "Beginning Where We Are: Feminist Methodology in Oral History," *The Oral History Review* 15, no. 1 (1987): 111.
53 Ibid., 109.
54 Greenspan and Bolkosky, "When Is an Interview an Interview," 439.
55 Ibid.
56 Anderson, Armitage, Jack, and Wittner, "Beginning Where We Are," 104.
57 Steve High's 2014 community-based digital oral history project that documented the stories of Montrealers displaced by war, violence, genocide and other such violations of human rights; Steven C. High, *Oral History at the Crossroads: Sharing Life Stories of Survival and Displacement* (Vancouver: UBC Press, 2014).
58 Sheftel and Zembrzycki, "Only Human," 199.
59 Mary Larson, "'We All Begin with a Story': Discovery and Discourse in the Digital Realm," in *Oral History and Digital Humanities: Voice, Access, and Engagement*, ed. Mary Larson and Douglas A. Boyd (New York: Palgrave Macmillan, 2014), 163.
60 Ibid.
61 See Michael Frisch, *A Shared Authority: Essays on the Craft and Meaning of Oral and Public History* (Albany: State University of New York Press, 1990).
62 High, *Oral History at the Crossroads*, 20.

63 See footnotes 45 and 46.
64 "Summary Form," The 1947 Partition Archive, accessed May 1, 2019, https://rb.gy/6mxurw.
65 Ibid.
66 "Leela Mamtani's interview."
67 Sanchia DeSouza and Jyothsna Latha Belliappa, "The Positionality of Narrators and Interviewers: Methodological Comments on Oral History with Anglo-Indian Schoolteachers in Bangalore, India," in *Beyond Women's Words: Feminisms and the Practice of Oral History in the Twenty-First Century*, ed. Katrina Srigley, Stacey Zembrzycki, and Franca Iacovetta (New York: Routledge, 2018), 64–73.
68 Deepra Dandekar, "Zeba Rizvi's Memory-Emotions of Partition: Silence and Secularism-*Pyar*," *Contemporary South Asia* 27, no. 3 (2019): 392–406.
69 Ibid., 394.
70 Ibid.
71 Ravinder Kaur, "We Best Remember Partition When We Connect the Dots from 1947 to 1984 and 2002," *The Wire*, August 15, 2016, https://thewire.in/communalism/how-not-to-remember-partition.
72 Examples of communal strife in India include the 1984 Sikh massacre, Godhra violence of 2002 and the communal riots of 2013 in Muzaffarnagar.
73 Kaur, "We Best Remember Partition."
74 Ibid., 395.
75 Dandekar, "Zeba Rizvi's Memory-Emotions of Partition," 396.
76 Ibid., 395.

Bibliography

Anderson, Kathryn, Susan Armitage, Dana Jack, and Judith Wittner. "Beginning Where We Are: Feminist Methodology in Oral History." *The Oral History Review* 15, no. 1 (1987): 103–127.

Boyd, Douglas, and Mary A. Larson. Introduction to *Oral History and Digital Humanities: Voice, Access, and Engagement*, edited by Mary Larson and Douglas A. Boyd, 1–16. New York: Palgrave Macmillan, 2014.

Butalia, Urvashi. *The Other Side of Silence: Voices from the Partition of India*. Durham: Duke University Press, 2000.

Dandekar, Deepra. "Zeba Rizvi's Memory-Emotions of Partition: Silence and Secularism-*Pyar*." *Contemporary South Asia* 27, no. 3 (2019): 392–406.

DeSouza, Sanchia, and Jyothsna Latha Belliappa. "The Positionality of Narrators and Interviewers: Methodological Comments on Oral History with Anglo-Indian Schoolteachers in Bangalore, India." In *Beyond Women's Words: Feminisms and the Practice of Oral History in the Twenty-First Century*, edited by Katrina Srigley, Stacey Zembrzycki, and Franca Iacovetta, 64–73. New York: Routledge, 2018.

Frisch, Michael. *A Shared Authority: Essays on the Craft and Meaning of Oral and Public History*. Albany: State University of New York Press, 1990.

Gluck, Sherna Berger. "From California to Kufr Nameh and Back: Reflections on 40 Years of Feminist Oral History." In *Oral History off the Record*, edited by Stacey Zembrzycki and Anna Sheftel, 25–42. New York: Palgrave Macmillan, 2013.

Greenspan, Henry, and Sidney Bolkosky. "When Is an Interview an Interview? Notes from Listening to Holocaust Survivors." *Poetics Today* 27, no. 2 (2006): 431–449.

Haskins, Ekaterina. "Between Archive and Participation: Public Memory in a Digital Age." *Rhetoric Society Quarterly* 37, no. 4 (2007): 401–422.

High, Steven C. *Oral History at the Crossroads: Sharing Life Stories of Survival and Displacement*. Vancouver: UBC Press, 2014.

Kaur, Ravinder. "We Best Remember Partition When We Connect the Dots from 1947 to 1984 and 2002." *The Wire*, August 15, 2016. https://thewire.in/communalism/how-not-to-remember-partition.

Kushner, Tony. "Holocaust Testimony, Ethics, and the Problem of Representation." *Poetics Today* 27, no. 2 (2006): 275–295.

Larson, Mary A. "'We All Begin with a Story': Discovery and Discourse in the Digital Realm." In *Oral History and Digital Humanities: Voice, Access, and Engagement*, edited by Mary Larson and Douglas A. Boyd, 157–171. New York: Palgrave Macmillan, 2014.

Larson, Mary A. "The Medium Is Political and the Message Is Personal: Feminist Oral Histories Online." In *Beyond Women's Words: Feminisms and the Practice of Oral History in the Twenty-First Century*, edited by Katrina Srigley, Stacey Zembrzycki, and Franca Iacovetta, 324–329. New York: Routledge, 2018.

Linden, Robin Ruth. "Reflections on 'Bearing Witness.'" In *Making Stories, Making Selves: Feminist Reflections on the Holocaust*, 70–83. Columbus: Ohio State University Press, 1993.

Malkki, Liisa. "News and Culture: Transitory Phenomena and the Fieldwork Tradition." In *Anthropological Locations: Boundaries and Grounds of a Field Science*, edited by James Ferguson and Akhil Gupta, 86–101. Berkeley: California University Press, 1997.

Menon, Ritu, and Kamala Bhasin. *Borders and Boundaries: Women in India's Partition*. New Delhi: Kali for Women, 1998.

Pandey, Gyanendra. "Community and Violence: Recalling Partition." *Economic and Political Weekly* 32, no. 32 (1997): 2037–2045.

Patterson, Monica Eileen. "The Ethical Murk of Using Testimony in Oral Historical Research in South Africa." In *Oral history off the Record*, edited by Stacey Zembrzycki and Anna Sheftel, 201–218. New York: Palgrave Macmillan, 2013.

Sheftel, Anna, and Stacey Zembrzycki. "Only Human: A Reflection on the Ethical and Methodological Challenges of Working with 'Difficult' Stories." *The Oral History Review* 37, no. 2 (2010): 191–214.

Sheftel, Anna, and Stacey Zembrzycki. "Slowing Down to Listen in the Digital Age: How New Technology Is Changing Oral History Practice." *The Oral History Review* 44, no. 1 (2017): 94–112.

The 1947 Partition Archive. "Citizen Historian Training Packet." Accessed May 1, 2019. www.1947partitionarchive.org/sites/default/files/Citizen_Historian_training_packet_March_2019.pdf.

The 1947 Partition Archive. "Collect Stories: Get Involved." Accessed May 1, 2019. https://in.1947partitionarchive.org/collect_stories.

The 1947 Partition Archive. "Home." Accessed May 1, 2019. https://in.1947partitionarchive.org.

The 1947 Partition Archive. "Mission: About Us." Accessed May 1, 2019. https://in.1947partitionarchive.org/our_team.

The 1947 Partition Archive. "Summary Form." Accessed May 1, 2019. https://rb.gy/6mxurw.

The 1947 Partition Archive. "The Interview Process: Share a Story." Accessed May 1, 2019. https://in.1947partitionarchive.org/interview_process.

15

PUBLIC BETWEEN THE STATE AND ACADEMIA

Cultural and Political Essentialism of Public History in Russia

Alexander Khodnev

Public history, having originated in the United States in the now distant 1970s, crossed the Atlantic and settled in Europe as part of the new cultural essentialism at the turn of the twentieth and twenty-first centuries. Public history in Russia began to develop at the beginning of the twenty-first century. Museums have changed their concept of the audience. Six Russian universities have

FIGURE 15.1   Red Square in Moscow in 2013, © Christophe Meneboeuf, public domain.

opened master's programs in public history.[1] The first program was launched in 2012 at the Moscow Higher School of Economic and Social Sciences. In 2020, the Kazan Federal University opened the seventh program with the profile "Public History: Contemporary Narrative and Visual Practices."[2] The first specialists in the field of public history have already received their diplomas. Graduates of the programs have acquired skills and competencies in the fields of applied history, modern media, and innovation processes in Russian and foreign education, as well as a wide range of humanitarian specialties. They are able to apply their skills as researchers, specialists in the social and cultural sphere, in the museum business, in state and local government bodies, and in tourism and excursion companies. Nonetheless, the relationship between academics and public history, as well as the concept of the public having a double role as both recipients and creators of public history are unclear in Russia. This new version of history, popular among the public and associated with non-academics, has placed academic historians in (for them) a new "servicing role, in marked contrast to their accustomed prestige as historical experts *par excellence*,"[3] as John Tosh has remarked concerning the British historians, which also accurately reflects the state of affairs in Russia.

In an article by Yegor M. Isaev published in 2016 on public history in Russia at the beginning of the twenty-first century, there is an important observation that without

> understanding how the public works, its demands and expectations regarding history analyzing dominant ideas and images of the past that require the participation of specialists in various fields of sociology, cultural studies, political science, etc., the development of public history is not possible.[4]

Indeed, the public plays a key role in the practices of public history.

The problem in respect to Russian society and its public stems from the focus of different specialists on Russian politics, sociology, cultural studies and history. The new Russian society has now existed for nearly three decades in the post-Soviet environment. There are great differences between the 1990s when the Russians initially enjoyed the new situation of freedom and absence of any ideology, and the period that began in the early 2000s with the gradual establishment of an authoritarian and personalist regime. During President Vladimir Putin's first term (2000–2004), the presidential administration denied any need for a state ideology. Putin cast himself as a non-ideological political figure, claiming to be working solely in line with technocratic objectives. In 2003, the authorities discussed the creation of a council for national ideology to convene major intellectual and cultural figures, but the project produced no concrete results and aroused little enthusiasm within state bodies. The new ideology promoted by the presidential administration was "labelled, as early as 2005, as conservatism, sometimes associated with qualifiers such as social conservatism or Russian conservatism."[5] Using this ideology, the Russian political elite hoped to unite the majority of the Russian public in a centrist form opposing liberalism and communism.

The state is actively engaged in constructing historical memory and making use of the past. The politics of history is an important part of the entire cultural context of the existence of history in Russia. Cultural essentialism in the field of preserving memory and using the past in Russia often gives way and is translated into propaganda and PR campaigns that influence the construction of a new collective memory. School history, according to Russian politicians, should support the "new historical memory" of Russia being introduced from above and imbibing ethnocentrism. In other words, in school textbooks, messages of power should be broadcast. While the "Historical and Cultural Concept of Teaching Russian History" that appeared in 2013 did not get an official support, the new version published in 2020 was approved by the Ministry of Education.

Public history or applied history with common global features, like any other field of history, has national characteristics. In Russia, the emergence of public history was a response to the desire of the state, since 2001, to monopolize the public sphere associated with the use of the past. On the initiative of state institutions, the dialogue between the society and the state is reduced to the politics of history.

Nevertheless, today we see in Russia the emergence of public history from below and a process of rethinking the role of history and the historian in public space, which is partly the result of a reaction to the historical policy pursued by the governing political elites. This chapter is devoted to discussing the uneasy relationship between the state and the history in Russia with special attention paid to cultural and political contexts of interactions of the public, history and professionals from academia.

Definition of the Term "Public" in Russian: Public and People

Russian writers and publicists in the nineteenth century laid the tradition of an ironic attitude to the community of people called the "public." The Russian writer Nikolai Leskov, "an authority on the Russian soul," spoke of them: "But I don't want to be liked by the public. Let her at least choke on my stories, and they read. I know how to please her, but I no longer want to please."[6]

Konstantin Sergeyevich Aksakov (1817–1860), a publicist, historian and one of the ideologists of Slavophilism, contrasted the public with the Russian people, like the West with old Russian society:

> The public orders thoughts and feelings from the sea, like a mazurka and polka; the Russian people draw from their own source. The public

walks in a German dress—the people are in Russian... The public is only a hundred and fifty years old, and you cannot count years for the people. The public is temporary; the people are everlasting.[7]

"Public" has been connected with the reforms of Peter the Great that caused Russia to turn to the West and to break with Russian patriotism in the eyes of Slavophiles. Aksakov's publication in the Slavophile newspaper *Molva* was very critical and, as Tsar Alexander II disliked the article, it led to the newspaper being shut down for censorship reasons in December 1857.[8] Nonetheless, Aksakov's arguments formed the basis of Russian conservatism in the nineteenth century. Many contemporary politicians spoke out in the same spirit, replacing the age of Peter the Great with the so-called dashing 1990s of Boris Yeltsin.

Aksakov was correct in explaining the etymology of the word "public." It appeared in the Russian language during the Petrine era. The word was borrowed from Polish, itself derived from French, going back to the Latin *publicus*—"public, popular," from which the term *populus*— "people"—originated.[9]

Clarifications on the use of the word "public" in German are contained in the "Dictionary of Historical Concepts" initiated by Reinhart Koselleck and translated into Russian from German. It says that the noun *publicum*, formed from the adjective *publicus*, was already common in classical Latin, but in Roman times it did not mean, as it did in the seventeenth century, the aggregate of citizens of the state, but rather a certain public sphere, precisely non-definable, that constitutes an opposition to the domestic one.[10] In the first half of the eighteenth century, when literary life in Germany became intense, the word *publicum*, in the sense of "readership," began to describe a new social phenomenon: the social stratum of educated readers, recruited mainly from the burghers.[11] In Russia, the reading public emerged in the eighteenth and nineteenth centuries as well. "The Explanatory Dictionary of the Living Russian Language" by Vladimir Dahl, published in 1880, gives the following definition of the word "public": "society, people, our public name is society, except mob, simple people... Public means nation-wide, announced, explicit, famous."[12]

In the "Great Russian Encyclopedia," there is no special article explaining the word "public," and no article devoted to "public history." There was no dictionary entry "public" in the famous nineteenth-early twentieth-century edition of "The Encyclopedic Dictionary of F.A. Brockhaus and I.A. Ephron." Moreover, the term "public history" has still not been included in encyclopedias and dictionaries. In reality, there is no precise definition of this concept, and the form used in the Russian language is borrowed from foreign languages.

Nowadays, we can see a new context around the public, people and society in Russia. As a result, the meaning of "public sphere" has begun to be re-evaluated.[13] This reconsideration stems from the wide distribution of new technologies, on the one hand, and on the other, the fragmentation of the public sphere itself, its disintegration into a number of "small" public spheres. Today, we can see how the internet changes the idea of the public into an object of influence of something. Everyone can take photos, write, sing, play or dance and post it on YouTube and other social media. This is the public that is beginning to take shape in a new communicative environment. It chooses, expresses its opinion and in some way pressures the historian to address it.

The present day turns the discussion on the meaning of the public into new terms and conditions connected with the IT era. For instance, Evgenii Dukov stated: "The public is the part of the population that runs a public life and meets in public space around public values."[14] The Russian section of Wikipedia gives the following definition of the word "public": "The public or the people are the totality of people who are the object of influence of something (art, propaganda, advertising, literature, entertainment, education, etc.)." Another explanation concerns the "mass audience"—a term widely used in relation to media audiences and to modern mass cultural phenomena.[15] Thus, in Russian the word "public" is perceived as a certain group of people subjected to influence: culture, fashion, propaganda, advertising, etc. As well, the observations of the usage of the term "public" confirm that public history as a special area of activity of society in Russia appeared at the beginning of the twenty-first century.

People, Public and History: External Observations and Observations from the Inside

In the early 1990s, a translation of Marc Ferro's book *Comment on raconte l'histoire aux enfants* was published in Russia. Ferro drew attention to the deep distrust—or even fear—by the Russian authorities toward historians. Soviet leader Nikita S. Khrushchev said that "historians are dangerous people and need constant supervision: they can turn all things upside down."[16] Hence, it comes as no surprise that the Soviet state created institutional structures to protect history from the dangers for the state hidden within it. The distrust of professional historians still exists in the political elite in Russia today.

Ferro made interesting observations about history during the period of *perestroika* and *glasnost* in Russia, and about how the old official historiography had lost all support in society. He emphasized that "the truth about the past" did not come from official historians and that historians, as certified commentators of official speeches, had "lost trust in themselves."[17]

In today's Russia, there is no politburo or ideology, but attempts by the current government to control history have continued. It is clearly engaged in the search for historical justification for the legality and prolongation of the present-day political regime which has obvious signs of autocracy, although without deep totalitarian symptoms yet.

Pro-government historians try to postulate that all revolutions, uprisings and revolts in the history of Russia have brought harm to the people and the state. The revolution of 1917 is shown as a disaster and anomaly. It interrupted the successful development of the Russian state, which retained its greatness and ability to fight during the First World War. The Russian state—the monarchy—was betrayed by the economic, political and cultural elite in 1917.[18] The Russian state in turn, in the view of these historians, always acted without mistakes and was eternally and deeply coherent with the spirit of the Russian people.

This was confirmed, for instance, in an article published in February 2019 by the high-ranking Kremlin official Vladislav Surkov. He claimed that at the beginning of the twenty-first century, a new model of the state was built in Russia: "the Putin state." This state, according to Surkov, corresponds to the "deep-seated people." President Putin has "the ability to hear and understand people, see through them, to the full depth and act accordingly." Therefore, his "state is effective and durable."[19] So, the state in Russia is populated with a "deep-seated" people that Putin understands very well, and therefore, the state of Putin will exist for a long time. Surkov also interestingly remarks on the significance of the state in the history of Russia, that the state "century after century provided the Russian World with a persistent upward movement."[20] Russian historiography, to which the author pays no attention, has developed a more complex attitude toward the dichotomy of the people and the state. Regarding the growth and durability of the Russian state in history, there is a famous phrase of one of the best and most authoritative historians of the late nineteenth–early twentieth century, Vasily O. Klyuchevsky: "The state was swollen, but the people got sick."[21] Klyuchevsky draws attention to the fact that the rapid expansion of the territory of Russia was draining the strength of the people, and there was a serious contradiction between the foreign policy of the state and the "internal growth of the people."[22] As a result, history developed in a completely different direction: there was no "deep-seated people" supporting the growth of the state. For most of its past, the Russian state did not know how to listen to its people, and often engaged in ventures that harmed the people.

Meanwhile, the modern attitude to history dictates completely different principles than those set forth in Surkov's article. Jörn Rüsen in the piece published in Russian in a leading journal emphasized the importance of equality in communication between the participants in the creation of a historical narrative. In this case, "with the help of this narrative, the social group asserts and explains its identity."[23]

Growth of Education, Public Movement and State Control

The first public society of history, the "Moscow Society of Russian History and Antiquities," appeared in Russia in 1804. It was an extremely upper-class organization and appeared in the academic atmosphere at the University of Moscow on the initiative of the German professor August Ludwig Schlötzer. While this society remained one of the most authoritative public organizations involved in the popularization of academic knowledge on the history of Russia, it was far from representing the broad Russian public. It tried to organize the activity of the educated part of Russian society, comprised mainly of the nobility, who were interested in history. All activities in the communication of historical knowledge within the society were aided by the Society's publications and by considerable government control. Boris N. Mironov has determined that the public readership in Russia totaled between 600,000 to one million people, which constituted only 1–1.5 percent of the Russian population in the middle of the nineteenth century.[24]

The end of the nineteenth century and the beginning of the twentieth century became a time when education in the Russian Empire "made a giant step forward."[25] The largest percentage of the literate population (over 50 percent) was represented by the central provinces with a large urban population—Moscow, St. Petersburg and Yaroslavl. Moreover, this situation was greatly influenced not only by economic factors, but also by cultural ones.

The growth of the literacy of the Russian population has precipitated a desire by the public for reliable information about both the outside world and the history of the country and its regions. In 1908, semiliterate Russia came third in the world in book publishing after Germany and Japan.[26]

Along with these new processes in Russian society, the public took an interest in museums, as well as historical monuments and their preservation. The idea of preserving cultural heritage, disappearing under the pressure of technological progress, appeared in Europe in connection with the rapid industrial development in the nineteenth century and it reached Russia as well. The public began to raise the issue of preserving the cultural heritage of the peoples of Russia. In 1884, the state established scientific archival commissions in a number of provinces of the country, with their number rapidly increasing to 40 in the provincial cities. In most cities, the commissions did not confine themselves just to archival research, but also examined collected material. In 1870, the Moscow Archaeological Society created a commission for the protection of ancient monuments,[27] and in 1910, the Society for the Protection and Preservation of Art and Antiquity Monuments in Russia was founded.[28]

At the same time, the importance of mass education and the formation of the public in Russia at the turn of the nineteenth and twentieth centuries should not be exaggerated. Social background and a high level of education were of great importance in this process. As a result, new associations singled out a privileged stratum from the population, creating new segregation in society, thereby hindering the creation of conditions for the emergence of a mass culture that would ignore the features of class and regional or religious subcultures.[29] All these changes in the role of history and the public raised the question of whether a civil society existed in Russia. Boris Mironov claimed that a civil society was understood as a group of nonprofit voluntary, independent and self-financed public organizations pursuing socially useful activities, corresponding to education, social welfare, the development of medicine, science, culture, and the public as the "advanced educated part of society."[30] Mironov believes that the main elements of a civil society in Russia had been formed by 1917: a mass of voluntary public associations, a critically thinking public, a free press, independent public opinion, political parties and parliament.[31] He states that the whole process was interrupted by the Bolshevik revolution in 1917.

Until the mid-1930s, a broad movement in local history developed in Soviet Russia, supported by unprecedented activity of the public from below. The study of local tradition in the 1920s, of course, cannot be called a purely social phenomenon as at the very beginning of that decade it was supported by the state. Many scientific and semi-scientific societies for the study of local regions were encouraged. The Academy of Sciences and the People's Commissariat for Education, as state structures, had the apparatus of the Central Bureau of Local History (CBLH). Local history activities were often led by people who worked in museums, educational bodies and organizations of a planned and economic nature. In December 1927, the state put forward the demand for the inclusion of local history work in the "general planned work of socialist construction."[32] Nevertheless, on the whole, regional studies developed, above all, as a phenomenon of public life. In 1930, according to some estimates, the public local history movement and local history network included 2,270 registered organizations, numbering 50,000–60,000 people.[33] The free, non-state mass public movement of people studying their own history aroused suspicion among the authorities in Moscow. On August 30, 1930, the Science Sector of the RSFSR People's Commissariat of Education sent out a circular to all regions, in which it was explained that "local history work is one of the forms of the involvement and participation of the working people in socialist construction." The document drew attention to the ideological shortcomings of the public movement: "There is no ideological leadership of the activities of local history societies and institutions, as a result of which the latter publish ideologically uncontrolled literature, and their organized expeditions are not always engaged in studying up-to-date issues of socialist construction."[34] Local historians were obliged to do the work of promoting the construction of the country's defense that was far removed from their plans to study the history of local places. The state pressed for the inclusion of local history in the system of arch-practical, urgent tasks of "socialist construction" and the creation of such a human resource base in which local history would cease to be the work of individual amateurs and become a "powerful revolutionary factor in the movement of the masses for culture, for socialism."[35] The independent mass public history movement was put in the same list of public defense and security movements controlled by the state in Soviet Russia as "Osoaviakhim" (Society for the Promotion of Defense, Aviation and Chemical Engineering) and the ideological "Soyuz bezbozhnikov" (Union of Atheists). In one of the definitions of 1930, the local history movement was described as

> one of the ways for the Soviet public to contribute to the socialist reconstruction of the USSR in their localities through a comprehensive, synthetic, and dialectical study of a relatively small area, a study entirely subordinated to the tasks of the dictatorship of the proletariat in general and the tasks of socialist construction in particular.[36]

The defamation and abusive criticism of leading specialists in local history that ensued is hardly surprising. In 1930, Mikhail I. Smirnov, the founder of the Pereslavl Museum, was called in publications "a terry bourgeois ethnographer," "a monopolist in the history of Pereslavl-Zalessk," "a preacher of kulak ideology" and "an adherent of religion and a hater of atheists" and was said to be "yearning for the tsar as a long-established counterrevolutionary."[37] In the same year, Smirnov was arrested, convicted and exiled to the Turukhansk region for three years. The public movement of local historians, semi-independent from the state, began to die out in subsequent years. On June 10, 1937, the Council of People's Commissars of the RSFSR issued a decree "On the reorganization of local history work in the center and localities," according to which the existence of central and local history bodies was recognized as inappropriate. All local history organizations were to be liquidated within two months.[38] During the period of Stalinist authoritarianism, mass movements in the field of historical and cultural heritage were under the rigid control of the authorities. The public did not have the opportunity to develop even semi-independent organizations nor to show any activity outside the established ideological framework.

Three Waves of Growing Public Interest in History and Heritage

The situation for public activity in the field of history and heritage began to change during the thawing period of Nikita S. Khrushchev. However, in general, the Khrushchev era was tough, when an unwise attitude to the historical past manifested itself, expressed in the struggle against the influence of the Russian Orthodox Church, the demolition of religious buildings and the destruction of architectural and archaeological monuments during new construction. In the second half of the 1950s and the early 1960s, the state cut funds for the protection and restoration of monuments, and the list of monuments under state protection was significantly reduced.

However, in the final decades of the twentieth century, there were three waves of strong interest in history within Russian society. This can be considered as growth in both public history and public interest in history and heritage.

The first wave was the rise of the mass movement of the mid-1960s for the protection of historical monuments in the Soviet Union. The society had a huge interest in the history of the Russian Orthodox Church buildings, including Andrei Rublev's frescoes and icons. This public interest was demonstrated in Andrei Tarkovsky's famous film *Andrei Rublev* (1969). The social movement spread quickly and was rather unexpected by authorities. Nonetheless, it was put under the ideological control of the Communist Party and the government, although without the same rigid domination as in 1930. After several years of public activities in large cities of Russia and active discussion about the problems of preserving historical heritage in the press, the position of state bodies began to change. On July 23, 1965, the Council of Ministers of the RSFSR adopted a Resolution on the creation of the All-Russian Society for the Protection of Historical and Cultural Monuments (VOOPIK) and formed an organizing committee for the congress. The founding congress took place in early May 1966 in Moscow. Vyacheslav I. Kochemasov, Deputy Chairman of the Council of Ministers of the RSFSR, was elected as the first chairman of the Society.[39] VOOPIK worked as an independent nongovernmental organization funded by member contributions. However, control by the government and ideological bodies of the CPSU still existed, and the election of Kochemasov confirms this. The Russian public was very active in VOOPIK activities and events in the 1970s–1980s.

The second wave was associated with the growth of the mass interest in the history of the Soviet period during Mikhail Gorbachev's period, 1985–1991. In fact, the Russian reading public first learned the term "public history" in 1985. The first Russian historian to pay attention to public history was Valery A. Tishkov who focused primarily on American professional historians from academia, although he did not ignore public history.[40]

This new wave of public history began with a history journalism campaign in the *Ogonyok* weekly magazine in 1987,[41] and was followed by *Novy Mir*, *October* and literary and cultural journals. The circulation of this kind of periodicals grew significantly as the people in their workplaces would discuss the so-called blank spots in Soviet history and would collectively subscribe to all "thick" literary journals and set up volunteer private resource centers for history. Vladimir V. Sogrin deemed this process as a revisionist trend in Soviet historiography. He claims, from a present-day perspective, that "the unity of propagandist, philistine historiography, as well as of many professional historians in the closing of 'blank spots' brought contradictory results in terms of the principles of historical research."[42] It is clear that academic historians were not satisfied with those publications.

The last, third wave of interest in history from the public related to the appearance of the New Russia changes in economy and private property and the development of the internet from the 1990s to the present. The 1990s were noteworthy for the creation of various independent public non-governmental organizations and movements of cultural and historical heritage protection in different Russian locations. The new media and the e-turn created a new cultural context for the field of history in Russia. One of the main issues on the agenda of this public history movement was how to cope with the politics of privatization of real estate and the "sweeping reorganization" of economic and cultural patterns of urban life.[43] In the old Russian cities like Yaroslavl, these changes led to quite acute conflicts on the issue of the preservation of historical spaces. Different groups of active citizens tried to draw attention of the broader public to the protection of the old city and started new forms of public history using earlier stories. As Blair A. Ruble has put it: "the Yaroslavl preservation zone is the result of a decade-long struggle involving mobilized citizen groups, professional architectural organizations, and intrenched planning bureaucrats."[44]

Mediators, Translators, or Creators of New Knowledge? The Public, the World of Academia and Public History

In 2008, Russian sociologist Lev Gudkov, answering the question "Does society exist in Russia?" explained: "In a sense, yes." While there are common symbols and beliefs and a certain sense of integrity, Russian society is very poorly organized, with the level of solidarity extremely low. "The whole integrity is held not so much by the inner sense of unity, but mechanically through the structures of state integration, state subordination."[45]

The television, controlled by the state, played an important role in the consolidation of the Russian public and its transformation into society. In the second half of the 1980s, radio, newspapers and magazines used a multitude of historical topics to expose the mistakes and mishandling by the communist state. The USSR was called the country that did the most reading in the world at that time. A significant proportion of the book circulation, however, comprised propagandistic literature that the public refused to buy and read. Today, the Russian public is losing interest in buying and reading books. Between 2003 and 2009, the number of people who regularly read books in Russia decreased from 26 to 16 percent. The number of adults who did not read books at all has grown from 34 to 50 percent.[46]

The interest of the public in reading has switched from books to new periodicals of *the glossy* trend. The magazine *Karavan Istorii* (*Caravan of histories*) pays a lot of attention to historical personalities, although undoubtedly this is a simplified history.[47] The gloss is associated with the pseudo-tragedies replicated on TV. Its "message" to the everyday viewer is based on sensationalism or on a beautiful picture replicated in an advertisement, a video or a series.

Russian professional historiography could not remain in an impregnable tower. Many professional Russian historians, especially those in academia, have tense relations with the type of history favored by public interest, but some of them do attempt to describe this new field of history. Vladimir V. Sogrin divided all modern Russian historical culture into three subcultures: popular subculture, reflecting the perception of history by mass public consciousness; the state political-historical subculture, born through state order with the purpose of keeping any other historical subcultures under its own control and forcing academic history to work in its favor; and academic subculture, created by professionals based on documentary sources and scholarly disciplinary criteria. V. Sogrin believes that only the third subculture of academic historical knowledge deserves recognition, and only it can be called historical science, in other words, "genuine history."[48] Another historian representing the Russian Academy of Sciences, Lorina P. Repina, believes that professional historians should coordinate and guide the movement of public history.[49] How professional historians will do this is not quite clear, because many historians from the academic world are far removed from the public and media projects and are not yet ready for this new informative activity and communication.

To conclude, public history is developing in Russia from below as an activity of the public, particularly the educated part of it. However, the possible pressure from the state in the direction of great statehood can cause a serious conflict, as in 1930 when the "great goals" of the country made the vast field of local history studies unnecessary.

Notes

1 "Portal publichnoy istorii. Obrazovatel'nye programmy v rossiyskikh universitetakh," accessed September 12, 2020, http://rupublichistory.ru/edu/edum.html.
2 "Kazanskiy Federal'nyi universitet," accessed September 12, 2020, https://kpfu.ru/imoiv/struktura/centr-magistratury-i-aspirantury/centr-magistratury/abiturientam.
3 John Tosh, "Public History, Civic Engagement and the Historical Profession in Britain," *History* 99, no. 335 (April 2014): 192.
4 Egor M. Isaev, "Publichnaya istoriya v Rossii: nauchnyi i uchebnyi kontekst formirovaniya novogo mezhdisciplinarnogo polya," *Vestnik Permskogo Universiteta* 33, no. 2 (2016): 11.
5 Marlene Laruelle, "Putin's Regime and the Ideological Market: A Difficult Balancing Game," accessed September 12, 2020, https://carnegieendowment.org/2017/03/16/putin-s-regime-and-ideological-market-difficult-balancing-game-pub-68250.
6 "'Pust' publika davitsya moimi rasskazami': Sud'ba pisatelya Nikolaya Leskova," *Argumenty i fakty*, March 5, 2016, http://www.spb.aif.ru/culture/person/pust_publika_davitsya_moimi_rasskazami_sudba_pisatelya_nikolaya_leskova.

7 Konstantin Aksakov, "Slavyanofil'stvo i zapadnichestvo: konservativnaya i liberal'naya utopiya v rabotakh Andzheya Valitskogo," in *Referativnyj sbornik*, ed. Konstantin V. Dushenko (Moscow: Rossijskaya akademiya nauk, INION, 1992): 79.

8 Aleksandr G. Dement'ev, ed., *Russkaya periodicheskaya pechat' (1702–1894): Spravochnik* (Moscow: Gosudarstvennoe izdatel'stvo politicheskoi literatury, 1959), 350.

9 *Etymological online dictionary of the Russian language Krylov G. A.*, "public," https://lexicography.online/etymology/krylov/п/публика.

10 Reinhart Koselleck, *Slovar' osnovnykh istoricheskikh ponyatiy: Izbrannye stat'i*, trans. Kirill Levinson, vol. 1 (Moscow: Novoe literaturnoe obozrenie, 2014), 325.

11 Ibid., 326.

12 *Tolkovyi slovar' zhivogo russkogo yazyka Vladimira Dalya*, vol. 3 (Sankt-Peterburg: Izdanie knigoprodavtsa-tipografa M.O. Vol'fa, 1882), 556.

13 Evgenii Dukov, "Novye razmyshleniya o publike," *Teleskop* 3, no. 93 (2012): 35.

14 Ibid., 34.

15 "Publika," Wikipedia, last modified February 19, 2016, https://ru.wikipedia.org/wiki/Publika.

16 Marc Ferro, *Kak rasskazyvayut istoriyu detyam v raznykh stranakh mira* (Moscow: Vysshaya shkola, 1992), 157.

17 Ibid., 192.

18 Vladimir V. Sogrin, "Professional'naya, propagandistskaya i obyvatel'skaya istoriografiya," *Novaya i noveyshaya istoriya*, no. 1 (2018): 192–193.

19 Vladislav Surkov, "Dolgoe gosudarstvo Putina," *Nezavisimaya gazeta*, February 11, 2019, http://www.ng.ru/ideas/2019-02-11/5_7503_surkov.html.

20 Surkov, "Dolgoe gosudarstvo."

21 Vasily O. Klyuchevskiy, "Kurs russkoy istorii," *Lekciya 41*, http://russiahistory.ru/vo-klyuchevskij-kurs-russkoj-istorii-lektsiya-41.

22 Ibid.

23 Jorn Rüsen, "Istoricheskaya ob"ektivnost' kak sostavlyayushchaya voprosa o social'nykh tsennostyakh," *Novaya i noveyshaya istoriya*, no. 4 (2012): 122.

24 Boris N. Mironov, *Social'naya istoriya Rossii perioda imperii*, vol. 1 (Sankt-Petersburg: Dmitriy Bulanin, 2003), 265.

25 Galina N. Ul'yanova, "Narodnoe obrazovanie. Pechat'," in *Rossiya v nachale 20 veka. Issledovaniya*, ed. Andrei N. Sakharov and Aleksandr N. Bokhanov (Moscow: Novyi khronograf, 2002), 577.

26 Ul'yanova, "Narodnoe obrazovanie," 609.

27 Aleksandr A. Formozov, *Russkoe obshchestvo i okhrana pamyatnikov kul'tury* (Moscow: Sovetskaya Rossiya, 1990), 71.

28 Ibid., 80.

29 Boris N. Mironov, "Grazhdanskoe obshchestvo v pozdneimperskoy Rossii: bylo ili ne bylo?" *Obshchestvennye nauki i sovremennost'*, no. 1 (2014): 143.

30 Ibid., 142.

31 Ibid., 146.

32 Vladimir F. Kozlov, "'Ogosudarstvlennoe' kraevedenie. Istoriya i uroki (Po stranitsam zhurnala 'Sovetskoe kraevedenie' 1930–1936)," *Vestnik RGGU. Seriya Istoricheskie nauki. Regional'naya istoriya. Kraevedenie* 110, no. 9 (2013): 55.

33 Ibid., 55.

34 Ibid., 58.

35 Ibid., 59.

36 Ibid., 62.

37 Ibid., 65.

38 Ibid., 80.
39 Viktor A. Livtsov, "Uchastie Vserossiyskogo obshchestva ohrany pamyatnikov istorii i kul'tury (VOOPIIK) v sokhranenii kul'turnogo naslediya narodov rossiyskoy federatsii," in *75 LET PAKTU RERIHA: Materialy mezhdunar. obshchest.-nauchn. konf. 2010*, ed. Lyudmila V. Shaposhnikova (Moscow: Mezhdunar. Centr Rerihov, Master-Bank, 2011), 322.
40 Valeriy A. Tishkov, *Istoriya i istoriki v SSHA* (Moscow: Nauka, 1985), 81.
41 Dmitriy S. Karataev, "Ogon'kovskaya legenda: k istorii publitsistiki pervykh let 'perestroiki,'" *Vestnik RGGU. Seriya: Istoriya. Filologiya. Kul'turologiya. Vostokovedenie* 4, no. 4 (2015): 62.
42 Sogrin, "Professional'naya," 186.
43 Blair A. Ruble, *Money Sings: The Changing Politics of Urban Space in Post-Soviet Yaroslavl* (New York: Woodrow Wilson Center for Scholars, Cambridge University Press, 1995), 2.
44 Ibid., 79.
45 Lev D. Gudkov, Boris V. Dubin, and Aleksei G. Levinson, "Fotorobot rossiskogo obyvatelya," *Mir Rossii*, no. 2 (2009): 22–23, http://www.civisbook.ru/files/File/Gudkov_Dubin.pdf.
46 Elena Veligzhanina, "Bestseller po trebovaniyu," *Rossiyskaya gazeta*, July 6, 2011, https://rg.ru/2011/07/06/reg-szapad/knigi.html.
47 Alexander S. Khodnev, "Istoriya v rossiskom glyancevom zhurnale 'Karavan istoriy,'" in *Sovremennye media: processy i konteksty*, ed. Evgenii A. Ermolin, Anastasiya A. Maslova, Tat'yana V. Yur'eva (Yaroslavl': Yaroslavskiy gosudarstvennyi pedagogicheskiy universitet im. K.D. Ushinskogo, 2015), 39.
48 Vladimir V. Sogrin, "Tri istoricheskie subkul'tury v Rossii," *Obshchestvennye nauki i sovremennost*, no. 3 (2013): 91–105; Sorgin, "Three Historical Subcultures in Post-Soviet Russia," *Russian Social Science Review* 55, no. 4 (2014): 71–96.
49 Lorina P. Repina, "Nauka i obshchestvo: publichnaya istoriya v kontekste istoricheskoi kul'tury ehpokhi globalizatsii," *Uchenyie zapiski Kazanskogo univeristeta. Ser. Gumanitarnye nauki* 157, no. 3 (2015): 62.

Bibliography

Aksakov, Konstantin. "Slavyanofil'stvo i zapadnichestvo: konservativnaya i liberal'naya utopiya v rabotakh Andzheya Valitskogo." In *Referativnyi sbornik*, edited by Konstantin V. Dushenko, 79. Moscow: Rossiyskaya akademiya nauk, INION, 1992.

Dement'ev, Aleksandr G., ed. *Russkaya periodicheskaya pechat' (1702–1894): Spravochnik*. Moscow: Gosudarstvennoe izdatel'stvo politicheskoi literatury, 1959.

Dukov, Evgenii. "Novye razmyshleniya o publike." *Teleskop* 3, no. 93 (2012): 31–35.

Etymological Online Dictionary of the Russian Language Krylov G. A. "Public." https://lexicography.online/etymology/krylov/п/публика.

Ferro, Marc. *Kak rasskazyvayut istoriyu detyam v raznykh stranakh mira*. Moscow: Vysshaya shkola, 1992.

Formozov, Aleksandr A. *Russkoe obshchestvo i okhrana pamyatnikov kul'tury*. Moscow: Sovetskaya Rossiya, 1990.

Gudkov, Lev D., Boris V. Dubin, and Aleksei G. Levinson. "Fotorobot rossiyskogo obyvatelya." *Mir Rossii*, no. 2 (2009): 22–23. http://www.civisbook.ru/files/File/Gudkov_Dubin.pdf.

Isaev, Egor M. "Publichnaya istoriya v Rossii: nauchnyi i uchebnyi kontekst formirovaniya novogo mezhdisciplinarnogo polya." *Vestnik Permskogo Universiteta* 33, no. 2 (2016): 7–13.

Karataev, Dmitrij S. "Ogon'kovskaya legenda: k istorii publitsistiki pervykh let 'perestroiki.'" *Vestnik RGGU. Seriya: Istoriya. Filologiya. Kul'turologiya. Vostokovedenie* 4, no. 4 (2015): 58–63.

Kazanskiy Federal'nyi Universitet. Accessed September 12, 2020. https://kpfu. ru/imoiv/struktura/centr-magistratury-i-aspirantury/centr-magistratury/ abiturientam.

Khodnev, Alexander S. "Istoriya v rossiyskom glyantsevom zhurnale 'Karavan istoriy.'" In *Sovremennye media: processy i konteksty*, edited by Evgenii A. Ermolin, Anastasiya A. Maslova, and Tat'yana V. Yur'eva, 37–40. Yaroslavl': Yaroslavskiy gosudarstvennyi pedagogicheskiy universitet im. K.D. Ushinskogo, 2015.

Klyuchevskiy, Vasily O. "Kurs russkoi istorii." *Lektsiya 41.* http://russiahistory.ru/ vo-klyuchevskij-kurs-russkoj-istorii-lektsiya-41.

Koselleck, Reinhart. "Slovar' osnovnykh istoricheskikh ponyatii: Izbrannye stat'i." Translated by Kirill Levinson. Vol. 1. Moscow: Novoe literaturnoe obozreniye, 2014.

Kozlov, Vladimir F. "'Ogosudarstvlennoe' kraevedenie. Istoriya i uroki (Po stranitsam zhurnala 'Sovetskoe kraevedenie' 1930–1936)." *Vestnik RGGU. Seriya Istoricheskie nauki. Regional'naya istoriya. Kraevedenie* 110, no. 9 (2013): 53–83.

Laruelle, Marlene. "Putin's Regime and the Ideological Market: A Difficult Balancing Game." Accessed September 12, 2020. https://carnegieendowment. org/2017/03/16/putin-s-regime-and-ideological-market-difficult-balancing-game-pub-68250.

Livtsov, Viktor A. "Uchastie Vserossiyskogo obshchestva okhrany pamyatnikov istorii i kul'tury (VOOPIIK) v sokhranenii kul'turnogo naslediya narodov rossiyskoy federatsii." In *75 LET PAKTU RERIHA: Materialy mezhdunar. obshchest.-nauchn. konf. 2010*, edited by Lyudmila V. Shaposhnikova, 317–336. Moscow: Mezhdunar. Centr Rerihov, Master-Bank, 2011.

Mironov, Boris N. "Grazhdanskoe obshchestvo v pozdneimperskoij Rossii: bylo ili ne bylo?" *Obshchestvennye nauki i sovremennost'*, no. 1 (2014): 141–150.

Mironov, Boris N. *Social'naya istoriya Rossii perioda imperii.* Vol. 1. Sankt-Petersburg: Dmitriy Bulanin, 2003.

"Portal publichnoi istorii. Obrazovatel'nye programmy v rossiyskikh universitetakh." Accessed September 12, 2020. http://rupublichistory.ru/edu/edum.html.

"'Pust' publika davitsya moimi rasskazami': Sud'ba pisatelya Nikolaya Leskova." *Argumenty i fakty.* March 5, 2016. http://www.spb.aif.ru/culture/person/pust_ publika_davitsya_moimi_rasskazami_sudba_pisatelya_nikolaya_leskova.

Repina, Lorina P. "Nauka i obshchestvo: publichnaya istoriya v kontekste istoricheskoi kul'tury ehpokhi globalizatsii." *Uchenyie zapiski Kazanskogo univeristeta. Ser. Gumanitarnye nauki* 157, no. 3 (2015): 55–67.

Ruble, Blair A., *Money Sings: The Changing Politics of Urban Space in Post-Soviet Yaroslavl.* New York: Woodrow Wilson Center for Scholars, Cambridge University Press, 1995.

Rüsen, Jorn. "Istoricheskaya ob"ektivnost' kak sostavlyayushchaya voprosa o sotsial'nykh tsennostyakh." *Novaya i noveishaya istoriya*, no. 4 (2012): 115–122.

Sogrin, Vladimir V. "'Publichnaya istoriya' i professional'naya istoriografiya." *Rossiyskaya istoriya*, no. 2 (2020): 139–148.

Sogrin, Vladimir V. "Professional'naya, propagandistskaya i obyvatel'skaya istoriografiya." *Novaya i noveishaya istoriya*, no. 1 (2018): 192–193.

Sorgin, Vladimir V. "Three Historical Subcultures in Post-Soviet Russia." *Russian Social Science Review* 55, no. 4 (2014): 71–96.

Sogrin, Vladimir V. "Tri istoricheskie subkul'tury v Rossii." *Obshchestvennye nauki i sovremennost'*, no. 3 (2013): 95–105.

Surkov, Vladislav V. "Dolgoe gosudarstvo Putina." *Nezavisimaya gazeta*, February 11, 2019. http://www.ng.ru/ideas/2019-02-11/5_7503_surkov.html.

Tishkov, Valeriy A. *Istoriya i istoriki v SSHA*. Mocow: Nauka, 1985.

Tolkovyi slovar' zhivogo russkogo yazyka Vladimira Dalya. Vol. 3. Sankt-Peterburg: Izdaniye knigoprodavca-tipografa M.O. Vol'fa, 1882.

Tosh, John. "Public History, Civic Engagement and the Historical Profession in Britain." *History* 99, no. 335 (April 2014): 191–212.

Ul'yanova, Galina N. "Narodnoe obrazovaniye. Pechat'." In *Rossiya v nachale 20 veka. Issledovaniya*, edited by Andrei N. Sakharov and Aleksandr N. Bokhanov, 577–623. Moscow: Novyi khronograf, 2002.

Veligzhanina, Elena. "Bestseller po trebovaniyu." *Rossiyskaya gazeta*, July 6, 2011. https://rg.ru/2011/07/06/reg-szapad/knigi.html.

Wikipedia. "Publika." Last modified February 19, 2016. https://ru.wikipedia.org/wiki/Publika.

PART V

Conclusion

16

THE PUBLIC(S) IN PUBLIC HISTORY—CONCLUSIONS

Joanna Wojdon and Dorota Wiśniewska

This volume has originated from the conference on "Public in Public and Applied History" organized in Wrocław (Poland) in 2019 within the framework of Jean-Monnet Network for Applied European Contemporary History, coordinated by the University of Jena.[1] The chapters by David Dean and Alexander Khodnev are based on the presentations delivered at that conference. The majority of other texts are based on the papers presented during the Second Public History Summer School held in the same year, also in Wrocław. They prove that the issues of the public in public history are of interest to young scholars in the field.

Many discussions within the Jean-Monnet Network have concentrated on the concepts of applied versus public history. The role of the public may be crucial in distinguishing between the two. Public history is not only "applied to," but also created "with" and "by" the public. To cite David Dean from this volume:

> it is about a shift from public history as history for and about publics to public history as history made by and with publics. It marks a move from a practice where historians speak to wider audiences to one where they work with them as collaborators and partners and in doing so embrace interdisciplinarity.

So far, most research in the field of public history has concentrated on history, understood as the representation of the past, and on the activities of public historians aimed at delivering the history-related content to the public.[2] Our book is focused on the public itself and presents it not only as an audience—an addressee and recipient of public history, but also as an actor, initiator, commentator, or modifier of public history. The chapters show that doing public history lies in interactions between the history and the public, with professional public historians sometimes serving as mere facilitators. Even if theirs is the initiative and the first message, the impact of the public on the results cannot be neglected. The public can change the meaning of public history endeavors. As the authors in this volume clearly show, we can speak of publics in the plural, rather than of one, singular, uniform public. The publics have various expectations and backgrounds based on their nationality/ethnicity, culture, history, age, gender, profession, life experiences, and a myriad of other factors, which form their interests (or disinterest) in certain elements of the past and the attitudes to the ways they are (to be) represented. For example, the reception of the core exhibition in the House of European History was different in Belgium, Germany, and Poland, and moreover, they did not necessarily follow national lines exactly.[3]

The researchers propose various definitions and typologies of the public, based on the role it plays in public history practices and on methodological approaches applied to particular research. Theories of memory and commemoration, pedagogy and psychology, sociology and history didactics, museum studies, and media studies have proved to be helpful in deconstructing individual case studies that served as a basis for or an illustration of more general observations or recommendations. Questionnaires, interviews, observations, and analyses of online activities and opinions are among the methods used. Both outsiders' (observers') and insiders' (participants') perspectives have been implemented, which is not unusual in public history scholarship.

Internet 2.0 gives researchers a chance to observe the public and its authentic behaviors in an inobtrusive way. Unlike in the traditional methods, such as interviews, questionnaires, or even participatory observation, the researched group is not concentrated on a researcher but behaves naturally in its own environment. Dorota Choińska not only discusses numerous caveats of such research schemes but also appreciates their advantages. The laboratory of internet 2.0 offers a multitude of research samples that can help understand various characteristics of public history publics.

However, research in the public history public(s) sometimes also reveals their uglier faces, for example of propagators of hate speech in internet arguments or of racists who misinterpret and abuse the past in order to erase the memory of their crimes.

Many authors pay attention to the role of the emotions of the public in doing public history. These can be negative emotions of hatred or trauma or positive emotions of engagement or even enthusiasm. Agata Moskwa refers to a very emotive exhibition at the Hiroshima Peace Memorial Museum and its impact on visitors who share their feelings and opinions about the dark past on Tripadvisor. Alexandra Zaremba discerns and discusses the following spheres of the public's engagement: sentimental, political, experiential, and intellectual. Such an approach can pave the way to a multilayered structure of future research.

Alexander Khodnev, Caitlin White, Paweł Ukielski, Ricardo Santhiago, and Jakub Šindelář all point to the national aspects of the public in public history, while Alexandra Zaremba, Dorota Choińska, Sugandha Agarwal, Linda Thomas, Ewa Woźniak-Wawrzyniak and David Dean focus on racial and ethnic issues. While most of the authors accept the Anglo-American perspective on the public, adopted when the concept of public history was born in the USA in the 1970s, Alexander Khodnev brings the Russian notions of public as opposed to private, and the public (educated, international, focused on impressing others) as opposed to the people (simple, deeply rooted in Russia, inner-oriented, "ours"), which place the public in a quite critical perspective.

Sugandha Agarwal and Olga Konkka discern three kinds of public: the public understood as "ordinary people" who share their memories of the past, the public understood as the audience (readership or other recipients) of public history projects, and the public understood as nonprofessional researchers of the past.

The case study presented by Caitlin White addresses the challenges posed by conflicting publics. While it is desirable and welcome to see the role of public history (and public historians) in building bridges between various kinds of public, in her case study the opposite took place, where public history had its share in creating the breach between rival publics. Not only White but also Dean, Agarwal, Woźniak-Wawrzyniak, and Thomas address the issues of the public(s) "owning" history and making legitimate claims on its representations in the public sphere.[4]

Marta Kopiniak stresses the impact on the biological age of the public and uses the conceptual framework of the twentieth–twenty-first-century generations: from baby-boomers to Generation Z in order to explain the needs, expectations, and reactions of various cohorts of the museum public. Ewa Woźniak-Wawrzyniak, in turn, examines the religious aspects in shaping the publics' reception of and engagement in public history. The importance of religion and church hierarchy is also stressed by Caitlin White and Alexandra Zaremba.

The public can play a more active part in public history. There are specific groups of the public, who take on the role of public historians themselves, such as nonprofessional enthusiasts engaged in historical reenactments.[5] In this volume, Jakub Šindelář demonstrates how players of video games communicate their interpretations of the gameplay to the broader public of their followers on a video channel. This kind of public history is happening for the most part beyond any control of professional historians. Research from the didactics of history done by Peter Gautschi in Swiss schools has shown how distorted interpretations were shared among the students as a result of deficits in their factual knowledge. His team recorded history lessons using multiple cameras and focused not only on the teacher but also on students' working groups. The teacher was not able to follow and control all the discussions going on in the classroom and, thus, had no chance to comment on the potential distortions.[6] In a similar way, professional historians are not able to monitor what is happening on all the history-related websites. In those cases, it is the public, and especially its more educated part, who serve as peer-reviewers. However, Dorota Choińska's analysis of the comments in online newspapers proves that this "peer review" may turn into hate speech, which breaks the public into hostile "tribes."

The active role of the public has been facilitated by the internet 2.0. Comments posted by the active part of the public(s) have their role in shaping the larger public's visions of the past as much as the core content provided (at least sometimes) by professional public historians. In services such as Tripadvisor or Let's Play, the active public is the only content provider. There is no "professional" input or supervision, and the authority of individual contributors is based solely on their experience in the service and the feedback from other users.

The internet can also serve as a powerful tool to mobilize the public for participatory practices. An active, participatory public is desired by many public historians and public history institutions. They proudly share information on successful participatory projects as proofs of their success. In our volume, Ricardo Santhiago presents a successful crowdsourcing project where the Brazilian public helps reconstruct the collection of the National Museum in Rio de Janeiro lost in a fire. Olga Konkka presents the role of the public in creating and maintaining school museums in Russia. Marta Kopiniak, in turn, enumerates various forms of participatory practices proposed by Polish museums and proves that not all of them represent the same level of public participation.

A question may be asked on the acceptable or desirable extent of autonomy of the public history public(s) versus the responsibilities of professionally trained public historians as providers, facilitators, or controllers of public history projects. Engagement of the public in public history can be both tempting and challenging, and therefore, ethical issues related to dealing with the public in public history deserve particular attention.[7] It is the central topic of the chapter by Sugandha Agarwal who draws attention to the threats of manipulation, trivialization, and traumatization, resulting from negligently handing oral history practices to an untrained public. Caitlin White refers to the role of the public leaders in interpreting the past in either a conflicting or peace-bringing way. Linda Thomas shows how one (in her case, white) public can "seize" the history of another (Native American) one and present its distorted interpretation to broader local publics within a framework of quasi-historical reenactment, with the general approval of the community leaders.

Public historians can try to meet the public's expectations or challenge them. The former seems to be easier and more tempting, but it does not necessarily bring ethically positive results. The knowledge of the public(s) can make public historians' work more effective, but it can also be used to manipulate them. Not only individual public historians, but also institutions, commercial companies, or governments can select historical contents and means of communication in order to achieve the desired reactions of the public, either in the sphere of activities or beliefs.[8] Tihana Kušter shows the simple tricks of a website publisher, while Paweł Ukielski describes a participatory strategy of a museum. Ewa Woźniak-Wawrzyniak discusses how messages about one historical figure depend on both their dispatchers and addressees. People supporting the erection of monuments in frequently visited public spaces shape historical memory. As well, those who engage in the alteration, devastation, or destruction of these structures take control over what is remembered and how it should be remembered. A historical perspective on the conflicts related to monuments, memory, and identity in Ireland is depicted by Caitlin White, while Linda Thomas discusses the American context.

As the research presented in this volume proves, however, most of the public is passive, uncritical, and open to the messages provided, especially when they are simple, positive, and correspond with the public's expectations. Contrary to the opinions of some enthusiasts of public history who see it as a chance to deal with contested local histories of marginalized groups, more often than not it turns out that the public(s) prefer simple, positive grand narratives of a glorious national past.

Notes

1 See the project's website: https://aec-history.uni-jena.de.
2 Cf. Jerome De Groot, *Consuming History: Historians and Heritage in Contemporary Popular Culture*, 2nd ed. (New York, London: Routledge, 2016); Faye Sayer, *Public History: A Practical Guide*, 2nd ed. (London: Bloomsbury, 2019); Thomas Cauvin, *Public history: A Textbook of Practice* (New York: Routledge, 2016); David Dean, ed., *A Companion to Public History* (Hoboken: Wiley, 2018).
3 Cf. Chantal Kesteloot, "The House of European History, Food for Thought and Reflection," *International Public History* 3, no. 1 (2020), https://doi.org/10.1515/iph-2020-2003; Christopher Garbowski, "The Polish Debate on the House of European History in Brussels," *The Polish Review* 65, no. 4 (2020): 60–70.
4 On tensions between the museum staff and the public related to "owning" history see Joanna Wojdon, "Who Owns the Museum Narrative," *Public History Weekly*, 6 (2018), with comments, https://dx.doi.org/10.1515/phw-2018-11623.
5 Cf. Vanessa Agnew, Jonathan Lamb, and Juliane Tomann, eds, *The Routledge Handbook of Reenactment Studies: Key Terms in the Field* (New York: Routledge, 2019).
6 Reflections of Joanna Wojdon on the presentation of raw data discussed in Peter Gautschi and Hans Utz, "Learning from Others: Considerations within History Didactics on Introducing the Cold War in Lessons in Germany, Sweden and Switzerland," in *The Cold War in the Classroom*, ed. Barbara Christoph, Peter Gautschi and Robert Torp (Cham: Palgrave Macmillan, 2019), 393–421.
7 On ethical issues in public history cf. Theodore Karamanski, "Reflections on Ethics and the Historical Profession," *The Public Historian* 21, no. 3 (1999): 127–133.

8 Cf. Cathy Stanton, *The Lowell Experiment: Public history in a Postindustrial City* (Boston: University of Massachusetts Press, 2006).

Bibliography

Cauvin, Thomas. *Public history: A Textbook of Practice*. New York: Routledge, 2016.

Dean, David, ed. *A Companion to Public History*. Hoboken: Wiley, 2018.

De Groot, Jerome. *Consuming History: Historians and Heritage in Contemporary Popular Culture*. 2nd ed. New York, London: Routledge, 2016.

Garbowski, Christopher. "The Polish Debate on the House of European History in Brussels." *The Polish Review* 65, no. 4 (2020): 60–70.

Gautschi, Peter, and Hans Utz. "Learning from Others: Considerations within History Didactics on Introducing the Cold War in Lessons in Germany, Sweden and Switzerland." In *The Cold War in the Classroom*, edited by Barbara Christoph, Peter Gautschi, and Robert Torp, 393–421. Cham: Palgrave Macmillan, 2019.

Karamanski, Theodore. "Reflections on Ethics and the Historical Profession." *The Public Historian* 21, no. 3 (1999): 127–133.

Kesteloot, Chantal. "The House of European History, Food for Thought and Reflection." *International Public History* 3, no. 1 (2020). https://doi.org/10.1515/iph-2020-2003.

Sayer, Faye. *Public History: A Practical Guide*. 2nd ed. London: Bloomsbury, 2019.

Stanton, Cathy. *The Lowell Experiment: Public history in a Postindustrial City*. Boston: University of Massachusetts Press, 2006.

Wojdon, Joanna. "Who Owns the Museum Narrative." *Public History Weekly*, 6, no. 11 (2018). https://dx.doi.org/10.1515/phw-2018-11623.

INDEX

Note: Page numbers followed by "n" denote endnotes.